The Role of Migration in the History of the Eurasian Steppe

Sedentary Civilization vs. "Barbarian" and Nomad

Edited by
Andrew Bell-Fialkoff

St. Martin's Press
New York

ISBN 0-312-21207-0

Library of Congress Cataloging-in-Publication Data
Bell-Fialkoff, Andrew (Andrew Villen), editor.
    The role of migration in the history of the Eurasian steppe : sedentary civilization vs. "barbarian" and nomad / Andrew Bell-Fialkoff.
        p.   cm.
    Includes bibliographical references and index.
    ISBN 0-312-21207-0
    1. Eurasia—History.   2. Migrations of nations.   I. Title.
DJK46. B45   2000
950—dc21   99–045059

Design by Letra Libre, Inc.

First edition: July, 2000
10 9 8 7 6 5 4 3 2 1

To Anna, while I can

Contents

Part III
Nomadic Migrations

Maps and Table

Acknowledgments

I am most grateful to the contributors: Christopher Kaplonski for his chapter on the Mongols; William Meyer for his elucidation of the role of climate, as well as constructive criticism and assistance in collecting data; the late Dean Rugg for his work on medieval German migrations and his persistence with the project, despite failing health and numerous problems; and Rebecca Wendelken for her contributions on the Scythians and the Russians in Kazakstan, both written in the middle of a dissertation. She has also provided me with valuable materials on the Huns.

I am also much indebted to Anna Bell for her unflagging support and help with the index. Finally, I owe many thanks to Michael Flamini, whose interest in the book made its publication possible.

Contributors

Andrew V. Bell-Fialkoff, independent scholar
Christopher Kaplonski, University of Cambridge and Rutgers University
William B. Meyer, Clark University
†Dean S. Rugg, University of Nebraska
Rebecca W. Wendelken, Emory University

Note on Spelling and Transliteration

Parts of the book derive from presentations at the conference of the American Association for the Advancement of Slavic Studies in Boston in November 1996 and of the American Historical Association in Washington, D.C. in January 1999.

A few words about spelling and transliteration. There is a bewildering array of systems of transliteration of various languages into English. As a rule of thumb, references to published works will reproduce the spelling of the original. Changes in spelling introduced by the newly independent states will be respected, e.g., "Ukraine" will lose its definite article, and "Kazakhstan" will become "Kazakstan." Chinese names will be transliterated according to the Wade-Giles system, Mongol ones according to contemporary Halh spelling; the spelling of Turkic names will follow the usage of *The Cambridge History of Early Inner Asia;* and Russian transliteration will follow the awkward and cumbersome system accepted by the Library of Congress, although I am sorely tempted to use my own system instead. Needless to say, long-established geographical and historical names will retain traditional spelling. Thus, Moskva will remain Moscow, and Warszawa will stay Warsaw.

Foreword

My interest in migration started in the fifth grade. The dramatic rise and fall of the Roman Empire caught my imagination. Battered by hordes of barbarians, from Gauls to Goths, Rome proudly withstood the onslaught for a thousand years.

Then it collapsed. A captivating picture in my textbook showed a hefty Germanic warrior in a horned helmet dragging an engagingly helpless Roman matron from a crumbling temple. Her torn *peplum* exposed a leg and much of the thigh but stopped precisely where propriety required.

The image was reinforced by stories of German brutality in World War II, leaving me to wonder about the continuity of Germanic assault on civilization and the problem of continuity in general.

Soon I learned that there were other assailants: Huns, Saracens, Vikings, Mongols. They came from all directions, converging on hapless Europe like swarms of locusts, pillaging, burning, killing, leaving death and destruction in their path. But a few pages later, the most bloodthirsty invaders would settle down, plough the fields, rebuild towns and villages, and learn to write, only to suffer, in the following chapter, an assault by rude newcomers.

My initial question was "Why?" The illustration in the textbook provided the answer (totally unintended by the authors, I am sure): sacking was fun.

I also wanted to know where all these barbarians had come from. I set out to read everything I could find about migrations, and was stunned by the sheer number of Volks wandering in the forests of Europe and by the countless nomads sweeping in from the steppes of Asia.

By the time I was in graduate school, I had enough background to write a term paper on migrations in the Eurasian steppe. That paper was the seed from which this book sprouted. By then, however, I was more concerned with the role that migration played in the history of Eurasia than the simple "whys" and "hows" that had already been answered by various historians.

When I started this project, I was hoping that each migration would be written up by a specialist. It was the most sensible approach, given the number of migrations under consideration and their wide diachronic and geographic span.

Unfortunately, most of the historians I approached had pressing commitments in the next two to five years. I did not want to wait that long.

After some hesitation, I decided that years of reading and studying had prepared me to write a coherent book on the subject, even if I could not be equally conversant on each topic. If a narrow specialist will find little here he or she does not already know, everybody else—historians, geographers, anthropologists, graduate and undergraduate students, and any educated person interested in the subject—will discover a wealth of information on a number of interconnected topics usually presented as independent (and disjointed) subjects. But even a narrow specialist may find it worth reading because the book attempts to apply to Europe Thomas Barfield's formula of the triangular relationship among China, the nomads, and the forest tribes.

The first chapter will provide the reader with the framework of the book: two migratory paradigms discernible in the history of temperate Eurasia in the last three thousand years and a brief historical overview to put them into context.

The following three sections, consisting of several chapters each, will discuss specific migrations and colonization movements by states, pre-state sedentary peoples of the forest zone (the "forest tribes"), and the nomads.

The last chapter will tie together various strands and issues addressed in the earlier narratives.

The book concludes with two appendices. The small but vitally important appendix A deals with the role of climate and climatic change as a factor in historical processes.

Appendix B addresses some of the controversies surrounding migration in several disciplines: diffusionism in archeology, the enormous ("Toynbeeesque" or "Spenglerian," depending on one's favorite *philosophe*) time span of its historical framework that may rile some historians, and accusations of essentialism from anthropologists and ethnic studies specialists. Although the book is not intended to definitively settle any of these issues, I will be glad if it contributes—if only indirectly—to the discussion.

The reader should keep in mind that this is not a history of individual migrations, but rather an examination of the role of migration in the history of Eurasia. Narratives of specific migrations include only enough details to clarify the dynamics of interaction between three types of civilization ("formations"). That is why complaints that this or that narrative is incomplete are misplaced.

Equally misplaced are complaints that the approach is superficial in its design and execution. An in-depth study is impossible in a book covering such a time span. Rather, this is a work of synthesis that aspires to give a new interpretation to some well-known facts and provide an all-encompassing approach to a phenomenon that is usually tacked on to other subjects.

Nomadism appeared later than sedentary society. According to Thomas Barfield, the horse was domesticated about 3200 B.C., and the chariot appeared by 1700 B.C. (Barfield 1989, 28). Other scholars date the domestication of the horse from about 4300 B.C., horseback riding by 4000 B.C.; and the appearance of carts and wagons by the middle of the next millennium (Anthony and Brown 1991, 22–38, in Bentley 1996, 756). But most agree that nomadic cultures based on transhumance appeared some time in the first two centuries of the first millennium B.C. With the appearance of nomadism, the stage was set for the interaction among the state, the forest tribes, and the nomads.

Migration played a crucial role in this interaction. Each type of civilization generated migratory flows. The dynamics of this process were peculiar to each type. But they had at least one thing in common: migrations expanded each type of civilization because migrants reproduced their *habiti* (from "habitus") even when they sought to escape from conditions imposed by their civilizations. Migrants originating from areas of developed civilization built cities, collected taxes, and reproduced forms of government and complex hierarchies that they were familiar with back home. Forest tribes who moved across Europe cleared forests, built villages, and brought new areas under cultivation—when they could not settle in the richer and more attractive areas of developed civilization. And nomadic migrants continued to practice pastoralism and recreate unstable confederacies thousands of miles away from their original home.

Of the three, migrants from areas of developed civilization were the most versatile: cities could be built in the deserts and in the forests, isles, and mountains. And trade and some form of agriculture could be carried on under almost any climatic conditions. The nomads, on the other hand, were the most circumscribed: pastoral nomadism was viable only on the steppe and only where it was reasonably well watered. Even the size of the steppe, as we will see in the chapters on nomadism, imposed severe restrictions.

Despite the limitations inherent in the internal structure of each formation and limits imposed by the political configurations, geography, climate, and the like, migration extended each formation far and wide. Ultimately, migration was a key instrument of historical change. Migratory flows created and destroyed empires, upset the balance of power, and changed ethnic and cultural composition of vast regions, making some developments possible but relegating numerous others to the proverbial dustbin of history.

Since we are interested in the interactions *among* various types of civilization, we will concentrate on inter-civilizational, rather than intra-civilizational, migrations.

The stage on which sedentary and nomadic civilizations collided was a vast stretch of the plains known as the Eurasian steppe. Historically, it has often functioned as a unit, in the sense that the nomads originating in Mongolia could end up in Pannonia, from where they would range all over Europe. However, the scope of migration in this region is too vast a subject for one book. We will limit ourselves "only" to Europe and China and the steppe corridor in-between—itself an enormous undertaking given our time frame. For the most part, we will leave out migrations that spilled into India and Iran, as well as conquests and migrations tangential to the area under consideration, such as the Scythian intrusion into the Near East or the Arab conquest-cummigration of the southern Mediterranean. Even Tamerlane's depredations, played out largely in the steppe, will be excluded, unlike the Seljuk and Osmanli intrusion into Asia Minor and Europe that proceeded for the most part outside the steppe. These decisions, where to draw the line, always difficult and sometimes, perhaps, infelicitous, were based on the role these invasions played in the history of the temperate Eurasia, migrations they generated, and, most importantly, the ways they could be incorporated into the conceptual framework of this book. Ultimately, it leaves "only" Europe and China.

Their response to the challenges presented by the forest-dwelling "barbarian" and nomad was highly dissimilar.

We should note that the earliest nomads—Cimmerians and Scythians—appeared in the western parts of the Eurasian steppe. From there they attempted to spread in all directions, for which there are historical records in the Near East and archeological evidence of burned villages in today's Poland. Their forays into the rich areas of the Near East took place in the eighth century B.C. Their thrust west occurred in approximately 500 B.C. It was only in the fourth century B.C. that nomads reached China (Barfield 1989, 29).

Here, they developed a highly symbiotic relationship with their sedentary neighbors. Anatoly Khazanov notes that the economy of the nomads is far less autarchic than the economy of the settled populations: the nomads cannot do without farming products and wares while farmers, on the contrary, don't need nomads (Khazanov 124, in Weissleder 1978). That is why nomads have always been eager to trade with sedentary populations. Since militarily, until the sixteenth century, the nomads had the upper hand, it was much cheaper to trade with them than keep them out. Thus, from very early on, the Chinese organized markets "in order to consolidate borders and . . . cut down defense expenditures" (Martynov 1970, 235, in Khazanov 124, in Weissleder 1978). The terms of trade were made easier when the Chinese were organized in a state with which nomads could negotiate treaties. "Nomadic imperial confederacies came into existence only in periods when it was possible to link themselves to the Chinese economy," notes Barfield (1989, 9). Wealth extorted from the state played a vital role in maintaining political stability of nomadic imperial confederations. Why would China pay tribute to the nomads, in effect subsidizing its enemies, precisely when it was strong and unified? Because it found it cheaper to buy off the nomads rather than engage in costly wars with an elusive enemy. Barfield asserts that the nomadic state maintained itself by exploiting China's economy, rather than exploiting its own population of "scattered sheep herders who were effectively organized by the nomadic state to make this extortion possible" (8).

The history of China and the northern nomads shows a striking parallelism: the unification of China brought about the creation of the nomadic empires; its dissolution was followed by their collapse (see table 1.1). The Han and the Hsiung-nu, the Sui and the First Turkic Empires, the Ming and the Oirats appeared, historically speaking, simultaneously.

The collapse of China and the nomadic confederacies enabled tribes in Manchuria (some of them sedentary forest tribes, others nomadic) to establish or reinvigorate small kingdoms in the frontier zone between China and Manchuria. When the ephemeral successor states established by the Chinese warlords and nomads in north China exhausted themselves in endless wars, the Manchurian kingdoms moved in for the kill. They would conquer them one by one until north China, and later (though not always) the entire country, acknowledged their rule.

Unlike the Han Chinese, foreign dynasties did not practice appeasement vis-à-vis the nomads. And since they faced much the same difficulties as did their Chinese counterparts, it suggests a cultural explanation for their stance against the elusive enemy. They sought to prevent the unification of the nomads and usually, with the exception of the Mongols, succeeded.

Eventually, the foreign dynasty would be ousted by an uprising of its Chinese subjects and/or conquest from south China where a native dynasty might have retained control. The unification of China under a native dynasty would then be followed by the creation of a new nomadic confederacy, and the cycle would start again.

There were three such cycles in Chinese history: (1) 221 B.C. to A.D. 581; (2) A.D. 581 to 1368; and (3) A.D. 1368 to 1949. (Technically, the Communist takeover was not a reunification under a native dynasty. But it does correspond to earlier unifications under a strong Chinese rule.)

Barfield notes that periods of instability after the fall of the native dynasty decreased with each cycle while the duration of foreign dynasties increased (1989, 11).

This configuration, state–nomad–forest tribe, came to an end in the eighteenth century when the nomads were eliminated as an independent

5

Table 1.1 Migrations and Conquests in Eurasia

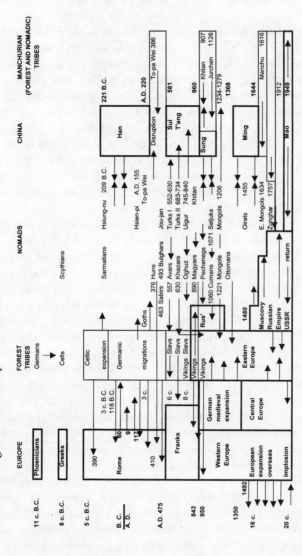

Key to Table 1.1

- Bold lines indicate areas of high civilization (e.g., Greeks)
- Thin lines indicate forest tribes (e.g., Celts)
- The names of nomadic tribes are not boxed (e.g., Scythians)
- Tribes that have been nomadic and forest appear in both categories (e.g., To-pa Wei)

power. And Manchuria, long closed to Chinese immigration by the Manchu emperors, has now been swamped by millions of Chinese migrants, leaving a small minority of 2.5 million Manchus in a population of 40 million. If China falls apart in the future, it will have to be a radically different process, without the input from either nomads or the Manchurians.

Throughout Chinese history, the northern frontier was largely static. But not for lack of Chinese efforts to expand north. Already in the Warring States period (455–221 B.C.) the Chinese governments used migration as a tool for integration of recently conquered areas. They sent migrants in all directions. In 221 B.C., Ch'in Shih-huang sent over five hundred thousand military colonists south (Lee 22, nn.8, 9, and 10 in McNeill and Adams 1978). Between the second century B.C. and the first century A.D., the Han governments transferred over 1.5 million people to the northern frontier (Lee 22 in McNeill and Adams 1978). Many of these migrants were settled in government colonies in Kansu and Inner Mongolia, with one thousand families per settlement (Lee 25, n.18 in McNeill and Adams 1978).

The Chinese government had acquired valuable experience in planning resettlement: "[W]hen the government moved people to far-away areas . . . they examined the climatic and water conditions [of the proposed site], inspected the local topography, and checked the supply of forest and pasture land. Only then did they organize camps and build cities, draw street and house foundation lines, build roads to the fields, and map the property boundaries. [After that] they first built houses for the migrants . . . when the migrants arrived, they had a place to live. When the time came to farm, they had land and agricultural tools" (Lee 23–24, n.13, in McNeill and Adams 1978). Settlement on this scale required enormous outlays financed by the "white deerskin" tax levied on all nobility (Lee 23–24, n.16, in McNeill and Adams 1978).

In addition to government-sponsored migration, powerful population movements originated as private initiative. And here, a significant proportion went south. The population, under constant threat from the north, shifted from the northwest to the southeast, toward the Yangtse River valley. Each major invasion set off a powerful migratory flow south. In the second to fourth centuries A.D., during the Age of Disruption, at least three million people—10 percent of the northern population—migrated south (Lee 29, in McNeill and Adams 1978). In the second and third centuries A.D., well over two million nomadic tribesmen moved from the northern steppe into the central plains (Lee 29, n.48, in McNeill and Adams 1978). Hundreds of thousands of the Chinese fled before their advance. Most went south, but some headed northeast, to Manchuria, where, by the early fourth century, there were two hundred thousand Chinese households (Lee 29, n.50, in Mc-Neill and Adams 1978).

Despite the continuous outflow, the North remained more populous until well into the T'ang period. In the 730s, the North: South population ratio was still 2:1 (Hucker 1975, 172). Of the 26 most populous prefectures in T'ang China, only six were in the south (173).

There were several factors, in addition to the nomad threat, that favored the South at the expense of the North. One was the greater availability of the agricultural land. Another reason was that passport regulations were more strictly enforced in the North, the old heartland. And the dessication, which gradually expanded the northern deserts (Lee 31, in McNeill and Adams 1978), also contributed to the shifting of the demographic center.

The South caught up with the North during the Northern Sung period (960–1126) when the Jurchen conquest of the North tilted the balance southward. A century later the Mongols reduced the northern share to no more than 25 percent, perhaps even 10 percent of the population (Hucker 1975, 330). Repopulating the North became a prime objective for the early Ming emperors. Their policies bore fruit in that the northern share reached almost a third by 1850 (331). And yet the North failed to catch up with the South despite increasing congestion, emigration, and strong local outflow to the west and the southwest.

In short, the Chinese state could not overcome the pressures from the nomad and forest tribes and was forced to direct its colonization south, away from the "perilous frontier." Chinese colonization was largely internal.

Developments in Europe were quite different. Here, a succession of civilizations generated external colonization flows that gradually expanded the area of developed civilization at the expense of forest tribes and nomads alike.

The beginnings, however, were similar. Rome was the European equivalent of the Han Empire in that it created an imperial entity that brought a large territory with a diverse population under its scepter and laid the foundations of a major civilization. And, like the Han, Rome faced the challenge of containing the nomads and the forest tribes. Like its Chinese counterparts, Rome had to establish a fortified frontier, although Roman *limes* (border) along the Rhine and the Danube were not as spectacular an undertaking as the Great Wall of China.

But the configuration of the triangular relationship among the state, the nomad, and the "barbarian" in the West differed significantly from that in the East. Here the empire and the forest tribes were the main players, the nomads being relegated to an important, but distinctly secondary, position. In a sense, "geography [was] destiny," for there was no wide zone of contact—and confrontation—between the sedentary state and the nomad, unlike the frontier separating Mongolia from China. Conversely, the zone of contact between the empire and the forest tribes was long and extensive, unlike the relatively limited zone of engagement between China and Manchuria. The nomads could reach Europe, but the only areas where they could "settle," if "settle" is the right word for pastoral nomads, were the Pontic steppe and Pannonia. Elsewhere in Europe, geographic and climatic conditions were inimical to the creation of nomadic confederacies.

The forest tribes were as aware of the attractions of developed civilization as their nomadic counterparts. First the Gauls, then the ancient Germans tried to invade and/or settle in the rich south. Those who could not gain entry into the empire settled along the frontier, within easy reach of imperial markets. Eventually, much of the Germanic population was concentrated in a narrow belt along the imperial frontier, creating a zone of what can be described as a "frontier culture." And Roman exports east and north, as far as Scandinavia, acquainted "barbarians" farther afield with the wealthy world to the south. It whetted their appetite.

Internal rot and external pressures led to the collapse of the West Roman Empire ("Western Empire") in the fifth century A.D. It had survived the Han Empire by some 250 years.

Nomads and forest tribes played an important role in its collapse. The pressure from the Germans, starting from about 120 B.C., was relentless. The nomads added to that pressure. When the Huns destroyed the Gothic kingdoms in the Pontic steppe circa 375, they sent thousands of refugees into the empire. Their subsequent move into Pannonia in 406 generated another wave that flooded the empire. Four years later Rome was sacked for the first time in eight hundred years. And 70 years later the Western Empire went under.

By that time the Huns were gone. But they had established a pattern of nomadic penetration deep into Europe that was to endure for a thousand years.

Like the preceding period (the empire building), the fragmentation in the West bears some similarity to that in China. In the East, small "barbarian" kingdoms based in Manchuria took over Chinese successor states in north China and gradually unified it. In the West, "barbarian" kingdoms were themselves destroyed by the nomads because many lay astride the steppe corridor or along the imperial frontier in a way that blocked nomadic inroads. "Barbarian" populations then sought refuge within the empire where they (re)created "barbarian" kingdoms. In the process, they carved up the imperial carcass, completing the destruction.

The next phase—a second barbarian dynasty unifying north China (Barfield 1989, 9)—was played out to the T: the Carolingians unified a large portion of the Western Empire. However, from here the Chinese and European paths diverge.

First, Byzantium (like south China, a part of the old empire that with-stood the onslaught) failed to reconquer the patrimony it lost to the "bar-barians." Second, the conquest of the southern Mediterranean and Iberia by the Arabs opened yet another front, something that did not happen in China. Later, Viking depredations completed the "encirclement" of Europe. It was assaulted from all sides, unlike China, whose east and south were se-cure. (And even in the west, despite occasional complications with Tibetans and Muslims, China did not face a major threat.)

Most important, however, was the fact that the Carolingian Empire in-corporated German areas beyond the old imperial *limes*. In other words, the area of high civilization in the period of imperial resurgence expanded be-yond the limits of the old imperial entity, something that China of the Sui, T'ang, and Sung periods failed to achieve. Finally, unlike China, the new imperial entity in the West was short-lived. In 843, it was divided into three parts. And the East Frankish kingdom, today's Germany, was transformed into a new imperial entity that was positioned to shield the West from fur-ther barbarian and nomadic depredations. It is as if the resurgent T'ang China expanded into Mongolia and established a new imperial polity that shielded the rest of China from nomads.

However, the expansion of the imperial territory further east brought areas of developed civilization into contact with the "outer" forest tribes in Scandinavia. One of the consequences was the era of Viking depredations in 700–1100.

With Avars and Magyars, Germany was much more successful. It took only 60 to 70 years to bring the Magyars to heel. In the process, they were sedentarized. And Pannonia, now Hungary, was definitively incorporated into the area of European civilization.

But Hungary was only one of several states that emerged on the fringes of European civilization at this time. It was a link in a string of small king-doms, an early *cordon sanitaire,* inhabited by former forest tribes (Poland, Bohemia) and sedentarized nomads (Bulgaria, Hungary) that functioned as marches of the German (Holy Roman) or Byzantine Empires (in fact, if not always in theory). To these we should add Scandinavian countries, which joined the European system of states at this time (roughly the tenth century).

The largest and easternmost of the new polities was Rus'. An East Slavic state created with the active participation of Scandinavians, it became an outer shield that covered eastern Europe that covered Germany that covered the West from attacks from the east. And Byzantium defended Europe from the southeast. In effect, some four hundred years after the collapse of the Roman Empire, medieval Europe had established a three-layer defensive shield.

The European achievement is all the more striking when compared to the Chinese: for most of its history, China sat it out behind the Great Wall. It had adopted a predominantly defensive posture. In European terms, the Chinese did not cross the Rhine and the Danube. (This is all the more remarkable since Europe, as had been stated earlier, was besieged on *all* sides: by Arabs from southeast and southwest (they reached Constantinople and the vicinity of Tours), Vikings from the north (reaching Constantinople and the environs of Rome), nomads from the east and southeast (Germany and Vienna). In these circumstances, the creation of a multi-layered defense system by a repeatedly inundated Europe was a truly remarkable achievement.

With the creation of the eastern European and Scandinavian states and their incorporation into the European system, the reserves of the forest tribes were effectively exhausted. There were still numerous forest tribes to be found east of Rus', all the way to the Urals and beyond, many of them Finno-Ugrians, but they were no longer a threat to developed civilization. By the year 1000, one of the combatants, the forest tribes—and in Europe they were one of the two main protagonists—were no longer a major factor. But the nomads remained for another 550 years. In fact, during this time, the assault on Europe intensified.

The battle of Manzikert in 1071 opened Anatolia to the Seljuk Turks. By 1529, their Osmanli successors were at the gates of Vienna.

While the Turks advanced across the Balkans, the Mongols smashed their way through Rus' and eastern Europe in one overwhelming blow in the middle of the thirteenth century. It was a close call since little stood in the way of a complete subjugation of Europe and, possibly, the demise of the European civilization as we know it. Europe was saved by the death of the Great Khan and the succession struggle that followed, which resulted in the recall of the Mongol troops.

Some 250 years passed before Europe's growing superiority in arms, economy, and organization made itself felt. But finally, in 1492, Spain completed the *reconquista* from the Muslims.

The fall of Kazan' and Astrakhan' in 1552 and 1556 marked the end of the nomadic predominance in the east. In quick succession, Russians crossed the Urals and "leaped" across Siberia, then the Russian Far East and on to Alaska. The eighteenth century witnessed the dismantling of the last successor state of the Golden Horde, the slave-trading Crimean khanate (1774–83). It also saw the last nomad migration—that of the Kalmyks—back to their ancestral homeland. In the nineteenth century, the entire steppe corridor, the breeding ground of the nomad, was brought under control and divided between Russia and China. Large, but ever-diminishing, pockets of nomad life remained in Kazakstan and Xinjiang, but they could no longer threaten sedentary areas. The tables were turned, and the nomads were now a threatened minority.

Only in the Balkans was the demise of the nomad delayed. Byzantium had long been a defensive rampart against nomads and Muslims. When Constantinople fell in 1453, the way was open to the heart of Europe. While the Spanish were preparing their assault on Granada, the last Muslim hold-out in Iberia, and the Russians were shaking off what was left of the Mongol yoke, the Turks opened the second (or third, if you wish) front by advancing to Vienna. The first siege of the Austrian capital, in 1529, stopped their advance. It was followed by 150 years of a "cold war," another siege in 1683, and then a slow rollback that lasted until 1918. The *reconquista* was least successful in the Balkans because the two European powers most closely involved—Austria and Russia—were rivals that often crossed each other while England and France often supported Turkey for their own reasons. But even now we keep hearing the distant echoes of the Balkan *reconquista* in Bosnia and Albania.

With the elimination of the nomad, the old paradigm came to an end. In Europe, it took some 1,500 years to eliminate the forest tribes (roughly 390 B.C. to A.D. 1000) and a comparable period to destroy the nomads (375 to 1918). (We have to keep in mind that when they besieged Vienna, the Turks were no longer "true nomads." Rather, they were a sedentary power with a nomadic *mythomoteur*. The same goes for most other nominally nomadic states, with the possible exception of the Crimean Tatars who continued raiding and slaving until 1769, to the very end of their semi-independent existence.)

By comparison, in China, the last nomadic confederation—the Zunghars—was eliminated only in 1757, and Manchuria was not effectively open to Han colonization until well into this century. Here, the elimination of both threats came late, very late, and the process was sluggish, its roots lying in faraway Europe.

What were the reasons for this disparity?

Undoubtedly, there were many, but we are primarily interested in one—migration.

The new states that joined Christian Europe around 1000 were sparsely populated while Germany, now at the geographical center of the European state system, had people to spare. Hence, a protracted German colonization in eastern Europe that lasted some four hundred years, from 950 until the Black Death, starting in 1348, killed off between one-quarter and one-third of the European population and stopped the colonization in its tracks. It was resumed in Bohemia in the seventeenth and Hungary and Russia in the eighteenth century but never achieved a comparable scope because by that time a new outlet appeared across the Atlantic.

The discovery of America and the beginnings of the European settlement in the colonies introduced an entirely new dimension into the pattern of migration flows. In fact, it was a new historical paradigm.

This paradigm was set into motion by the completion of the *reconquista* and the discovery of America. For Iberian powers, the colonization of the Americas grew out of the *reconquista*. For other colonizing powers on the Atlantic seaboard—England, France, Holland—it was an entirely new venture. In any case, the colonization created a powerful migratory movement overseas.

A similar population outflow developed across Siberia. A rapid demographic expansion of the Russian population, adverse agricultural conditions in central Russia, and the sparse population in Siberia led to massive colonization along the entire steppe corridor. In a sense, the two flows, one across the ocean, the other one across Siberia, were mirror images (see Treadgold). Both were part of the same process: European demographic explosion that spread in all directions but, due to political, economic, and geographic constraints, was directed mostly west and east. And in the east, the new trend, migration fueled by the colonization and the industrial revolution, overlaid the old one (in a curtailed form, encompassing only the state and the nomads).

For a while, in the sixteenth to eighteenth centuries, both paradigms coexisted. But gradually, the new configuration hastened the end of the old one: the demographic explosion, largely the result of the demographic transition, provided excess population and the technical means of settling huge areas that had been the preserve of the nomad. They rendered the nomad's defeat inevitable.

Two factors (among many) played an important role in shaping and promoting migratory movements. One was the expansion of areas controlled by developed civilization; the other was the disparity in the standards of living.

The expansion, predicated on colonial conquests, was underwritten by European technological superiority. It opened up whole continents to European settlement. These vast areas had been thinly settled in the first place (with some notable exceptions, such as central Mexico or the heartland of the Inca Empire) and were further emptied by the spread of European diseases. The availability of virtually empty lands allowed the rural-to-rural migration of the earlier period (roughly, until 1800), which created the largely agricultural population that served as the demographic foundation for further development. This foundation, although impressive, was numerically modest: by the middle of the eighteenth century, there were 1.5 million English colonists in North America (Wartik 1989, 43). (They had far surpassed their main competitor, the French, whose numbers reached only 65,000, a disparity that clinched the outcome of the struggle for North America.) By 1800, after two centuries of colonization, North America had fewer than five million whites and about one million blacks (Crosby 1986, 5). (And South America was far behind: its southern portion comprising Argentina, Chile, and Uruguay, with some adjacent areas, had less than five hundred thousand whites—after nearly three centuries of colonization! [5]

After 1800, rapid expansion of European populations and the opportunities offered by overseas colonies attracted an increasingly large number of migrants. From 1800 to 1914, some 50 million Europeans moved overseas; and if we count return migrants, at a 30 percent return rate, then the total number could easily reach 65 million (Tilly 58, in McNeill and Adams 1978). This was no longer a rural-to-rural, but increasingly rural-to-urban and urban-to-urban migration. It was predicated upon faster economic development in some colonies, particularly North America. Toward the end of the nineteenth century, faster development created an increasingly large gap in the standards of living.

This factor, the attraction of areas with a higher standard of living, was a constant one at least since Antiquity, although its relative importance fluctuated. (We must keep in mind its relativity: in the nineteenth century, Britain was one of the most developed areas in the world, yet it provided at least one-third of all migrants to America in this period [Tilly 58, McNeill and Adams 1978]. Clearly, there were other factors involved: different push factors for different social strata [for not every émigré was poor—some were professional people and even well-to-do]; the availability of information and support in the new place [chain migration]; fluctuations in business cycles; and many others.)

In general, North America and western European countries industrialized earlier and developed more rapidly than other regions. As a result, they achieved a higher standard of living and started to attract migrants from less-developed areas of Europe, migrants who earlier would have gone east. Migration in Europe "turned around."

This was an uneven process, spatially. In the post-medieval world, the line separating areas of advanced civilization from less-developed regions was no longer the clear-cut imperial *limes*. Rather, industrialization spread unevenly in all directions, creating concentric belts and patches of industrialized zones initially centered on coal-mining and iron-smelting areas.

The first signs of the turnaround appeared in Germany in the eighteenth century. Large-scale German migrations to Hungary and, after 1763, to Russia, were the last German movements east. (There were smaller ones later: an attempt by Wilhelmine Germany to reinforce the German element in Posen, plans for German settlement in the Baltic after World War I, and Hitler's colonization schemes in the East; all came to naught.)

While fewer Germans could be induced to move east, an increasing number turned west. Many migrated overseas, particularly to North America, where there was a substantial German colony already in the eighteenth century. But, as development in Germany took off, many more relocated within the country, especially to the more economically vibrant west.

Industrialization and urbanization in the nineteenth century reinforced this trend since the largest concentration of industry in Germany, the Ruhr valley, happened to be in the western part of the country. By the end of the century, the pull of the west began to affect Poland as thousands of peasants, attracted by higher wages in the industries, streamed into the mines of the Ruhr and Upper Silesia (then part of Germany). Initially limited to the Poles of Germany, the migration by the first decade of the twentieth century included an increasing number of migrants from Russian and Austrian Poland. (Polish economic migration had been preceded by political emigration of the 1790s, 1830s, and 1860s. But numerically, the economic migration was much larger.)

This was a worldwide phenomenon: everywhere peasants flocked to the industrial areas. It just so happened that western Europe was more developed; hence population flows were directed west (in southern Europe they were directed north and in Scandinavia and Scotland south; Irish migration was a mixed bag, to England and overseas).

By the end of the nineteenth century the pull of the west reached Russia. After 1881, an increasing number of Russian Jews started leaving the empire, 1.9 million by the start of World War I (Gitelman 23, in Lewin-Epstein, Ro'i, and Ritterband 1997). They fled poverty, pogroms, and persecution. Most other migrants from Russia also belonged to various minorities: Poles, Lithuanians, Finns, Germans. Ethnic Russians and most of their East Slav cousins continued to migrate east in the ever-increasing numbers, although industrial centers, such as Moscow and St. Petersburg, also attracted thousands of migrants.

World War I marked the next stage in the migratory process. (We will leave out population movements generated by the war. They were directed away from the front; west and south in France, east in Russia. Latvia alone lost about 800,000, out of the prewar population of 2.5 million, to evacuation and flight.)

After the war, several million Germans and some three million Hungarians suddenly found themselves under alien rule. Many could not or would not accept it and went west to their historic homelands. Within the first postwar decade, more than half of Germans in Poland moved to Germany (Schechtman 1946, 259). By 1926, the German urban population in Posen and Pomerania had declined by 85 percent (Blanke 1993, 34, in Brubaker 1996, 163, n.53). Some 300,000 Sudeten Germans emigrated to Austria and Germany (de Zayaz 1988, 25). In Hungary, the 424,000 "returnees" (Mócsy 1973, 8–9, in Brubaker 1996, 157, n.34) from Romania, Yugoslavia, and Czechoslovakia amounted to 5 percent of the country's postwar population (Brubaker 1996, 158). This was no longer a migration of excess rural population motivated largely by economic considerations, but an ethnic exodus rarely seen since the time of the Völkerwanderung. ("Völkerwanderung" is a term borrowed from German historiography. In the narrow sense, it refers to Germanic migrations of the first five centuries A.D., but, more broadly, it can be applied to any mass migration involving whole tribes/ethnies.)

Two other factors made this period unusual: the closure of the Russian borders in the early 1920s and the closure of America to mass immigration in 1924. These closures, virtually simultaneous, left European populations with few options of escape. They created a vast cauldron with no safety valves and have immeasurably contributed to the economic disasters and political extremism that marked Europe in the interwar period.

The closure of the Soviet borders created a "wall of China" cutting across eastern Europe. To the west of the wall, migration west continued, although it was now more intra-European, since America was now closed (e.g., the Polish migration to France, which involved 218,000 people in 1919–25; the number of Poles residing in France increased from 45,000 in 1921 to 508,000 in 1931 [Kulischer 1948, 139]). On the other side of the wall, in the Soviet Union, migratory streams continued to flow east unabated. It is likely that the closure of the borders had artificially prolonged and enhanced traditional patterns of the Russian migration and settlement in the Eurasian steppe and beyond because it left only the eastern option open.

But not for long. World War II confirmed and enhanced many of the earlier trends in population movement and distribution. First, the mass murder of Jews and Gypsies and the postwar expulsions had greatly simplified the ethnic mosaic of Eastern and Central Europe. Second, the flight and transfer of some 14 million Germans and their replacement by 3.5 million Poles and 1.9 million Czechs (Magocsi 1993, 165) in 1945–48 moved the Slav-German borderline back to where it had been roughly a thousand years earlier. Finally, about two million Poles flocked from Lithuania, Belarus, and Ukraine into Poland (167) while two million Russians moved west into the Baltic republics, former eastern Poland, and Bessarabia (165). It was the avant-garde of a huge Russian migration that was to follow. (We should not oversimplify the postwar migrations. Some two million Soviet citizens and 520,000 Poles were repatriated from Germany in the same period (167). However, most of these people had been imported by Germany as (in)voluntary laborers. In effect, it was a temporary labor deportation. In that respect, these migrants differed from Poles migrating to Poland and Soviet citizens migrating to the western areas of the Soviet Union. Another interesting aspect of the post–World War II settlement is that it doubled and duplicated the "wall of China" that emerged after World War I. There were now two walls, the outer one separating Eastern Europe from the West, and the inner wall cutting off the Soviet Union from its East European satellites; the inner and outer defensive rings of Fortress Russia. Migration west was reduced to a trickle.)

Thus, in the first postwar years there were three major migratory waves west: Germans, Poles and Czechs, and Soviet citizens (mostly Russians). Once they had subsided, a new pattern emerged: migration west from Eastern Europe was artificially contained and broke out in spurts only in times of crisis (Hungarian refugees in 1956, Czechs and Slovaks in 1968). But within the Soviet Union, migration west gained strength sapping and undermining migration east. This was the continuation of the great turnaround that started in Germany in the eighteenth century.

Migration east, artificially sustained by megaprojects, such as the Virgin Lands settlement, sputtered on until the early 1960s when falling birth rates among Slav populations and continued migration west finally brought it to an end. Before long, toward the second half of the decade, an outflow from the east began, spurred in the early 1990s by the collapse of the Soviet Union; ethnic tensions in Central Asia, Transcaucasia, and Kazakstan; and the harsh living conditions in Siberia and the Far East. Half of former Soviet Germans have left, and Russia continues to receive thousands of migrants, most of them from the East. (But also from the Baltic: by 1998, the non-Latvian population of Latvia was down by 110,000 ([Internet, www.lat-net.lv, Population].)

What we are witnessing in Europe right now is a three-pronged process.

At one level, there is a return of colonial settlers and post-imperial disentanglement of various ethnies in Russia and the former Soviet Union. This process is centered on Russia and to some degree involves other Soviet successor states as well.

At another level, we are witnessing the completion of the "turnaround," which has now reached the eastern end of temperate Eurasia. The massive outflow from Eastern Europe to the West, predicted and feared by so many, did not materialize. It can be partly explained by the fact that Fortress Europe is well locked. But it is also the consequence of European demographic exhaustion on both sides of the former Iron Curtain.

Migration overseas has virtually ceased, despite the re-opening of Fortress America in 1964. The legacy of the *trente glorieuses,* a high standard of living, a slower population growth, and greater familiarity with the United States stopped the outflow. On the contrary, the aging European population can no longer satisfy the requirements of industry. Millions of non-European migrants had to be brought in. By now, there are some 3 to 4 million Arabs in France; 2.5 million Indians, Pakistanis, and West Indians in Britain; 2 million Turks in Germany; thousands more in the Netherlands, Sweden, and Switzerland. And in the last ten years or so Italy, Spain, and even Greece have begun to attract migrants.

In fact, what we are witnessing is a grandiose demographic implosion of Europe. The first signs appeared in France in the second half of the nineteenth century: zero or negative population growth, aging population, relative sluggishness in rates of economic growth. The two world wars shattered not only France but the entire continent. The catastrophe was partly concealed by massive infusions of American funds that made postwar economic prosperity possible. But if one looked closer, the signs were unmistakable: the division of Europe by the superpowers, loss of colonies, demographic wilting. It was exacerbated by the completion of the demographic transition to low death/low birth rates.

The transition and the implosion mark the end of a five hundred year period of an explosive European expansion. But before we can discuss its significance and try to predict what comes next, we have to go to the beginning and take a closer look at migrations generated by each of the three formations.

PART I

Migrations from Areas of Advanced Civilization

In this section, we will discuss how migration contributed to the expansion of advanced civilization.

The choice of examples may strike many readers as odd: colonization in Antiquity (Phoenicians, Greeks, Etruscans, Romans), medieval migration from Germany, and Russian imperial expansion, plus an example of how Russian colonization worked in one area (Kazakstan). What do they have in common? What kind of a smorgasbord is this?

Indeed, these civilizations differed profoundly, perhaps in everything except three things: they qualify as high (advanced) civilizations in that they had reached the level of statehood and developed writing, urban centers, and complex hierarchies; they generated powerful migratory movements that greatly expanded their area and influenced the course of history; and they all interacted with the forest tribes and, except for the Phoenicians and Etruscans, with the nomads of the Eurasian steppe.

CHAPTER 2

Migration and Colonization in Antiquity

The Phoenicians

The area of Phoenician colonization lies outside our area of interest, but it developed in a close conjuncture—and constant rivalry—with Greek colonization and needs to be mentioned.

The motor behind Phoenician colonization was a lack of vital resources in Phoenicia, especially metals. A search for metals sent Phoenicians to all corners of the Mediterranean and beyond. It led to the establishment of trade posts, first temporary, then permanent, and, eventually, to colonization.

Even at this early date—according to the Phoenician tradition, Cadiz was founded in the beginning of the eleventh century B.C. (Mansuelli 1967, 101)—Phoenician trade in the southern Mediterranean followed a classical pattern of trade between developed and underdeveloped countries: finished products from Phoenicia in exchange for raw materials.

Land trade routes were long and dangerous because they passed through areas controlled by numerous tribes. Trade caravans have always been vulnerable, their vulnerability increased manifold by political fragmentation. By comparison, the maritime trade, despite the ever-present threat of piracy, was on the whole safer.

Even with the maritime trade, the length of the trade routes and all the dangers involved, required a network of strongholds providing storage and trans-shipping facilities, as well as bases for military operations.

The best trade posts were located at the juncture of land and maritime routes and combined several functions. Cadiz, for example, served as an outlet for the products of Iberian mines and as an emporium for tin from Cornwall.

The great mercantile expansion was led by Tyre. It can be dated from the second half of the tenth century B.C. (Katzenstein 1973, 124). By then, Tyre had developed into a leading Phoenician city with a large fleet and extensive international connections. Its rise as a sea power is probably linked with the eclipse of the People of the Sea who had succumbed to the nascent Jewish kingdom. But Tyre was not an exclusively maritime trading city. It had trading quarters in Damascus and Samaria as well (I Kings 20:34).

Tyre was one of the first trading polities. From the time of Hiram I, the state—the king and the great merchant princes—had become the entrepreneur (Katzenstein 1973, 125). Directed and assisted by the state, Phoenician outposts sprang up in Cyprus (Menander, ch. V, in Katzenstein 1973, 125), Libya, and Spain. Their trade network covered Greece (although they never attempted to establish emporia there), Malta, western Sicily, and Sardinia. Carthage, founded in present-day Tunisia in 814/13 B.C., became the main outpost in the western Mediterranean, eventually founding its own colonies in the Balearic Islands (circa 654 B.C.) and elsewhere (Katzenstein 1973, 293).

Tyre held its colonial "empire" in a tight grip. The fact that it was the only colonial power in Phoenicia certainly helped, although it raises the question of why other Phoenician powers, like Sidon, did not emulate it.

Despite its early success, Tyre's capabilities were severely limited. It was a small city-state located perilously close to the coast that served as the major "highway" of the Near East. Tyre was no match for the predatory empires— Egypt, Assyria, Babylon—that periodically fought for the possession of the Fertile Crescent. In the earlier periods, the city could buy a degree of autonomy, as it did circa 731/29 B.C. from Assyria (222, n.14), but after 574, the Neo-Babylonian Kingdom and later Persia tightened their grip on the Phoenician coast. Although Tyre became a major port and maritime outlet for the Persian Empire, it was unable to hold on to its colonies, especially in the western Mediterranean, where it was supplanted by Carthage (Mansuelli 1967, 103).

The takeover by Carthage was facilitated by the fact that Tyrian colonies issued from the same metropolitan center and were used to being part of a unified network. Thus, when Tyre went into a decline in the sixth century B.C., it was easier for Carthage to impose unity on other Phoenician colonies (104). In contrast to the Greeks, the Phoenicians managed to avoid internecine squabbles.

The rise of Carthage inaugurated four hundred years of struggle, first against the Greeks, then Rome.

At its zenith, Carthage controlled the coast of North Africa from Syrtes to Numidia, eastern Iberia, western Sicily, Sardinia, Corsica, and the Balearic Islands. In effect, Carthage controlled the central and most of the western Mediterranean.

Its far-flung interests brought it into conflict with the Greeks. This conflict had long antecedents. In the seventh century B.C., Greeks, particularly those from Miletus, competed with Phoenicians in Egypt, while Phoenicians tried to expand their commerce to the Black Sea area. Phoenician subjection to Assyria was an unexpected boon for the Greeks. It even allowed Dorians from Thera, under Cretan leadership, to gain a foothold in Cyrenaica (Mansuelli 1967, 104).

The period around 600 B.C. was a time of transition: Tyre was already weakened but Carthage had not yet taken over its possessions in the western Mediterranean. It was this "interregnum" that allowed Greeks from Phocas to establish a colony at Massalia (Marseille). In the 570s B.C., Rhodians and Cnidians tried to establish a colony at Lilybaeum, near an existing Phoenician town of Motya (in west Sicily), but they were chased away and had to settle in the Lipari Islands (Boardman 1980, 215).

From Massalia, Greeks threatened Carthaginian holdings on the islands (Massalia founded a colony at Alalia in Corsica in 565 B.C. [214, n.195]) and in Iberia. They could rely on local rulers who were often less than happy with Phoenician monopoly (i.e., king Arganthonios of Tartessos) (Mansuelli 1967, 104).

But Carthage had several important advantages. First, it possessed a strategically important colony on the island of Ibiza. Second, community of interests allowed it to conclude an anti-Greek alliance with the Etruscans. Finally, the occupation of Phocas by Persia in 546 deprived Phocaeans—the main element in the Greek expansion in the western Mediterranean—of vital support from their home base. The battle of Alalia in 540 B.C., against a combined force of Etruscans and Carthaginians, was won by the Greeks, but it was a Pyrrhic victory. Soon, Corsica was lost to the Etruscans; Sardinia was lost to the Carthaginians; and Spain was virtually closed to Greek trade (Boardman 1980, 215). By the end of the sixth century B.C., Greeks hardly ventured west of Sicily; a de facto delimitation into spheres of influence had taken place (Mansuelli 1967, 105). (The delimitation between Carthaginian and Etruscan spheres was more formal, by a treaty [Boardman 1980, 215, n.200].)

The Greeks

The earliest Greek colonies, like their Phoenician counterparts, were trading posts. Already Minoans and Myceneans had established several trading stations along the coasts of Asia Minor and Syria (23; Desborough 1964, ch. 8–10). Myceneans, in particular, lacked adequate supplies of tin and copper. These metals had to be imported from Cyprus and the Cyclades.

The destruction of the Mycenean palaces in the twelfth to tenth centuries B.C. led to the cessation of trade. But the upheavals in continental Greece created large numbers of refugees who sought to start a new life across the

Aegean. Tradition mentions several migratory streams—Aeolian, Ionian, and Dorian (Cook 1962, ch. 1–2; Sakellariou 1958)—and the distribution of Greek dialects on the islands and on the coast of Anatolia seems to bear this out. Among the settlements (re)established by migrants or refugees were Rhodes, Halicarnassus, Ephesus, and many others. Many of these sites show a previous Mycenean occupation with later arrivals building settlements on the same site or in close proximity.

The early colonization provided "training" for later ventures overseas and schooling on how to deal with local people. Toward the end of the ninth century B.C., Ionian cities banded together in a league that included 12 members (Miletus, Ephesus, Phocaea, Samos, Chios, etc.) (G. L. Huxley 1966).

By the eighth century B.C., Greek settlements in western Asia Minor were well established and rapidly outgrowing their territory and local resources (Boardman 1980, 33). Population spread to the islands that were still unoccupied (by the Greeks)—Tenedos, Samothrace, and others—where earlier Thracian inhabitants were peacefully absorbed by Aeolian Greeks arriving circa 700 B.C. (85). Offshore islands built settlements on the mainland across the water (known as *peraiai,* from *pera,* "opposite" [85]).

Continental centers, such as Athens, also experienced explosive growth. Their populations needed more corn and wood than the limited local resources could provide. Hence, early imports of grain from the Black Sea and wood from the Caucasus. By the fifth century B.C., Athens had to build "clerouquies," outlying settlements that combined the functions of a military stronghold and a colony. They were peopled by the excess population of poor peasants (Mansuelli 1967, 102).

Although colonization was an effective means of draining off excess population, trade remained an important motive in Greek expansion overseas. It was greatly enhanced by the introduction, in the seventh century B.C., of larger ships that could transport more merchandise (112). Naucratis, a Greek emporium in Egypt, was a trading center par excellence. According to Herodotus, Pharaoh Amasis established it as a commercial headquarters for anyone who wished to settle and trade in Egypt (Herodotus 2, 178–79, in Boardman 1980, 117, n.31). (But archeological evidence shows that the town had been founded long before Amasis' reign.) We should note that Amasis was married to a Greek princess from Cyrene and relied on Greek mercenaries (nor was he the first Egyptian ruler to do so). On the other hand, Egyptians seem to have disliked Greeks as much as they disliked other foreigners: "No Egyptian, man or woman, will kiss a Greek, or use a Greek knife, spit, or cauldron, or even eat the flesh of a bull known to be clean, if it has been cut with a Greek knife" (Herodotus 2, 41, in Boardman 1980, 139, n.111). Unwelcome, Greeks banded together: the largest Greek sanctuary in Naucratis was built jointly by Ionians from Chios, Teos, Phocaea, and Clazomenae; Dorians from Rhodes, Cnidus, Halicarnassus, and Phaselis; and Aeolians from Mytilene (Boardman 1980, 117). It shows a degree of intra-Greek cooperation that is truly astonishing, certainly unlike Greek infighting elsewhere. But then, Naucratis was in many respects a special case. It was neither a true colony, that is, "an independent self-supporting town which had come to terms with the local population" (131), nor a simple trading station like Al Mina at the mouth of the Orontes in Syria.

Also, Greeks rarely encountered a strong state. In that sense, Naucratis was an exception while their settlement in Cyrenaica (today's Libya) is more typical. Here, Greek settlers came from a small island of Thera that could not support a large population. Despite the barren soil, many were reluctant to leave. Migrants had to be chosen by lots, one adult male per family (154). A Cretan guided them to a small offshore island where they spent the first two years trading with natives. Once friendly relations had been established, the Greeks moved to the mainland and then, six years later (circa 630 B.C.), to a better location further inland. Relations with the natives continued to be friendly; the Greeks married local women. The community was so prosperous that a century later the settlers invited new colonists from the Peloponnese and the Dorian islands (155). (Later, when the north African coast came under Carthaginian domination, further attempts at colonization failed. A band of settlers under Spartan Dorileus tried to establish a colony at Kinyps in Libya in 514 B.C., but they were driven out by Carthaginians and their local allies [215, n.203].)

Greek ventures in Magna Graecia—Sicily and southern Italy—had early antecedents. Remains of Cretan and Mycenean trading posts from as far back as 1600 B.C. have been found in the Lipari islands and parts of Sicily. A flourishing colony existed at Tarentum between 1400 and 1200 B.C. (164). However, these trading posts came to an end with the collapse of the Mycenean civilization.

The Greeks "returned" in the eighth century B.C. when Dorians and Ionians founded the first batch of some 30 colonies throughout the region. Here, the pioneers were the Euboeans (as they had been in the east [165].) They and the Corinthians (who founded the largest and richest Greek city in Sicily, Syracuse, in 733 B.C. [172]) built stations that controlled the best farmland in east Sicily, the Straits of Messina, and access to Etruria. The next batch was built by the Achaeans (from northwest Peloponnese) on the western coast of Italy. They commanded overland routes between the Ionian and Tyrrhenian Seas bypassing the Straits of Messina (178). The Greek grip on the area was consolidated in the seventh century B.C. By this time, some colonies were so large and prosperous that they could establish colonies of their own. Thus, Syracuse founded Helorus, Acrae, Casmenae, and Camarina. With the foundation of Acragas in 580 B.C., Greek colonization in Sicily was complete (185).

Unlike Cyrenaica, Greek relations with natives in Magna Graecia were much less friendly. Greek colonists frequently chose sites already occupied by the Sicels. And when the colonies began to expand in the seventh and sixth centuries, they expanded at the expense of the indigenous population (189, n.109). Despite the tensions, Greek trade brought prosperity, not only to the Greeks, but to natives as well. Hellenization was not far behind. Boardman believes that economic advantages and a strong cultural influence curtailed and ultimately destroyed a strong anti-Greek reaction that developed among the Sicels in the fifth century B.C. (190).

As we know, the Greeks did not stop in Sicily but went on to explore Sardinia, Corsica, and the southern coast of today's France. Here, not far from the mouth of the Rhône, the Phocaeans founded Massalia circa 600 B.C. Very quickly, the colony grew into an important trade center that connected the Mediterranean with central Europe, northern Gaul, and the British Isles via the Rhône. A maritime route followed the coastline, but here the way was barred by the Phoenicians. Massalians founded Emporion (Ampurias) in north Spain, but could not advance much further (218).

But Massalian preeminence was short-lived. When the trade routes shifted circa 500 B.C., its trade with the interior came to a halt.

For some reason, the Adriatic played a peripheral role in Greek colonization. The first settlement, on the island of Corcyra (Corfu), was a way station on the route west to Magna Graecia (Beaumont; Vallet; Braccesi; all in Boardman 1980, 225, n.1). Then, Euboean settlements up the Illyrian coast prompted a response from Corcyra and Corinth: in 627, they founded Epidamnus (today's Durres) (Boardman 1980, 226). Thereafter, the adversaries "hip-hopped" along the Illyrian coast until, by 600 B.C., they reached the northern tip of the sea.

On the other side of the Adriatic, the Greeks encountered Etruscans who were attracted by the fertile lands of the Po valley. By the time the Greeks reached the area, a number of Etruscan settlements centered on Felsina (Bologna) were already in place. Etruscans had also established a lively trade with central Europe via Adria at the mouth of the Po (which may have contributed to the decline in the trade of Massalia). It is unclear whether Greeks were admitted to either Adria or Felsina, but they were a prominent element in another port, Spina, on the southern arm of the Po delta (228). (Several authors mention Demaratus, a Corinthian noble who left home in the middle of the seventh century B.C. because of a political crisis and settled at Tarquinii. He married a local woman. His son, Tarquinius Priscus, became the fifth king of Rome [Blakeway; Pliny; Livy; Dionysios; all in Boardman 1980, 202, n.152].)

Another area where colonization was delayed was the Greeks' own back-yard, the Macedonian and Thracian coast. The reason, unlike with the Adriatic, seems clear: lack of good harbors. However, the coastal plains are fertile, if marshy, and, until recently, malarial. Once the colonies had been established—here, once again, the Euboeans were pioneers—a lively trade developed. The core Greek areas were being rapidly deforested, so the northern timber came in handy. So did Thracian horses, wine, and gold and silver from Mt. Pangaeum (Boardman 1980, 230). (It is interesting that a Phoenician presence has been uncovered on Thasos. It was corroborated by Herodotus [Herodotus 6, 47, in Boardman 1980, 230, n.32].)

The last area of Greek colonization is the Propontis, Black, and Azov Seas. Here, literary sources indicate the foundation of Sinope in the middle of the eighth century B.C. (Drews, in Boardman 1980, 240, n.76), but archeological evidence suggests the early seventh century for the Propontis and the late seventh for the Black Sea, although both areas must have been explored before settlement.

The most active colonizer in the Propontis was Megara, a small city-state north of Corinth whose population needed land (Megara had already es-tablished a colony in Sicily in the eighth century B.C. [Boardman 1980, 241]). In the Black Sea, the initiative belonged to Miletus, which also ex-perienced rapid population growth and, it seems, a series of crop failures (241). A number of colonies—Byzantium, Tomis (Constanza), Olbia, Chersonesus, Panticapaeum, Sinope, Trapezus (Trebizond)—grew into sub-stantial urban centers that played an important part in the history of the Black Sea region. The most remote foundation, Tanais, at the mouth of the Don, was an important emporium for trade with people in the Pontic steppe and further north.

To summarize, the primary motive for Greek colonization, like the Phoenician one, was trade and the search for raw materials. However, there were other important factors, such as growing population in Greek urban centers; the threat from Persia; and internal political turmoil, the fight be-tween democracy and oligarchy in many Greek city-states, which led the losers to migrate. Thus, Tarentum was founded by political exiles from La-conia, and the tradition that made Dido a fugitive hints that similar processes may have occurred among Phoenicians (Mansuelli 1967, 103). Fi-nally, there was what poet Archilochus called a "Panhellenic bastard" (103)—an adventurer who sought fortune overseas and, occasionally, helped to found new colonies. This type has a lot in common with later Vikings.

Eventually, possession of many colonies became a matter of prestige. Some cities started to recruit foreigners and mercenaries led by a few citizen families that formed the elite of the new colony. That is how even small cities like Megara managed to create an impressive number of colonies (103).

Before long, relations and conflicts generated by the colonization movement became exceedingly complex. They developed on several levels: between the metropoles, between colonies, between the metropole and its colonies, between the metropole and someone else's colonies, and any combination of the above. To these must be added conflicts between Dorians and Ionians and later the pan-Hellenic conflict between Athens and Sparta. The very pattern of colonization, which planted colonies of diverse origin in close proximity, created a situation favorable to conflicts. Finally, in the great struggle between democracy and oligarchy the oligarchy often lost. For that reason, colonies were often settled or at least led by the oligarchs while the metropoles were democratic or aristocratic. These factional/class differences created yet another framework for conflicts. By the sixth century B.C., conflicts of all kinds and at all levels raged in the Greek world (103).

If we compare Greek colonization with the Phoenician one, Greek holdings were more spread out, mostly because Greek colonization originated from many centers. (Achaeans were the least adventurous: they did not venture farther than southern Italy. Dorians too colonized southern Italy, but also planted colonies in Thrace, the Black Sea area, and Cyrenaica. Ionians were the most adventurous, ranging from Tanais on the Don to Naucratis in Egypt to Mainake in Andalusia [107].)

Another threat, to all colonization movements, was the struggle against indigenous peoples. Although occasionally Greeks reached satisfactory agreements with locals (e.g., in the Crimea), in other places, such as Sicily and southern Italy, they fought them tooth and nail (107). This did not prevent eventual infiltration and a gradual takeover by the locals. Greek disunity contributed to this process. Phoenicians, more united, could better withstand the pressure. With the rise of Syracuse, Greeks acquired a major center comparable to Carthage. But it started later in the process, and the diversity of Greek colonies was too great. The city never succeeded in centralizing Greek colonies the way Carthage had centralized the Phoenician ones.

By the fifth century B.C., virtually the entire shoreline of the Mediterranean, except Etruria and Egypt, was jam-packed by colonies.

The colonization unified the Mediterranean world and lay the foundations for the Roman Empire. At the same time, immediate contact created by colonization seldom exceeded 100 kilometers. As a result of the geopolitical constraints, the movement hugged the coast. But the trade routes inland were in the hands of the locals. For example, tin was transported to Massalia from Britain via the Seine, the Saône, and the Rhône by Celts, since the maritime route was in the hands of Carthage. This way the Mediterranean civilization penetrated inland via the rivers. It acquainted northern "forest tribes" with rich southern lands.

Greek and especially Etruscan traders also traveled far inland from at least the second half of the sixth century B.C. Increased trade also attracted "barbarian" traders to the Mediterranean colonies and settlements. In many colonies, such as Emporion, whole city blocks inhabited by indigenes grew around the Greek core (111).

Thus, colonization introduced urbanization into agricultural tribal societies. It also exposed indigenous populations to new political and social ideas. Even the colonists were not immune because colonies were more open societies than the old metropoles. Merchants and entrepreneurs who were often the leading element in the new foundations were different from hereditary nobility predominant in the metropole even if they eventually acquired land and became landowners. De Sanctis showed that the spirit of freedom and individualism had a better chance to develop in colonies (De Sanctis in Mansuelli 1967, 113).

Finally, despite the discord, the colonization promoted among Greeks the concept of Hellenism.

The Etruscans

Unlike Phoenicia, Etruria was rich in metals. It had copper, tin, and lead near the coast (Colline Metallifere) and rich deposits of iron ore on the island of Elba (Barker and Rasmussen 1998, 76). Naturally, it exercised a considerable attraction on Greek and Phoenician traders. But they failed to establish long-lasting colonies. The fact that there were no Greek or Phoenician settlements north of Cumae testifies to the strength of Etruscan city-states. The situation in Etruria confirmed the rule that, when Greeks or Phoenicians encountered powerful states, as they also did in Egypt, they limited themselves to establishing trade colonies. However, Etruria, like Syria but unlike Egypt, was not a major power. And it was disunited. It seems that any polity that had established a state presented a sufficient barrier to Greek and Phoenician colonization.

Etruria was decentralized and politically fragmented to a degree comparable to Greece or Phoenicia. Centers close to the Tyrrhenian coast—Cerveteri, Tarquinia, Vulci, Veii—traded with the west and south; those close to the Adriatic coast, centered on Felsina, directed their attention east and north. Populonia and Vetulonia had very close links with Sardinia, with both the indigenous powers and Phoenicians stationed there (76–77), while Spina and Adria, at the mouth of the Po, traded with central Europe.

From very early on, the luscious lands of Campania and a lively trade with Greeks further down the coast pulled the Etruscans south. There are indications that they may have founded Capua circa 800 B.C. (139). Their penetration proceeded along the coast as well as inland routes. Coastal towns like Fratte and Pontecagnano were probably settled from the coast of southern Etruria, while inland centers like Nola and Capua were more likely offshoots from the area around Veii, the southernmost of the Etruscan states (Cristofani 1979b, 384, in Barker and Rasmussen 1998, 140, n.59). At the height of their power, in 616–509 B.C., even Rome was ruled by the (Etruscan) Tarquin dynasty (139).

Eventually, competition with Greeks and Carthaginians led to a struggle for the mastery of the Tyrrhenian Sea in which the Etruscans held the balance of power. Ultimately, Etruscans sided with Carthage because Greeks were a closer and a major threat. In the battle at Alalia, a combined Puno-Etruscan fleet fought it out with the Phocaeans. And, as we know, although the Greeks won, their losses precluded further expansion.

Despite the continuous enmity, trade with Greeks continued at Greek trading enclaves on the coast (Cristofani 1983a, in Barker and Rasmussen 1998, 135, n.48). Epigraphic data preserves the names of Etruscanized Greeks whose names—Larth Telicles, Rutile Hipucrates—were found scratched on seventh-century pots (136, n.49). Many seem to have come from eastern (i.e., west Anatolian) Greece. Some were probably refugees fleeing the Persians. And the site at Alalia (modern Algeria), where Greek expansion in the Tyrrthenian was stopped, shows a town with sizable Carthaginian, Etruscan, and Greek components (Jehasse and Jehasse, in Barker and Rasmussen 1998, 137, n.55).

As the competition in the south stiffened and the spheres of interest were delimited, it was natural that the Etruscans would turn north, to the valley of the Po. Here, there were Etruscan speakers already toward the end of the seventh century B.C. (C. Morigi Govi, in Cristofani 1985a, 87, in Barker and Rasmussen 1998, 140, n.62). A number of reversals suffered by the Etruscans in the south—the expulsion from Rome in 509 B.C.; the defeat of a major Etruscan force at Aricia by a combined army of Latins and Greeks, which closed off Latium to the Etruscans and isolated those in Campania; and, finally, the defeat of an Etruscan fleet off Cumae by the Greeks in 474 B.C. (Barker and Rasmussen 1998, 140)—made the northern option the only one available.

Within a short time, Etruscans colonized the area south of the Po; built a major urban center at Felsina (Bologna); and established important trading emporia at Adria and Spina.

Unfortunately for the Etruscans, this option was not open for long. Around 400 B.C., the incoming Gauls closed off the north, leaving the Etruscans between the Roman hammer and the Celtic anvil.

Rome

Rome started as a polis. At this earlier stage its development did not differ significantly from general trends and patterns of other city-states. But its rapid expansion and eventual transformation into an empire posed the problem of absorbing the conquests and integrating diverse populations. And here colonization played an important part. Thus, in Rome, colonization was primarily an instrument of imperial expansion, not trade. In motivation, it was quite different from earlier colonizing movements by the Etruscans, Phoenicians, and Greeks.

Initially, Rome borrowed the pattern of land-based colonization from its earlier masters, the Etruscans. But its colonies and their relations with Rome and Roman citizens were organized according to a statute, *lex data,* that specified their rights and obligations. For example, citizen soldiers planted in Roman colonies retained full citizen rights. Mansuelli calls them "veritable little Romes placed in subjugated countries" (Mansuelli 1967, 299). Agricultural colonists from Latin cities had more restricted rights. But whether Latin or Roman, the ties between the colonies and the metropole remained bilateral.

The development of the colonies went hand in hand with the integration of Latins. When the Latin League was broken up in 338 B.C. (Grant 1978, 57), some Latin cities retained formal independence. In others, Rome granted male inhabitants a new sort of right, citizenship without franchise (*civitas sine suffragio*). This was a partial, halfway Roman citizenship by which they could not vote in Roman elections but had private (civic) rights in relations with Romans: they could conduct relations according to Roman law (*commercium*) and were entitled to marry a Roman without forfeiting inheritance of paternity rights (*conubium*) (Grant 1978, 58). This idea developed from the guest-right privileges granted to Etruscan Caere some 40 years earlier, was tried out on member towns of the Campanian League, and was then extended to Latin cities and the Sabines (59). The objective was to maintain control over Latins without offending their sensibilities.

Among Latin colonies established during the previous century and a half, seven were authorized by Rome to retain special privileges. The rest were granted the halfway status (59). In Cales (near Capua), for example, plots of land were allotted to more than two thousand families, a mixture of Latins, Romans, and Campanians (59). With time, these colonies, many of them strategically located, multiplied, becoming an effective bulwark against the empire's enemies.

Purely Roman colonies appeared toward the end of the fourth century B.C. and were originally located along the coast, as coast guard stations. They were linked to Rome by a continuous stretch of Roman territory, which meant that they needed fewer defenders and could operate with fewer settlers (60). One of the reasons was that Rome did not want to disperse its manpower. Another, that comparatively few Romans wanted to leave the City. Roman colonies comprised only 300 families each, compared to 2,000 in the Latin ones. If we combine both types of colonies plus individual allotments outside the colonies, some 60,000 holdings were established in 343–264 B.C.; taken together, they increased the area under effective Roman control threefold to some 50,000 square miles (61).

Another subdivision of colonies separated those that were settled by Roman citizens (the "settlement" colonies) and existing towns that were granted the status of a colony (the "titular" colonies). Only a settlement colony was a true colony (Vittinghoff 1951, 23). Their inhabitants belonged to Roman tribes and retained Roman citizenship. But from the time of Trajan and Hadrian, titular colonies multiplied and gained in importance. Starting in 90/89 B.C., transpadanian cities were promoted to the status of Latin colonies without any Latin settlements therein. Such promotions could be granted for exceptional service (27) or from political considerations.

Yet another subdivision separated the veteran colonies from "proletarian" colonies (53). Many veterans were rewarded with land grants and settled in newly acquired provinces or in old ones after a suppression of rebellions. Such colonies played an important role as military outposts that strengthened the imperial defenses. In general, settlers were considered manpower reserves that helped the army in time of need. Sulla (early first century B.C.) settled about one hundred thousand of his veterans in large colonies in Italy (Grant 1978, 187). For comparison, in 70/69 B.C., there were 910,000 citizens liable for military service (Phlegon Olymp. 177,3; Liv. Epit. 98 [900,000]; in Vittinghoff 1951, 62, n.1). And in 43 B.C., land for 170,000 men had to be found (App. 5, 3, in Vittinghoff 1951, 98, n.3).

But Rome also faced a perennial problem of urban "proletariat," a largely parasitic *plebs urbana* that posed a serious political and economic problem. In 46 B.C., 320,000 Romans (not counting wives or children) received state corn subsidies (Suet. Iul. 41, 3; Plut. Caes. 55; in Vittinghoff 1951, 57, n.2). By resettlement and pruning the lists of the eligible, Caesar reduced the number of recipients by more than half. However, not all those taken off the public dole were willing to relocate: the total number of those resettled by Caesar amounted to only 80,000 (Suet. Iul. 42, 1, in Vittinghoff 1951, 24, n.1).

Under Augustus, the number of those on the dole grew again to no less than 200,000, perhaps even 250,000 (Vittinghoff 1951, 57, n.5). Augustus founded 28 colonies in Italy spending 600 million sesterce there; in the same period 260 million were spent in the provinces (98). In 29 B.C., Augustus settled 120,000 men in colonies (99, n.4) and 300,000 were sent back to their places of origin (99, n.5).

Colonization was also an important instrument of integrating the newly incorporated territories. Here is how the formerly Celtic (and before that, Etruscan) land south of the Po (Cispadania) was integrated.

After the defeat of the Senones, the Romans lay the groundwork for the conquest of *ager Gallicus*. The first step was the foundation of the Latin colony at Ariminum in 268 B.C., on the border between the old land of the Senones and the Boii (Livy *Per.* 15; Vell. Pat. 1.14, in Dyson 1985, 27, n.102). It was populated by several thousand families from several parts of central Italy.

Four years after the capture of Mediolanum, in 218 B.C., Romans founded Placentia and Cremona, six thousand families each. Placed on the opposite sides of the Po, they controlled the river at its juncture with the Adda interrupting communications between the Insubres and the Boii. Placentia had an additional task of keeping watch over the Ligurians who sided with the Gauls at this time (Dyson 1985, 32–33). During the Second Punic War both colonies held out but not without difficulty. By the time of the final victory over the local Gauls, in 190 B.C., many settlers had left (Livy 37.46.9–37.47.2, in Dyson 1985, 40, n.172). Now they could return. New colonies were founded at Bononia/Felsina in 189 B.C. (Livy 37.57.7–9, in Dyson 1985, 40, n.173) and at Parma and Mutina in 183 B.C. (Livy 39.55.6–8, in Dyson 1985, 40, n.173). In 187 B.C. a major road between Ariminum and Placentia was built (Livy 39.2.6–7, 39.2.10–11, in Dyson 1985, 40, n.174), and in 173 B.C. more *ager publicus* land, consisting of land confiscated from the natives, was divided among new settlers (Livy 42.4.3–4, in Dyson 1985, 40, n.175). These principal foundations were supplemented by a network of smaller settlements, especially along Via Emilia. Although officially not colonies, they quickly became foci of social and economic life linking local markets with major roads. They also helped settlers to mix with remnants of the local population, advancing their Romanization (Dyson 1985, 40–41). Thus, the area south of the Po was made part of Italy.

With the advent of the empire, granting Roman citizenship personally benefited the emperor since he acquired clients. Not surprisingly, the pace of "naturalization" quickened. In the second half of Augustus's rule, from 8 B.C. to A.D. 14, the number of male Roman citizens over 17 increased by 17 percent, from 4,233,000 to 4,937,000 (Vittinghoff 1951, 97, n.1). Altogether, from 69 B.C. to the time of his death in A.D. 14, the total number of Roman citizens increased from 2.7 million to 14.8 million (139, n.3). Most of the increase could be attributed to citizenship grants rather than a frenetic population growth. (But, according to Michael Grant, Augustus raised the number of citizens from about 5 to more than 6 million, and in the provinces from about 1 million to nearly 2 [Grant 1978, 247].)

The pace in the founding of colonies shows a similar pattern.

When Caesar came to power, there were only 7 colonies: 2 in Corsica, 2 in the Baleares, 2 in Iberia, and 1 in Gaul. Caesar founded 32: 5 in Gaul and Narbonensis, 10 in Iberia (plus 2 municipia), 8 in Africa, 3 in Macedonia,

4 in Asia Minor. Augustus founded 74 (plus 33 municipia): 4 in Narbonensis (plus 4 municipia), 11 in Iberia (Baetica, Tarraconensis, Lusitania) (plus 10 municipia), 27 in Africa and Mauretania (plus 8 municipia), 7 in Sicily and Sardinia (plus 8 municipia), 5 in Illyria (plus 2 municipia), 7 in Macedonia (plus 1 municipium), 1 in Crete, 10 in Asia Minor (Asia and Galatia), and 2 in Syria (148–50).

Roman colonization was profoundly different from that of the Greeks, Etruscans, or Phoenicians. Although at the earliest stage of the Roman state the pattern was borrowed from the Etruscans, the main distinction was the imperial nature of the Roman state, even before it was formally transformed into an empire. The Roman colonies were not trade stations but military outposts and instruments of imperial control. As such, they were the cornerstone of Roman power and its expansion, ensuring political integration and economic exploitation of outlying territories.

In addition to securing control over vast areas, Roman colonization pursued several other objectives. One was to reward the veterans, providing them with the means of sustenance in their declining years. This policy not only ensured their loyalty, it also assured the state a supply of future manpower since veterans' sons frequently followed in their fathers' footsteps. Ironically, this policy sometimes worked against interests of state because many veterans preferred Italy, where funds of available land were inadequate. As a result, land sometimes had to be confiscated from other Roman citizens and allies, creating deep resentments among whole strata of Roman citizens whose loyalty the state was eager to retain.

Another objective was to alleviate the pressure from the parasitic and prolific urban plebs, which, already by the middle of the first century B.C., numbered in the hundreds of thousands. This was a problem of relative overpopulation and as such, on a par with population problems in some Greek cities, although its scale dwarfed anything experienced even by the largest Greek urban center.

Finally, the granting of citizenship promoted the process of Romanization. If one can generalize (but one can't, because it differed from province to province and from epoch to epoch), Romanization in the west was slow but solid because it was not imposed. Locals could keep their languages, customs, and religion for as long as they wished, as long as they were loyal subjects. Of course, Roman citizenship carried enormous prestige. It was the envy of everyone, the state to which everyone aspired. Even where local civilization was on a comparable (Etruria) or higher (Magna Graecia) level, people chose to Romanize.

However, in the East, all the power of the state and the attractions of Roman citizenship and civilization were powerless before the prestige of the

Greek language and culture. The decay of the West, the transfer of the capital to Constantinople, and the emergence of the alternate, culturally Greek center, prevented a similar Romanization of the East. Here, *"Graecia [capta] ferum victorem cepit"* (Greece captive captured her rough conqueror) (Horace, *Epistles,* 2.I.156).

CHAPTER 3

German Migrations East

†Dean S. Rugg

Introduction

The interaction of different cultures in the Eurasian steppe is an interesting and important subject. One thinks most often of the migrations of peoples from the east, especially the Mongols, but the movement of German settlers from the west was no less significant.

The purpose of this chapter is to place the German migration and its relationship to other cultures in its historical context. First, I will deal with German settlement in eastern Europe and then with German migration into Russia.

Eastern Europe, an area on the western margins of the Eurasian steppe, was affected by German migration and its consequences until World War II. Many Germans fled the area during the war but after 1945 most of the remaining Germans (some 12 million) were forced to leave under the Potsdam agreements. Only the relics of this settlement remain today. However, after 1990, the reunification of Germany created an economic giant that, although peaceful in nature, may affect the Eurasian steppe in the future.

Although my treatment of this subject in my book (Rugg 1985, ch. 3) covered only German medieval settlement, I believe it is necessary to broaden the scope to include the interrelationships between Germans and their eastern neighbors in later periods.

The German settlement in Russia was quite different from that in eastern Europe. The Baltic areas of the Russian Empire had been settled during the Middle Ages, but were Germanized by force of arms, unlike Poland, Bohemia, and Hungary, where German settlers came by invitation from local rulers. The mostly agricultural settlement on the Volga and in the southern regions of European Russia was done on invitation from the Russian tsars, but occurred much later, mostly in the eighteenth century.

The impact of these two groups of Germans, in Eastern Europe and Russia, has been evident in what German geopoliticians called a Deutscher Kulturraum ("German culture area"), which is shown on map 3.1. My long stay in Germany and frequent travels in Eastern Europe and the Soviet Union have convinced me that the concept retained validity in the German mind through World War II.

A model of settlement by Germans in both eastern Europe and Russia, together with their interrelationships to other cultures, should prove helpful:

German Colonization	*Conditions in Eastern Europe*
Eastern Europe	
German medieval colonization (ninth to fourteenth century)	Cooperation with some Germanization
German colonization as imperial policy (sixteenth to twentieth century)	Serfdom and Germanization
Russia	
German settlement in Russia, especially in the early eighteenth century and in 1763–1860	Baltic Germans as part of Russian society and farmer colonists in isolated villages in European Russia
Russification of Germans and the later effects of communism on these groups	Deportation of Germans to the east with loss of language and culture

Eastern Europe—Medieval Colonization

Relations between Germans and Other Ethnic Groups

C. T. Smith's (1978, 183) statement adequately explains the change from German medieval to imperial colonization: "The conditions which affected German settlement in the east changed considerably after the end of the Middle Ages. . . . During the seventeenth and eighteenth centuries the dynastic policies of the Habsburgs, Brandenburg-Prussia, and particularly of Frederick II put a new and different emphasis on rural colonization in the lands which had been acquired from the Slavs." German colonists came to eastern areas that had received settlers during the Middle Ages, but now they became part of a more systematic state-controlled movement rather than one that had been voluntary and even cooperative with the Slavs and the Hungarians. Thus, the interrelationships between Germans and eastern Europeans changed, with Germanization now promoted by the state. However, these interrelationships differed from area to area.

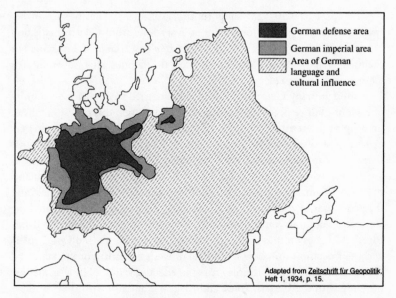

Map 3.1   Area of German Influence

Aubin, a recognized scholar of German colonization in the east, points out two types of interaction during the medieval period. First, "on old-settled land, the native and German ways of settlement interacted, and the native way was to some extent immediately transformed." Second, "where absolutely new land was won, especially on bogs and marshes, as on the lower Elbe, in the Harz lowland . . . and in the delta of the Vistula about Danzig . . . only German immigrants were qualified . . . for forest clearing" and draining of land (1966, 458).

Here I should mention that a new interpretation of the interaction between Germans and eastern Europeans has been proposed by a group of historians. They have tried to show that the interaction was more peaceful than generally thought (Graus et al., 1970). While conflict was frequent, especially in East Prussia controlled by the Teutonic Knights, peaceful interaction was more often the case. Indeed, Gieysztor (Graus et al. 1970, 12) says that the dominant feature of this contact "was not a collision of civilizations but the emergence of a common civilization; and where there were conflicts, it was much more class than national or ethnic affiliations . . ." Or, as Barraclough (9–10) states, "as a result of political and cultural interchange, of trading links, and, perhaps above all, participation in a common religious experience, a single civilization embracing both East and West . . . came into existence."

Thompson (1928, 528) supports this assessment. The interaction between settlement groups took place at every level from field to castle and church, and the common civilization was often best seen in architecture. For example, Veit Stoss of Nurnberg created the famous altar in St. Mary's Church in Cracow, Poland.

Although many German and Slav scholars tried to emphasize the unity of each of their respective groups in the Middle Ages, this cohesion fails to hold up under scrutiny. Within German and Slav areas, many differences existed in state organization and religion. Even the notion of *Drang nach Osten* (drive to the east), a symbol of German imperialism, did not have this aspect in medieval colonization. Bosl (54–57, Graus et al. 1970) remarks that "Christianization was carried out by agreement with native princes and magnates, not by the sword. This voluntary religious decision prepared the way for a voluntary integration into the political system of medieval Europe." Bosl goes on to say that "the strength and genius of individual rulers and their decision to follow the model of western institutions in state and church definitely united the Slav tribes in effective states." This was the case not only with the Czechs, Poles, and Magyars, but also with the East Slavs in Kiev Rus' during the tenth century. Originally, a strong conviction existed, especially among German historians, that as a result of Germanization, the Slavs acquired the foundations of higher civilization by assimilating the more progressive techniques of the West. "In reality, the German eastward movement in the thirteenth and fourteenth centuries was successful because the Slavs were already Christians and already had civilized standards. . . . The rulers of eastern Europe were interested in reforming the economy and social structure of their countries, in order to compete with the West, and for this purpose they invited western settlers, artisans, miners, and traders to settle in their kingdoms" (Bosl 61, Graus et al. 1970). Thus, it appears an important group of European historians are leaning toward the hypothesis that much of the east-west integration between German colonists and native peoples was voluntary and cooperative. Pounds (1969, 85) provides some support to this thesis when he states that "at no time were the two cultural worlds, the German and the Slav, sharply divided. The one merged into the other through a region of mixed language and divided loyalties."

But this German medieval colonization varied from place to place. Mass settlement of immigrants took place in what later became the principalities of Brandenburg, Mecklenburg, Pomerania, and western Silesia. Farther east, particularly in East Prussia, despite the power of the Teutonic Knights, and in eastern Silesia and Bohemia, the German settlement was not numerous enough to supplant the predominantly Slav element. German colonization in Bohemia seems to have been encouraged by the Slav rulers to counteract the power of the native aristocracy (*Germany,* Geographical Handbook, Naval Intelligence Division, II, 1944, 90). Poston (144, Graus et al. 1970) expresses it well when he states that "the main achievement of German colonization was not so much to displace the existing Slav population as to introduce a large additional stratum of peasant immigrants and thereby to create a wholly new agrarian economy on land hitherto unoccupied or else occupied very sparsely."

Even more important was the role of German migrants in urbanization. Many towns throughout eastern Europe, from Riga to Plzeň, were founded by Germans.

One special class of medieval German colonists was invited by the Hungarian kings because they brought mining, trade, and frontier security to areas in what are now parts of Slovakia and Romania. They enjoyed a privileged status and lived a rather exclusive existence in walled towns and villages, where they resisted any centralizing tendencies of governments and retained German language and culture for hundreds of years. Kuhn (1937, 810) called these areas Volksräume (ethnic areas) because they represent a different type of interrelationship between man and land than was found in other areas of eastern Europe. One of the reasons they were able to remain isolated enclaves of German settlement was their status as privileged peoples, a contrast to what we have mentioned above for many German colonists. However, toward the end of the Middle Ages, in the fifteenth and sixteenth centuries, the situation changed radically. In western Europe, feudalism declined as people were freed of former obligations, while in the east feudalism was altered as the peasants were reduced to the level of serfs. The effects of this radical change are essential in understanding the interrelationships between Germans and other cultures in eastern Europe.

Characteristics of Medieval Colonization

From northern Poland to Transylvania, a distance of seven hundred miles, there exists a series of landscape relics that are derived from a single process—the colonization of eastern Europe during the Middle Ages by German-speaking peoples. The process lasted about four hundred years (950 to 1350) and took place at different rates and with varying degrees of intensity. It was essentially one process and has been described as the greatest single transformation of the eastern European landscape. The Germans transformed the economy of eastern Europe by clearing and settling the land, opening up mines, and creating networks of trade and urbanization. In the steady expansion of a frontier and settlement to the east, this colonization resembled that of the American frontier, but differed in important aspects, too.

Political Organization, Terrain, and Routes

The Holy Roman Empire formed the political base for the first German colonization in Eastern Europe. However, the actual process took place in the kingdoms of Poland, Bohemia, and Hungary to the east. The unstable nature of the empire's eastern border before the tenth century forced the establishment there of Marken (marches) as defensive frontier provinces against the incursions of the Slavs and Hungarians. After the ninth century and for some four hundred years, the Germans colonized the East and the marches became jumping-off points. The colonization became systemic over this period, resulting in the pattern shown on map 3.2 with three prongs extending into Pomerania on the Baltic Sea coast, up the Oder River valley into Silesia, and down the Danube River valley through Austria. To the north in Poland, the prongs of colonization took place on the northern European plain dominated by glacial topography in the north and center, and the fertile loess soil in the south. These three areas of the Northern European plain represent an extension of the Eurasian steppe to the west. In Bohemia and northern Hungary, settlement occurred in the basins and forested mountains, as shown on map 3.2. In these mountains, the diffusion of mining technology became important as it extended from Goslar through Freiburg. A mining school developed at Kuttenberg (Kutná Hora). Even today, mining relics remain in Iglau (Jihlava), Kremnitz (Kremnice), Schemnitz (Šemnice), Offenberg (Baia de Argeş) and other German, Czech, Slovak, and Romanian towns.

Besides the *Bergbau,* or mining settlements, along the southern route of colonization, the Grenzer (border) settlements of the Zips, Siebenbürgen (Transylvania), and Burzenland (Romania) deserve mention (Kuhn 1937). In these areas, scattered German colonies existed for hundreds of years as Volksräume where they established solid connections to the land.

Two other political units must be mentioned in connection with German medieval colonization of 950–1350. The Teutonic Knights moved into the area of the southeastern Baltic Sea (later East Prussia) and settled in fortified towns like Marienburg where they attempted to Christianize the heathen Prussians. Here, German influence was enhanced by the Hanseatic League, a voluntary association of some 80 towns that promoted trade around the Baltic Sea and beyond. Although not all were German, the Germanic element predominated.

As expected, the routes holding together these Germanic colonies were more numerous in the north, across the European plain, than in the south, in central Europe, and the Balkans. In the north, four routes diverged from Halle, a clearing point for trading networks within the Germanic settlements. On map 3.2, two of these four routes correspond to two prongs of settlement mentioned above: (1) along the Baltic Sea coast to Danzig and

Map 3.2 German Medieval Migrations

Königsberg and (2) the Hohe Strasse ("High Street") paralleling the fertile loess belt of the upper Oder River to Lublin. The third route, located between these prongs, runs from Berlin to Thorn on the Vistula. The fourth east-west route crossed the Mittelgebirge from the Bohemian Forest through Prague to the Moravian Gate and Cracow. North-south roads connected the east-west routes; some converged on the fair towns of Leipzig and Posen (Poznań). In the south, only two routes became important, both connecting Vienna to Constantinople. The first route kept to the west of the Danube River from Budapest to Belgrade and Sofia. The second left Budapest through Grosswardein, Klausenburg, and Kronstadt. Later, the levying of duties displaced Vienna, and trade moved along north-south routes, especially the Kupferweg (copper route) through Kaschau (Košice) to Budapest.

The Process of Colonization

The process of German colonization occurred in the context of feudalism, a social order in which mutual obligations existed among lord, vassal, and peasant. This political system rested on the foundations of manorial economy that involved the duties of the lord's demesne, but also allowed the peasant to work for himself. The system provided order in a world where central authority was either weak or nonexistent; and the economy, at least in early feudalism, was a self-sufficient one.

The system was harsh. And German colonization in the east gave the settlers an opportunity to escape from oppressive obligations and higher population densities in the empire (the push factors) to an area where both were much lower (the pull factors).

The colonization was communal in character: farmers, craftsmen, miners, and clergy formed a group that moved as a unit. By relocating to Poland, Bohemia, or Hungary, these groups transformed preexisting institutions of agriculture, commerce, mineral production, and religion. Perhaps the most important aspect of this institutional change involved the diffusion of German town law that gave rights and obligations to settlers. Although the legal system was stratified among the three estates—gentry, clergy, and peasantry—a peasant could still rise socially and economically to become a free landholder.

A "locator" or promoter coordinated each group, recruiting settlers, acquiring the land by purchase or grant, dividing it, handling the legal problems, and dealing with indigenous people. For his contribution, the locator received rewards in land and other benefits. Similarly, the colonists benefited in terms of lower rents, less labor, exemptions from dues for 20 years, and rights to sell land and move. For that reason, residents of the western part of the empire differed in their perceptions and ideologies from settlers in the East. Only later, in the fifteenth century, did the situation in the east deteriorate as feudalism and serfdom worsened.

Landscape Relics

Numerous relics of German colonization in the eastern European landscape helped to motivate my research in this area. The colonization transformed society in the east and led to a certain amount of uniformity in all settlements. Some of these relics still exist, in contrast to German settlement in Russia. The village forms of German origin—Strassendorf, Angerdorf, Wald- or Marschhufendorf, and Runddorf—are well known and still visible throughout the area. In eastern Europe, the three-field system (grain, feed, fallow) has disappeared as individual strips in most areas replaced it. Communist collectivization with its large fields replaced the strips in Czechoslovakia, Hungary, and Romania, but these countries have largely reverted to strips since 1990, and in Poland collectivization never incorporated them. In 1960, in eastern Poland, I saw one of the last relics of the three-field system.

German-founded towns show their origin in three outstanding land-marks—castle, cathedral, and town hall/market place—which represented the three estates of medieval society: aristocracy, clergy, and people. Roman-ian Sighişoara (in Transylvania), called Schässburg by Germans, is a good ex-ample. These relics, along with remnants of town walls, remain visible in the "old towns" or city centers of today. The diffusion of monasteries from the west often left an imprint, as seen, for example, in Chorin northeast of Berlin. Mine relics of a chain of Bergbau (mining) settlements also persist, perhaps most strongly in Kuttenberg (Kutná Hora) and Kremnitz (Kremnice), today in the Czech and Slovak Republics respectively. Finally, relics of trading set-tlements endure in the Zips towns like Leutschau (Levoča) in Slovakia.

Eastern Europe—Imperial Colonization

Relations between the Germans and Other Ethnic Groups

The late rise of serfdom in eastern Europe radically altered the interrela-tionships among its peoples. As the position of the peasant in western Eu-rope improved, it deteriorated in the East. It was rulers in western Europe who, acting independently of the nobility, established norms of feudal oblig-ations. As feudalism withered, work obligations were converted into rent payments, and serfs gradually became free. In the East, however, the rulers became more dependent on the lords in rural areas and thus allowed them to increase their powers over the peasants. The rationale was producing grain for export, a lucrative undertaking. As a result, the bond between lord and serf ceased to be one of mutual obligation and degenerated into one-sided exploitation (Rugg 1985, 72–73). The process was characterized by four main factors: (1) the increase in the political power of the nobility; (2) growth of seigniorial jurisdictional powers over peasantry; (3) the shift by lords from being rent receivers to becoming producers for the market; and (4) the decline of the cities and urban middle class (Blum 1957, 807–36).

These changes began to take place in the fifteenth century with a long pe-riod of depression and contraction. The slump had started with the decrease of the migratory inflow from the West, as population pressure eased in west-ern Europe due to plagues, wars, invasions, feuds, civil strife, and crop fail-ure. Within the depopulated villages in the East, the lords tried to compensate their smaller income by imposing newer and heavier obliga-tions, notably in the form of labor dues and cash payments. Encroachments were also made on peasants' right to move. Thus, by the end of the fifteenth century, the peasants were well on their way to becoming serfs.

The important thing about refeudalization in the East is that its ratio-nale was economic, not ethnic. The nobility of Germany, Poland, Bohemia,

Hungary, and Russia all began to (re)enserf the peasant regardless of nationality. It could do it because of the increase in its political power (Blum 1957, 836).

Characteristics of Imperial Colonization

With the rise of serfdom in the East, German colonization changed its character.

The absolutist period in Prussian history began with Frederick Wilhelm in 1660 and ended effectively with the death of Frederick II (Frederick the Great) in 1786 (Mayhew 1973, 163–65). These Prussian rulers held the mercantilist belief that the economy should be directed and protected by the state. Economic growth was seen as the cornerstone of political expansion, and the key to this growth was thought to lie in agriculture; so these rulers invested heavily in the improvement and expansion of the existing agriculture into the poorer areas, although industry and commerce were also encouraged.

It was Frederick the Great who developed more fully the Prussian policy of increasing rapidly both population and the area available for settlement. Reclamation and settlement took place in the bog areas of the Oder, Warthe, and Netze valleys (today northwest Poland), and colonization of upland areas of Silesia. Frederick the Great is reputed to have been responsible for the creation of nine hundred new villages and the settlement of three hundred thousand colonists. These projects gave a quick return on invested capital. The forms of this state-directed colonization differed somewhat from the older forms of the medieval colonization in that the village forms and field patterns were quite regular. The Habsburg Empire followed a similar policy of imperial colonization in the eastern areas liberated from the Turks. Here, the Strassendorf (street village) and Streckhof (extended court) house type became the chosen method of rapidly expanding colonization in depopulated areas like the Banat of Yugoslavia and Romania today.

The process of change in the East is illustrated by the Junker noble class of Prussia. Muncy (1944, 3–40) has fully described the role it played: in the early days of the fifteenth and sixteenth centuries, the Junkers obtained complete economic and social domination over their estates and immediate localities. The institution of the Gutsherrchaft, or a proprietor cultivation, existed now throughout the area and is to be differentiated from the Grundherrschaft (or rental system), which had come to characterize economic relations in western Europe. Hintze (1914, 499–500) states that the new Junker nobility of the East "frequently demanded compulsory service from their bound peasants in place of dues. . . ." Later, as the Hohenzollern kings of Prussia began to exercise strong control, they had to come to an agreement with the Junkers. During the reign of Frederick the Great, the nobles exercised control in rural areas but had to serve the Prussian government in the military and administration. Muncy (1944, 19) states that it was now possible "to reconcile absolutism at the center of the state with feudalism at the base. . . ." In the nineteenth century, pressure for land reform led to the Stein-Hardenberg reforms but the Junkers were able to get around these by acquiring much of the peasant land and forcing the peasants to work on the estates as landless laborers whose condition differed little from serfdom.

Eventually, however, economic development, accompanied by the advance of individual liberty, equality, and the liberal changes in western Europe spread east and forced the Junkers on the defensive. New forces of nationalism, constitutionalism, and representative government; industrial capitalism; and a rising middle class did much to destroy the Junkers as a political power. Gradually, this class began to lose influence, although some members remained prominent in the government, the military, and the diplomatic corps as late as World War II.

Final Remarks about German Medieval Settlement

German colonization represented a new form of spatial organization in eastern Europe. Gerhard (1959) contrasts this colonization with that of the American frontier, where individuals received blocks of land to settle. Settlers in America represented a variety of denominations with very little central authority. In eastern Europe, medieval towns became the focal points of diffusion of German town law. In this they differed from the United States, where town formation was not systematic.

German settlements in eastern Europe persisted until the end of World War II. They retained German language and culture to a remarkable degree. During World War II, settlers were under strong pressure to support the Nazi cause and often collaborated with German armies of occupation. Many became a veritable fifth column.

After 1945, under the Potsdam agreements, more than 12 million Germans were sent to Germany, almost eliminating this ethnic group from Eastern Europe. Today, only some five hundred thousand Germans remain in the region. Many of those who remain are part of mixed marriages.

The Settlement of Germans in Russia

The movement of Germans into Russia includes two groups, both of which were quite different from comparable migrations into eastern Europe. The first group was comprised of Germans who settled largely in and around St. Petersburg after 1700. Many of these came from earlier German settlements in the Baltic region founded by the Teutonic Knights and the Hanseatic League (see Giesinger 1981, 47 and ch. VIII). Their movement was encouraged by Peter the Great (1689–1725), who was determined to westernize Russia; he changed the capital from Moscow to St. Petersburg and invited many westerners, including Germans, to move to Russia (Maynard 1962, 142–44). There had been a German suburb (Nemetskaia sloboda) near Moscow. With the transfer of the capital to St. Petersburg, many Germans moved there. Thus started the long and persistent involvement of Germans, particularly Baltic Germans, in Russian affairs, including administration, the diplomatic service, and the military. Baltic nobility was overwhelmingly German but proved itself loyal to the tsar on many occasions. Their contribution was out of all proportion to their numbers and was occasionally resented.

The second group was much larger and had a profound effect on the Eurasian steppe. This group consisted of farmers who arrived after 1763 at the invitation of the German-born empress of Russia, Catherine the Great. The migration continued for almost a hundred years.

More than 1.8 million Germans lived in the Soviet Union at the time of its collapse, but many of them have lost their language and culture, having been completely or partially assimilated into Russian life. Their experience of pioneer settlement lasted more than two hundred years, and although similar in some ways to German colonization in eastern Europe, was quite different. It also differed from migrations into the American West. Despite notable success in the first one hundred years, this movement was ultimately a failure. The reasons for this failure are largely the result of growing Russian nationalism and problems of empire consolidation facing Russian and Soviet governments. Despite the ultimate failure, the impact of German migration on the steppe was substantial. However, while many relics of German colonization in eastern Europe remain, they are very few in Russia today.

Political Organization, Terrain, and Routes

Unlike earlier German migration into eastern Europe, the movement to Russia took place within the framework of one political unit. The colonists did not have to deal with various jurisdictions. Instead, their status was determined by the original manifesto of Catherine the Great.

The movement was controlled by Russian authorities. Migration spread over a very large area. No marches existed as jumping-off points as in the earlier migrations. A large proportion of migrants to Russia were farmers. They also traveled in groups but lacked the diversity of professional and class composition of medieval migration. The mostly steppe terrain, although flat, was difficult to plow, and no established routes to settlement destinations existed.

The Colonization Process

Much as their medieval predecessors, migrants to Russia were subject to push and pull factors.

In 1763, Catherine the Great issued a manifesto inviting Germans to come to Russia and settle unpopulated steppe areas. Thus, these German migrants did not compete with Russian peasants since the latter were bound to large estates as serfs. Indeed, the German settlers called themselves "colonists," not peasants, and considered themselves above the native peoples (Bartels 1928, 7–9). At the time, Catherine found many Germans willing to take risks of pioneer settlement because they suffered under feudal burdens, religious persecution, wars that had little relevance for them, destruction caused by foreign armies, high taxes, poverty, malnutrition, and unemployment. But the pull factors were equally important in attracting settlers: land allotments for peasants who had had none, freedom of religion, exemptions from taxation and military service.

The Manifesto of 1763 was characterized as a "masterpiece of immigration propaganda" and became the cornerstone of Russia's colonization policy for a century (Giesinger 1981, 5; Klaus 1897, 22–26). Later on, when problems developed, colonists referred to the manifesto and the promises it contained.

The manifesto presented an attractive picture of Russia as a country with large tracts of fertile land, virtually uninhabited, in accessible, well-watered regions. Catherine hoped that the progress made by the colonists would serve as a model for Russian peasants. Stumpp (1978, 9) also reports that the Russians envisioned these settlements as a protective wall against Asiatic tribes. Russia sent agents to western Europe to spread information about the manifesto, especially to Germany, with its pattern of fragmented states, persistent conflicts, religious intolerance, land shortages, and serfdom.

Map 3.3 from the American Historical Society of Germans from Russia shows the distribution of German settlements after the first one hundred years from the issuance of the manifesto. Maps in Stumpp (16–19) show the names of German settlements in European Russia and their places of origin in the west. The colonies, mostly villages, extended over a vast area of European Russia, particularly in the south, where few agricultural settlements had existed. Thus, German settlers had relatively infrequent contacts with other ethnic groups, especially in the first one hundred years. The major mother colonies were located along the Volga River in both the hilly west and the flatter east and in the Black Sea region (the Pontic steppe) that had been conquered from the Ottoman Empire. Major colonies also evolved in Bessarabia; Volhynia, where scattered settlements came to predominate in the forested terrain; and some areas in the Caucasus. By the 1860s, there were some 3,500 German villages with more than one million people. The Russian peasants, still serfs bound to the land, were impoverished and illiterate; on the other hand, many Germans were literate and liked to think of themselves as farmers, not peasants. Some villages contained flour mills and, in larger places, industries producing textiles, metals, agricultural implements, and even carriages. German colonists also resided in some 50 cities.

The First One Hundred Years

From the invitation of Catherine the Great in 1763 until the 1870s, when the German colonists lost their exemption from military service, their experience was on the whole favorable. For the most part, they had established closed villages and built churches and schools to preserve their culture and religion. Their agriculture concentrated mainly on growing wheat and raising cattle and sheep, although other specialties, like growing grapes, also existed. These colonists made a notable contribution to Russia's economic life.

Still, problems abounded, although nothing like they were going to experience in the next one hundred years.

Nature. The colonists found the natural conditions on the steppe difficult to master (Stumpp 1978, 23). First of all, they had a long trek of some two thousand miles to the point of settlement. Secondly, the climate, as in any prairie area, was unpredictable, precipitation irregular, and winds frequent. However, Germans were good farmers and gradually learned to meet the challenges.

Settlement. Conditions for the establishment of villages in the steppe were difficult from the beginning. Colonists were used to forested terrain in Germany. In their new place of domicile little wood was available. Draft animals and farming equipment were lacking. Great distances separated the villages from each other and from towns where necessary supplies, including tools, could be had. Stumpp (24) reports that wheat harvests had to be hauled far to railheads or ports. The colonists had little money to build and support churches and schools, which were so scattered that services were irregular even if clergy were available.

Land hunger. The need for land increased as the villages expanded or new pioneers arrived. In addition, the birth rate was high. The shortage was less apparent in the Volga River region, where the colonists periodically redistributed land among heirs so that plots grew smaller and smaller (Klaus 1887, 43–43, 189–95). However, in the Black Sea area, where the youngest son inherited the land, the other heirs were left without land and had to

51

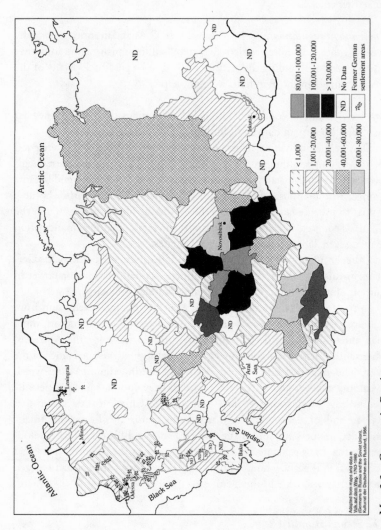

Adapted from maps and data in
Volk auf dem Weg, 1763-1996
(Germans in Russia and the Soviet Union),
Kulturrat der Deutschen aus Russland, 1996.

Map 3.3 Germans in Russia

seek it elsewhere, frequently through the establishment of daughter colonies, a common practice in this pioneer settlement. Altogether, by the 1870s, there were some 300 mother colonies and more than 3,000 daughter settlements.

Government regulations. The actions of the Russian authorities gradually became more and more restrictive, thereby stifling much of the initiative. Loans given for founding the settlements had to be paid back. Many of the promises made in the manifesto were not kept.

Famine. Drought conditions often led to famines that were somewhat eased by the German custom of building grain storage facilities.

Despite the difficulties, in general, the first one hundred years were good for the colonists, although anti-German feelings began to manifest themselves among the Russian population already at this time. This trend became stronger in the 1860s, when Alexander II emancipated the serfs who now wished to procure land, often from the Germans. The former serfs and the Germans competed against each other. At the same time, the emancipation created severe labor shortages on landed estates.

Other anti-German feelings resulted from the influence of the Baltic Germans in Russian affairs, the rise of a united Germany as a major power in Europe, and the output of Slavophile and Pan-Slav publicists.

In the 1870s, Tsar Alexander II canceled the colonists' exemption from military service. Given the choice of military service or emigration, more than three hundred thousand colonists opted to leave for the Americas, where authorities were seeking new pioneer settlers for the open lands of the West. The migration began in the 1870s and continued until World War I. Even after the war and after the Communist revolution, some got permission to leave or escaped over the Amur River to China. It is estimated that over 1.5 million descendants of these German emigrants live in the Americas today, about 1 million in the United States and Canada. The developments after 1870 generated much bitterness among the colonists. They had been loyal to their new homeland; it was Russia, they felt, that had reneged on the promises made in the manifesto.

The Second Hundred Years

The history of Russian Germans after the 1870s differs from the previous one hundred years. The two periods, so unlike each other, may seem unique when taken as a whole. But the history of German settlement in many other areas of eastern Europe, e.g., Bohemia, shows the same pattern: successful settlement followed by anti-German reaction.

The second period presents a picture of growing discrimination, Russification, hardships caused by two world wars, the Communist revolution and, finally, the liquidation of almost all of the German settlements in European Russia.

Major changes affected the German colonists after the 1870s.

Anti-German feelings among the Russian population and programs of Russification. The anti-German feelings in Russia became evident in the reign of Tsar Alexander II but intensified after Alexander III came to power in 1881. Unlike the earlier tsars, Nicholas I and Alexander II, the new emperor had strong nationalist leanings; he meant to eliminate non-Russian influences from the government and assimilate his non-Russian subjects as rapidly as possible. Riasanovsky (1963, 433–38) and Seton-Watson (1967, 460–546) provide details on these policies, including Russification of subject nationalities, such as Poles, Ukrainians, Finns, Jews, Germans, and others. Unlike the previous tsars who had been pro-German in their sympathies, Alexander III was influenced by his anti-German Danish wife and by the propaganda of the Slavophile Russian intelligentsia. His Russification policies met with public support. Many Russians felt that this foreign group could become dangerous; they were also jealous of the privileges granted earlier to the colonists and their economic success. Alexander III also feared the growing power of imperial Germany. Many Germans, especially Baltic Germans, were gradually eliminated from positions of power in the government, army, and diplomatic service, although many remained until World War I and even later. Alexander III also promoted Russification by supporting free Russian schools and appointing land captains, a measure that allowed the government to interfere in the local affairs of German colonists. And their reluctance to interact with their Russian neighbors, as well as resistance to assimilation, did not help their cause. Finally, Russian nationalist publications spread anti-German propaganda and accusations of disloyalty and pan-Germanism. By the beginning of the twentieth century, many German settlers felt that all of Catherine the Great's promises had been abrogated.

Religious problems. From the beginning of the settlement colonists faced religious problems. In 1897, some three-fourths of the colonists were Protestant, mostly Lutheran, the rest being largely Catholic (Broedrich-Kurmahlen et al. 1916, 38–53). Villages were strictly segregated according to religion. The Mennonite settlements, amounting to less than 4 percent of the colonists, were particularly cohesive. A major problem for all colonists was the lack of funds to construct churches, schools, and training facilities. The colonists made great sacrifices to build churches and schools.

Because they were scattered over a vast area, they faced a perennial problem of finding enough clergy. Catholics faced additional burdens because Russian authorities, interested in protecting the Russian Orthodox Church against the power of Rome, were suspicious of the Catholics. They were always under fire.

Revolution, War, Communism. Despite all the difficulties and disappointments, by the beginning of this century German colonization was, on the whole, a success story. Many colonists did well, not only in agriculture but also in manufacture and trade. Stumpp (1964, 25) states that in 1914 the Germans cultivated 25 million acres, a total only 5 million acres less than that of Germany in 1937. Later, however, they inevitably suffered through all the vicissitudes of Russian history in this century. Already during the uprisings of 1905, unrest surged all around them. Strong anti-German feelings ran high.

The start of World War I in 1914 was accompanied by veritable anti-German pogroms in Moscow and St. Petersburg. Still, many Germans expressed loyalty to Russia and even volunteered to fight for it. But as the war turned against Russia, Germans were often blamed because Germany was the main opponent. As a result, many Germans were deported from Volhynia to Siberia. Families were separated. Starvation that followed the war and revolution reduced German (and non-German) population.

By 1922, the Bolsheviks had won the civil war and took complete control. The German settlers along the Volga River formed the Volga German Republic with some local autonomy. Kolarz (1967, 67–76) gives a good account of the Soviet nationalities program as it applied to minorities, including Germans. Russian peasants seized German colonist land, religion was prohibited, and even speaking German was restricted. The anti-German drive was temporarily softened by the rapprochement between Germany and Russia at Rapallo. But then the collectivization hit the colonists especially hard as many of the better farmers were considered "kulaks" and were liquidated. The purges of 1936 did not bypass the German settlers either. Many were deported to Siberia and Central Asia or to slave labor camps.

World War II created new problems for German colonists still settled in the European parts of the Soviet Union. The German-Soviet treaty of August 1939 dividing eastern Europe into spheres of influence softened some of the anti-German animus. But after Germany attacked Russia in June 1941, most of the Germans under Russian control were banished to Siberia and Central Asia. (Those who found themselves under Nazi occupation faired very well.) Particularly catastrophic was the liquidation of the Volga Republic in 1941. Altogether, some 650,000 German settlers were evicted and exiled. Their forced migration is shown on map 3.3.

After the tide of war turned against Germany, many German settlers in the occupied areas tried to flee west ahead of the Red Army. However, some 280,000 were captured and sent east.

German fate in Russia after World War II was filled with uncertainty. But gradually, one can discern a tendency toward rehabilitation. The first public mention, in 1951, praised their good work on collective farms in the east. After Stalin died, Russian Germans were granted an amnesty (in 1955). Under Khrushchev conditions seemed to improve further. Konrad Adenauer, chancellor of the Federal Republic of Germany, made an effort to have the Soviet Union return to Germany prisoners of war, and his initiative was partly successful. But attempts to secure the expatriation of German colonists who wished to emigrate to Germany were refused on the grounds that these people were Soviet citizens. The USSR census of 1969 (*Volk auf dem Weg,* Sept. 1971, 2, and Oct. 1971, 7–8) listed some 1,846,000 Germans living in the Soviet Union, but of these only some 120,000 lived in German villages. The vast majority continued to reside in regions of internal exile, about 810,000 in Siberia and 800,000 more in Central Asia. The distribution of German settlements in the Soviet Union is shown on map 3.3 issued by the American Historical Society of the Germans from Russia (1962).

Today, about half of the Germans live in urban areas. Only two-thirds of this population listed German as a mother tongue. Of some 3,500 German villages that existed in European Russia all are gone except as shown on map 3.3. Many Germans are now engaged in non-agricultural activities, and although there are no German churches or schools, these people have some limited cultural associations, newspapers, and theater groups. One publication states that it is now possible to speak of a scattered German culture distributed over vast areas (*Volk auf dem Weg* 1986, 7).

Ironically, the collapse of the Soviet Union, while easing the burdens of enforced Russification, may have sounded the death knell of Russian Germandom. Before the collapse of the Soviet Union, only a few elderly Germans with close relatives in Germany were occasionally given permission to emigrate. With gradual liberalization under Gorbachëv, restrictions on emigration were lifted even before the collapse. As a result, from 1987 to 1993, 851,000 Germans left the former USSR (Schmaltz, *Volk auf dem Weg: Deutsche in Russland und in der GUS, 1763–1993,* 32, in *Nationalities Papers* 26, No. 2 [June 1998]:237, n.116). According to Heinrich Groth, one of the former leaders of the Wiedergeburt (Rebirth) movement, around 1993, the emigration of Russian Germans was regulated at 225,000 per year, and the admission is guaranteed until the year 2001 (Olt, in Schmaltz 1998, 236, n.110). In other words, all Russian Germans, plus large numbers of people of mixed origin, will be able to emigrate.

Given the economic collapse in Russia, persistent nationalism, and a much higher standard of living in Germany, it is quite possible that most will.

Landscape Relics

Unlike the German colonists in eastern Europe who left a number of important relics in the landscape, the Germans in Russia left almost none. The deportations from the original villages on the Volga and Black Sea and in other areas meant that these villages were given over to Russians, who changed them completely. Stumpp (1978) provides descriptions and pictures of the villages as they existed in the nineteenth century. The American Historical Society of Germans from Russia is located in Lincoln, Nebraska, and arranges trips to the areas that their ancestors left; visitors report that almost nothing is left of previous German occupants. Nevertheless, they are thrilled to see the landscape where their ancestors settled and to appreciate the difficulties they encountered in Russia.

Conclusions

What does this brief analysis of the German migrations into eastern Europe and Russia tell us about the impact they had on the Eurasian steppe, the subject of this book? To me, two of the major characteristics involve contrasts between the two migrations. The Germans in eastern Europe are largely gone, having been expelled to Germany in a cleansing under the Potsdam agreements. But their effect on the development of eastern Europe was enormous.

On the other hand, the Germans who migrated to Russia are still there (this may soon change, however, as migration from Russia is gathering steam), but their contribution, while important, was much less pronounced. The paradox is that one German group is gone, but its relics still exist, while the other group is still there, but its relics and culture are gone.

One interesting aspect of these migrations is the persistence of German ethnicity and culture in many eastern European and Russian societies. (However, assimilation on a large scale did take place. Between 1890 and 1914, about four hundred thousand Germans were assimilated in Hungary [Hanák 1974, no. 1–2, in Niederhauser, in Teich and Porter 1993, 261, n.34].) In Romania, in 1961, my interpreter was a German whose main task, as a Romanian anthropologist, was to reduce the Isolierung (isolation) of the Germans in Romanian society. This mostly applied to the Germans of Transylvania (Siebenbürgen) who had been settled there for almost eight hundred years as part of their original migration in the Middle Ages. And for over a hundred years, the lack of assimilation of Germans in Russia was even greater. This phenomenon differs from that in America, where by the second or third generation, descendants of migrants generally assimilated, often losing their language and culture.

Thus, one could ask why the slowness of assimilation in the case of some Germans in eastern Europe and especially those in Russia? One answer seems to lie in the position of Germans in society. In Romania, in the Transylvanian areas where the Germans settled, their villages remained closed for hundreds of years. The same was true in Russia and even in Latin America. In those areas, the German settlers felt superior to the locals. But in North America they did not and assimilated after a generation or two. The school system in the United States helped. So even here, where some German settlements remained closed, the children attended public schools where they had to "sink or swim" in classes held in English.

What was the impact of German migrations on the steppe? For the German colonists in eastern Europe, I have cited authorities who feel that their migrations transformed areas of Poland, Bohemia, and Hungary, so that by the fourteenth century they were fully integrated into European civilization. For some four hundred years, German colonists brought progress and a measure of stability to the western fringe of the Eurasian steppe.

German migration was cut short by the Black Death in the middle of the fourteenth century. Gradually, the position of Germans deteriorated, especially under the impact of anti-German reaction (e.g., the Hussite wars in Bohemia). When German migration resumed (Hungary after its liberation from the Turks), it took place within an imperial framework and was directed by the government.

In Russia, migration was different. In the Baltic, it followed the conquests of the Teutonic Knights in the thirteenth century. Germans were the upper class and the leading element of Baltic societies for some three hundred years, well into the sixteenth century. Socially and economically, they dominated the area until the twentieth. In Russia proper, along the Volga, migration resembled its counterpart in Hungary in the eighteenth century, except that Russia was not a German-dominated empire like Austria. Eventually, an anti-German reaction developed in Russia as well. Inevitably, it led to forced assimilation and Russification. In the twentieth century, world wars, revolutions, and Communism devastated the German communities, leading to deportations and starvation.

Where do these two German migrations fit in the geographic history and theory of pioneer settlement? The most common question asked is their relevance to the concept of the American frontier, set out in 1893 by Frederick Jackson Turner (Turner, 1894). Turner's thesis held that the development of the Western frontier had a profound effect on the institutions of the United States and on the characteristics of the American people. Settling this frontier area, he believed, was responsible for many of the characteristics that we hold dear, including individualism, freedom of religion, widening opportunity, social equality, and lack of government interference. This frontier thesis had been applied to Eurasia, South Africa, Australia, and Canada. However, its application to Russia has been limited to the Siberian expansion by Russians, and only Treadgold (1957) and Gerhard (1959) have utilized this thesis in comparing German settlement in eastern Europe with American settlement in the West. Gerhard also makes (1959, 224–26) some interesting comparisons between the United States frontier, as Turner saw it, and the advancing frontier in Siberia, which seems applicable to the subject of this book. Here he emphasizes above all the strong contrast between the freedom on the American frontier and the Siberian frontier, where state control and direction persisted (but were less pronounced than in European Russia). Gerhard also notes the lack of church activity in Siberia versus the Protestant zeal in the United States. He feels that the American frontier gave rise to a modern and more mobile and non-stratified society, in contrast to Siberia, where there was adherence to custom, less mobility, and acceptance of social stratification (Treadgold would contest that [1957, 244–45]). Gerhard mentions the lingering effects of hostile groups from the east in Russia, especially the Tatars. Finally, he feels that the Russians in Siberia borrowed a great deal more from civilizations they encountered than the American frontiersman ever did from the Indians. But the Americans had better tools on the frontier.

Germans who settled in eastern Europe for about a thousand years and those who came to Russia some two hundred years ago had a great influence on the Eurasian steppe. Now, the Germans in eastern Europe are mostly gone while the ones in Russia have been greatly Russified, many of them losing their language and culture. Nevertheless, the impact of these settlers is part of the heritage of Eurasia that needs to be clarified.

CHAPTER 4

Russian Migrations in the Sixteenth to Twentieth Centuries

Migration and colonization played an outstanding role in Russian history. This was noted by many historians, Russian and non-Russian alike. In 1887, Michael Kulischer, a Russian historian and ethnologist, published two articles in *Vestnik Evropy* in which he traced the role of major population shifts in Russian history (M. Kulischer 1887, in E. Kulischer 1948, v). Another noted Russian historian, Vasilii Kliuchevsky, wrote that "Russia's history, throughout, is the history of a country undergoing colonization. . . . Migration, colonization constituted the basic feature of our history, to which all other features were more or less directly related" (Kliuchevsky 1937 [1948], v:20–21, in Treadgold 1957, 14). Among westerners, Sumner, Pipes, and many others reached similar conclusions. "Throughout Russian history one dominating theme has been the frontier" (Sumner 1947, 9, in Treadgold 1957, 14).

Migration of East Slavs up the Dnieper valley in the sixth to eighth centuries laid the foundation of Kievan Rus' (see chapter 8 on early Slavs). Later expansion to the northeast, toward the Kama and the Volga, prepared the ground for the emergence of Muscovy.

The Mongol invasion of 1236–41 and the Mongol Yoke that followed (effectively till 1380, nominally till 1480) stopped the East Slav expansion. It was resumed only three hundred years later, when the conquest of Kazan' and Astrakhan' in 1552 and 1556 opened the way east. In 1581, the *pervo-prokhodtsy* (Russian for "pioneers") crossed the Urals, and by 1639 they had conquered Siberia.

While it was expanding east, Russia was also engaged in a continuous struggle against the Crimean khanate to the south. Originally a part of the Golden Horde (until the 1440s), it was an independent entity for a generation, then, after 1475, a vassal of the Ottoman Empire. The khanate proved to be a persistent and dangerous foe. At least twice, in 1382 and 1571, the

Crimean Tatars burned Moscow. Even worse were their incessant slave raids deep into Russian territory. Trade in slaves was the cornerstone of the Crimean economy. Slave raids on Muscovy and Poland-Lithuania reached great intensity in 1474–1534 (Armstrong 1982, xxxiii) and again in 1700 (Armstrong 1982, xxxv), as they did against Transylvania in 1717 (Cadzow et al. 1983, 17). In only one raid during the reign of Ivan the Terrible, the Tatars took 130,000 captives (Pares 1926, 114–15). As late as 1713, a raid on the relatively thinly settled Kiev area led to the capture of 14,000 people (Stokl 1953, 54; Ferguson 1954, 141). (The last raid into Russia took place in 1769 [Armstrong 1982, xxxv].) It is surprising that severe depopulation had not undermined Muscovy.

Successive Russian governments tried various measures. In 1571, the Russians built a line of defensive stockades from the Donets to the Irtysh, the Russian answer to the Great Wall of China, to protect newly settled areas from the nomads (Pipes 1974, 14).

Ultimately, only the conquest of the Crimea could eliminate the constant drain on Russian human resources. But the khanate, supported by the Ottomans, was a tough nut to crack. Azov, a key fortress at the mouth of the Don, where Greek Tanais and Genoese Tana once stood, was taken in 1637, lost again, and finally captured for good in 1696.

Toward the end of the seventeenth century, an insecure "Belgorod line" near the present Russian-Ukrainian frontier was established (Armstrong 1982, 79). But such arrangements were inadequate. As late as 1735, Russians had to settle for a defensive *glacis* north of the Sea of Azov, a no-man's land where no one lived (Armstrong 1982, 79). Only the incorporation of the Crimea in 1774–83 finally eliminated the menace. The annexation of the Crimea coincided with the exodus of the Kalmyks in 1771. For the first time since its foundation, the first time in a thousand years, Russia did not have to fear the devil's horsemen.

The pacification of the nomad (although by the eighteenth century the Crimean Tatars had long been sedentarized) opened vast stretches of the Eurasian steppe to Russian settlement. This was a third Slav migration (the first one, in the fifth to seventh centuries, took them to the Elbe and down the Balkans; the second, by East Slavs, consolidated Slav hold on the Dnieper basin and laid the foundation for Muscovy and its later expansion).

The Russian migration can be subdivided into two periods. In 1552–1861, most migrants were either internal political exiles, such as the Decembrists or participants in the Polish uprisings (in 1823–62, the number of "politicals" reached 356,000 according to Kuznetsov [Treadgold 1957, 24, n.17]; or serfs transferred, sometimes against their will, by the state (although one could also find settlements of fugitive serfs). After the emancipation of the serfs in 1861, all nonpolitical migrants came of their own free will.

With the elimination of the nomad threat, the main push factors were economic, not unlike the situation in western Europe, and the desire of the government to settle thinly populated lands. As a result, in the seventeenth and eighteenth centuries, more than 2 million serfs were moved south while 400,000 went east, to Siberia and the Urals (Pipes 1974, 15). From 1724 to 1859, the number of Slavs in the New South (corresponding, roughly, to the Pontic steppe) increased from 1.6 million to 14.5 million (Lorimer 1946, 10), while the number in Siberia went up from 400,000 to 3.4 million (10).

After 1861, the purely economic factors predominated. These included, but were not limited to, relative overpopulation in the Russian heartland; backward agriculture; the decline of available agricultural land per person; restraints imposed first by a semifeudal system and then, after the emancipation, by the communal ownership of land; and the like. Most important was the fast population growth that far outstripped economic resources. The demographic transition in Russia started early, around 1750, and in the next one hundred years its population quadrupled, to 68 million reaching 170 million by 1914 (Pipes 1974, 13). The end result was gradual impoverishment in the Russian heartland—and large numbers of willing migrants.

For 1801–1914, Lorimer estimated the number of migrants to the New South at 12–13 million, for Siberia and Central Asia at more than 4.5 million (Lorimer 1946, 26). (Treadgold put this number at 7 million [Treadgold 1957, 13]; Obolensky-Osinsky at 5.7 million, of whom nearly 1 million were prisoners and exiles [1928, 84, in Treadgold 1957, 33].) This compares with 35 million who crossed the Atlantic (Hansen 1945, 11). This is a conservative estimate. Crosby (1986, 5) put the number at 50 million for 1820–1930, and even 65 million if we count returnees) and several million Chinese who settled in Manchuria in 1880–1930 (Young 1932).

The influx of eager migrants was such that occasionally, as in the 1840s, there was not enough land available (officially, only surveyed land could be allotted to settlers). In 1846, the government even tried to stop migration—but could not (Treadgold 1957, 29).

By the end of the nineteenth century, when there was no land left in the southern steppe, Siberia remained the only part of the country where it could still be found (31). Despite its harsh climate, Siberia was very attractive because the new Siberian society was more prosperous and less socially rigid than that of European Russia (7). "Siberia escaped the gentry, and so it escaped serfdom" was Treadgold's verdict (26).

In the late 1850s, many peasants postponed resettlement in the hope that the coming emancipation would solve their problems. During the 1860s, many hoped that the emancipation (1861) would be followed by other legislation (73). When it became clear that such hopes were misplaced, migratory flows increased dramatically. If 30,000 settlers entered Kuban' in 1870, by 1881, their numbers increased to 237,000 and then to 800,000 in 1900 (Kaufman in Treadgold 1957, 77, n.23).

Particularly dramatic was the increase in the numbers of "irregulars," that is, migrants who were not sponsored by the government, especially in the south. After 1889, they constituted the great majority of migrants. In 1890, the irregulars reached 70 percent in Tomsk and 80 percent in Tobol'sk (Treadgold 1957, 80). By 1894 they reached 78 percent of the entire migratory movement. (But their share fluctuated: it fell to 24 percent in 1895 before rising again a few years later [112].)

For some 30 years following the emancipation, the government tried, but failed, to control migration. The extent of its failure is demonstrated by the fact that it repeatedly legalized violations of its own regulations (112).

Early migrants to Siberia came mostly from two areas: the central agricultural region (Kursk-Tambov-Voronezh) and the middle Volga area (90). As many as two million people from the central provinces migrated annually to the south (Pontic steppe) to perform agricultural labor, but as the south "filled up," there was less need for their services. They were redirected east (91–92).

Not all migrants were impoverished: the landless amounted only to 15.7 percent of the total in 1895. A plurality of 36.5 percent had up to three desiatinas (a measure of land of 2.7 acres) (Kolonizatsiia Sibiri, 151, in Treadgold 1957, 93, n.27), compared to the average size of 11 desiatinas per household in European Russia (Blagoveshchensky 1893, in Treadgold 1957, 93, n.28). Only 2.4 percent had more than 10 desiatinas (Treadgold 1957, 93, n.27). Thus, most migrants were poor but not destitute. If they were, they could not afford the total cost of resettlement, which Iadrintsev, in 1881, estimated at three to five hundred rubles (Iadrintsev 612, in Treadgold 1957, 98, n.41).

By the beginning of the twentieth century, the issue of migration was politicized. The annual increase in the population of European Russia was now two million. Even rapid industrialization experienced by Russia at this time could not provide employment to the new cohorts that joined the labor market each year. The Right believed that migration was the answer (Volshchinin 1912, 28–29, in Treadgold 1957, 189, n.19). The Left, on the contrary, was against migration because, in its estimation, it made a revolution less likely since it provided an outlet for the discontented.

However, neither the Left nor the war with Japan nor the first revolution could stop the outflow. The completion of the Trans-Siberian railroad greatly facilitated migration. The results were spectacular: if, in 1897, the population of Asiatic Russia was 13.5 million, by 1911 it reached 20 million! (Turchaninov, 64–68, in Treadgold 1957, 227, n.1). Among other things, it fully Russianized vast areas of the empire. The percentage of Russians in the total population reached 86.5 percent in Siberia, 74 percent in the Far East, 40 percent in the Steppe (compared to 19 percent in 1897), and 6.3 percent in Turkestan (Treadgold 1957, 227). In other words, by the beginning of the century, Siberia and the Far East had been fully incorporated and integrated into Mother Russia with the steppe region not far behind.

The disasters of the 1910s and early 1920s—World War I, two revolutions, and the Civil War accompanied by famine—brought migration to a standstill. In 1914 there were 242,000 migrants going east. The number was down to 6,000 in 1917. It revived somewhat in 1918, but there was no migrant registration in 1919. Migration resumed in 1920–21, then dropped down to zero during the famine, then shot up to 95,000 in 1925 (Obolensky-Osinsky, 127–28, in Treadgold 1957, 236, n.22).

The upheaval brought an enormous dislocation. More than 7 million soldiers were sent to the front while over 3 million refugees fled east. At the same time, hundreds of thousands of people moved to the cities, where defense industries provided employment to 2 million workers by 1916 (plus over 430,000 prisoners of war) (Kulischer 1948, ch. 3). But after 1917, the collapse of the economy and spreading hunger led to a massive return to the village (Treadgold 1957, 237) which depopulated large cities, especially St. Petersburg.

Interrupted by the upheavals of 1914–22, the Great Migration resumed under the new regime. From 1926 to 1941, 1.164 million migrants went to Siberia, 1.023 million to the Urals, and 899,000 to the Far East (Lorimer 1946, 164). Between 1928 and 1936, 1.7 million migrants settled in Kazakstan and Central Asia (Rywkin 1990, 59).

Mass evacuation of civilian population in the early phases of World War II added momentum to the movement. Some eight million people fled or were transferred east (Magocsi 1993, 164). As a result, even a Muslim heartland city like Samarkand was only 39.5 percent Uzbek and Tajik by the 1950s, with Slavs accounting for 36.9 percent (Rywkin 1990, 61).

Migration was further enhanced after the war by vast industrial and agricultural projects like the Virgin Lands development scheme in 1954–64, which, along with other similar undertakings, attracted 1.5 million migrants to Kazakstan and Central Asia in 1959–70 (Bruk 1971, 28, n.4, in Rywkin 1990, 61, n.6).

The massive outflow of Russian and other Slav population from the heartland was a safety valve in a period of high population growth in the nineteenth and early twentieth centuries. But with increasing urbanization, industrialization, and the spread of education, Slav population growth rates began to sag. Slav population in the core area could no longer adequately reproduce itself.

Demographically, the history of the Russian heartland in the last century falls into two sharply delineated periods. Up until the late 1960s, the prevalent pattern was dispersal. In effect, the Russian heartland was being drained: the percentage of all Russians living in the heartland area around Moscow decreased from 25.6 percent in 1897 to 19.5 percentage in 1970 (Lewis et al. 1976, 208, 211) while the percentage of Russians residing in the traditional areas of Russian settlement in European Russia decreased from 80.2 percent to 59.8 percent (206). Correspondingly, the proportion of Russians residing in Siberia increased from 5.5 percent to 12.4 percent, in the Far East from 0.3 to 3.4 percent, and in Kazakstan from 1.4 to 4.3 percent (206). On the other hand, the spreading out made the geographical distribution of the Russian population more even and contributed to the integration of the colonized areas. This was probably a factor in preserving the Russian, and later Soviet, Empire.

By the 1960s, however, the core regions had been demographically exhausted. Since they also happened to be the most industrially developed and had a higher standard of living, the Center (around Moscow) and the Northwest (around Leningrad) began to attract migrants from other areas of the country. This trend was even more pronounced in the two largest cities. In the 1980s, Moscow and Leningrad, with only 7 percent of the population, attracted 45 percent of all migrants (Zaionchkovskaya, 17, in Azrael and Payin 1996).

In addition to lower birth rates, the flow east in the post-1945 period was weakened by the acquisition of a belt of territories in the west, some of them part of the Russian Empire before World War I (the Baltic republics), others an entirely new acquisition, like West Ukraine. Some of these areas had attained a much higher level of development prior to their acquisition by the Soviet Union. They were also badly damaged during the war. Rebuilding and reconstruction requirements, as well as the general attractiveness of the newly acquired European areas, pulled thousands of prospective migrants west, rather than east. Some nine hundred thousand Russians, not counting other Russophones, settled in Latvia alone.

The outflow west and plunging birth rates (9.4 to 14.4 percent among Slav nationalities, compared to 46.3 to 52.9 percent among Muslims in 1959–70 [Kozlov 1988, 5]), inevitably led to a decrease in the share of the Russian population in the east: in Kazakstan, for example, Russians peaked at 42.73 percent in 1959 (due in part to heavy losses sustained by the Kazak population during collectivization, losses that amounted to almost one-fourth of all ethnic Kazaks), then slowly subsided to 37.82 percent by 1989 (Table 1C, Olcott in Hajda and Beissinger 1990, 263). Similar declines were seen in Kyrgyzstan (from 30.1 to 21.53 percent), Turkmenistan (from 17.32 to 9.52 percent), Uzbekistan (from 13.46 to 8.34 percent), and Tajikistan (from 13.26 to 7.60 percent) (Table 1C, Olcott in Hajda and Beissinger 1990, 263).

The turnaround was not instantaneous. It took about 15 years, from 1945 until 1960, with the period of 1960–65 marking the high point of Russian penetration east.

There had always been returnees (*obratniki,* remigrants). In this, Russian migration east was no different from any migratory flow, including the one into the United States, where return rates among some ethnic groups exceeded 50 percent. But before the 1960s, the balance of migration in the east had been positive. As late as 1961–65, the Russian Socialist Federated Soviet Republic (RSFSR) lost 861,000 people while all the republics of Central Asia gained migrants (Table 18, Rywkin 1990, 79). But in the second half of the decade, the positive balance precipitously declined: from 602,000 to 90,000 in Kazakstan, from 105,000 to 25,000 in Kyrgyzstan, from 120,000 to 18,000 in Tajikistan (79). At the same time, the negative balance of migration from RSFSR almost doubled to 1,567,000. In other words, the outflow from RSFSR continued, but it had by then decisively switched west. As a result, the balance of migration to Ukraine increased from 150,000 to 399,000 (Shpiliuk 1975, 76, in Rywkin 1990, 79), although return migration of Ukrainian migrants from the east may have been partly responsible for this.

In the 1970s, *obratnichestvo* (return) gained momentum. According to Rywkin, *obratnichestvo* began in Kyrgyzstan around 1970 and spread to the rest of Central Asia by the mid-1970s. In 1971–75, the republics of Central Asia and Kazakstan lost 199,000 people (Arutiunian, Bromlei, 1986, 30, in Rywkin 1990, 77, n.41).

It was particularly pronounced in rural areas. In 1970–79, for example, virtually all Russian settlers in the villages of Karakalpakia left the area while the Russian population in the environs of Tashkent (a major urban center, the largest in Central Asia), was reduced by half (Pain 1983, 11, in Rywkin 1990, 81, n.51). By the early 1980s, more than four hundred thousand European settlers had left Kazak rural settlements (Shkaratan 1987, 147–48, in Rywkin 1990, 81, n.52).

Higher levels of education among native populations contributed to the Russian and Slav outflow. From the mid-1960s, Russians were squeezed out of many occupations, except industry and construction. In 1989, in Kyrgyzstan, for every 205 Kyrghyz physicians, only 98 Russians were hired; the ratio for lawyers was 38:16, for scientific personnel and college professors 197:105 (Zaionchkovkaya, 28, n.8, in Azrael and Payin 1996).

Among migrants going west, Muslims were a small minority. Among those resettling in Kiev, in 1967 they amounted to only 7 to 10 percent (it is interesting that ethnic Ukrainians amounted to only 20 to 30 percent; the majority were Europeans of other, presumably mostly Russian, ethnic origin [Onykiienko 1973, 39, 152, in Rywkin 1990, 79, n.48]). This flight from Muslim areas spilled into all "Russian" areas, since 7.3 percent of migrants arriving in the Far East came from Central Asia, Kazakstan, and, significantly, the Caucasus (Rybakovsky 1973, 61, in Rywkin 1990, 79, 81, n.49).

In the 1980s, these tendencies were reinforced. In 1979–89, the RSFSR, Ukraine, and the Baltic republics all showed positive migratory balance, with the RSFSR far ahead (1,768,000 compared to second-place Ukraine with 153,000) (Diuk and Karatnycky 1990, 267), an indication that many, if not most, migrants were Russophones. Altogether, during the 1980s, nearly three-quarters of positive net migration was directed to Russia, with an additional 15 percent going to Ukraine and 10 percent to the Baltic (Zaionchkovskaya, 17, in Azrael and Payin 1996). All other republics lost: Kazakstan 784,000, Uzbekistan 507,000, Armenia 321,000, Azerbaijan 266,000, and the like. (Diuk and Karatnycky 1990, 267). And while it is true that Armenia, Azerbaijan, and Moldova lost a significant proportion of migrants due to ethnic conflicts, the general picture is clear: a massive population reflux from the east and south to the west and north.

These tendencies were further reinforced by the collapse of the Soviet Union when 25 million Russians and millions of Russophones belonging to other ethnic groups suddenly found themselves outside Russia, not unlike Germans and Hungarians did in 1918. What came next was a typical post-colonial "sorting out."

Many Russians, as well as mostly Russophone non-titular minorities, wanted to leave the now independent colonies. The total net migratory losses from the non-Slavic republics for 1990–94 amounted to 4 million people, of whom about 1 million emigrated to the West and more than 3 million relocated to the Slavic republics (Zaionchkovkaya, 26, in Azrael and Payin 1996).

Russia was the main destination: in 1989–96, it accepted 2.3 million people, compared to Ukraine (382,000) and Belarus (65,000). All other former Soviet republics, except Armenia, had negative balances. Kazakstan, for example, lost 1.3 million people. Percentage-wise, Kyrgyzstan lost 8.6 percent of its 1989 population; Kazakstan 7.9 percent; and Azerbaijan and Tajikistan 5.5 and 5.2 percent, respectively (Heleniak 1997, 16). Losses of ethnic Russians were even higher, especially in areas of armed conflict: 42 percent of Russian residents left Tajikistan and 37 percent left Transcaucasia (Zaionchkovkaya, 27, in Azrael and Payin 1996). Altogether, 21 percent of Russians in Central Asia and 14 percent of all Russians in the former Soviet republics left their place of residence in 1990–94 or, in absolute numbers, 1.7 million. Many more would like to leave, and not only Russians. Of those surveyed, 75 percent of non-titular non–Central Asian families in Uzbekistan, 66 percent in Kazakstan, and 62 percent in Kyrgyzstan expressed a desire to emigrate, while 14 percent, 24 percent, and 28 percent, respectively, would choose to stay (Vitkovskaya, 114, in Azrael and Payin 1996).

It is interesting that 50 percent of Ukrainian respondents in Uzbekistan would rather relocate to Russia than Ukraine (7 percent); the same holds true for Kazakstan (80 percent vs. 11 percent), and Kyrgyzstan (50 percent vs. 10 percent). Among Belarusians the number is 50 percent, among Armenians 80 percent, among Koreans in Uzbekistan 60 percent, and even among Germans in Kazakstan 57 percent (although for many Germans Russia will be a way station to Germany (Vitkovskaya 122–23, in Azrael and Payin 1996). Many, if not most, of these migrants are Russophones, and that makes Russia more attractive than their historic homelands.

Another interesting fact is that although in each of the Central Asian republics Russians have the strongest desire to migrate, Ukrainians have much less, less than the Tatars (Vitkovskaya, 124, in Azrael and Payin 1996). Evidently, cultural distance is not always a decisive factor; the loss of status suffered by Russians is more significant. Yet, distance should not be entirely discounted either: the exodus is much larger from well-to-do, but culturally more distant, Uzbekistan than it is from impoverished Ukraine (Payin and Susarov, 53, in Azrael and Payin 1996).

Incidentally, Ukraine, in 1994, experienced the first negative migration balance in postwar years, mostly due to the emigration of Russians to Russia (Pirozhkov, 69, in Azrael and Payin 1996). But this phenomenon did not seem to affect Belarus, which absorbed approximately 90,000 immigrants in 1991–93 (often from areas of ethnic strife) (Tikhonova, 80, in Azrael and Payin 1996).

Migration accompanying the postcolonial sorting-out did not bypass the Baltics. In 1990–95, 50,000 left Lithuania; 95,000 Latvia; and 60,000 Estonia (Vashanov, 65, in Azrael and Payin 1996). (Latvian official data indicate that Latvia's population decreased from 2,673 million in 1990 to 2,458 million in 1998 [Internet, www.latnet.lv].)

Another phenomenon typical of postcolonial sorting-out was that in 1992 all titular nationalities began to leave Russia for their respective homelands (Zaionchkovskaya, 29, in Azrael and Payin 1996). The same thing occurred in central and southeastern Europe and in the Balkans when empires collapsed in 1918.

However, we should not oversimplify a very complex process. Even after the collapse of the union, migration was not all unidirectional. Some 122,000 Russians immigrated to Kazakstan in 1992, compared to 128,000 who left (Kolstoe 1995, 246, in Davis and Sabol, *Nationalities Papers* 26,

No. 3 [Sept. 1998]:484, n.33). And in the first half of 1994, among immigrants, 63.8 percent were Russian (Davis and Sabol, *Nationalities Papers* 26, No. 3 [Sept. 1998]:484, n.34). The major reason seems to be economic (personal communication from S. Davis).

After the collapse of the Soviet Union, an entirely new trend in migration became visible: the abandonment of the North and the Far East. Altogether, in 1990–94, the Russian Far North and adjacent areas lost 770,000, or 8 percent, of the population (Zaionchkovskaya, 32, in Azrael and Payin 1996). Chukotka and Magadan were the hardest hit, losing 22 and 15 percent in 1993–94, respectively (32). It is interesting that attempts to link this reflux with declines in production and rises in unemployment were unsuccessful. More fruitful were correlations with the development of the private sector elsewhere, which provided better opportunities in other regions (Zaionchkovskaya, 33, in Azrael and Payin 1996).

While Slavs leave, the Chinese are coming in. At the end of the nineteenth century, there were about 500,000 Chinese living in the Russian Far East in a total population of 1.5 to 2 million (Minakir, 86, in Azrael and Payin 1996). The influx of Slavs and tight border controls imposed after the revolution stopped the inflow of the Chinese when Slav expansion in the Far East reached its high point. There was a small, mostly temporary, influx after World War II when Chinese experts and students were trained in the Soviet Union. This influx came to an end after the rift emerged between two Communist giants. The situation changed radically with the collapse of the Soviet Union. The Russian Far East experienced a sharp economic decline while Chinese economic reforms took off. The Chinese private sector, specializing in consumer goods and foodstuffs, needed raw materials and machinery that the Russian Far East could supply. Thus, the economies on each side of the border began to complement each other. With political accommodation achieved in 1989 during Gorbachëv's visit to Beijing, the road was wide open for cooperation, although trade between the two countries was not immune from ups and downs (as in 1994). Trade and the general opening of post-Soviet Russia facilitated a Chinese influx. Initially, in 1991–92, Russian regulations were lax. This, and the encouragement by the Chinese government, allowed some Chinese to petition for residency permits and Russian citizenship on the basis of family ties. Many Chinese came to study Russian in Khabarovsk, Vladivostok, and Blagoveshchensk (Minakir, 92, in Azrael and Payin 1996). Others were employed in agriculture, construction, and other areas where demand exceeded local labor resources. Between 1990, when employment of the Chinese began, and 1992, the number of Chinese workers almost trebled (Minakir, 93, in Azrael and Payin 1996). The influx awoke perennial Russian fears of the "yellow danger," and by the end of 1992 a new anti-Chinese campaign, instigated by Russian nationalism and business competition, was underway. Although the total number of Chinese immigrants in the Far East in 1992–93 probably did not exceed 50,000 to 80,000 (including 10,000 to 15,000 contract workers and 10,000 to 12,000 students), estimates ranged from 200,000 to 2 million (Minakir, 94, in Azrael and Payin 1996). These numbers were a gross overestimation since the entire population of the four major host regions did not exceed 1.8 million (94). And mass hunts on illegals in Khabarovsk and Amur provinces yielded only 5,000 to 6,000 each (94). By the end of 1994 it became obvious that the anti-Chinese campaign had boomeranged, and in 1995 ties were largely restored. The Russian Far East badly needs Chinese trade and investment, and that means accepting Chinese immigration at a level that makes local Russians far too uncomfortable.

East Slavs knew three periods of great migration. The first, up the Dnieper valley and further north, laid the foundations of Kievan Rus'. With the establishment of the state, the "natural" direction of expansion was south, into the fertile Black Earth belt. The desire of Slav farmers to expand south was enhanced by the Scandinavian elite's greed and the desire to trade with Byzantium and the Muslim world. But Kievan aspirations were thwarted by the nomads who controlled the Pontic steppe.

Unable to expand south, Slavs turned north and northeast, always within the confines of the forest zone. This second phase, the Kievan colonization, continued under the Mongols and laid the foundations of Muscovy.

The destruction of the Golden Horde successor states in the middle of the sixteenth century opened the way east; the annexation of the Crimea opened the south, a thousand years after the initial push. This Third Great Migration gained in intensity in the nineteenth century with industrialization and improved transportation. Before the emancipation of 1861, many migrants were political criminals, government serfs transferred by decree, and runaway serfs. After 1861, the great majority of migrants were free peasants.

However, already toward the end of the nineteenth century migration of ethnic minorities from the western fringe of the empire was redirected west. The loss of much of the western fringe after World War I and the closing of Soviet borders preserved the eastern direction for another generation. But after 1945, Russians increasingly migrated west and south. Their plunging birth rates undercut further expansion. The turning point occurred in the 1960s in Transcaucasia, in the early 1970s in Kazakstan, and in the mid-1970s in Central Asia (Zaionchkovskaya, 16, in Azrael and Payin 1996). After that, more and more Russians started to leave Turkestan, Siberia, and the Far East. The collapse of the Soviet Union reinforced this trend.

Migration built up the Russian Empire. Now it may complete its destruction.

CHAPTER 5

Russian Immigration and its Effect on the Kazak Steppes, 1552–1965

Rebecca W. Wendelken

The history of the Kazak steppes is primarily a story of the relationship between the nomad and the settled. Sometimes the interaction was peaceful. More often it was not, as the two groups struggled over how to utilize the vast steppelands. The arrival of Russian peasants had an enormous impact on the modern history of the Kazak steppes. Their movement into Asia has been compared to the western expansion of America—a sort of Russian "manifest destiny."[1] Like America's, Russia's frontier region already contained numerous peoples with a variety of economic cultures, ranging from nomadic to settled farmer.[2] Beginning in the late nineteenth century, waves of settlers from European Russia immigrated to the Kazak steppes.[3] Their motivations for this perilous journey were simple—land and freedom.[4] But the land was occupied. Russia came to see these nomadic peoples as obstacles in the path of settlement and later as her own "white man's burden." At that point Russia, like other imperialistic European powers, succumbed to the apparently inescapable urge to remold the Kazaks in a European image and make them into agricultural peasants. This urge, which continued into the Soviet period, dramatically altered Kazak society, culture, and economy.

Russia's presence in the Kazak steppes before 1965 can be divided into several stages and should be viewed in the context of the general Russian expansion to the east. The first stage lasted from the mid-1550s until the 1830s and was a defensive and commercial venture, one of containment rather than control. The second and third stages overlap somewhat. The goal of the second stage was pacification, and this was largely achieved by the late nineteenth century. The third stage, from the late 1880s until 1914, was a period of government-promoted colonization and settlement during which large numbers of Russian settlers migrated to the steppes. From World War I until 1926, bridging the tsarist and Soviet periods, civil and political turmoil caused a sharp decline in the Kazak population and reflux of the Russians back to their homeland. During this short twelve-year period, the region experienced the 1916 Kazak revolt, the Russian revolutions, the Civil War, and several years of famine. During the fifth stage, from 1926 to 1939, the new government attempted to sovietize both the Russian and the Kazak populations. Collectivization in the 1930s and the gulag period from 1934 to 1939 forced many Kazaks to leave the country. During the same period and extending through World War II, there was a new type of immigration as many "suspect" people from European Russia and the Russian Far East, such as Germans and Koreans, were forcibly relocated to the steppes. The largest influx of Russians, however, occurred during the sixth stage, from 1954 to 1964. During the Virgin Lands Project, the Russian population increased so rapidly that this period has been referred to as Kazakstan's second colonization.[5]

The numerous stages of Russian involvement and their varied goals help account for the divergence of views on whether Russia's presence was a positive or a negative one for the region. The controversial aspect of Russia's impact is mirrored in its ethnocentric and heavily politicized historiography. In some cases, the writings are colored by the availability of source materials. For example, details of the annexation of the Kazak steppes by Russia come entirely from Russian administrative papers, which have an understandable, if not always extractable, bias.[6] This has led to conflicting views of how Kazakstan became part of the Russian Empire. Soviet and Russian writers stress the voluntary nature of Kazakstan's assimilation into the Russian Empire, arguing that the Russians were invited into the steppes to protect the Kazaks from hostile outsiders, such as the Zunghars.[7] In this scenario Russia's presence has been a positive one that brought urbanization, industrialization, modernization, and education. The opposing argument, found primarily in the writings of Westerners and Kazak nationalist writers, emphasizes the negative aspects of the Russian presence. While all but the most nationalistic of Kazaks concede the Russians were invited into the country in 1731/32, most would agree that once they arrived, the Russians acted like boorish guests. Although modern-day Kazaks are no longer nomadic and many cannot speak Kazak, these two factors continue to constitute their primary identity markers. In the eyes of nationalists, it was the Russians who destroyed Kazak traditional life and culture.[8]

Like most highly polarized topics, each viewpoint on the history of the Kazak steppes contains some element of truth, but each is limited in scope.

Russian policies over time showed a remarkable amount of inconsistency and actual contradiction, which adds to the confusion. For example, Russian historians argue that the Kazaks were reluctant to settle and adopt agriculture. While it is true that nomadic pastoralism in its pure form is not compatible with modern industrial society, the process of sedentarization had already begun in some areas before the arrival of Russian settlers.[9] Recently a third trend has emerged that examines the tsarist and Soviet periods in a broader historical context, addressing factors such as geography and environment, religion, other external contacts, the limitations of nomadism, interethnic conflict, and the nature of traditional society itself.

Who were these nomads? The Kazaks, a Turkic people, have occupied the area south of Russia between the Caspian Sea and Lake Baikal since the mid-fifteenth century. They developed a primarily oral tradition and considered themselves Muslim, with a deep attachment to the cult of Sufi saints. Their economy centered around pastoral nomadism with herds primarily composed of sheep and horses. Kazak society was segmented, a system that provides "stability without government," allowing internal order to be maintained even though their system of social differentiation was not elaborately developed.[10] They retained the Mongol-style social divisions between the "white bones," or nobility, which traced its decent from Genghis Khan, and the "black bones," or commoners.

Although a Kazak khanate existed between the 1550s and the 1720s, the Kazak political organization was very loose, consisting of three "hordes" or *zhuz*. The *Ulu* (greater or elder) *zhuz,* the *Orta* (middle) *zhuz,* and the *Kishi* (little or younger) *zhuz* each had their own territory, leadership, and history. During the early nineteenth century a fourth group, the Inner or *Bukiev* Horde, was formed when Russia allowed a part of the Kishi Zhuz access to Russian pastureland between the Ural and Volga rivers. Each zhuz was composed of several tribes, each with a number of clans. Clans contained a number of *auls,* or migratory villages. The *aul* was the most important division for the average Kazak. It governed all aspects of daily life, including the assignment of migratory routes, grazing areas, and winter quarters. The Russian government conducted its dealings with each zhuz, and sometimes with each tribe, independently.

The Kazak population was mainly concentrated in the northern part of the steppe, where fertile soil and comparatively abundant rainfall produced rich grasslands. Consequently this was the same area that received the heaviest Russian settlement. As one moves southward, soil fertility and average yearly rainfall decreases until the land becomes desert. Beyond that are foothills and mountains that can support some agriculture.[11] Unlike peasant farmers, nomads used the land on an extensive, rather than intensive, basis. Even in the more temperate areas, they required a large land area in order to keep their herds continually fed. Sheep are especially hard on pasture land. Their protruding teeth are able to nip the grass down to the roots. It may take several years for the grass to recover sufficiently enough to allow grazing again.

Although Russians were, and still are, often blamed for putting nomadic pastures under the plow, the Kazaks' range was being compressed even before Russian colonization began.[12] Their loose political organization and thinly spread-out population prevented them from mounting an effective resistance to outside forces.[13] The Uzbeks pressed them from the south, and the Kalmyks made raids from the southeast and the southwest. Decreased pasturage meant smaller herds and in times of disease or drought; a group's entire livelihood could be wiped out in a single season.

Imperial Russia's interest in the steppes began in the sixteenth century as a combination of defense and commercialism. In the 1550s, Moscow conquered Kazan' and Astrakhan', opening up the whole course of the Volga for trade with Bukhara and Persia. Russians began to recognize the economic potential of this vast unexplored territory and to become involved in steppe politics. By playing allies off against each other, and by strategically placing settlements along the frontiers Russia slowly gained control of the steppe. In 1722, Peter I devised a plan to extend Russian influence into Asia that contained the following instructions: "The Kazak hordes constitute the door and the key to the whole of Asia. Consequently we must, without fail, take them under Russian protection."[14]

The Cossacks were the first Europeans to permanently settle in the Kazak steppes. Often confused with the Kazaks because of the similarity of their names, the Cossacks were formed during the sixteenth century by peasants fleeing enserfment. Their bands were later joined by more escaped serfs and dissenters from the Orthodox Church. These people intermarried with the local population and over time developed a new identity.[15] By 1560, a large band of Cossacks had settled on the northwestern border of the Kazak steppes. They traded service to the tsar in the form of troops and border defenses for title to their land and local autonomy. The Russian government viewed borders in terms of security: if the border areas were thinly populated, they were vulnerable to invasion; if they were peopled by other ethnic groups, they were equally vulnerable.[16] Russia's objective was to create a stable frontier. Over time more and more Cossack outposts were created to protect the border from raiding Kazaks, until eventually the Cossacks gained ownership to a narrow strip of land along three sides of the Kazak steppes. Although they practiced some agriculture in addition to trade and fishing, the Cossacks used only a small portion of their land. As time went on, they began to supplement their income by renting the remainder to Russian peasants or to settled Kazaks. The Cossack forts, such as Omsk, Orsk, Orenburg, and Petropavlovsk, served as nuclei for future Cossack and Russian settlement.[17] A southern line, completing the circle around the Kazak steppes, was established to protect Russian traders and to control raids by slavers from Central Asia. The encirclement had a destabilizing effect on the Kazak. The line blocked the traditional migration routes and sometimes access to water and winter pastures as well. Many Kazaks, those who were unable or unwilling to adapt, lost most or all of their livestock and were forced to settle, either farming the land themselves or working as agricultural laborers.

Long before the Cossack line was completed, however, raiders from Central Asia had already begun to limit Kazak movement. In 1723, the Zungharian Kalmyks, long enemies of the Kazaks, crossed the Talas Valley into the southern Kazak steppes. They surprised the Ulu Zhuz camping there and forced them to flee, leaving most of their possessions and livestock behind. It has been argued that Kazak nomadism never recovered from this blow, known as the Aqtaban Shuirindi, or Great Retreat.[18] Realizing the Kishi Zhuz was in danger as well, their khan applied to Russia for protection from their enemies. In 1730, the khans swore loyalty to the Russian empress. Similar agreements were made by the khans of the Orta Zhuz in 1740. The agreements had two problems for the Kazaks. First, none of these agreements clearly defined Kazak territory, and second, it is unclear whether the khans swore personal loyalty or spoke for the entire *zhuz*. Once the agreements were signed, the Kazaks became members of the social category known as the *inorodtsy*, or aliens. The term applied to any group in the Russian Empire who were considered too different from Russian society to be integrated into it.[19] The *inorodtsy* had fewer rights than Russian citizens, but were also exempt from certain duties, such as military service. However, the possibility remained that they could, if they converted to Russian Orthodoxy and adopted Russian culture, be fully integrated into Russian society.

In the 1830s, Russia began an active military conquest of the steppes that resulted in the actual incorporation of the Kazak steppes into the Russian Empire. General Perovskii's unsuccessful military campaign against Khiva in 1835 demonstrated the importance of the Kazak steppe for military ventures to the south. New fortifications were built inside the original Cossack line, which allowed the region to be divided into smaller, more manageable administrative units.[20] Because these new forts were built without the permission of the Kazak khans, the Kazaks were victims of Russian conquest, not members of a voluntary union with Russia.[21] Russian administration of the area was never particularly strict, although the "Rules on the Siberian Kyrgyz," crafted by Michael Speranskii in 1822, redefined how the region should be administered. These rules, which applied only to the Orta Zhuz, instituted a type of local self-rule with combined Kazak and Russian administration at the higher levels. Perhaps the greatest change was not the type of administration, but the requirement that Kazaks pay taxes to fund it. These taxes, which had to be paid in cash, introduced the cash economy. Some Kazaks see this as the beginning of the real decline of Kazak society.

The Crimean War briefly interrupted Russian military expansion into Central Asia. This process was finally completed in 1885 when the Turkmen were subdued after many long and bloody battles. While fighting in the Kazak steppes was not as intense as in Central Asia, many Kazaks actively resisted Russian rule. The most famous and long-lived of these revolts was led by Sultan Kenesari Kasim, known in Russian history as Kenisary Qasimov. His nine-year revolt of the Orta Zhuz began in 1837 and ended with his submission.

Russian presence also affected the power structure of Kazak society. Once the khans accepted Russian protection, the Russian authorities had the final say in disputes. Whether the authority of the khans had already begun to erode by this time or whether Russian subjugation actually began the process is unclear. Russian reforms did undercut the prestige of the Kazak aristocracy as the khans became more closely identified with Russia. Power shifted away from them and toward the traditional local leadership of the *bais* and the *aksakals* (village elders). Crushing this leadership became one of the primary goals of the early Soviet period. From 1740 to 1840, much of the Kazak nobility were slowly assimilated by the Russians or, at least, they became strongly Russified. They were courted by the Russian government and often received lavish gifts of money, property, and titles. Their male children were sent to government boarding schools where they received a Russian education. Some of these educated Kazaks, like ethnographer Chokhan Valikhanov, retained contact with their people. Others became, if not alienated, at least distanced from Kazak culture. In the 1860s, Russia introduced the concept of European-style elected officials. It separated the administrative and legislative functions formerly performed by the khans and elders, but the *adat,* or traditional law, continued to be used on the local level. This dual law system often created confusion, and internal conflicts developed. As open migration areas decreased in size, disputes could no longer be settled by the traditional method of simply splitting off to form a new group. The result was destructive infighting.[22]

As Russian control solidified, the Cossack fortifications along the steppe lost much of their military importance. Regular towns began to develop in these border areas, but few Russians immigrated into the interior.[23] In 1868, the tsarist government formally annexed the Kazak steppes. Administratively the region was divided into six provinces, or oblasti, which fell under three separate jurisdictions. Syr Darya and Semirechye were governed by the governor-general of Turkestan, Ural'sk and Turgai by the Orenburg governor-general, and Akmolinsk and Semipalatinsk by the governor-general of

Western Siberia. Each of the three major population groups in the region, the Russians, the Kazaks, and the Cossacks, had different administrative structures, which complicated interethnic relations, especially when disputes arose. Again, Kazaks were taxed to fund the administration, and local taxes were added to pay for roads, schools and other infrastructure.

In 1891, the four northern oblasti, Turgai, Ural'sk, Akmolinsk, and Semi-palatinsk, were united under one administration under the new governor-generalship of the steppe.[24] The governor-general commanded the Russian occupational forces and also oversaw the civilian political, economic, judicial, and administrative systems. Each oblast' was divided into counties, or *uiezdy*, administered by Russian officers with the assistance of local Kazak notables. Further internal divisions were made similar to those already in existence. Locally elected officials were responsible for the lower divisions. A dual court system was imposed, with both a native court and a Russian criminal court at the *volost'* and *uiezd* levels.[25] While the Kazaks were now, in principle, responsible for their own local government, with officials elected rather than appointed by the village elders, bribery and unkept promises made to secure votes increased demoralization and disillusionment.[26] The most damaging aspect of the 1891 Steppe Statute was the section that declared all land in excess of Kazak needs to be state property. The official explanation was that the land was "surplus."[27] A formula was divised to compute the amount of surplus land. Each Kazak was allotted 30 hectares, an inadequate amount of land to support a single Kazak in most areas of the steppes. The number of Kazaks in a given area was multiplied by 30, and that number was subtracted from the total number of hectares. The remainder was declared "surplus." This action catalyzed a shift in the basic fault line that had always existed between the settled tribes and the nomads. The strongest division now became that between the Russians and the Kazaks.[28]

The true extent of Russia's early migration is difficult to analyze because no records of immigration were kept until 1896, when the Resettlement Administration was established. The 1897 census showed Russians comprised about 12 percent of the total population of Kazakstan, or around 600,000.[29] It is estimated that the total number of settlers moving to the Kazak steppes before 1897 was between 300,000 and 500,000.[30] This number increased dramatically after 1896 due to the work of the Resettlement Administration, famine conditions in European Russia, and the completion of the Trans-Siberian Railroad to Omsk, the major point of entry for immigrants into Kazakstan. From the end of the nineteenth century to 1916, approximately 1,400,000 European Russians arrived in the Kazak steppes. By 1911, Russians comprised 40 percent of the steppe oblasti's population.[31]

The Russian peasant settlers fell into three broad groups. The first were those authorized by the government. They were, in principle, prepared for their new life. Their number was limited by law, and to obtain authorization they were required to pay off all their debts before permission to resettle was granted. This alone was an insurmountable burden in most cases. High debt ratios and continued obligations to the commune meant that only the very wealthy could afford to immigrate legally.[32] Those who did not or could not pay their debts probably comprised the bulk of the second group, the "self-willed" or unauthorized settlers ("irregulars"). Their numbers were swelled by harvest failures during the 1890s. The third group was primarily peasants who had been authorized for another area but had failed to make a go of it there. Rather than return to European Russia, they headed for the steppes and a second chance to start over. Although illegal immigration was a criminal offense and unauthorized or illegal settlers were supposed to be returned home, regulations against them were rarely enforced.[33]

The urge to immigrate generally involves both "push" and "pull" factors. Russian peasants were "pushed" by the relative lack of freedom they experienced in European Russia and by the heavy political control they experienced there. They also wanted to escape the problems of rural overpopulation, land shortages, and recurring famine. The seemingly limitless land and relative freedom of Siberia and the Kazak steppes were strong "pull" factors. The government played a key role in promoting Siberia as the land of opportunity and plenty. Publications and tracts sought to appeal to both the peasant farmer and the industrialist seeking new opportunities. This was especially true after 1906, when the more heavily populated Russian provinces disseminated resettlement information as well in hopes of relieving the population pressure and preventing further civil unrest. As more settlers went east, news of the new land was transmitted by word of mouth.[34] The Russian government also offered loans for authorized settlers and liberalized its migration policies, but perhaps its greatest contribution to resettlement was the building of railroads.[35] These allowed rapid access to the newly available lands and speeded the immigration process. Legally immigrating families were often given their railroad tickets free or at a reduced rate, subsidized by the government.

The average settlers came as family units. Persons under the age of 18 formed one of the largest cohorts, and males dominated in all age groups. The new settlers exhibited varying degrees of preparation. Some peasants departing for the great unknown simply pulled up stakes and set out for the new land. Others made a more planned effort. Rather than relying on luck, they hired "land scouts," paid individuals who went ahead to claim the best land.[36] But even the best planning could not always ensure success or happiness. Between 1896 and 1916, Demko estimates that 22 percent of the migrants to Kazakstan returned to European Russia. Some found the available land unsuitable or were unable to grow their accustomed crops in the new soil and climate. Others were unable to make a living on their new allotment.[37]

As the number of settlers surpassed the amount of land available for settlement, new lands had to be found. The 1891 Steppe Statute seizing "surplus" land only applied to Akmolinsk, Semipalatinsk, and Semirechye. In 1892 it was extended to Turgai and Ural'sk as well. This statute marked a change in official policy. No longer concerned with merely controlling the nomads' movements and pacifying the Kazak steppes, the government now began an active campaign to settle the nomads, or at least greatly restrict their movements. Central authorities continued to argue that there was an abundance of land, far more than the Kazaks needed, and that this surplus land should be freed up for colonization.[38] A. N. Kulomzin, coordinator of peasant resettlement in the late tsarist period, actively supported land seizure.[39] The government, he argued, could requisition almost 2.5 million desiatinas (one desiatina equals 2.7 acres) of land and still "guarantee that [the Kazaks'] minimum dietary and economic needs would be met!"[40]

Despite the numerous statutes on "surplus" land and the dramatic increase in Russian population, Russian rule in its colonial areas retained a certain amount of "indirectness" and continued to be based, in principle, on a policy of non-interference and self-rule. Like the British "indirect" rule system, this system allowed Kazaks to hold titular posts while the real power was wielded by Russian administrators.[41] The policies proposed by St. Petersburg were often contradictory, a result of overlapping administrations and an ignorance of the local situation. For example, although the government wanted to see the nomads settled, farmers were taxed at a higher rate than nomads. Some groups insisted on retaining nomadic status in spite of their actual situation in order to be assessed at a lower tax rate. As "nomads," however, they could not sell land or use it as security for loans in times of difficulty.[42]

In spite of all the problems, the late nineteenth century was a time of relative peace on the steppe. Although the slow chipping away of land restricted their movement, it did not create a great alarm for most Kazaks. Essentially, except where taxes or other direct interaction with the government were concerned, they were left alone, albeit within the confines of their continually shrinking territory. As Russian settlement in the northern regions increased, fertile land became more and more scarce. This land shortage resulted in "spillover" of immigrants into the southern *uiezdy*. The numbers of Russian settlers were increasing so rapidly that Semirechye was closed to immigration from 1896 to 1910, until the government could decide how to handle land distribution between settlers and natives.[43] Restrictions and regulations did little to affect the influx of illegal immigrants, who continued to arrive in large numbers.

Some Kazaks, especially those in the areas of greatest Russian settlement, adapted to the shrinking pasturage by supplemental farming. Some took advantage of Russian markets and improved transportation by switching from sheep to cattle, a meat preferred by the Russians. These cattle were driven to railheads and those that were not consumed locally were shipped to other cities and towns. Cattle did have a drawback. Unlike sheep, they were less suited to the climate of the steppes and needed supplemental feeding during the winter months. This increased the number of Kazaks who began to grow fodder crops and grain for supplemental feeding during the winter or drought periods.

Although relatively large urban areas developed in the northern border, the majority of the population remained rural. In 1897, only about 7 percent of the population was urban. Although these towns and cities began as centers for regional administration and trade, these "cities" became centers of industry and manufacture as well.[44] Omsk is an example of how quickly urbanization took place. In 1903, Omsk was the only city in the steppes with more than 50,000 inhabitants. Seven years later, its population had more than tripled.[45] As industry increased, many peasants whose agriculture was marginal moved to the cities, where they sought jobs in the new factories.

Had settlement occurred in an organized manner or at a leisurely pace, its negative impact might have been lessened. Neither was the case. Rules were frequently ignored and the whole process became chaotic.[46] Complaints were generally sent to St. Petersburg in the form of petitions, and there they often became lost in the bureaucratic shuffle, thus increasing distaste for the imperial authorities. St. Petersburg's inability to organize resettlement was exacerbated by local officials who lacked the necessary powers and "seemed reluctant to use what little influence they possessed."[47] By 1908, complaints became so frequent that they could no longer be ignored, and a government commission was dispatched to investigate. Headed by Senator Count K. K. Pahlen, the commission strongly criticized settlement implementation, reporting that the process was not in accordance with the current laws; that it often removed settled Kazaks from their land, thus discouraging nomad settlement; that land formerly under irrigation was often lost because the settlers refused to continue the practice; and that crops planted were frequently unsuitable to the climate and soil. Land farmed by sedentary Kazaks and even Cossacks was often confiscated and given to Russian settlers to quell disturbances. The settlement system was fraught with fraud, and loans were often made to ineligible applicants.[48] It found the settlers were unprepared, underfunded, and of generally poor quality.[49]

As the Kazak/Russian divide solidified, tensions mounted. The old steppe conflict between settled and nomad reappeared with a new twist. Many new settlers brought with them an animosity toward the Russian government. They also soon developed contempt toward the Kazaks, who, they felt, were being maintained on the land at the settlers' expense. Anyone who held coveted land, including indigenous peasants, Cossacks, and settled Kazaks, was seen as a stumbling block in the path of the new settlers. As peasants scrambled for more and more land and the government became increasingly unable to organize resettlement, the general atmosphere became that of a land rush, not an organized effort. To escape with their herds intact, many Kazaks along the border moved to Chinese territory.[50]

Those Kazaks who remained tried to adapt in various ways. As discussed previously, some completely abandoned nomadism or supplemented pasturage with grain or fodder in the winter. Those who could not make a go of it were forced to give up herding altogether. They sought employment as farm laborers or as miners in some of the developing copper or coal mines, but these were menial jobs at pay scales well below that of Russian workers. The impoverishment of many Kazaks caused a greater economic stratification in Kazak society. It also meant a social polarization, as those who abandoned nomadism, whether by choice or not, were viewed as inferior by their nomadic brothers.[51]

The Russian Empire at the beginning of the twentieth century was in a state of flux, and some members of the tiny Kazak intelligensia saw in Russia's weakness the potential to advance their own cause. Russia was torn by revolution. Continued land shortages, the unsolved problems of emancipation, and the difficulties of modernization came to a head during the disastrous Russo-Japanese War of 1904. A few intellectuals began to examine the idea of the formation of a Kazak. The difficulty was that the leadership was deeply divided over the future of their people. Among the intellectuals, there were supporters for both modernization and westernization, and for a return to nomadism.[52] The modernizers saw Russia as an attractive model of western civilization, one that could be adapted to Kazak needs. Their opponents were against Russian rule and believed the future of the Kazaks could only be assured if they returned to their traditional lifestyle. The traditional leaders, the *beys, sultans,* and *aksakals,* were equally divided. Some wanted to overcome economic, cultural, and religious supremacy of the Russian outsiders and to protect Kazak land. Others, who owed their wealth or position to the empire, were uninterested in revolutionary political activity. Having no desire to participate in a radical political opposition, they were chiefly interested in local cultural and religious autonomy within the Russian Empire.

During the summer of 1905, the more sophisticated members of the Kazak elite overcame their differences. They realized that while the Kazaks shared few of the workers' and peasants' demands, the time was ripe to advance their own agenda. They demanded the return of all land seized from the Kazaks and protection from further seizures. They also asked for the return of control of forests and fisheries and the assurance that mineral extraction would be solely by the Kazaks for their own benefit.[53] The government unsurprisingly failed to respond. Religious leaders were somewhat more successful. They persuaded St. Petersburg to yield to long-standing Kazak religious and cultural demands. The powers of the local Muslim clergy were broadened to establish a muftiate of the steppe region.[54] Newspapers and other periodicals in the Kazak language were permitted, and Kazak was allowed to become the primary language for religious instruction.

Politically, Kazaks were given representation in the new Imperial Duma created in 1906. Educated Kazaks benefited from their participation and, although their role was limited, they received an introduction to the democratic process. In the first Imperial Duma, four Kazaks and four Russians represented the steppe. In the second Duma, there were four delegates from the steppe, at least two of whom were Kazak. However, a new electoral law in 1907, designed to quell ideas unpopular with the tsar and his advisors, denied the Kazaks, and indeed many formerly represented peoples, representation. The Kazak intellectuals were disappointed that no legislation beneficial to the Kazaks was ever passed, "although they did use the Duma as a forum to attract increased attention to the Kazak plight" (quoted in Pierce 1960, 258).[55] They continued to work for change within the system, and the cessation of peasant colonization, and the return of Kazak lands continued to be at the top of their list of demands.[56]

Even before the 1905 Revolution, the government had liberalized immigration requirements. In June 1904, a new migration law, replacing the regulations of 1889, favored some groups of peasants, particularly those who wanted to go to areas of low population, especially if these were strategically important, and those who were coming from areas of intense land shortages. Both received financial support. The new policy marked a change. In the past, immigration regulations favored rich or well-off peasants. Now they especially encouraged poorer peasants to resettle as well.[57] By easing up on immigration restrictions, they hoped to stifle the revolutionary and antigovernment activities among peasants in European Russia. Russian debate on the policies of immigration did not actually develop until after 1905. As migration increased, state supporters continued to voice their view that the Russian influx would strengthen border areas, while leftists feared that it might lessen the possibility for revolution by easing population pressure in European Russia itself.[58] The flood of new settlers reached new highs after the implementation of the Stolypin Reforms. These reforms, which were formulated in the wake of the 1905 revolution, were aimed at abolishing the hold of the commune over its members in European Russia. Peasant allotments were consolidated in an effort to make agriculture more efficient. These reforms made it easier for a peasant to leave the commune. Individual ownership of the land could replace joint family control, redemption payments from the emancipation process were abolished, and credit institutions provided loans for land purchase.[59] Many European peasants were prompted to sell their small holdings and emigrate to the steppes, where they received a larger land allotment. Between 1906 and 1914, over one million immigrants are believed to have resettled in Kazakstan. Once they arrived, some peasants resumed farming while others sought employment in the steppes' newly emerging industries. Foreign-owned mines such as Spassky, Atbasar, and Kyshtym drew a small but influential workforce that brought with it revolutionary ideas and attitudes. A few Kazaks also sought work in these mines, but they were restricted to the most menial jobs at low pay.

After 1914, thanks in part to the war, the flow of Russian settlers slowed to a trickle. Eligible males who had immigrated were drafted into the military. The early years of the war had little effect on the Kazaks. As aliens, they were exempt from military service. By 1916, Russia desperately needed manpower. In June of that year, Kazak males between the ages of 19 and 43 were conscripted for the first time.[60] Instead of being given cavalry duty as they requested, Kazaks were placed in manual labor brigades and used as forced labor on Russian-owned farms. These "volunteers" were badly treated, prompting the few Kazaks who could afford it to purchase an exemption.[61] The forced draft caused a panic among the Kazaks, and anti-Russian sentiment finally boiled over. Nomads along the border moved their herds into Chinese territory for protection.[62] Those Kazaks employed in industry or agriculture fled into the interior of the steppes and formed armed bands. They raided Russian settlements, killed stock, and burned buildings. The rebellion quickly spread to Central Asia, but there the primarily urban outbreaks were easily suppressed.[63] In the Kazak steppes violence occurred primarily in rural areas. Inadequate transportation made it difficult to bring in troops to quell the rebellion. The heaviest Kazak resistance was in Semirechye and Semipalatinsk, where *volost'* leaders who tried to enforce conscription were frequently killed. In retaliation for Kazak raids, vigilante groups of Russian peasants, armed by the military, were formed. It was these groups that committed the majority of the atrocities. Losses were heavy on both sides, but the Kazaks bore the brunt of the damage. Russian peasants killed Kazaks and slaughtered their herds. Famine spread among the Kazaks and many more died of starvation. The heavy losses sustained by the Kazaks during the 1916 revolt had a decided affect on their inability to defend themselves during the Russian Civil War.

After the 1917 February revolution, Russians throughout the empire, including Kazakstan, were divided between support for the new government and allegiance to the old. Kazaks shared the hope of many other Central Asians that the wrongs committed under the tsarist government would be righted. Some Kazak intellectuals formally established Alash Orda, the nationalist party, and hopes were high that changes would be implemented. However, as the Provisional Government continued to drag its feet throughout the summer and into the fall, both Kazaks and Russians began to lose hope that their grievances would be addressed.

The Bolshevik takeover in October 1917 was mainly supported in urban, industrialized areas with high concentrations of Russians.[64] It found little support among the Kazaks. This is not surprising as the Bolsheviks generally ignored the interests of agricultural workers and nomads, who, they felt, had not "reached the 'proletarian' level of consciousness."[65] When they did attempt to organize in villages and *auls* in Kazakstan, they were hampered for a variety of reasons. One major reason was that the Bolsheviks were virtually all Russians, and anti-Russian sentiments made the Kazaks unreceptive to their propaganda. Additionally, Kazak traditional leadership resisted the Bolsheviks, who, they rightly felt, were trying to force them out of power.[66] All this was despite the fact that the Bolsheviks offered reason to hope for improved conditions for Kazaks under their government. Lenin and Stalin's "Message to Working Muslims in Russia and the Orient," published in December 1917, promised to redress past wrongs and to allow ethnic groups to retain their own customs and religion. As they had in 1905, some Kazak intellectuals saw Russia's chaotic situation as an auspicious time to take matters into their own hands. Retaining their allegiance to the Provisional Government, they created their own quasi-republican autonomous government called Alash Orda, which lasted from December 1917 to mid-1919.

Alash Orda's constitution was fairly liberal. It proposed freedom of speech, press, and assembly; a militia funded by a graduated tax; separation of church and state; and free universal education in Kazak. It also sought to address Kazak grievances, including return of all seized land.[67] Despite its proposed policies, the new government had its opponents in the Kazak community. They began to coalesce around Kolbai Togusov, who became the leader of the largest Kazak opposition party, Ush Zhuz (Three Hordes). Although Alash Orda had republican leanings while Ush Zhuz was essentially socialist, the real split may have had more to do with personal rivalry combined with commoner vs. aristocratic origins of the leaders of the two groups rather than with political ideology.[68]

With the fate of European Russia in question, other groups began to assert their autonomy. Five different groups, the Provisional Government (Whites), the Bolsheviks (Reds), the Kazak Nationalists (Alash Orda), the Cossacks, and the peasants (Greens), claimed control of the steppes. Civil war was inevitable. Initially, Alash Orda supported the Russian Provisional government. The Bolsheviks soon realized that their cause could be greatly advanced in the steppes if they were recognized by Alash Orda. Lenin and Stalin invited Alash Orda's leadership to Moscow, where they tried to convince them that the new Bolshevik government supported their autonomy. The Kazaks and the White Guard continued to fight side by side until the middle of 1919, when Bolshevik victories, continuing famine, and the collapse of the Whites left Alash Orda little choice but to seek accommodation with the Bolsheviks. Most members of the former Kazak government subsequently joined the Bolshevik party.

The near continual fighting in the Kazak steppes from 1916 into the 1920s had a profound effect on the entire population. All sides suffered heavy losses and were deeply affected by the economic collapse. The nomads' migrations were disrupted as opposing armies crisscrossed the steppes trying to gain control of strategic objectives. Herd sizes were greatly reduced. Continued fighting over key agricultural areas meant that crops could not be planted, and those that were frequently went unharvested. War losses freed up some of the land in European Russia, and some Russian peasants moved back to these more peaceful areas. The economy was further devastated because the infant industries of the region were mostly destroyed.[69] With no food and no money to purchase any, there was a wide ranging famine that lasted until 1922.[70] *Auls* with wealthier *bais* faired better during the difficult times because the *bais* were obligated to assist needy relatives. This not only benefited the community but tended to reinforce the *bais*' traditional authority as well. For most Kazaks, however, the economic difficulties proved insurmountable, and they sank deeper into poverty. For the Cossacks it was the beginning of their end. They suffered losses in the early 1920s similar to those of the Kazaks. Within 20 years they were either eliminated or assimilated.

After two years of bloody civil war the Bolsheviks triumphed. Initially, administration of the Kazak steppes, now called Kazakstan, was placed in the hands of a Moscow-appointed Revolutionary Committee, but in 1920 the new government began to organize political territories. The areas of present-day Kazakstan and Kyrgyzstan were united to create the Kyrgyz Autonomous Soviet Socialist Republic. Kazaks still called for the return of all land seized from them and also sought means to preserve the tattered remains of their native culture as well. Despite their conflicting agendas, the new Bolshevik government was forced to include both Alash Orda officials and officials of the old regime in their new government.[71] Also under NEP (New Economic Policy), businesses that had been suspended during World War I or damaged during the Civil War were revived, especially those dealing with already identified natural resources, such as copper, coal, and oil. This increased the number of available jobs, but was of little benefit to the

Kazaks, as most positions were filled by Russians. The Kazaks, for the most part, lacked Russian language skills, and because they were marginalized by the primarily Russian urban population, few Kazaks were ever trained for skilled jobs.[72] Despite the lack of jobs, both Russians and Kazaks continued to migrate from the rural to urban areas between the 1920s and 1930s, drawn by hopes of a better life. Urban population grew rapidly for other reasons as well. Continued immigration of European Russians and the deportation of *kulaks* from other areas of the Soviet Union swelled the population of Kazakstan's cities.

In 1924, the Soviet government reorganized, and provided each major ethnic group or nation with an area of separate administration. Stalin's program was based on his concept of a nation as "an historically evolved, stable community of people arising on the basis of a commonality of language, territory, economic life and psychological makeup as manifested in a common culture."[73] Despite this, the Kazaks, Kyrgyz, and Karakalpaks, who shared a common culture and relatively similar languages, were separated. A dialect was made the official language for the Kyrgyz, and a standard written language was developed for the Kazaks. The Soviets hoped to stifle the development of a Turko-Muslim identity and to lay the groundwork for a future Soviet state. Their plan was to gain political control by instituting social change, that is, sedentarization; stamping out traditional identities, customs, and religion; and destroying the power of the traditional leadership. Dividing the three groups would make the task easier. Kazakstan was originally placed under the Russian Soviet Federated Socialist Republic (RFSFR) in 1925. Eleven years later Kazakstan received union republic status.[74]

Having sown the seeds to destroy any possibility of a common identity among Turkic groups, the government next sought to sovietize the Kazak *aul.* In 1927, a six-point program was adopted that vowed to equalize land holdings, decrease the traditional power of the *bais,* introduce co-ops into livestock breeding, and fill positions in local government with Kazaks.[75] Low literacy rates made it difficult for Kazaks to qualify for administrative positions. Party penetration of traditional structures, such as clans and religious organizations, was resisted. The sovietization project was unsuccessful. Land redistribution and confiscation of livestock from the *bais* failed, as did co-op livestock breeding. The Bolsheviks found "harmful" customs, such as *kun* (blood revenge), *kalym* (bride price), leverate and sororate marriages, and marriage contracts difficult to eradicate. Although severe penalties were enacted against these activities, village soviets were frequently headed by traditional local leaders who were loath to destroy the customs and traditions they cherished. In general, the laws were poorly enforced or ignored. Over time many "banned" customs did become largely symbolic, not because of

Soviet laws, but because the impoverished Kazaks could no longer afford to practice them.[76]

To undermine the traditional power of the *bais* and Islam, the Bolsheviks closed mosques and *madrassahs*. This policy was successful in almost completely eradicating doctrinal Islam in Kazakstan, but mostly because Islam had never held much influence among Kazaks anyway. In its place, a different kind of Islam developed, combining Kazak customary practice and Islamic rituals. Despite the government's best efforts over a nearly 70-year period, this form of Islam remained an important part Kazak identity. In the post-Soviet period there has been a resurgence of doctrinal Islam as well, as evidenced by the great numbers of mosques and madrassahs under construction in Kazakstan today.[77]

Another leg of the government's program to undermine tradition and politicize the masses was a massive education and literacy campaign. Standard Bolshevik practices were modified to fit Kazak lifestyle. In 1922, Red Caravans traveled through the nomadic areas lecturing on the goals of the Communist Party. Red Yurts, primarily directed toward educating women in reading and communist politics, were also established.[78] The literacy campaign was initially unsuccessful. By the end of the 1920s, less than 10 percent of Kazaks could read. This was in part due to resistance from the Muslim clergy, but also because of repeated changes in the official alphabet. Prior to 1920, the Kazak language was written in Arabic. In 1926 a Latin alphabet was adopted, and, finally, in 1941 the Cyrillic alphabet became official. Each change, in effect, destroyed any previous progress, necessitating a new wave of literacy campaigns.

The blame for sovietization's failure had to fall somewhere. In 1928, an All-Union Central Committee decreed that wealthier cattle owners were subverting the sovietization of the Kazak *aul*. Their cattle, the committee determined, should be confiscated. Six hundred and ninety-six persons/households were originally targeted, but the numbers soon rose to between 55,000 and 60,000 thousand. Of these, 40,000 were actually "dekulakized," that is, had their property seized. Many were killed. Others were deported. Those who escaped fled with their herds into China.[79]

The period between the revolution and 1926 was devastating for the entire population of Kazakstan. Infant death rates rose to 90 percent of all births in some parts of Kazakhstan, and birth rates for both Russians and Kazakhs plummeted.[80] The mean death rate for Kazaks doubled, from 26.2 per 1,000 in 1910 to 54.6 in 1917.[81] Russian population figures show they were even more dramatically affected, due in large part to war losses.[82] Urban populations fell, although overall the total population figures did not vary much, largely due to mass Russian immigration.

The process of collectivization, which began with the First Five-Year Plan in 1928, had a devastating effect on the entire population of Kazakstan, both Russian and Kazak alike. However, once again the Kazaks bore the brunt of the damage. The Kazak Central Executive Committee decided to settle 56,000 nomadic and 54,000 semi-nomadic households by force, if necessary.[83] This period has been described as one of "immense human tragedy" for the Kazaks."[84] Their traditions were under constant attack and their population continued to decline. The Kazaks had the sharpest rate of population drop of any ethnic group of the USSR between 1926 and 1939.[85] The number of Kazak households fell from 1,233,000 in 1929 to 565,000 in 1936.[86] The total loss to Kazak population during this period is estimated to have been as high as 2.5 million or more.[87] What happened to them? Once again some Kazaks escaped to China, although there is evidence that many of these returned to Kazakstan when the situation cooled. Others fled to Uzbekistan.[88] But the majority died as a result of famine, purges, and general repression associated with collectivization. The famine was especially costly. Kazaks slaughtered large numbers of cattle and sheep rather than allow the government to seize them, and more died of disease and starvation. In the worst period of 1929–1930, the government refused to bring in food supplies for the Kazaks, hoping to force them into submission. At the same time, the Russian population was saved because of large shipments of food imported from Russia.[89] The drop in the Kazak population combined with Russian in-migration began to shift the ethnic proportions of the republic. The percentage of Russians increased from 19.7 percent in 1926 to 40.3 percent in 1939.[90] As Russian population increased, resettling in Kazakstan became a more attractive prospect for other Russians. While the ethnic composition of the countryside during the early Soviet period continually shifted in the Russians' favor, that of the cities was hardly affected. They continued to be primarily Russian. Distrust of Russians and industry, plus a general distaste for manual labor and low level of education, insured that most Kazaks remained firmly entrenched in the most menial jobs.[91]

Collectivization and the formation of kolkhozy was more successful in grain-producing areas where there were concentrations of Russians.[92] It was a disaster in the primarily Kazak animal breeding areas and in the regions that remained nomadic. Despite apparent attempts by the authorities, the two communities maintained their ethnic and economic segregation.[93] Collectivization was often confused, and even the most rudimentary supplies were lacking. Most kolkhozy had no plows or supplies, and in many cases no water. By March 1930, 56.6 percent of the overall population of Kazakstan was collectivized, but the figure was only 20 percent in the nomadic areas.[94] Its slow progress gave the government an excuse to rid itself of nonsupporters. The first to be targeted were the former leaders of Alash Orda.

They were implicated in a "plot" in 1930 to resist collectivization. By the end of 1932, most of their leadership had been removed from official positions. Other purges of party and government officials effectively removed both Russian and Kazak leadership, and the purging of wealthy Kazaks and Russian kulaks made further inroads into the Kazak population. Between 1932 and 1936, the Kazak Communist Party membership, which included both Russians and Kazaks, decreased from 53,869 to 25,302.[95] A succession of purges continued from 1932 to 1939, as one by one an entire generation of Kazak intellectuals, authors, politicians, and academics were executed. Russians were not exempt either. Purges of non-Kazak populations resulted in a loss of an estimated 700,000 people.[96] The losses were offset by a massive movement of Russians from the countryside to the cities.

There was another migration to Kazakstan in the 1930s and 1940s, albeit an involuntary one. Entire ethnic groups, or parts thereof, were deported from their ancestral homelands. These included the Karachis, Kalmyks, Chechens, Ingush, Balkars, Crimean Tatars, Volga Germans, Meshkhetian Turks, Kurds, and Koreans. The exact reasons for these deportations remain unclear, although some groups were accused of treason and crimes against the state, including collaboration with the Germans during the war. The deportees were resettled in Kazakstan and Central Asia, where they were placed under surveillance in labor camps or special settlement areas mostly located in the northern and eastern part of the republic. Many died during transport or in the first five years, with death rates as high as 24 percent for those from the northern Caucasus. Even after they were freed from MVD (Ministry of Internal Affairs) surveillance, which, in the case of the Germans, was not until 1955, they were not allowed to return home until the 1990s.[97]

World War II provided a respite from collectivization for the Kazaks. Although the Soviet government did not pursue its goals as strongly as in the 1930s, they remained the same—end "feudal" leaders' authority and religious authority through mass education, scientific atheism, and attacks on customary practices. The government retreated on its antireligious campaign at the beginning of the war to help mobilize the entire country and decrease anti-Russian sentiment. This "retreat" lasted until 1946 and provided a brief respite for the Kazaks.[98] The war itself had a profound effect on all population groups.[99] The military draft made no allowances for population losses that had occurred since the revolution but, unlike World War I, there is no evidence that either Russians or Kazaks resisted the draft.[100] The quotas for both produce and manpower, enacted as part of the war effort, placed heavy demands on the entire population. The military draft had caused a domestic labor shortage. Moscow was not able to provide the technical or material assistance that local industries needed. What they could and did supply was labor. Kazakstan's location, far from German-held territories, made it a perfect refuge for evacuees. By the summer of 1942, more than 400,000 Russians and Ukrainians, mostly women and children, had been evacuated to Kazakstan and Central Asia. Not only people, but entire factories were relocated to protect them from the advancing German army. These factories opened up some opportunities, but despite this the economy remained stagnant.[101]

The postwar period and the atomic age provided new roles for the land of Kazakstan. Its deserts became atomic test sites, but repeated atomic blasts made vast areas uninhabitable. Kazakstan also became the home of the Soviet space program, a somewhat less destructive role. The Cosmodrome at Baikonur is still the launch site for Russian cosmonauts. Both of these programs required large numbers of scientists, technicians, and skilled workers, positions that could not be filled by the less educated Kazaks. Russians and other educated people moved to the steppes. Many of them made permanent homes in Kazakstan.

During the postwar period there was also an attempt to bolster Kazakstan's agricultural production. Between 1946 and 1953, the smaller farms were consolidated to increase farming efficiency. Experts were brought in to study the problems, and there was even an attempt to solve the rural labor problem by demobilizing some Soviet army units in Kazakstan.[102] Suddenly in 1953, Stalin died. In Moscow, Communist leaders grappled over who would become his successor. Agriculture in the Soviet Union had not yet recovered from the war, while in Kazakstan agricultural productivity was still at an all-time low. There were widespread food shortages. To enhance his position, Nikita Khrushchëv set out to solve the food problem by devising a plan to grow grain on the Kazak Steppes. Its title, the Virgin Lands Project, implies that the land was unexploited and empty. This was misleading. Much of the land was, in fact, being used by the Kazak livestock industry. Besides its obvious benefits to Khrushchëv's career, the project provided an opportunity to reward his supporters and replace his opponents. Many leaders in the Kazakstan Communist Party, and especially the Kazak party's first and second secretaries, who opposed the project, were targeted. In 1954, Khrushchëv's supporters replaced both secretaries and local party officials in the six Virgin Land oblasti. Leonid Brezhnev was named the second secretary. The path was now clear to place the steppes under the plow.

The Virgin Lands Project had the enormity of scale typical of Soviet undertakings. In its first year, three hundred new state farms were begun. A total of 3.5 million hectares were plowed for the first time. However, the project faced several obstacles. The first was finance. Many areas of the Soviet Union had not even begun to repair war damage, and some officials argued that reconstruction of those areas would make better use of the country's limited funds. The second problem was the age-old problem of infrastructure. Without massive road and railroad construction, how could supplies be brought to the new fields, and even more important, how could the agricultural products, once harvested, be shipped to markets or processing plants? The solution for the third problem was easier. There was still a rural labor shortage in Kazakstan. Until sufficient population could be built up in these regions, young people from the cities and universities were recruited to work on the farms. Some came for only short periods, while others settled permanently.[103] Besides recruiting youths, "patriotic work brigades" were dispatched to Kazakstan to assist with the development. Once they arrived, however, they were not officially allowed to leave until the late 1950s, when internal migration regulations were eased.[104]

The initial harvests were promising, but production soon began to drop. The thin topsoil of the steppes, loosened by plowing, simply blew away. Shortfalls in the program's quotas were blamed on the new Kazak Communist Party first secretary, who now supported one of Khrushchëv's rivals. He was replaced in 1955 by Brezhnev. Once Kazak dissenters had been ousted from party leadership, the next step was to create sovkhozy to combine growing fodder crops with livestock breeding. Feed lots to fatten cattle for market were introduced. Former pastureland was sown in corn. The 1959 Seven-Year Plan set new higher milk and meat quotas but could not replace the soil. Each year's harvest proved worse than the one before. The 1963 harvest was particularly disastrous. Each new failure was followed by a wave of accusations, higher quotas, and a flurry of dismissals of highly placed officials. Meat production increased somewhat, but nothing could raise the production of grain. The 1964 plenum adopted a resolution calling again for dramatic increases in the production of meat and milk—200 to 300 per cent. It was impossible. The Virgin Lands Project had been Khrushchëv's ticket to power, and it became his demise as well. In October 1964 he was released from his party and government duties. Although the program was enormously successful for a period of time, this era of economic experimentation, like others before it, ended in failure.

The Virgin Lands Program brought large numbers of European Russians to Kazakstan. Because of it Kazakstan had the greatest rural population growth of any union republic between 1939 and 1959.[105] However, the percentage of Kazaks in the total population continued to fall. By 1959, Kazaks comprised only 30 percent of the total population, becoming the only ethnic group that was a minority in its titular republic.[106] The impact was so severe that it can easily be argued that the Virgin Lands Program had a greater negative demographic impact on the Kazak population than any other policy, with the exception of collectivization.

Then, slowly, Kazaks began to recover as Russian immigration slowed and the Russian birth rate declined. By 1970, Kazaks had risen to 32.6 percent of the total population. Today, due to substantial Russian out-migration after the collapse of the Soviet Union, Kazaks are once again the most populous ethnic group in their own country.

Conclusion

The impact of Russia and the Soviet Union on the Kazak steppes was both dramatic and long lasting. While it would be difficult to argue in a nationalist vein that it was entirely negative, the Soviet view that it was inherently positive is equally problematic. The changes that did occur were largely accomplished by the immigration, voluntary or otherwise, of large numbers of European Slavs and other ethnic groups from Russia. But, as has been shown, the demise of Kazak nomadism was not entirely due to Russian settlement and policy. Certainly, the Russian presence limited the land available for grazing and brought with it modernization, which is inherently incompatible with nomadism, but there were other factors as well. These factors did not occur uniformly throughout the steppe, but their presence affected how the different groups of Kazaks reacted to the changes in their society. Many of these factors have not been adequately studied. Areas that are ripe for additional exploration and research include the effect of geography and environment, the nature and structure of the individual native groups, the limits of nomadism, the effects of agriculture, and the impact of external contacts other than Russia. Equally fascinating and unstudied is the question of adaptation versus resistance on the part of the Kazaks. It is possible that many questions concerning the Kazaks and Russians may never be answered, for example the key question of the Khans in 1730. When they signed the agreements with the Russians, did they do it in their own name or for the entire Kazak people, and did they do it to save their own people or their personal position?

The relationship between Russians and Kazaks has always been an imperial one. It was a question of power in which St. Petersburg/Moscow set the rules and defined the game. The tsars used the Kazak steppes to guard their southern borders and as a dumping ground for excess or unwanted population. The Soviets, on the other hand, believed they were fighting imperialism. They saw Kazakstan as a model of the Soviet East, but their policies were either extractive or exploitative.

The policies of both the tsarist and especially the Soviet government helped consolidate Kazak identity. Many peoples, the Kazaks included, had little grasp of ethnicity, in the formal sense, before the Soviet period. Because their own ethnicity and that of the Russians were evolving at the same time, they form an interwoven mass, inextricably interlocked, but without a consistent pattern or form. This continues to be a problem in Kazakstan today and is exacerbated by the continued use of ethnic designation on passports and by other government policies. The situation is not conducive to a "melting pot" in which eventually all will emerge with one nationality. Old questions and concerns will continue to remain important to the survival of Kazakstan as an independent republic, and population dynamics will continue to play a key role in its development.

Notes

1. Donald W. Treadgold, The Great Siberian Migration: Government and Peasant in Resettlement from Emancipation to the First World War (Princeton, NJ: Princeton University Press, 1957), 4.

2. I. A. Gurvich, *Pereselenie Krest'ian v Sibir'* (Moscow: Izd. pereselencheskago upravleniia ministerstva vnutrennikh del, 1899).

3. These Europeans included ethnic Great Russians as well as Ukrainians, Belarusians, and other ethnic groups. The Kazaks viewed them all as "Russians," just as the Russians viewed all the peoples of the Kazak steppes and Central Asia as one group. This us/them relationship played out throughout the period in question.

4. Robert A. Lewis and Richard W. Rowland, *Population Redistribution in the USSR: Its Impact on Society, 1897–1977* (New York: Praeger, 1979), 5.

5. George Demko, *The Russian Colonization of Kazakhstan, 1896–1916* (Bloomington: University of Indiana Press, 1968), 3.

6. Baymirza Hayit, "Some Reflections on the Subject of Annexation of Turkestani Kazakhstan by Russia," *Central Asian Survey* 3, no. 4 (1984): 62; Michael Khodarkovsky, *Where Two Worlds Met: The Russian State and the Kalmyk Nomads, 1600–1771* (Ithaca: Cornell University Press, 1992), 4.

7. E. B. Bekmachanova, *Prisoedinenie Kazakhstana k Rossii* (Moscow: Akademiia Nauk, 1957), 117–19.

8. Bhavna Dave, "Inventing Islam—an Islamic Threat—in Kazakhstan," *Transition* xx, no. xx (29 December 1995): 22; Anatoly M. Khazanov, *Nomads and the Outside World,* 2d ed (Oxford: Clarendon Press, 1994), 244.

9. Khazanov, *Nomads and the Outside World,* xviii.

10. Ernest Gellner, *State and Society in Soviet Thought* (Cambridge: Cambridge University Press, 1988), 173–74; Khazanov, *Nomads and the Outside World,* 145.

11. Demko, *The Russian Colonization of Kazakhstan, 1896–1916,* 12–19; S.P. Suslov, *Physical Geography of Asiatic Russia,* trans. Noah Gershevsky (San Francisco: W. H Freeman and Company, 1961), 413–16; Boris A. Litvinskii, "The Ecology of Ancient Nomads of Soviet Central Asia and Kazakhstan," in *Ecology and Empire: Nomads in the Cultural Evolution of the Old World,* ed. Gary Seaman (Los Angeles: University of Southern California Press, 1989), 65.

12. Martha Brill Olcott, *The Kazaks*, 2d ed (Stanford: Stanford University Press, 1995), 2.

13. Demko, *The Russian Colonization of Kazakhstan, 1896–1916*, 31–33.

14. Hayit, "Some Reflections on the Subject of Annexation of Turkestani Kazakhstan by Russia," 68.

15. Paul Kolstoe, *Russians in the Former Soviet Republics* (Bloomington: Indiana University Press, 1995), 26.

16. Ibid., 24–25.

17. James Forsyth, *A History of the Peoples of Siberia: Russia's Northern Asian Colony, 1581–1900* (Cambridge: Cambridge University Press, 1992), 121; Demko, *The Russian Colonization of Kazakhstan, 1896–1916*, 36.

18. Olcott, *The Kazaks*, 26, 90; G. E. Taijakova, *Kazaki Istoriko-Ethnograficheskoe Issledovanie* (Almati: Kazakstan, 1995), 4.

19. Andreas Kappeler, "Czarist Policy toward the Muslims of the Russian Empire," in *Muslim Communities Reemerge*, ed. Edward Allworth (Durham, NC: Duke University Press, 1994), 150.

20. Demko, *The Russian Colonization of Kazakhstan, 1896–1916*, 39.

21. Hayit, "Some Reflections on the Subject of Annexation of Turkestani Kazakhstan by Russia," 69.

22. Elizabeth E. Bacon, *Central Asians under Russian Rule: A Study of Cultural Change* (Ithaca: Cornell University Press, 1966), 39.

23. Bacon, *Central Asians under Russian Rule: A Study of Cultural Change*, 94; "Russian Military and Civilian Settlements, 1824–1917," *Central Asian Review* VI, no. 2 (xxxx): 147.

24. Olcott, *The Kazaks*, 78.

25. Ibid., 78.

26. Count K.K. Pahlen, *Mission to Turkestan* (London: Oxford University Press, 1964), 178.

27. J.N. Westwood, *Russia, 1917–1964* (London: Batsford, 1966), 133.

28. Alexander and Chantal Le Mercier Quelquejay Bennigsen, *Islam in the Soviet Union* (New York: Praeger, 1967), 15; Cyril Black and Louis Duprée, *The Modernization of Inner Asia* (Armonk, NY: M. E. Sharpe, 1991), 78.

29. *Aziatskaya Rossiya* (St. Petersburg: Resettlement Administration, 1914), 82.

30. Demko, *Russian Colonization*, 76.

31. Ibid., 121, 230.

32. Kolstoe, *Russians in the Former Soviet Republics*, 27.

33. D. S. M. Williams, "Russian Peasant Settlement in Semirech'ye," *Central Asian Review* xx, no. 2 (1966): 111.

34. Treadgold, *The Great Siberian Migration: Government and Peasant in Resettlement from Emancipation to the First World War*, 240; Demko, *The Russian Colonization of Kazakhstan, 1896–1916*, 93, 74.

35. Demko, *Russian Colonization*, 97.

36. Ibid., 88.

37. Ibid., 84.

38. Ibid., 58–59, 121, 123; Williams, "Russian Peasant Settlement in Semirech'ye," 111, 114.

39. Steven G. Marks, "Conquering the Great East," in *Rediscovering Russia in Asia: Siberia and the Russian Far East* (Armonk, NY: M. E. Sharpe, 1995), 25–26, 33.

40. Ibid., 33.

41. Martha Brill Olcott, "The Settlement of the Kazakh Nomads," *Nomadic Papers*, no. 8 (1981): 13.

42. Bacon, *Central Asians under Russian Rule: A Study of Cultural Change*, 104.

43. Demko, *Russian Colonization*, 91, 93, 103.

44. Ibid., 105, 140, 146.

45. Ibid., 62; Richard A. Pierce, *Russian Central Asia, 1867–1917: A Study in Colonial Rule* (Berkeley: University of California Press, 1960), 105–06.

46. Williams, "Russian Peasant Settlement in Semirech'ye," 117.

47. Ibid., 120–21.

48. *Pereselencheskoye Delo*, Otchet po revizii Turkestanskogo kraya, proizvedennoy po vysochayshemu poveleniyu senatorom gofmeysterom grafom K. K. Pahlenom (St. Petersburg, 1910), 96–110.

49. *Pereselencheskoye Delo*, 64–67.

50. Pahlen, *Mission to Turkestan*, 208.

51. Bacon, *Central Asians under Russian Rule*, 48; S.N. Pokrovskii, "Iz istorii Vtorogo semirechenskogo oblastnogo krest'ianskogo s'ezda," *Vestnik Akademii Nauk Kazakhskoi SSR* 11, no. 9 (1955): 14–15.

52. Bennigsen, *Islam in the Soviet Union*, 29.

53. Olcott, *The Kazaks*, 111–12.

54. Ibid., 111.

55. Ibid., 113.

56. Alisov, "Musul'manskii vopros v Rossii," *Russkaia Mysl'* VII (1909): 34.

57. Kolstoe, *Russians in the Former Soviet Republics*, 29.

58. Ibid., 36.

59. Jerome Blum, *Lord and Peasant in Russia: From the Ninth to the Nineteenth Century* (Princeton, NJ: Princeton University Press, 1961), 620.

60. *Vosstanie 1916 Goda v Kazakhstane: Dokumenty i Materialy* (Alma Ata: ANKazSSR, 1947), 97.

61. G. M. Broido, *Vosstanie Kirghiz v 1916 g.* (Moscow: 1925), 19.

62. G. F. and K. Nurpeisov Dakhshleiger, *Iz istorii krest'ianstva sovetskogo Kazakstana* (Alma Ata: Nauka, 1985), 94.

63. Broido, *Vosstanie Kirghiz v 1916 g.*, 15.

64. Kolstoe, *Russians in the Former Soviet Republics*, 18.

65. Ibid., 743.

66. Dakhshleiger, *Iz istorii krest'ianstva sovetskogo Kazakhstana*, 19.

67. Olcott, *The Kazaks*, 138, 141.

68. Ibid., 137.

69. Ibid., 144–50.

70. T. R. Ryskulov, *Revoliutsiia i korennoe naselenie Turkestana, 1917–1919 gg* (Tashkent: 1925), 70.

71. Kolstoe, *Russians in the Former Soviet Republics*, 74. They had little choice because there were only a very few local Bolsheviks or proletarians. In effect, they

simply mapped their new administration over the existing social and political leadership.

Another group that formed during the Civil War was less accommodating. Anti-Bolshevik forces called the Basmachi led a resistance movement that lasted well into the 1930s. The movement was centered in Central Asia, but Basmachi bands were formed in Kazakstan as well. Operating in guerrilla fashion they made quick raids on Russian settlements and military installations and then withdrew into the steppe or crossed the border into China. Perceptions of their role exemplify the dichotomy in Kazak historiography. Soviet scholars depict them as counterrevolutionaries while Western scholars tend to see them as "freedom fighters." The Basmachi threat tended to wax and wane based on the repressiveness of Soviet policy, so it was strong from 1917 to 1922, weakened during NEP, and increased again (Kolstoe 1995).

72. Kolstoe, *Russians in the Former Soviet Republics,* 155.

73. Joseph Stalin, "Sotsial'naia demokratiia natsional'nyi vopros," *Prosveshchenie,* no. 3, (5 March 1913): 179.

74. Lawrence Krader, *Peoples of Central Asia* (Bloomington: Indiana University Press, 1963), 111–12; Hélène Carrère d'Encausse, *The Great Challenge: Nationalities and the Bolshevik State, 1917–1930* (New York: Holmes and Meier, 1992), 178; Ronald Wixman, "Applied Soviet Nationalities Policy: A Suggested Rationale," in *Turco-Tatar Past, Soviet Present: Collection Turcica IV,* ed. G. Veinstein, Ch. Lemercier-Quelquejay, and S. E. Wimbush (Louvain: Éditions Peeters and Paris: Écoles des Hautes Études en Sciences Sociales, 1986), 455.

75. Olcott, *The Kazaks,* 169.

76. Olcott, *The Kazaks,* 197.

77. Teresa Rakowska-Harmstone, "Soviet Moslem Nationalism in Comparative Perspective," in *Turco-Tatar Past, Soviet Present: Collection Turcica IV,* 475; Olcott, *The Kazaks,* 197.

78. Olcott, *The Kazaks,* 172.

79. Robert Conquest, *The Harvest of Sorrow: Soviet Collectivization and the Terror-Famine* (New York: Oxford University Press, 1986), 192.

80. Peter Rudolf Meffert, "The Population and Rural Economy of the Kazakh Soviet Socialist Republic," Ph. D. Diss. (Stanford University, 1988), 145.

81. Meffert, "The Population and Rural Economy of the Kazakh Soviet Socialist Republic," 141.

82. Meffert, "The Population and Rural Economy of the Kazakh Soviet Socialist Republic," 141–42.

83. B. A. Tulepbaev, *Torzhestvo leninskikh idey sotsialisticheskogo preobrazovaniya sel'skogo khozyaystva v Sredney Azii i Kazakhstane* (Moscow: Akademiia Nauk, 1971), 199.

84. Conquest, *The Harvest of Sorrow: Soviet Collectivization and the Terror-Famine,* 190.

85. Dakhshleiger, *Iz istorii krest'ianstva sovetskogo Kazakhstana,* 7; Lewis, *Population Redistribution in the USSR: Its Impact on Society, 1897–1977,* 370.

86. Conquest, *The Harvest of Sorrow: Soviet Collectivization and the Terror-Famine,* 190.

87. Conquest, *The Harvest of Sorrow: Soviet Collectivization and the Terror-Famine,* 190.

88. Meffert, "The Population and Rural Economy of the Kazakh Soviet Socialist Republic," 160.

89. Meffert, "The Population and Rural Economy of the Kazakh Soviet Socialist Republic," 250.

90. Meffert, "The Population and Rural Economy of the Kazakh Soviet Socialist Republic," 157.

91. d'Encausse, *The Great Challenge: Nationalities and the Bolshevik State, 1917–1930,* 201.

92. Olcott, *The Kazakhs,* 178.

93. Dakhshleiger, *Iz istorii krest'ianstva sovetskogo Kazakhstana,* 7.

94. Conquest, *The Harvest of Sorrow: Soviet Collectivization and the Terror-Famine,* 193.

95. Olcott, "The Settlement of the Kazakh Nomads," 220.

96. Meffert, "The Population and Rural Economy of the Kazakh Soviet Socialist Republic," 161.

97. Helsinki Watch Report, *"Punished Peoples" of the Soviet Union: The Continuing Legacy of Stalin's Deportations* (New York: Human Rights Watch, 1991), 7–10.

98. Olcott, *The Kazaks,* 194; Kappeler, "Czarist Policy Toward the Muslims of the Russian Empire," 169.

99. Meffert, "The Population and Rural Economy of the Kazakh Soviet Socialist Republic," 363.

100. Meffert, "The Population and Rural Economy of the Kazakh Soviet Socialist Republic," 291.

101. Olcott, *The Kazaks,* 189.

102. Meffert, "The Population and Rural Economy of the Kazakh Soviet Socialist Republic," 303.

103. Lewis, *Population Redistribution in the USSR: Its Impact on Society, 1897–1977,* 20.

104. Meffert, "The Population and Rural Economy of the Kazakh Soviet Socialist Republic," 259.

105. Lewis, *Population Redistribution in the USSR: Its Impact on Society, 1897–1977,* 370.

106. Meffert, "The Population and Rural Economy of the Kazakh Soviet Socialist Republic," 498.

Can We Discern a Pattern in the Expansion of High Civilization?

At first glance, migratory movements from areas of high civilization may seem to lack cohesion. They are too diverse, too different in goal, design, and execution, too unlike each other in duration and motivation. They have developed in radically different circumstances. Indeed, what could be the common element in Phoenician, medieval German, and Soviet population movements?

Once we try to discern some patterns, we can see that migration flows originating from the areas of high civilization fall into two major categories that we may call "early" and "imperial."

Early migrations—Phoenician, Greek, and Etruscan—originated in small city-states that lacked (with some notable exceptions) natural resources. These early migrations were a by-product of the search for raw materials and trade and were largely motivated by economic considerations. To these we may add fast population growth in times of prosperity, as well as internal and external political instability. Population growth frequently outstripped the limited local resources of a small polis; internal strife often forced the losing party to emigrate; and the imposition of foreign rule (e.g., Persian in Phocaea) was sometimes unacceptable to large segments of the population. In short, there was a wide array of underlying factors even though economic considerations were primary, political and social factors were far from negligible.

The "imperial" migrations, for which Rome is a prime example, developed in the context of aggressively expanding empires. The goal was the consolidation of conquests and the integration of diverse populations within the imperial organism. Here, the primary objectives were largely political and strategic, although economic ones cannot and should not be written off.

Each empire and period had a peculiarity of its own. In Rome, there was a periodic desire on the part of the government to reduce the number of the Roman plebs; another was the pressing need to settle and remunerate thousands of veterans. When planted in an alien milieu, Roman colonies became islands of Roman life and civilization supported by the prestige of the mighty state. They were effective promoters of Romanization.

In contrast, the German Empire in its medieval incarnation failed to achieve the degree of cohesion that characterized its Roman predecessor. In fact, much of the settlement was carried out by private or semi-private means. And yet, despite the lack of state support, the colonization movement was both long-term (it lasted for some four hundred years) and, initially at least, highly successful.

If the German settlers could not always count on imperial support, they could often find local rulers interested in German immigration. This was especially so in Bohemia, Hungary, and Poland. Fully aware that their countries were underdeveloped and underpopulated, many eastern European rulers showed a keen interest in German skills and settlers. Their crucial role in promoting German immigration can be seen in comparison to Italy where imperial German conquests did not lead to colonization, despite the attraction that Italy had always exercised on northerners. With imperial and local support lacking, German settlement was limited to a few Alpine valleys.

But if rulers in eastern Europe were well disposed to German migrants, large segments of the indigenous population were not: they found themselves in a stiff competition with immigrants. Even the upper classes were not exempt because, occasionally, wealthy German burghers were in a position to buy and/or marry their way into the aristocracy, as in Bohemia in the fourteenth century. When sufficiently numerous, they were perceived as a threat. Eventually, low-intensity tensions led to confrontations that flared into open war (such as the Hussite wars).

German migration east promoted urbanization, mining (especially in Hungary, but also in Bohemia), and town law, each factor playing an important role in the development of the European periphery. These factors were still valid in the eighteenth century when Russia also invited German settlers, a rare example of an empire using alien population for imperial expansion.

There were several periods when German settlement in the East had imperial support—when expansion was fueled by a strong ideological component. In the early Middle Ages it was religion. While there were still significant pagan populations within easy reach, as in Brandenburg in the tenth century or in the Baltic in the twelfth, the expansion (and migration that followed) took the guise of Christianizing the heathens. With the conversion of the Lithuanians, there were no more pagans left to convert. Attempts to invade Russia (in 1240 and 1242) failed, and the Crusades were ultimately unsuccessful.

The later German migrations in the seventeenth and eighteenth century were also carried under a religious banner, but this time as an instrument of the Counter-Reformation promoted by Catholic Austria. This occurred mostly in Bohemia, but also, to a limited extent, in Hungary, where the main preoccupation of the Austrian government was the repopulation of a country devastated by 150 years of wars and Turkish occupation.

The last instance of German imperial migration east was the settlement promoted by the Third Reich. It was a purely imperial venture colored by racist and totalitarian ideology of the time and was, mercifully, very short. The collapse of the Reich led to the loss of most of the lands acquired during the previous seven hundred years.

Thus, if German migrations have any binding element, it is a strong ideological component—Christian Crusade, Counter-Reformation, Nazi—depending on the epoch and the prevailing ideology of the time. Another constant was the desire of eastern European rulers, from Bohemian kings in the twelfth century to the Russian rulers in the eighteenth, to invite German settlers.

With Russian migrations in the sixteenth to twentieth centuries we again encounter a strong empire interested in incorporating vast areas. But here the peculiarity is the state ownership of serfs (until 1861) that facilitated administrative population transfers, industrialization in its early stages and, after 1917, a strong ideological component: Russian marxism. The wonder is that migrations continued unabated in all three periods (before 1861, 1861–1917, and after 1917), which testifies to the presence of some underlying factors. They are: poor soil in the Russian heartland, explosive population growth in the era of the demographic transition, and the availability of vast underpopulated lands, which determined the direction of migratory outflow.

Ultimately, one cannot speak of *the* mode of expansion of high civilization. Migrations and their underlying factors were too numerous and too diverse. And yet, they show a number of distinct patterns that vary from one historical period and civilization to another. We may even say that each epoch and/or civilization created its own mode of expansion. The only thing that binds them together is the continuous expansion itself.

PART II

Migrations of the "Forest" Tribes

The next section covers migrations of the "forest tribes": Celts, ancient Germans, Slavs, and Vikings.

This category includes sedentary tribes of the forest zone that have not achieved statehood. This statement may seem to imply a certain teleology, a notion that many scholars may find objectionable. I believe that in this case such objections are invalid. Historically, the general direction taken by most societies has been from a prestate level to statehood until the system of states has become global. Whether one discerns elements of a "grand design" in this millennial process or a chaotic confluence of diverse factors is immaterial for the purposes of this book. What is undeniable, however, is that the "stateless" tribes were historically at a disadvantage vis-à-vis the states. They had a choice: to achieve statehood or go under. Their success or failure depended, to a significant degree, on their interaction with the existing states and state systems, as well as their proximity to the dangerous nomads of the steppe. Both factors were largely determined by their location (accusations of geographical determinism!), but if geography was destiny, it could be changed by mass migration with often unforeseen consequences for the forest tribes, the states, and the nomads. In the following four chapters we will see how migration by some major groups of forest tribes impacted the triangular relationship.

CHAPTER 6

The Celts

Archeological evidence suggests that the Celts descend from the Bronze Age Tumulus culture (circa 1550–1250 B.C.) and the Urnfield culture (circa 1200 B.C.). The earliest remains of a fully Celtic civilization, the Hallstatt culture, derive from the eighth century B.C. According to John X. W. P. Corcoran, "there is little to distinguish the Urnfield people from their descendants of the Hallstatt culture, other than the latter's use of iron" (Corcoran, 1970, in Ellis 1998, 17).

Although Hallstatt emerged on the upper Danube in today's Bavaria and was originally a Bronze Age culture (James 1993, 20), some scholars believe that the Celtic nucleus probably came into being on the middle Rhine in Hunsruck and Eiffel (deVries 1960, 9, in Demougeot 1969, 27, n.18).

Early Celtic society was organized in small chiefdoms. An unmistakable sign of social stratification—wealthy burials—appeared in the eighth century B.C. along with the introduction of iron. Another indicator of social disparity, fortified strongholds, appeared at this time (Hallstatt C, dated 800–600 B.C.). They were spread across the upper Rhine, Bohemia, and western Hungary (James 1993, 21).

In the last phase, Hallstatt D (600–475 B.C.), the core Hallstatt area shifted into eastern France (upper Rhône, upper Seine, upper Loire) and southwest Germany. The new heartland lay at the intersection of major trade routes along the Rhône and the river valleys that connected the Mediterranean with Central Europe and the British Isles, an important source of tin and lead.

The late Hallstatt elites derived much of their wealth from trade with Massalia. The Greek colony, founded circa 600 B.C., played a pivotal role in the subsequent development of Gaul. The shift of the Celtic core area west and the transition to La Tène culture are probably connected with the establishment of Massalia.

The Roman historian Justinus wrote that "from the Greeks the Gauls learned a more civilized way of life. . . . They set to tilling their fields and walling their towns. They even got used to living by law rather than force of arms . . ." (Justinus 43, 41–2, in Boardman 1980, 218, n.223). It was Greek settlers who introduced the vine and the olive to the south of France. The complex process of cultural interaction is visible in many settlements. One, on Mt. Garou, between contemporary Marseilles and Toulon, initially a Hallstatt foundation, shows Etruscan, Greek, and Phoenician pottery by the early sixth century B.C. (219, n.226). Later, Greek wares became predominant, indicating that the region passed into the Greek sphere of influence.

Soon, all the luxury products of the Mediterranean were pouring up the Rhône valley from where they spread into Celtic lands. Even silk from China was found in some graves (James 1993, 23). Naturally, only the upper crust could afford such luxuries. However, a parallel process of social differentiation was taking place in Bohemia, which was far removed from the zone of interaction with the Mediterranean. Clearly, one cannot explain all processes in the Hallstatt world by contacts with Greeks (25). But the profound influence of Greek civilization on the Celtic world is undeniable.

About 520 B.C., a wave of destruction spread from the upper Danube into the Rhine valley, and from there to eastern France, the valley of the Rhône, and northern Italy (Herm 1976, 114). The old hill forts were largely abandoned. The Greek trade based on Massalia collapsed. Herm notes that "the whole network of market places and trade routes that had arisen in the previous centuries was torn apart" (Herm 1976, 114). The trade route from Etruria was also abandoned; instead, Etruscan merchants turned east, building new emporia at Spina (in 480 B.C.; Demougeot 1976, 38) and Adria.

The pattern of Celtic expansion also changed. In the earlier, Hallstatt, phase, it was directed mostly west, to Gaul, the British Isles, and Iberia, as well as south into Switzerland and northern Italy, bringing about a patchy Celtization of these areas. It is interesting that in Gaul the Celtization worked hand in hand with Hellenization because both followed the same trade routes (37). In the new La Tène phase expansion was directed mainly south and southeast.

One can only speculate about the nature of the collapse of 520 B.C. Was it caused by invasion(s) or rebellions? Whatever it was, the upheaval and the shifting trade routes led to the decline of Hallstatt. The old elites lost their incomes and power while new ones, in chiefdoms that had earlier been on the periphery, gained.

About 400 B.C., the Celts embarked on a series of migratory movements south.

This date is not universally accepted. Among modern historians, G. Dobesch argued for an earlier start of migrations in the sixth century B.C. (Dobesch 1989, in Ellis 1998, 19). And Alexandre Bertrand placed it even earlier, at the start of the first millennium B.C., largely because he did not discriminate between Celts and Umbrians (Bertrand 1879, in Ellis 1998, 19).

Among the "ancients," only Trogus Pompeius, himself of Celtic origin, and Livy, who came from Cisalpine Gaul (and used Trogus as one of his sources), pointed to circa 600 B.C. (21). The rest—Cornelius Nepos, Polybius, Dionysius of Halicarnassus, Diodorus Siculus, and others—date it between 396 and 386 B.C. (21–22).

Why did the Celts migrate? Many authors cited overpopulation. According to Trogus Pompeius, when the population grew too large, young men of 20 were expelled and had to seek their fortunes elsewhere (23). (This was the custom of *ver sacrum* practiced by ancient Latins and some Greeks). This version was shared by Livy, Pliny the Elder, Marcus Porcius Cato, Appian of Alexandria, Aulus Gellius, and others (23).

But the lure of the rich south should not be underestimated. Polybius wrote that "the Celts, who were much associated with the Etruscans because they were their neighbors, cast envious eyes upon the beauty of their country, and suddenly seized upon some trivial pretext to attack them with a large army, drove them out of the valley of the Po and occupied the area themselves" (Polybius, in Ellis 1998, 29).

Pliny and Plutarch chose a more frivolous explanation. Plutarch: "At last they got a taste of wine, which was then for the first time brought to them from Italy. They admired the drink so much, and were all so beside themselves with the novel pleasures which it gave, that they seized their arms, took along their families, and made off to the Alps in quest of the land which produced such fruit . . ." (Plutarch, in Ellis 1998, 24). If only they had abstained from wine!

This is, of course, nonsense, because Greeks of southern Gaul had been exporting wine into Celtic areas for some two hundred years. But the attraction of the south is undeniable. "The migrations may have been triggered by internal pressures, but their direction was governed by the lure of the warm, rich lands to the south" (James 1993, 31). Eventually, out-migration affected the entire Celtic world, for even in Bohemia, at the periphery, there was a marked reduction in population around 400 B.C. (It is known that the Boii, who gave their name to Bohemia, were among the early Celtic invaders of Italy. Their name survives in Bologna, from Boii-nonia. But we have no proof that they came to Italy directly from Bohemia [30].)

Ligurians and Etruscans were the first victims of the Celtic onslaught. When the Celtic Senones besieged the Etruscan city of Clusium (in 390 or 387 B.C.), the Etruscans turned to their old adversary Rome for help. But the Romans too were defeated at the river Allia, and Rome itself was sacked. "Legend has it that the Capitoline hill held out," writes James, "but this is probably a patriotic fiction" (34). In any case, Rome had to pay a heavy indemnity to make the Celts leave.

It is surprising that they did, even though they needed land to settle. The reason given by Polybius was that they came under pressure from the Veneti, who, in turn, were being pressured by their neighbors to the north (Polybius 2.17, in Rankin 1987, 106–107). This was the domino effect frequently encountered among the nomads but, evidently, not limited to them alone.

The Celts took over the valley of the Po that had been, until then, an Etruscan preserve and most of northern Italy. Etruscan Melpum became the main town of the Insubres; as Mediolanum (Milan), it was to play an important role in Roman and Italian history. The Cenomani are believed to have founded Brescia. Other tribes that settled south of the Alps were the Lingones, the Senones, and the Boii (James 1993, 35). Much of the earlier population of the newly conquered areas seems to have stayed in place. Excavations of numerous Celtic sites show settlements of mixed ethnic character. L. Homo argued that the Celts who had settled south of the Po were quickly Etruscanized, while those to the north of the river were not (Homo 1925, in Ellis 1998, 31).

The defeat at the Allia destroyed Roman overlordship of the Italic peoples. Rome had to spend the next 30 years rebuilding it (Polybius 2.18, in Rankin 1987, 107). What's more, Celts and Greek Syracuse concluded an alliance. Syracusan rulers (Dionysius I and II) encouraged Celtic attacks on Rome and employed Celtic mercenaries stationed in Apulia. Even without the Syracusan intrigues, Rome remained a prime target. Celts attacked it in 367, 365–63, and 348 but were repulsed each time (Rankin 1987, 107–109).

The changing balance of power led to the agreement of 334 B.C. The Celts needed some time to recoup their losses while Rome wanted to "finish off" the Italics.

By 300 B.C., the Celts of northern Italy (Cispadania) grew sufficiently wealthy to attract the envious eye of other, poorer, Celts living in the mountains. However, the Cispadanian Celts, by bribes and appeals to common origin ("ethnic solidarity"), managed to redirect their "country cousins" against Rome. They and some Etruscans joined in (109). In 299, 297 (together with the Samnites), 295 (at Sentinum), 284, 283, and 282, Celts and Romans fought it out. Although they suffered an occasional defeat, the Romans emerged victorious from the contest and assured themselves more than 40 years of peace (111).

A generation later, however, the old story repeated itself. Again, Celts from the Alps and the mountains of Provence were covetous of Cispadanian wealth. And again the Cispadanians tried to redirect their cousins against Rome. But this time they were less successful because they were now split into two camps, one favoring an attack on Rome, the other one against it.

In 232 B.C., alarmed by an impending war against Carthage, the Romans seized the land of the Senones and parceled it out among the landless citizens of Rome (35). And a few years later they granted full Roman citizenship to Roman colonies in northern Italy (113).

The Celts counterattacked in 225. That year, the mountain Celts (Gaesati) descended from the Alps into the Po valley. Once again, the Celts were divided. The Insubres and the Boii joined them, but the Cenomani and (the non-Celtic) Veneti did not. In the great battle at Telamon, in Etruria, the main part of the Celtic force was destroyed.

Telamon proved to be a watershed. It broke the back of the Celtic resistance to Rome. The Boii were subdued in 224, the Insubres in 222 (James 1993, 122).

After 225 B.C., the Celts no longer constituted a major threat to Rome. They joined Hannibal when he invaded Italy. But his defeat was theirs as well: they were left alone facing a much stronger and better organized enemy. And even though Rome had to retake the region after the Second Punic War in 203–191 B.C., by 190 B.C. even the Boii, the strongest of the Cispadanian tribes, were brought to heel (Rankin 1987, 114–15).

In the Danubian basin, like in Cispadania, Celtic artifacts preceded the Celts (James 1993, 35, 37). They could have been brought in by merchants or, perhaps, Celtic warrior bands that roamed the area. Two Celtic embassies to Alexander the Great, one in 335 B.C., the other one in 323 B.C., show that Celts already had extensive contacts with the Greek world (Green 1991, 130). In fact, Alexander's father Philip had been killed by a Celtic sword (105).

The defeat at Sentinum in 295 B.C. made it clear that the growing power of Rome made further depredations in Italy increasingly costly. It was also clear that their final subjugation was only a matter of time. And although some sort of guerrilla warfare against Rome in northern Italy continued until about 175 B.C. (Herm 1976, 288), Celts had to look elsewhere.

Already circa 310 B.C., there were clashes between Illyrians and the Celts coming down the Danube. In the decade following Sentinum, Celtic activity on the Danube increased (Rankin 1987, 87). There were exploratory incursions, such as the one under Bolgius in 281 B.C. (88).

Two years later, a major Celtic force invaded Macedonia and Greece. The Greeks tried to stop the invaders at Thermopylae but the Celts, like the Persians in 480 B.C., bypassed the defenders along the same path and made for the treasure house of Delphi. Although they reached the sanctuary, they failed to take it. In this case, gods were clearly on the Greek side. They launched earthquakes, thunderbolts, rockslides, and snow that kept the invaders at bay. The Celts retreated.

Antigonos Gonatas of Macedonia defeated another Celtic invasion in 278–77 B.C., the last one into Greece (James 1993, 39). Pockets of Celtic power in the Balkans remained (e.g., the kingdom of Tylis, which survived until 212 B.C. [189]). But they gradually declined and were absorbed by the local population.

Although the main thrust into the Balkans was directed against Greece, three tribes—Tectosages, Tolistobogii, and Trocmi—went to Anatolia.

They were invited by Nicomedes of Bithynia in 278 B.C. He was at war with Antiochus I and needed allies. But Antiochus defeated them as well (in 275 B.C.). However, by this time they were firmly implanted in central Anatolia, around today's Ankara, and Antiochus failed to dislodge them.

If this migration proves anything, it is that archeological record is not always reliable. By 1993, only three brooches identifiable as La Tène metalwork have been discovered in the area (James 1993, 40). If we did not have Greek and Roman records, this migration would have remained unknown to us.

Galatia, as the area came to be known, was, according to James, a "robber kingdom" (41). The invaders divided Anatolia into "spheres of depredation" (Livy 38.16.12, in Rankin 1987, 193). They raided their neighbors, looting and taking prisoners for ransom. Soon, it became a major center of slave trade. The Celts committed such gruesome atrocities against prisoners, including human sacrifice (James 1993, 41), that people would kill themselves rather than fall into their hands. Special taxes (*ta Galatika*) were introduced to ransom prisoners taken by the Galatians (*Orientis Graeci Inscriptiones Selectae* [ed. Duttenberger], 223, in Rankin 1978, 189).

Gradually, their neighbors' resistance stiffened. Attalus I of Pergamon defeated them around 240 B.C. (Powell 1958, 10) but could not dislodge them. Finally, by 232 B.C., the Celts reached an agreement with other powers in the area who were eager to settle the troublesome newcomers (Rankin 1987, 190).

Celts who settled in Galatia formed a ruling class. The indigenous population of the region consisted of partly Hellenized Phrygians whose ancestors came to Asia Minor from the Balkans. From the tenth until the seventh century B.C., Phrygia was independent. It was then weakened by the Cimmerian invasion(s) and was eventually absorbed into the Persian Empire (in the middle of the sixth century B.C.). By the time the Celts arrived on the scene, the Phrygians were an old, civilized people, no match for the "warrior pastoralists" (190–91).

In the early stage of their penetration, the Celts destroyed many of the existing cities of Galatia. Instead, they built hill forts and strong points not unlike those of their Hallstatt ancestors in central Europe and Gaul. It took some time before the Celts and the indigenes began to mix. In the second century B.C., a tragedy by Plutarch (*De Virt. Mul.* 22, in Rankin 1987, 192) shows a Galatian heroine who was kind to the subject people.

We need not follow all the vicissitudes of subsequent Galatian history. Romans gave them a good thrashing in 189 B.C. but did not stop their expansion (south). Politically, hemmed in on all sides, Galatia oscillated between alliances with Pergamon, Pontus, and Rome. But if its political orientation was flexible, culturally strong Celtic and Hellenistic/Phrygian tendencies prevailed. For a long time the country remained a foreign implant. It is interesting that Roman cultural norms were more readily adopted by the Galatians than the Greeks (201). Given the assimilationist record of the Celts in the West, it seems that there was something in the Celtic cultural makeup that predisposed them toward Rome. "In general the Gauls were not ill prepared by the nature of their own way of life to adopt many of the ways of Roman civilization" (Salway 1981, 15, in Rankin 1987, 132). And their pantheon (like German and Greek) was relatively easily translatable into that of the Romans.

In the first century B.C., rivalry with Mithridates and his treacheries pulled Galatia into the Roman camp. It was annexed in 25 B.C., was made a Roman province, and seemed well on its way to complete assimilation. But in the second century A.D. the pace of Romanization slowed considerably. The Celtic language survived till at least A.D. 400, when St. Jerome (331–420) wrote that "the Galatians have their own language, and it is almost the same as that of the Treveri" (in eastern Gaul around today's Trier) (James 1993, 123). Under the Eastern Empire, Galatia remained a well-defined province well into the eighth century A.D. (Rankin 1987, 206).

According to Herodotus, Celts entered Iberia by the fifth century B.C. However, few Hallstatt or La Tène artifacts have been found there. From very early on, Celts intermarried with the indigenes, producing a thoroughly mixed population known as "Celtiberians," making them archeologically hard to distinguish (James 1993, 42). Aside from some tribal names and linguistic residue, there is little direct evidence of the Celtic presence in Iberia (43).

Such is not the case in Britain.

When Caesar explored the island in 55 and 54 B.C. (it was not definitively conquered until A.D. 43), he found a land much like Gaul (48).

Early British archeologists detected three distinct Celtic invasions. This approach has fallen into disrepute in the last 30 years. Some general tendencies in archeology, such as anti-migrationism and *indigenismo,* as well as genuine discoveries—for example, Ian Stead showed that the Arras culture of east Yorkshire was of local provenance (Stead 1979)—worked against the invasionist models.

But the record is mixed. Place names show that in Caesar's time most of Britain was already inhabited by Celtic speakers (Salway 1981, 17, in Rankin 1987, 214). Even if we take only the last wave of Celtic migrants, the Belgae, we have contradictory evidence. On the one hand, Caesar wrote in his *De Bello Gallico* that Belgae had settled eastern coastal regions and were in the process of conquering the island. Coinage also suggests that by this time the Belgae had been immigrating into southeast Britain for about 60 years (Cunliffe 1973, 11, in Rankin 1987, 214). On the other hand, archeologically, the Belgae in Britain are almost invisible. Only the name of Winchester, Venta Belgarum, indicates their presence (James 1993, 48). (In this, the Belgae are similar to Galatians.)

Much the same goes for Ireland: there is a strong continuity from the Bronze Age, followed, quite late, by the adoption of the La Tène artistic traditions. Hallstatt C swords reached Ireland, Hallstatt D and early La Tène metalwork did not. In fact, La Tène-style artifacts appeared only by 250 B.C. If the archeological materials are patchy, linguistic evidence and Roman records indicate that by the first century B.C., Britain and Ireland were part of the Celtic world but, like Spain, peripheral and highly distinctive (49).

When Rome and Greece blocked the way south, some Celts migrated north. Thus, some of the Boii moved from Bologna to Bohemia (Demougeot 1969, 43). After 250 B.C., there was a remarkable expansion of Celtic settlement in Silesia and southern Poland (J. Rosen-Przeworska 1962, 125–64, in Demougeot 1969, 41, n.45). But a hundred years later, toward the middle of the first century B.C., we notice Celtic reflux from Silesia. It coincided with the Celtic movement west, across the Rhine, which had started somewhat earlier. These movements show a growing pressure from the north clearly attributable to the Germanic advance south (Demougeot 1969, 43) that also pushed the Belgae toward Britain.

By this time, migration and assimilation had turned Gaul into the Celtic heartland. But even here they could find no rest, hemmed in as they were between the Roman rock and the Germanic hard place.

Roman involvement in southern Gaul goes back to at least the Punic wars in the third century B.C. The eviction of Carthage from Iberia and the acquisition of new provinces in the peninsula made it imperative to establish a secure land corridor between Italy and Iberia. The pretext was provided by Massalia, which found itself at war with the tribe of the Saluvii and called upon Rome for assistance. The Romans obliged. They destroyed the main Saluvian stronghold at Entremont in 124–23 B.C. and built their own fortress at Aquae Sextiae (Aix-en-Provence). The establishment of a Roman colony at Narbo (Narbonne) in 118 B.C. and the construction of a strategic road from Italy to Spain laid the foundations for the province of Gallia Transalpina (James 1993, 46).

The Germanic penetration was almost simultaneous with the Roman one. Already in 105 B.C. the newly established province was overrun by the Cimbri and the Teutons (124).

Soon, the Celts, disunited and quarrelling, involved the Germans in their endless internecine squabbles. In 71 B.C., the Arverni and Sequani invited a Germanic tribe, the Suevi, into Celtic territory to help them against the Aedui. When the war ended, the Suevi refused to leave. This was a pattern all too familiar in the Celtic world. It would facilitate the Saxon conquest of Britain some five hundred years later. This is the best known example. Others are plentiful: Tacitus (24), in the *Agricola*, mentions an exiled Irish prince who tried to have Romans help him regain his lost possessions. And in the twelfth century, a princely quarrel in Ireland would lead to Anglo-Norman interference (Rankin 1987, 20).

Toward the middle of the first century B.C., the pressure from both sides increased. In 58 B.C., the Celtic Helvetii, under Germanic threat, tried to move further west, away from the perilous Gallo-German frontier. Caesar, who was a consul in 59 B.C., blocked their way. The weakest of the triumvirs (the other two being Pompey the Great, the leading warrior, and Crassus, the richest financier), he needed fame and money. And here was his chance.

Caesar defeated the Helvetii and sent them back. Then, after seven years of war and the suppression of Vercingetorix (in 52 B.C.), he completed the first phase in the conquest of Gaul. He found fame and money. But for Celtic Gaul, this was the beginning of the end.

Celts were an indigenous Indo-European people with long local antecedents. They originated in the triangle between the upper Danube and the upper Rhine in southwest Germany.

Trade with Massalia introduced them to the riches of the Mediterranean civilization and made them aware of the possibilities for loot and settlement in the south. It is unclear to what extent contact with Greek civilization induced the transition from Hallstatt to La Tène. However, it was probably instrumental in transferring the Celtic heartland south and west. And the upheavals of 520 B.C. may have resulted from the differentiation between the increasingly rich areas that traded with the south and their country cousins on the periphery.

Two major factors seem to have determined the Celtic "explosion": population pressures and the attraction of the south.

From the start, Celtic aspirations were directed toward areas of developed civilizations in the south, mostly Italy and the Balkans. Their foray into Iberia in the fifth century B.C. does not contradict this trend: by then, southern and eastern Iberia had long been colonized by Greeks and Phoenicians and was no less developed than Italy. The discrediting of the "invasionist" models in Britain, if true, offers another proof of the importance of the southern connection, that is, the importance of high civilization for forest tribes.

Celtic intrusions into Italy started around 400 B.C. and continued roughly until the battle of Telamon in 225 B.C. Already at this stage, an interesting pattern emerged: the closer the Celts were to areas of high civilization, the wealthier they were. Eventually, the wealthier Cispadanian Celts became a magnet for their poor mountain cousins, a pattern that would be later replayed with Germans and other forest tribes.

Although the struggle against Rome continued till about 175 B.C., it was increasingly clear after Sentinum (295 B.C.) that they were powerless against Rome. They could beat Etruscans and could mix, on equal terms, with Iberians, but Rome was a nut they could not crack.

The only other way south was down the Danube. Clashes with Illyrians started no later than 310 B.C., but it was only a generation later, around 280 B.C., that the Celts swept across the Balkans to Greece and Asia Minor. Their venture in Greece was unsuccessful, but three tribes managed to carve out a substantial chunk of real estate in central Anatolia. Here they established themselves as "robber barons" in hill forts, recreating the lifestyle familiar to them in central Europe. Defeated by Attalus in 240 B.C., they were forced to settle down and turned into the upper class of a multiethnic state. Eventually, it was absorbed into the Roman Empire, and the Galatae were gradually assimilated.

Meanwhile, in Italy, the growing power of Rome made a substantial number of Celts to emigrate north. In a sense, this was a return migration, to areas that their ancestors came from. There had been a marked reduction in the population of Bohemia around 400 B.C., at the time of the first Celtic intrusion into Italy. Now, between 250 B.C. and 150 B.C., there was a substantial flow "back" (e.g., the Boii). There was also a spread of Celtic settlement in Silesia. However, an increasingly strong German pressure from the north cut it short.

"Belgian" migration to Britain, starting about 110 B.C. or even earlier, was another consequence of the German pressure. Although migrationist models are decidedly out of fashion right now, it is unlikely that the Belgae were the first Celtic migrants to Britain because Caesar, arriving only 60 years later, found it thoroughly Celtic.

By the first century B.C., the Celts found themselves reduced to Gaul, which was now their heartland, and some adjacent areas. But even here they were hemmed in between Rome and the Germans. Gaul failed to escape either one. Conquered and thoroughly Romanized for some five hundred years, it was eventually overrun by various Germanic tribes who then used it as a foundation for a new empire.

As for the Celts, only Ireland and northern Scotland escaped Rome. Here, as well as in Wales and Brittany, Celtic remnants survived into our own time.

CHAPTER 7

Early Germanic Migrations

Pytheas from Massalia, in the fourth century B.C., was the first known traveler of Antiquity to encounter Germanic tribes (Musset 1965, I, 48).

Musset placed their Urheimat in southern Scandinavia in the late Bronze Age, an area where no pre-Germanic linguistic substratum had been found (4). From there, some Germanic tribes spread along the Baltic coast, toward the Oder. Others followed the coast of the North Sea, toward the Weser. By 1000 B.C., according to Musset, German habitat stretched from Ems to central Pomerania. (Demougeot dated their appearance in Pomerania much later, from 400 B.C. [Demougeot 1969, 45].) If we follow Musset, by 800 B.C., Germans reached Westphalia in the west and Vistula in the east. And three hundred years later they could be found on the lower Rhine, in Thuringia and Lower Silesia (Musset 1965, I, 4)

The separation of eastern and western Germans occurred no later than 400 B.C. (Demougeot 1969, 51). By this time, they were well established in northern Germany, northeast Netherlands, and northern and western Poland.

Their advance south brought them into contact with the Celts, who were, since about 250 B.C., moving back north. For whatever reasons, the Germans proved stronger, (48) and, from about 200 B.C., the Celts were losing territory. As some Germanic confederations (e.g., Suevi) expanded into Saxony and Thuringia while others (those from Schleswig-Holstein and Mecklenburg) moved into central Germany, the Celts retreated toward the Main, eventually seeking refuge across the Rhine. In the process, some of them intermarried with their Germanic adversaries (the Belgae, who had crossed into Gaul some time before 150 B.C., claimed a partly Germanic origin) (49).

Germano-Celtic hostilities considerably slowed the Germanic advance south (Musset believed it was brought to a halt in 500–200 B.C. (Musset 1965, I, 49). The Celtic migration north was also thwarted and then deflected west.

Celtic resistance in the west probably accounts for the fact that the first Germans to reach areas of high civilization were eastern tribes of Bastarni and Skiri that appeared at the walls of Olbia by 230 B.C. (50, n.1; Trogus Pompeius, in Demougeot 1969, 47). It is interesting that they were accompanied by the Celts, who were well familiar with the valley of the Danube by that time. Evidently, hostilities in central Europe did not preclude cooperation elsewhere. Or, it is also possible that both tribes were members of a Celtic confederation that would also account for Germano-Celtic mixing. In any case, it looks like the Celts opened the door south to the Germans. (Both tribes remained in the Black Sea area, their "center of gravity" located somewhere in the eastern Carpathians. Romans defeated the Bastarni in 29 B.C., but they remained in place till at least the third century A.D. The Skiri were later caught up in the Gothic migrations at the end of the fourth century but retained independence till 469. Odoacer came from their ranks [Musset 1965, I, 50–51, n.1].)

By the middle of the second century B.C., the Celtic resistance east of the Rhine had been broken, and the German pressure south was resumed. That, inevitably, brought Germans into contact with Rome.

About 120 B.C., a vast horde of several Germanic tribes—the Cimbri, the Teutons, and the Ambrones—descended from Denmark. They first went up the Oder to Bohemia but were rebuffed by the Boii. Then they went south and reached Noricum, whose principal town, Noreia, they sacked in 113 B.C. Further advances south and east were repulsed by Romans and Illyrians. They returned to the upper Danube, where they were joined by Celtic Tigurini, and from there they descended upon Gaul. Beaten by the Belgae, the invaders poured down the valley of the Rhône, where they inflicted several defeats upon the Romans in 109, 107, and 105 B.C. From the Rhône valley they went west, devastated Aquitaine, and tried to enter Spain but could not overcome the Celtiberians. Finally, they returned to Gaul, where the Teutons were annihilated by consul Marius at Aix in 102 B.C. Their allies the Cimbri moved on into Italy, where they were destroyed at Vercelli in the valley of the Po the next year (Demougeot 1969, 56–58).

The first encounter of Germans with Rome is highly significant for several reasons. It shows that the forest tribes—and Germans were forest tribes par excellence—could range over vast distances in the earliest phase of their migratory movement; their wanderings could last many years; they could combine with non-Germans; and could be contained only with great difficulty and at high cost.

As Germans kept up the pressure, the Celts continued to move west. Many of the Belgic tribes migrated to Gaul and England, and the Helvetii made their unsuccessful bid in 59–58 B.C. At the same time, Germanic tribes at the fringe of the Germanic world were being pushed from behind by other tribes. This constant pressure accounts for the relentless spread of the Germans.

Roman conquest of Gaul was but the start of the contest. Rome responded to the Germanic challenge with a counteroffensive that lasted roughly from 61 B.C. to A.D. 117. The first salvo was the war against the Suevi under Ariovistus. Caesar defeated them in 58 B.C. and beat back new Germanic attacks from across the Rhine in 55 B.C. These victories allowed Caesar to subdue Gaul in four years and suppress Celtic uprisings in 52 and 51 B.C. (63). By the end of the century the Germans were on the defensive as Roman armies first under Domitius Ahenobarbus and then under Tiberius penetrated deep into Germany, as far as the Elbe (65). For a short time, the territory between the Rhine and the Elbe became a Roman province (Dvornik 1956, 16).

In A.D. 9, however, the Romans suffered a major setback in the Teutoburg forest (Burns 1984, 4), where Germans under Arminius eliminated three legions under Varus. Although impressive, Roman defeat was not as decisive as it may seem. The Germans still lacked basic military skills: not only did Arminius fail to take a small fort, Aliso, on the Lippe, he also failed to cross the Rhine (Demougeot 1969, 110).

Still, Tiberius decided that the empire was overextended. He abandoned the region between the Rhine and the Elbe (Dvornik 1956, 16) and, instead, proceeded to establish a string of client states along the Rhine and the Danube, in A.D. 17–37 (Demougeot 1969, 114).

The frontiers stabilized in 117–160 (187). And the stabilization facilitated and promoted the development of symbiosis between the adversaries. Although the Roman army retained the upper hand for at least two centuries (Bury 1984, 6), the relentless assault forced Rome to adopt a defensive posture. The line of defensive walls and moats was gradually expanded. From the end of the third century the emphasis shifted to rear defenses. Towns built walls; the main defense armies were stationed in the interior (Lot 1945, 39–40). Increasing use was made of soldier-peasants.

Why this relentless assault *after* the stabilization? As with the Celts, there were probably two sets of factors. One was internal population pressures (the "push" factors), since Germans expanded in all directions (except the north). But there was also the "pull" of the easier, more comfortable life in the area of developed civilization. The fact is that life in the empire proved irresistibly attractive to many barbarians.

Some Germans volunteered for duty in the Roman army, individually and as tribes; others took civilian jobs of all kinds. German merchants were actively engaged in trade exporting Roman merchandise across the border and importing those barbarian wares that were in demand in Roman towns and military camps.

Many barbarians wanted to settle inside the empire. Already in 39–38 B.C., Agrippa installed small Germanic groups (the Ubii) within the empire (Demougeot 1969, 64). By the time of Ammianus (circa 330–395), almost all "barbarians" in western Germany outside the empire lived in villages within ten miles of the river (Burns 1984, 7, n.22). Archeological evidence supports him (11).

As Germans and Romans both adjusted to living in close proximity, the frontier gradually developed into a hybrid civilization with its own tastes, fashions, and linguistic borrowings (12). Intermarriage was widespread. Inevitably, some Romans regarded German "infiltration" with suspicion, and Constantius II, Julian, and Valentinian I tried to reverse it, or at least slow it down (7–8).

But Roman influence did not stop at the frontier or even within the zone of hybrid civilization. It extended far into the forest zone interior. As trade enriched tribes living at the border, it created an increasing disparity with tribes who lived farther away. It had been so with Cispadanian and mountain Celts. Now the story repeated itself with Germans. And the population within the empire was wealthier still. The disparity in wealth explains, to a large extent, the constant movement of the forest tribes into the empire (Heather 1996, 50).

The proximity to the empire also influenced social developments among Germans. Early Germans lived in small groups of, at most, a few hundred people (Hachmann 1970 and 1971, in Burns 1984, 19, n.1). When they "encountered" Rome, "the ensuing warfare favored the evolution of war bands that fused elements from both the familial and gift-exchange bonds into military units of increasing scope and duration" (21, n.7). Already Tacitus, in *Germania,* noted that the closer the tribe was to the sphere of Roman influence, the more durable and complex was its social organization (n.7). "The evolution of Germanic groups from small localized units, often fleeting in duration and cohesion, to larger regional conglomerates under warrior nobilities, themselves at the head of ever stronger and more specialized war bands, and then to increasingly permanent confederations with complex ranking and advancing stratification, is the dominant sociopolitical theme among a variety of Germanic peoples. The Alamanni, the Quadi, the Gepids, the Goths, and the Lombards all traversed the same paths of social and political development" (Burns 1984, 10–11).

In the long run, the contact with the more developed civilization promoted evolution of Germanic tribes toward more complex forms of social organization. For ordinary Germans, the Roman frontier was a land of opportunity: it offered service in the army and remunerative work in towns and camps; it offered a primary stimulus for barbaric migrations (21–22). The early Germans did not seek to destroy the empire. They wanted a share of the fruits and amenities of a higher civilization. And if they could have them for free, by pillage and rapine, so much the better.

If the interaction of Rome with early Germans in the west presents a picture of a tumultuous assault by new tribes arriving on the scene from the "darkest" Germany, the scene in the east was dominated by the Goths.

After the arrival of the Bastarni and the Skiri in the Black Sea area in the third century B.C., there was a let-up in Germanic migrations in that direction. This, most likely, was related to the fact that Celtic resistance in central Europe had been broken, and the Celts were now in retreat. Another factor was the relative proximity of Italy and other areas of high civilization to central Europe. It was only when Rome erected a strong barrier along the Rhine and the Danube that the Germans, once again, turned east.

Gothic tradition, related by Jordanes (*Getica*), Cassiodorus (*Gothic History*), and Ablabius (all in Heather 1996, 9–10; see also Heather 1991, I, 1993; Momigliano 1955, and Goffart 1988), traced their origin to the isle of Scandza, that is, Scandinavia. From there, they migrated across the Baltic to what is now northern Poland and settled in Pomerania and at the mouth of the Vistula. It was there that Tacitus (*Germania* 43–4), Ptolemy (*Geography* 3.5.8), and Strabo (*Geography* 7.1.3) placed them in the middle of the first century A.D. (Heather 1996, 21).

Archeological evidence, however, is inconclusive. It does confirm the existence of the Gotho-Gepidan culture in Pomerania and lower Vistula at this time (the so-called Wielbark culture) and links it to seven specific elements. But only one of these can be archeologically traced to Scandinavia (Shchukin 1989, II, ch. 4; Oxenstierna 1948; Kmieciński 1962, 1972; Hachmann 1970, all in Heather 1996, 14). Even more significant is the fact that the Wielbark culture had already acquired its distinctiveness by the time of the putative Gothic migration from Scandinavia. These considerations make some scholars doubt the veracity of the Gothic tradition (Wolfram 1980, 12).

And yet, there are several factors that support the traditional version. First, East Germanic languages (of which Gothic was one) were closer to North Germanic (i.e., Scandinavian) tongues than to West Germanic ones. Such affinity implies a close relationship, if not direct derivation. The toponymics of the island of Gotland, as well as the modern Swedish provinces of Öster- and Västergötaland, where the Goths had supposedly originated, also show linguistic affinity (Carlo Alberto Mastrelli, *I Goti* 1994, 276). Second, Count Oxenstierna excavated incineration burials in Oster- and Vastergotaland that, numerous in the second and first centuries B.C., suddenly became rare after about 50 B.C. (Oxenstierna 1958, 5, in Demougeot 1969, 361). This would suggest a disappearance of a significant portion of the previous population. Why did it happen? Pressure from other population groups is unlikely: in Scandinavia, as elsewhere, the non-Germanic populations have been retreating under Germanic pressure. A famine, perhaps due to deteriorating climatic conditions, is more likely. A famine around A.D. 800 caused a massive out-migration across the Baltic to the Daugava (Demougeot 1969, 362, n. 37). Heather writes that we can probably speak of a limited migration of a few aristocratic clans from Scandinavia (Heather 1996, 26) that may have organized the local population and given it their name, similar to what the Vikings accomplished in Russia and Normandy a thousand years later. But the disappearance of the incineration burials in the Gotaland provinces suggests that the migration affected all social strata rather than a few clans. As for the local provenance of most elements of the Wielbark culture, it may indicate that the Scandinavian migrants were rapidly assimilated by the numerically preponderant local population, as indeed happened everywhere Scandinavians settled. Even in Normandy and Rus' the Vikings left relatively few traces. If we didn't have records, such as annals, and other documentary evidence, these traces could be ascribed to trade or cultural influence, leading some scholars to deny the possibility of conquest and migration.

If the Goths did originate in Scandinavia, why did they go to the southern Baltic? One possible reason is that they followed the Amber Way, an old trade route linking southern Scandinavia with the eastern Mediterranean as early as 1800 B.C. (Demougeot 1969, 20). Another possible reason is that geographically and historically the populations on the territory of today's Sweden "looked" east and south. The southern Baltic was their traditional area of interest. Finally, it could also be something random, a matter of chance, like a tribal chief's youthful adventures in Pomerania, that acquainted him with the local people and their tribal elites, perhaps a matrimonial alliance that led to involvement or interference in a power struggle and made later migration possible.

In any case, the Goths could be found in the area of the Wielbark culture by A.D. 5–6 at the latest, but did not occupy the entire area (Volker Bierbrauer, *I Goti* 1994, 31). Their ethnogenesis occurred in the area between the Oder and the Vistula (Wolfram 1980, 37, n.22), under some Celtic influence. In the first half of the first century A.D., Goths or Gutones were a small people, a tributary of the (Germanic) Lugii, who were themselves tributaries of the Celtic Boii and their king Marbod (Strabo, *Geographika* VII, 1, 3, in Wolfram 1980, 38, n.32). As "vassals of the vassals," they were intimately involved in the Boii internal politics.

By the middle of the first century, their culture had acquired coherence, and for the next one hundred years the density of the Wielbark sites continued to increase (Heather 1996, 23).

About A.D. 100, the Gutones escaped the Lugii-Vandal overlordship and moved from the Oder to the Vistula (Wolfram 1980, 38). After A.D. 150, the Wielbark culture started to expand south, up the Vistula, into the territory of the so-called Przeworsk culture. Heather believes that this phase had something to do with the Marcomannic war of 169–71, although the exact nature of that connection is impossible to ascertain.

From the Vistula, the Goths went up the valley of the Bug and the San, from where they penetrated into Belarus and Ukraine, ultimately settling in a vast area between the Don and the Danube (basically, modern Ukraine, Moldova, and Romania). The Wielbark sites appeared along the Bug and the San in 160–220; during 180–220 they spread across northwest Ukraine. And by 250–300 they reached into south Ukraine, covering the entire area of the Cherniakhovo culture, which arose shortly after the migration (Heather 1996, 38–39).

Several factors indicate that it was a migration, rather than a cultural transmission. First, the density of the Wielbark sites that had been steadily increasing in northern Poland until the middle of the second century, decreased thereafter. Second, elements of the Wielbark culture traceable in the Cherniakhovo area are numerous and distinctive, suggesting a transfer "not just of certain objects but of basic beliefs and norms" (23). Particularly significant was the continuity in the female dress (48), indicating that the entire population had moved. Finally, the Roman historians mention a major Germanic migration, including the Goths, to the Pontic steppes.

The first Gothic attack known from historical records is the sack of Olbia in 238 (Demougeot 1969, 256). Bratianu states that already in 214 the Goths launched an attack against Roman territory (Bratianu 1969, 106), but Heather believes that this notion is derived from Deuxippus's mistaken reference to Histria at the mouth of the Danube (Heather 1996, 40).

Although few scholars doubt the fact that the migration to the Black Sea area took place, certain aspects of this migration are open to interpretation. Thus, some scholars believe that an exploratory migration of 160–220 was followed by settlement in Volhynia in 220–30 and south Ukraine in 260–70 (Bierbrauer, *I Goti* 1994, 32–35). It does seem that bands of young warriors went first, later followed by a large segment of the general population (Heather 1996, 49). We should also keep in mind that the Wielbark culture was comprised of many groups, not only Goths but also the Heruli, the Gepids, the Rugii, and others (43). The migration was a movement of many tribes. In the process, new tribes were created (e.g., the Taifali), others disappeared (e.g., the Ampsivarii, the Bructeri) (45).

The Goths settled in the forested steppe with fertile soil and, at the time, abundant rainfall. Although historical tradition divides them into two groups, the Tervingi (probably "men of the forest") who lived west of the

Dniester and the Greuthingi ("men of the steppe," akin to the Anglo-Saxon *greot,* "flat") who lived east of that river, there may have been half a dozen (semi-)independent political units in the Pontic steppe (56–57). The situation was further complicated by the fact that the invading Goths intruded into an area where Dacians, Sarmatians, and Greek city-states led a life of uneasy coexistence where strife was a constant. It was inevitable, since "neither the immigrants nor the inhabitants of the small villages . . . had much ethnic unity or coherent political organization: the Goths were probably bound together in small raiding bands, whereas the indigenous populations were clustered around their agrarian communities" (Ionita 1975, 77–78, in Burns 1984, 24, n.20). Goths also clashed with other Germanic tribes that had migrated earlier. In 291 alone the Tervingi were at war with the Vandals, Gepids, and others (Burns 1984, 33). In the light of this strife and turmoil it is amazing that all the diverse and disparate cultural elements—Germanic, Sarmato-Scythian, Pontic Greek, and others—were soon amalgamated into a new and distinct Cherniakhovo culture. Pockets of indigenous cultures lingered, but the heterogeneous Germanic groups quickly absorbed most of these (24).

Despite constant infighting among barbarians, the rich lands of the empire were the main attraction. For 40 years, from 238, when they sacked Olbia, until 277, the Goths fought against the empire. The struggle came to be known as the Gothic Wars.

Already in 238, the Goths and their allies (subjects?) the Carpi (relatives of Dacians) crossed the Danube. The *limes* of Wallachia were abandoned, and new ones were established along the Olt (Bratianu 1969, 107).

In 249–51, once again, the Goths breached the Danube and swept across the Balkans. Philippopolis, a major urban center, fell in 250 (Demougeot 1969, 410).

By 253, they were masters of the Crimea, having captured the Bosporan fleet and the Bosporan capital Panticapaeum (418), although, according to Bratianu, the Bosporan kingdom probably survived till 343 (Bratianu 1969, 107).

In 256, the Goths pushed into Greece. Their campaigns there culminated in the sack of Athens by the Heruli in 267 (Burns 1984, 29), the date that probably marks the end of Antiquity in that great city, or at least the beginning of the end.

Their depredations were not limited to land operations. They were equally effective on the sea. They had probably learned their maritime skills on the Baltic for it would be impossible for a land-borne people to adapt to maritime warfare so fast. Already in 255–57 they launched major sea raids around the Black Sea. In 268, a huge sea-borne expedition of Goths and their allies forced the Dardanelles and spilled into the Aegean, where they robbed and looted at will. Although a counterattack led by Aurelian defeated them in 271, other sea-borne raids in 276–77 reached as far as Galatia and Cilicia (Heather 1996, 41–42).

By 270/71 the Goths and their allies appear to have been beaten. That the war dragged on for another seven years can probably be ascribed to reinforcements from new Germanic migrants from the Baltic who arrived in the area at about this time, the Heruli, who settled by the Sea of Azov, and the Gepids, who appeared on the scene circa 269 (Bratianu 1969, 107).

Years of warfare weakened the Roman grip on the transdanubian provinces. Dacia had to be abandoned (in 270, according to Grant 1978, 520; 271–72 according to Demougeot 1969, 454–55; and 275, according to Burns 1984, 30). Toward 280, the situation stabilized, and in the next one hundred years the Pontic steppes between the Don and the Danube saw the emergence of economic and cultural unity under a loose Gothic overlordship.

Much like in the west, relations with Rome were close, although frequently hostile. Many frontier rulers received periodic subventions, to keep their men in line (Heather 1996, 59). The empire meddled in Goths' affairs, taking sides in their enmity with the Carpi and Sarmatians in the 330s. It also utilized their manpower: on at least three occasions, Gothic contingents fought on the Roman side against Persia (58–59).

When the empire turned Christian, Rome tried to promote Christianity among the Goths, provoking a strong anti-Christian reaction, especially among the Tervingi (whose lands bordered on the empire and who were more sensitive to any interference). In 369–72, the Tervingi persecuted "their" Christians and expelled bishop Ulfila and many of his Christian followers (61). It appears that constant interaction with Rome and other adversaries created a strong sense of identity among the Goths, particularly among the Tervingi.

If Rome's relations with east Germanic tribes stabilized after 280, those in the west show a pattern of unremitting conflict that continued, with various degrees of intensity, until the collapse of the empire.

The brief period of relative peace in the west (117–160) came to an end in 161–62 with attacks by the Chatti (Demougeot 1969, 211). It was followed by a massive upheaval in 166, probably caused by the east Germanic migration from Poland to the Pontic steppes. And then came the Marcomannic war of 166–68, when the Quadi and Marcomanni broke through in northeast Italy while the Costoboki and Bastarni showed up in Achaea and Asia (Musset 1965, I, 52). It is very likely that all three were interrelated. Perhaps some internecine struggles among the Marcomanni caused some of their allies/vassals, Goths among them, to flee, while others, perhaps a defeated party, invaded imperial territory. In any case, from then on the troubles on the western frontier were endemic: the great Germanic war of 169–74 was followed by another one in

177–80; smaller clashes after 180 were followed by wars with the Alamanni in 213 and 234–35 (Demougeot 1969, 215–250).

Thus, by the time the Goths burst on the scene in 238, Rome had already been at war with their western cousins for more than three hundred years. It is unlikely that the attacks from east and west were coordinated, but they often occurred simultaneously, and their effect on the empire was deleterious. While the Goths were on the attack in 238–80 and later, their western cousins invaded the empire in 254–56 (piercing the *limes* in upper Germany); 259–60 (breakthrough in Belgica, Alamanni invaded Italy); and 268–78 (repeated assaults on Gaul, another Alamannian invasion in Italy) (Musset 1965, I, 53). These were mostly pillaging expeditions, although in 269–70, the Franks and the Alamanni almost reached Rome (Demougeot 1969, 463–64). Then came the great invasions of 275–80 (521). Gaul was devastated, and Italy, the imperial heartland, was so ruined that Aurelian did not celebrate his victories (515). The struggle became critical in 337–75 (Lot 1945, 36).

It is well beyond the scope of this chapter to present a detailed picture of Germanic migrations in the first centuries of our era. Musset counted four major waves in the epoch of the empire's collapse: (1) Goths, Vandals, Suevi, and Burgundians in the fourth and fifth centuries; (2) Franks, Alamanni, and Bavarians (fifth and sixth centuries); (3) Lombards (sixth and seventh centuries); and (4) Angles, Saxons, and Jutes (maritime, fifth and sixth centuries) (Musset 1965, I, 328).

If we compare Germanic migrations against the empire on both flanks, we will notice that they went through similar phases:

West	East
Early migrations (late second century B.C.)	Early migrations (third century B.C.)
Roman counteroffensive (60 B.C.-A.D. 117)	Gothic migrations (160–238)
	Gothic wars (238–277)
Stabilization (117–160)	Stabilization (277–375)
Renewed migrations (after 161)	Renewed Gothic migrations under pressure from the Huns (after 378)

But the early migrations in the east were "aborted" by the opening in the west. When they resumed, Rome was a mature polity interested in the status quo; a major counteroffensive was beyond its strength. Hence a shortcut to stabilization, bypassing the counteroffensive stage in the east altogether.

It is pointless to speculate what would have happened if the interaction between Rome and the forest tribes had been allowed to continue. It is likely that the unremitting assaults in the west would have worn the empire to the point where Germanic tribes in the east would have easily joined in dismembering the carcass. On the other hand, by the middle of the fourth century, the attacks in the west had been going on for two hundred years while the relative peace in the east continued to hold.

This *entente peu cordiale* was rudely interrupted by the arrival of the Huns.

They will be dealt with in more detail in a subsequent chapter. Here we will only trace their impact on the Goths and the empire.

The Huns probably appeared in Europe some time in the middle of the fourth century. Around 350 they subdued the semi-nomadic Alans, the Goths' eastern neighbors across the Don; then a quarter of a century later, in about 375, they smashed the Goths. In 376, the Tervingi under Alavivus and Fritigern and Greuthingi under Alatheus and Saphrax sought refuge in the empire. They were followed by other Greuthingi under Odotheus ten years later and then still other Goths under Radagaisus in 405/6 (Heather 1996, 108). Archeological evidence suggests an influx of the Cherniakhovo refugees into the Transylvanian uplands after 380 (Heather 1996, 102–103).

Although many Goths fled, many remained (or had to remain) under the Huns. We should keep in mind that the arrival of the Huns was not a furious one-time onslaught *à la mongole*. Rather, it was a movement that extended over an entire generation, an avalanche in slow motion with a gradual build-up and release. As late as 395, their core area was still somewhere between the lower Don and the Volga; it was from there that they crossed the Caucasus and raided far into Armenia, Cilicia, and Syria (103). "While the Goths who came to the Danube in 376 certainly were retreating under Hunnic pressure, these events were only the first act in a slowly unfolding drama. . . . Their retreat westward provoked a similar response from many of their neighbors. . . . These groups were not closely pursued by massed Huns . . . only from 400 is there clear evidence of Huns as a permanent presence on or around the Danube frontier. Sometime between 395 and 420 the bulk of the Huns moved to Pannonia (104). Even in 406, some 30 years after the initial "contact," there were still Gothic groups independent of the Huns.

The years 405/6 were marked by massive invasions-cum-migrations. The Gothic king Radagaisus invaded Italy; Alans, Burgundians, Suevi, Vandals, and many others crossed the Rhine. And Huns under Uldin crossed the Danube. These invasions represent a large-scale exodus from the middle-Danubian areas west of the Carpathians. "What contemporaries witnessed in 405/6," wrote Heather, "was an outpouring of peoples from the middle Danubian region west of the Carpathian ring" (107). The emptying of Pannonia was the direct result of the intrusion and settlement of the Huns.

The Roman Empire survived the massive onslaught of 405/6 by 70 years. Although the deposition of Romulus Augustulus in 475/76 is merely an arbitrary date in the long process of decomposition, it is a convenient point for historians.

The Goths survived as well, and their subsequent story is truly fascinating. After the first Tervingi and Greuthingi were admitted into the empire in 376, the local Roman commander Lupicinus (Little Wolf— Wölfel—Ulfila?) invited Gothic leaders to dinner, then treacherously murdered them. If he had counted on decapitating his dangerous guests, he had miscalculated. When the treachery became known, the enraged Goths raided all over the Balkans and dealt a crushing defeat to emperor Valens on August 9, 378 (Heather 1996, 134).

Eventually, however, both sides came to an understanding. The Goths were settled in the Balkans, within the empire, where they were joined by the latecomers who arrived in 386 and 405/6. These Goths came to be known as Visigoths.

They were a restless lot. In 391, they threatened Constantinople; in 397 they raided Peloponnesus; and in the next ten years made their unwanted presence known in Italy, Epirus, Pannonia, and elsewhere. In 408 and 409 they joined Alaric, took part in the siege of Rome, and finally entered the city on August 24, 410 (Wolfram, *I Goti* 1994, 287).

In 412 the Visigoths left Italy and moved to southern Gaul where, in 418, they cobbled together a kingdom centered on Tolosa (Toulouse) (288). By 475, a greater part of Gaul between the Loire and the Rhône was in their hands. They had also expanded into Iberia. However, they soon came under strong pressure from the Franks, who crossed the Loire in 496. Goths started to migrate to Spain in increasing numbers, first in 494–97, then 498. By the time the kingdom of Tolosa was destroyed in 507, the Visigoths had acquired a foothold in Iberia, where they put together another kingdom, that of Toledo (290–94). It lasted from 569 till 719 and fell under the onslaught of the Arabs. By that time, the Visigoths had largely assimilated into the local Ibero-Roman population.

The other Goths, those who remained under the Huns, had a no less extravagant history. The Huns seem to have settled them in Pannonia (formerly an outlying Roman province, now the core of the Hun "Empire") in a series of separate groups firmly under Hunnic control. By the time of Attila's death they numbered about 50,000 (Heather 1996, 151). In the chaos that followed Attila's demise, these Goths, now known as Ostrogoths, shook off the Hunnic domination and migrated south, to the Balkans, where they took part in the struggles of 473–79. In 474–76, they were temporarily settled in Macedonia, west of Thessaloniki (154, 156).

By the early 480s it became clear that they and Constantinople were on a collision course. In 487 they threatened the city. Emperor Zeno was anxious to get rid of them at almost any price. The next year, he reached an agreement with their king Theodoric that they would move to Italy (216–17). And indeed, by 493, Italy was secured. However, the Ostrogothic kingdom there did not endure. In 535, Justinian sent Belisarius against the Ostrogoths (263). After a long and listless campaign, in May 540, Belisarius took Ravenna, the Ostrogothic capital. But the war dragged on. In April 552 another Byzantine general, Narses, advanced into Italy. Between 558 and 560, imperial control was reestablished across northern Italy. And in 561 the last flicker of Ostrogothic resistance was extinguished in Brescia (266–71).

What happened to the Goths who remained? Those in the West seem to have assimilated by the middle of the eighth century. In the East, small groups seem to have lingered on for a while. In the ninth century, a western Frankish writer and poet, Walafrid Strabo, mentioned Goths living in Dobrudja. They still spoke their language and used Gothic translation of the Bible (Walafrid Strabo, in (ed.) A. Knoepfler 1899, 20, in Vasiliev 1936, 38, n. 1).

Another group seems to have survived in the Crimea, where they lived in the mountains in an area that came to be known as "Gothia." These Goths probably descended from those who did not flee to the empire and had somehow survived under the Huns. Too small to stand on its own, this Gothia passed from Byzantium to nomads and back. Its inhabitants, living under Byzantine rule for long periods of time, were strongly Hellenized. St. Antonius the Roman, when he was in Novgorod (twelfth century), met a Hellenized Goth merchant (*grechanin Gotfin*) who spoke fluent Latin, Greek, and Russian (St. Antonius the Roman, in (ed.) Kushelev-Bezborodko 1860, 265, in Vasiliev 1936, 123, n. 4).

We have later evidence from 1436–37 from an Italian traveler, Giosafat Barbaro, who had spent sixteen years in Tana and the Crimea; his German servant, supposedly, could converse with local Goths in German (Vasiliev 1936, 219–20). Finally, from the middle of the sixteenth century we have an account written by Ogier Ghislain de Busbecq, a Flemish noble, who came to Constantinople as ambassador of Emperor Ferdinand I in 1554. This gentleman met two Crimeans (in Constantinople) who asserted that there were still many people who used the Gothic tongue in the Crimea at that time. They even gave Busbecq a list of German words (269–71, n. 2). This is the last (and rather flimsy) testimony that we have of the survival of Gothic remnants.

Expansion south, from the southern Scandinavian core area, characterized Germanic migrations from the Late Bronze Age.

From the Jutland peninsula the tribes followed the coastline, which, naturally, sent them in two directions: west, following the North Sea, and east, following the Baltic. The penetration farther inland followed the course of major rivers.

Toward the middle of the first millennium B.C., Germanic tribes encountered the Celts. It is possible that the destruction of the Hallstatt strongholds in Gaul and southern Germany was the result of Germano-Celtic wars. It may have also played a part in the emergence of La Tène (if only because the Hallstatt centers had been destroyed).

Toward the middle of the third century B.C., the Celtic pressure on the Germans increased because the Celts had been beaten in Italy and Greece, the road south was blocked, and Celts were moving north in droves. This was the time of the expanding Celtic settlement in the east, Bohemia, and Silesia. It is also possible that the Celtic pressure precipitated the first Germanic migrations from the Baltic to the Black Sea area.

However, some time around 200 B.C., the German won the contest with the Celt in central Europe. And by the middle of the second century B.C., Celts were fleeing west.

The first Germanic invasion of western Europe at the end of the second century B.C. shows basic traits of subsequent Germanic migrations: continental scope (from Jutland to Bohemia to the upper Danube to Gaul to Spain back to Gaul, then Italy), mass movement, the ability to stay together for long periods of time (good organization), warriors followed by families.

Germanic expansion west and Roman expansion north led to a contest for Gaul. Here, at first, Rome was victorious. It won Gaul and went on a counteroffensive, penetrating deep into Germany. However, the cost of the occupation was deemed too high, and Rome retreated behind a defensive perimeter along the Rhine and the Danube. A short period of equilibrium and stabilization was followed by renewed Germanic attacks in the west, which, eventually, after three hundred years of incessant warfare, led to the collapse of the empire.

In the east, the crumbling of the Celtic resistance and the opening in the west brought early migrations to a halt. They resumed when the road west was closed again, this time by Rome. We should note that it did not resume right away, but rather occurred in the context of the collapse of the equilibrium between Rome and Germans. The beginning of Gothic migrations coincided with assault by Chauki against Rome (both around A.D. 160). Both were also tied with internal strife among the Marcomanni (then in Bohemia) and, probably, the collapse of a mighty tribal confederation under Marcomannic overlordship.

Migrations east went through similar stages as migration west, a period of wars followed by an equilibrium and stabilization. But there was no

Roman counteroffensive, largely because Goths "caught" Rome at a different point on the imperial trajectory, when it was no longer an expanding power.

It is hard to tell whether Goths would have renewed their attacks on the empire like their western cousins. The "natural" course of development was interrupted by the arrival of the Huns. The Goths were overcome and splintered. Some sought safety within the empire, others submitted to the Huns. The first group, after brief sojourns in the Balkans and Italy, reached Gaul, where they managed to establish a kingdom. When it was destroyed by the Franks, they relocated to Spain, where they built another kingdom, which survived till the Arab takeover. The second group, first stranded in Pannonia under the Huns, also moved to the Balkans and on to Italy, where their kingdom was destroyed by the Byzantines in the middle of the sixth century.

At least three things should be noted here: the attraction exercised by high civilization, in this case Rome, on forest tribes; the role of trade; and the frontier.

Trade sent imperial wares deep into the forest zone, as far as Scandinavia. During the period of stabilization, a great trade route led from Aquilea on the Adriatic to the Baltic via Carnuntum; the other one connected Gaul with Jutland, partly along the Rhine, partly along the coast. The exotic merchandise reached people in the remotest hamlet in the wilderness of Scandinavia or an east European forest and made them aware of the existence of a more developed, richer civilization.

At closer range, in Germany, this role was played by the frontier. It offered opportunities for gainful employment and trade. Increasingly, populations outside the empire gravitated toward the frontier. By the fourth century, a very large proportion of the German population lived in a narrow belt about ten miles wide along the frontier. This stretch of territory developed a hybrid civilization with its own customs and lingo. Frequent intermarriage contributed to the process of hybridization. Not all Roman rulers were happy about the infiltration of the barbarians, but no one could bring it to a halt.

One truly amazing thing stands out: the ability of early Germans to "transport" and recreate their state structures over vast distances of space and time. In a sense, early Germans could "outnomad" the nomads. The Goths, for example, erected primitive state(s) in the south Baltic; recreated them in the Pontic steppe; and recreated them again in Gaul, Italy, and Iberia. These "portable" states indicate great organizational ability. They also suggest a very strong sense of identity (which is not to say that *all* Goths migrated or that some of them did not assimilate).

On the other hand, we have evidence of frequent tribal/ethnic transformations: the Chauki, who renewed Germanic assault in the west, moved to the coast of the North Sea, where they abandoned their old name and became Saxons. In the beginning of the third century B.C., tribes in central Germany formed the Alamannic confederation, those along the lower Rhine turned into Franks. In the fourth century, Hermunduri evolved into Thuringians, in the fifth, Bavarians coalesced from several smaller tribes. In Jutland, Cimbri, Teutons, and Charudi disappeared, while Heruli emigrated, leaving the Danish islands to the Jutes and Danes (Musset 1965, I, 53–54). The contrast between relatively stable identity and constant turmoil is one of the fascinating aspects of early Germans.

CHAPTER 8

The Slavs

There are two main contenders for the original area of the Slavs: Poland and the middle Dnieper valley around Kiev. The regions are "connected" by the Bug and the Pripiat' rivers.

The question has never been definitively settled. P. J. Šafárik, writing in 1837, placed the original Slavic homeland north of the Carpathians and in western Ukraine (Galicia, Volhynia, Podolia) (Safarik 1837, in Gimbutas 1971, 21, n.4). Lubor Niederle, 65 years later, located it in the middle and upper Dnieper (Niederle 1902, vol. I, in Gimbutas 1971, 21, n.5). Many Polish scholars (surprise!) prefer Poland: Lehr-Spławiński identified Proto-Slavs with the Trzciniec culture while Hensel identified them with the Lusatian culture (Dolukhanov 1996, 145).

Tree and river names have been much used to settle the argument. All Slavic languages share Indo-European names for birch, oak, ash, aspen, elm, maple, and a few other trees (Gimbutas 1971, 22). In Gimbutas's opinion, "this supports the view that the Slavic homeland must have been located in a climatic zone where natural conditions did not differ much from those of the Indo-European homeland" (22). But this could merely point to the Indo-European origins of the Proto-Slavic language. More significant are names borrowed from other language groups: beech, larch, yew. They all grow to the west and south-west of the presumed Slavic homeland (23).

The tree distribution allows us to draw a line from Kaliningrad to Odessa. Hence, the Slavic homeland must have been located in the Pripiat' marshes (Dvornik 1956, 3). However, the Pripiat marshes acquired reasonably dense settlement only by the end of the first millennium B.C. and beginning of the first millennium A.D. Besides, climatic conditions in that part of Europe are unstable, so that the tree distribution could have been drawn further west than today. This would allow the Lusatian culture to remain a distinct possibility, an idea supported by John Szekanowski, L. Kozlowski, J. Kostrzewski, and T. Sulimirski (8). Niederle did not preclude this possibility either (Niederle 1923, 20, in Dvornik 1956, 8).

Another argument in favor of the Lusatian culture is based on loan words in Proto-Slav that give us an indication of the relative position of that language vis-à-vis other early languages. These data indicate that the Proto-Slavs bordered on Proto-Germans, Proto-Balts, and Proto-Thracians. If the original habitat of the Proto-Germans was in southern Scandinavia and, a bit later, included the Baltic coast to the Oder, and the Proto-Balts lived east of the Vistula while the Thracians were located south of the Carpathians, then the Proto-Slavs had to be in Poland (based on Dvornik 1956, 5–8).

The river names paint a different picture. Max Vasmer's study located early Slavs in Galicia, Volhynia, Podolia, and the middle Dnieper region (Vasmer 1941, in Gimbutas 1971, 22, n.7). Other studies of river names (Moszyński 1957 and Trubachëv 1968, in Gimbutas 1971, 22, n.8) also located the oldest area along the Pripiat', the middle Dnieper, and further east along the Sejm river. Toporov and Trubachëv (Gimbutas 1971, 25, n.12) placed the oldest Slavic river names in the eastern middle/upper Dnieper catchment, south of the Balts. There is also some evidence that Slavs were moving from the south, from the Dniester and the Southern Bug, to the north, along the Dnieper and its tributaries (Dolukhanov 1996, 151).

Among major Indo-European groups, Balts are the closest relative. Linguistic affinity, as well as a relatively slow rate of cultural change, led some scholars to postulate a Balto-Slav linguistic unity at some early point (Gimbutas 1971, 25, n.13; Birnbaum 1983, 18, in Dolukhanov 1996, 140). But this hypothesis did not win a universal acceptance (Senn 1966; Klimas 1967, in Gimbutas 1971, 25, n.14).

When we turn to the anthropological evidence, we have to put aside a large number of craniological studies that are now out of favor. That leaves physical measurements of the skeletal remains (also suspect) and other indicators, such as blood groups.

If we go by the skeletal remains, they indicate that the forest-steppe people differed from the Scythians but were closely related to the medieval eastern Slavs (Velikanova, in Gimbutas 1971, 47, n.19). Similarities in blood groups are also noticeable between later Slav groups in the south of the Russian plain, the Scythian forest-steppe groups (i.e., "Scythian ploughmen") and the Cherniakhovo culture, but the evidence is inconclusive. It may simply indicate proximity and intermarriage, since similarities in blood groups exist between Russians in the Pskov area and some Baltic groups, such as Prussians and Yatvyagians (Benevolenskaya 1985, in Dolukhanov 1996, 140); eastern Slavs and some eastern Finno-Ugrians; western Slavs and neighboring Germanic groups, and southern Slavs and several Balkan groups (Alexeyeva 1973, in Dolukhanov 1996, 140–41).

Archeological evidence shows a remarkable cultural continuity throughout the Bronze (2000 B.C.–750 B.C.) and Early Iron Ages (750 B.C.–500 B.C.)

(Gimbutas 1971, 20). The earliest culture that covered most of the Slav homeland was the Komarov complex (1500–1200 B.C.), which shows a strong central European influence in metallurgy and trade (33).

The Komarov complex was followed by the Proto-Slav Bilohrudivka culture (Terenozhkin 1951; Berezanskaia and Titenko 1952 and 1954, in Gimbutas 1971, 28 and 36, n.8), which existed at approximately 1000–800 B.C. At this time, the western influence had decreased, but bronze hoards indicate some western contacts (37).

At the beginning of the eighth century B.C., Bilohrudivka gave way to the Chernoles complex, named after a hill fort on the river Chernoles. This culture was synchronous with Hallstatt (750–500 B.C.). This was an Early Iron Age culture with unfortified settlements and large ash mounds, similar to the Late Bronze phase (39). At some point, the Chernoles culture expanded into the Proto-Scythian area (40). Here one finds small hill forts at strategic locations: high river banks, river bends, or the confluence of two rivers.

In the fifth century B.C., Herodotus placed the "Royal" Scythians in the Pontic steppe. They were pastoralists whose economy was based on stock-breeding (Dolukhanov 1996, 134). To the north, that is, in the former Chernoles area, lived "Scythian ploughmen" who practiced agriculture and even grew corn for sale (Herodotus, *History*, Book IV, 17, in Gimbutas 1971, 46). This information allowed some scholars (46; Rybakov 1979, in Dolukhanov 1996, 135) to identify these "ploughmen" as Proto-Slavs.

The population grew rapidly at the end of the Bronze Age and the beginning of the Early Iron Age. In the second half of the eighth century B.C. the Proto-Slavs started moving east, colonizing the valleys of the Sula, upper Sejm, Psël, and Vorskla rivers. Shortly thereafter they were conquered by the Scythians, who exercised a strong influence in the next few centuries. Gimbutas believed that Slavs lived under Scythian rule and came to be known, by Herodotus' time, as the "Scythian ploughmen" (Gimbutas 1971, 56).

During the fifth through third centuries B.C. the forest steppe culture had close ties with the Scythian steppe and the Greek cities in the Pontic area (47). However, archeological evidence suggests that the Scythians and the Proto-Slavs did not mix (48). Their contact was limited: seminomadic Scythians extracted tribute in the form of agricultural surplus. Gimbutas also noted the "striking conservatism of the Proto-Slav farming culture" (49).

Until the first century A.D. there is no epigraphic evidence of the Slavs. The first mention comes from Ptolemy (circa A.D. 100–178), who wrote, in *Geography*, that the northern part of Scythia, until the Imaos (Ural) mountains, was inhabited by the Alans, Soubenoi, and Alanorsi (58, n.2). "Soubenoi" is taken to mean "Sloveni," since the hard "l" followed by a closed "o" would sound like "slu/swu/su" to a Greek while "b" and "v" had become interchangeable in Greek by this time.

In his description of Sarmatia, Ptolemy also mentioned the "Serboi" who lived, along with some other tribes, between the northeastern foothills of the Caucasus and the Volga (Ptolemy, *Geography* V, 8, in Gimbutas 1971, 60). Moszyński derived the name from Indo-European *ser-*, *serv-*, that is, "guard, protect," a cognate of Latin *servus*. Originally, it probably meant "guardians of animals," in other words, "shepherds." In Sarmatian, *serv-* turned into *xarv-*, very close to "Hrvat," "Croat." P. S. Sakać discovered Persian inscriptions of the time of Darius, mentioning a Persian province and its people close to modern Afghanistan, Harahvaiti, Harahvatis, Horo-hoati. It is possible that some "Croats" did not migrate to Iran but stayed in the Caspian steppe, or between the Caspian and the Aral Sea (Sakać 1949, 313–40, in Dvornik 1956, 26, n.1). This name, in the form of "Horoathos" and "Horouatos," appears in two Greek inscriptions from Tanais from the second and third centuries A.D. (Gimbutas 1971, 60, n.3). It is possible that the "Horoati" and their cousins the Serboi fled from the Huns to southern Poland (where the area around Cracow was known as White Croatia in the early Middle Ages) and southeast Germany, where they were assimilated by the surrounding Slavs (and where the remnant of the Slav-speaking popula-tion is still known as "Sorbs"). By the time they moved to the Balkans in the seventh century they had been thoroughly Slavicized. Croatian toponyms from the ninth to eleventh centuries are known in Galicia, White Croatia around Cracow, Saxony, the Saale valley, the upper Elbe, the vicinity of Olo-mouc in Bohemia, Styria and, of course, Croatia in the Balkans. And "Ser-bian" place names are encountered in Little Poland, Pomerania, and the area in-between (108–09).

Another people who may have been of Slav or partly Slav origin are the "Antes." They were mentioned by Pliny the Elder (A.D. 23–79) in his *Nat-ural History* (VI, 35, in Gimbutas 1971, 60) among the people living be-tween the Sea of Azov and the Caspian, in an area that was at that time ruled by the Sarmatians. Ptolemy in the second century and Greek inscriptions from the third place the "Antas" on the Kerch peninsula in east Crimea, on the shores of the Azov, and at the mouth of the Don. These early inscrip-tions do not specify their ethnicity, but Jordanes, in the sixth century, indi-cated that the "Antes" and the "Sclavini" spoke the same language and comprised the "Venedi": " . . . they all come from the same tribe but are known under three different names: the Veneti, the Antes, and the Sclaveni" (Jordanes, ch. 23, pp. 119–20, in Conte 1995, 9, n.7).

The Antes lived to the east of the Sclavini, between the Dniester and the Dnieper. Procopius (d.562), a Byzantine historian and a contemporary of Jordanes, mentioned their invasion into the lower Danube in his history of the Gothic wars in 536–37 (Gimbutas 1971, 58).

Some linguists derive "Antes" from "Viatichi" (*Vetici*). If so, the name could be a variant of "Venedi." The fact that Finnish "Venaja" denotes "Russia" and "Wend" is an old Germanic term for Slav, as well as another term for Sorbs, lends support to this theory. Another indication are the "Wantit," who are found in the works of some Arab and Persian historians and geographers (61). Finally, the root also appears in Old Church Slavonic *vesti* (venshti) (greater), Polish *więcej* (more), and various male names like Venceslav, Viacheslav, and the like.

The Antes were later annihilated by the Avars (61).

As for the Venedi, they were first mentioned by Tacitus in *Germania,* 46. "His" Venedi were robbers who lived in the forests and mountains between the Peucini (Germanic "Bastarni") in the east Carpathians and the Fenni (Finns) in eastern Russia. Jordanes also mentions them, as the "Venethi," living on the northern slopes of the Carpathians at the source of the Vistula. They were defeated by the Gothic king Ermanaric. He lists them together with the Sclavini and the Antes (Jordanes XXIII, 119, in Gimbutas 62, n.7). Yet, cautioned Gimbutas, not all Veneti mentioned in the earlier historic records (Herodotus, Tacitus, Pliny the Elder, Ptolemy) can be identified as Slavs (Moszyński 1961, in Gimbutas 1971, 62, n.8). There were Illyrian Veneti in northeast Italy (hence Venice) and even Celtic ones in Brittany (Simon James 1993, 48, 119).

Finally, the Russian Primary Chronicle, probably compiled in the twelfth century, said that " . . . the Slavs [had] settled along the Danube, the present-day location of the Hungarians and the Bulgarians. It is from there that the Slavs spread out . . ." (Conte 1995, 5, n.2). But this version did not win wide acceptance.

The archeological culture that most closely corresponds to the epigraphic evidence is the Zarubintsy culture. It bridged the valleys of the Vistula and the Dnieper, stretching along the Bug and the Pripiat', connecting the two likeliest areas of the original Slav homeland.

Dolukhanov describes it as a link in "a chain of local cultural entities, variously affected by the Graeco-Roman civilization [that] emerged on the fringe of the Roman Empire" (Dolukhanov 1996, 148). Discovered by V. V. Khvoika in 1899 (149), the culture was dated 200 B.C.–A.D. 100 (Gimbutas 1971, 66), the period that immediately preceded the earliest epigraphic evidence.

The Zarubintsy complex had close contacts with the Scythians (Dolukhanov 1996, 150). Much more surprising is the great number of late La Tène fibulae of provincial Roman manufacture found at Zarubintsy sites (150). This indicates close trade ties with the Roman world.

Khvoika identified Zarubintsy as an early Slav culture. His opinion is still shared by some (mostly Russian) archeologists. Terenozhkin (1955) derived it from the Bilohrudivka and the Chernoles cultures; Pobol' (1970) thought it had emerged from the Baltic Milograd complex (both 151).

But Kukharenko (1961, 1964) believed that the Zarubintsy culture was an offshoot of the Pomeranian (Pomorian) group of the Lusatian culture in the Vistula basin. Gimbutas supported his conclusions. In her opinion, he had shown "more or less conclusively that the Zarubinets complex bears no relation at all to the preceding culture in this region during the Scythian or pre-Scythian era, that is, with the culture of the 'Scythian farmers' and Chernoles. Genetically, it can be affiliated only with the Pomeranian group" (Kukharenko 1964; Tretyakov 1959, in Gimbutas 1971, 67, n.4).

Others took a middle-road approach. Tretyakov wrote that the Zarubintsy culture resulted from a "cultural-ethnic integration" of various local Iron Age groups (Tretyakov 1966, 217, in Dolukhanov 1996, 151). Or, according to Dolukhanov, the Zarubintsy culture was a "poli-ethnic entity which resulted from the transition of various Middle Dnieper groups to a plough-type agriculture and their inclusion into an agricultural forest-steppe 'Scythian' network. In its turn, this led to the gradual inclusion of these groups into the sphere of provincial Roman-Celtic interaction. It is very probable that this conglomerate of local ethnic groups used Slavic dialects as a means of communication" (151).

The Zarubintsy culture was submerged in the Cherniakhovo complex (discussed in the previous section).

It is only at the end of the fifth century A.D. that we can identify a clearly Slav complex. At this time, the Slav settlement was concentrated in today's west Ukraine. The early Slavs did not venture into the steppe. For one thing, they were no match for the nomads. But there was also another reason: their ploughs could not open the hard soils of the steppe and the black earth belt.

The earliest Slav sites fall into two groups: one, on the river Teterev in Volhynia, reaching into southeast Poland (Gimbutas called it "Zhitomir," Dolukhanov "Prague-Korchak"); the other one, around the Dnieper rapids but also extending west to the middle Prut ("Pen'kovka" in Gimbutas's nomenclature, "Prague-Pen'kovka" in Dolukhanov's) (Gimbutas 1971, 80, and Dolukhanov 1996, 161, respectively). Dolukhanov designates both groups "Prague" because they were first identified from a type of pottery found near Prague (Borkovský 1940, in Dolukhanov 1996, 160).

The economy of both groups was based on agriculture and cattle breeding.

According to Shchukin (1994), the so-called Kiev-type sites, synchronous with Cherniakhovo, played an important role in the emergence of several groups of early Slavs (Dolukhanov 165). And Sedov (1982) wrote that the pottery and the house types of the eastern ("Pen'kovka") group show direct antecedents in the Cherniakhovo complex. (He also noted the similarity of certain types of ceramics and the burial rite of Prague-Korchak sites with those of the Przeworsk culture [Sedov 1982, in Dolukhanov 167].) Perhaps that would also explain a relatively large number of Gothic loan words in Slav languages (Gimbutas 1971, 77–79).

We should also add that the eastern part of the Zhitomir complex corresponds to the area of the Zarubintsy culture. Perhaps, the people of the Zarubintsy culture were Slavicized at some point. And their close ties with the Lusatian culture facilitated their early spread west.

Dolukhanov suggests the following scenario for the earliest phase of Slavic migration in the fifth and sixth centuries: "The increasing aridity of the climate in the forest-steppic zone caused a considerable decline in agricultural productivity in that area [but he also writes, on page 146, that this period saw an increase in precipitation!]. At the same time, this area became the target of repeated invasions on the part of various nomadic groups (the Huns and many others)" (Dolukhanov 1996, 165–67). The nomads established an overlordship over the Slavs and imposed a harsh taxation on their agricultural resources. The combination of ecological and political pressures pushed the agricultural populations north and west, away from the steppe. In the process, once Slavs "had gained substantial political and military experience in their dealings with their warlike nomadic assailants, [they] emerged as a dominant force and established a new socio-political network in the entire area of central and southeastern Europe. . . . One may suggest that economic power stood at the bottom of this newly emerged Slavic sociopolitical network. An intensive exchange of goods and communication, as in all similar cases, bound together various ethnic groups involved in this network. The Slavic language functioned as a common information medium" (Dolukhanov 1996, 165–67).

This scenario is less than satisfactory for several reasons. Forest tribes did not carry on intensive trade with each other because they produced the same or similar kinds of products. Their natural trade partners were areas of high civilization—which would not promote cohesion among these tribes (witness Celts and Germans). That their language "functioned as a common information medium" for groups of impoverished swineherds fleeing the nomads also hardly matters. Its spread is much more plausibly explained by their numerical superiority, the low density of population in the areas where they expanded (due in part to the outmigration of the Germanic tribes), and the lack of a strong imperial power. Where the power was later reestablished, as in Greece, Slavic dialects disappeared. Finally, the role of climate is ambiguous: after a cooling period in 900–300 B.C., the climate grew warmer. Roman records show that the cultivation of vines and olives spread north (Gribbin 1978, in Dolukhanov 1996, 146). Throughout the entire first millennium the temperatures were on the increase. And starting in the fifth and sixth centuries, there was also an increase in precipitation, which cancels the argument that aridity drove early Slavs out of their original habitat.

Perhaps all one can say about early Slavs is that their roots go back to the Zarubintsy culture (whether its carriers were originally Slav or not) and the Cherniakhovo complex, as well as a substantial Scythian influence. Perhaps these two sources, Zarubintsy and Cherniakhovo, explain the subdivision of early Slavs into two areas. They may also explain the western and eastern orientation of the Zhitomir and Pen'kovka areas, respectively.

The Huns "opened" Europe to the Slavs, although it is possible that some Slavs had arrived on the Hungarian plain as unwilling Sarmatian auxiliaries a century earlier (Ammianus Marcellinus; Zasterova 1966, in Gimbutas 1971, 98, n.1).

After the raids, the nomads returned to the plains, their natural habitat, while the Slavs stayed and colonized. Yet, there is little direct evidence of the Slav presence among the Huns. One reference comes from Priscus, a member of a Byzantine delegation that visited Attila's court in 448. He described a local people who lived in villages, sailed in boats made from hollowed tree trunks (*monoxyles*), and drank mead and *kamon* (a drink made from barley), all traits later associated with Slavs. These people had a language of their own, although they could also communicate in Hunnic, Gothic, and Latin (Ivanka, in Gimbutas 1971, 99, n.3). And Jordanes mentions a Hunnish feast called *strava*, which sounds like a Slavic word, in connection with Attila's funeral (the timing and location seem to imply that it was a wake) (Jordanes, in Gimbutas 1971, 99, n.2).

Some time in the early sixth, or maybe even late fifth, century, Slavs took part in early Bulghar raids against the Byzantines. The first one, according to Dvornik, occurred in 517 (Dvornik 1956, 34). But the real deluge started ten years later, under Justinian. At this time, Byzantium concentrated all efforts on reconquering western provinces; its Danubian frontier was stripped bare.

In 528, the Sclavini crossed the Danube and swept into Thrace. Chilbudius, *magister militum* of Thrace, managed to contain them until 533. But from 540 on, Bulghars and Sclavini were constantly raiding all over the Balkans, as far as Illyria and Greece. Initially, the towns were spared because the marauders lacked the necessary skills. But they learned soon enough, and by 550/51 threatened Constantinople and Thessaloniki.

They were a beastly lot: if they took too many prisoners, they burned them together with oxen and sheep. They also impaled their captives on sharp stakes or fastened them between four posts and killed them with maces (Procopius, in Gimbutas 1971, 100).

Faced with unruly hordes, the Byzantines resorted to an old practice of fighting fire with fire: they made an alliance with the Avars, who conquered

Bulgharian Utigurs and annihilated their Slav allies the Antes (then living between the Dnieper and the Danube). By 561, the Avars were on the Danube, demanding land south of the river. And in 567 they helped the Langobards to destroy the Gepids in Pannonia (101).

The emptying of Pannonia (the Langobards soon departed for Italy) allowed other Slavs to occupy (as Avar allies?) parts of the former Gepid territory between Orşova on the Danube and the river Olt in Romania (Barada 1952, in Gimbutas 1971, 102, n.11). The departure of the Langobards opened the way up the Danube into Moravia and Bohemia, and from there, by way of the Elbe, into Germany. It is possible, even probable, that in the west, like in the Balkans, the nomads opened the way for the Slavs.

It is hard to generalize about Slav/nomad relations. Evidently, some tribes allied themselves with the nomads, others fought them. *Renversements* were also frequent. Thus, while the Antes had been annihilated, other Slavs joined the Avars, as they had earlier joined (or were forced to join) the Utigurs. At one point, some Slavs stopped paying tribute to the Avars and even killed their envoys. Enraged, the Avars destroyed the Slavs who had settled south of the Danube in what used to be Byzantine territory (102).

But enmity with one tribe did not hamper alliance with another. When khaqan Baian captured Sirmium (a major Byzantine center on the river Sava, modern Sremska Mitrovica), Slavs once again joined the Avars. Together, they overran the entire Balkan peninsula. Slavs reached Salona (on the Adriatic coast) in 536, Dyrrhachium (Durres) in 548 (Dvornik 1956, 36). In 549, for the first time, large numbers of Slavs spent the winter on imperial territory (Musset 1965, II, 85). Thereafter, invasions of Illyricum followed in quick succession: 549, 550, 559 (Dvornik 1956, 36). In 551, Slav hordes were at the gates of Adrianople and Constantinople (Musset 1965, II, 85).

Even Athens was not spared, although the city remained under Byzantine control (Thomson 1959, in Gimbutas 1971, 103, n.13). By 578, Slavs reached Corinth (Musset 1965, II, 31) and Peloponnese. In 587, as new tribes arrived, Slavs began to settle in the vicinity of Thebes and Athens (Dvornik 1956, 40).

While the interior of the Balkan peninsula was repeatedly overrun, the Adriatic coast seems to have been largely spared. The lull ended with the Langobard-Avar-Slav raid on Istria in 600 when Archbishop Maximus of Salona wrote to the Pope about the great danger from *de Sclavorum gente* (Bulić 1904, in Gimbutas 1971, 105, n.18).

We should note the truly surprising level of cooperation and coordination among barbarians: according to Paulus Diaconus, the Avars sent Slavs from Carinthia and Pannonia to help the Langobardian king Agilulf take Cremona, Mantua, and other cities in northern Italy in 603 (Paulus Diaconus, in Gimbutas 1971, 105, n.19).

Emperor Maurice managed to stem the tide for a while by paying hefty tributes to the Avars. But he was assassinated in 602, and the attacks resumed. Sometime around 614, Slavs swept down Dalmatia destroying Salona, the largest Roman city on the Adriatic coast, and a number of other important centers, such as Epidaurum. Those inhabitants who managed to escape built new towns in better-protected areas: Ragusa (Dubrovnik), Cattaro (Kotor), and others (n.20). Between 610 and 626, Thessaloniki, the second city in the empire, was sacked. Attacks reached into the farthest recesses of Greece, including the Aegean islands (Lemerle 1953, in Gimbutas 1971, 103, n.14). Eventually, Byzantium had to abandon virtually all of Illyria and much of Macedonia, Greece, and Thrace (although it did not abandon claims to these territories). By the middle of the seventh century its de facto control was limited to Thessaloniki (103) and a few Dalmatian ports: Zadar, Trogir, Split, Dubrovnik, Kotor, and Durres (Dvornik 1956, 41).

The Slavs did not stop in the Balkans. They also made their way to Italy and Asia Minor. In 641, they tried to disembark in Apulia (Musset 1965, II, 86). Eventually, several Slav migrations succeeded in establishing a foothold in southern Italy. It is known that Robert Guiscard recruited Slav soldiers from Calabria in the middle of the eleventh century (Conte 1995, 59, n.90). And an Arab traveler, Ibn Hawqal, mentioned a "Slavic district" in Palermo in the tenth century (then Arab territory) (n. 91).

Slavs also showed up in Bithynia, deep in Asia Minor, in 650 (Musset 1965, II, 31). It was later used as a dumping ground for Slav prisoners of war. Thus, Justinian II transferred 250,000 Slavs to Asia Minor after his victory in Macedonia in 688 (the numbers are probably inflated). Another 200,000 were sent there in the middle of the eighth century. So numerous were the Slavs in Bithynia in the tenth century that the area was called Sclavisia (Conte 1995, 39). As late as the beginning of the twelfth century, Serb prisoners were being transported to Nicomedia (Izmit) (38).

The Avar attack on Constantinople in 626, joined by Slavs, Bulghars, and even Persians (who approached the city from the east), was the high point of Avar power. The Avars soon began to weaken, while Slavs continued to increase.

They were now scattered over vast and largely depopulated territories whose earlier inhabitants had fled (*Chronicle of Monemvasia,* in Charanis 1950, in Gimbutas 1971, 104, n.16). Bishop Isidore of Seville wrote that "Slavs took Greece from the Romans" (*Sclavi Graeciam Romanis tulerunt* [Isidore Hispaniensis, in Gimbutas 1971, 104, n.15]).

By the middle of the seventh century Slavs had a de facto control over the entire Balkan peninsula, and the invasions petered out (105). The Bulghars who reached Thrace around 670 found an alliance of several Slav tribes.

They conquered the Slavs but, like the Franks in Gaul, were eventually assimilated (106).

Rivers served as highways for Slav penetration in the Balkans. The distribution of place and river names shows a massive Slav influx in west and northwest Bulgaria while the east and southeast were spared. It is interesting that about 70 percent of large rivers in the area retained Thracian nomenclature, with only 7 percent Slav. The percentage of Thracian names dips to only 15 percent for medium-sized rivers while the share of Slav names increases to 56 percent (108).

While the invaders colonized the interior, the earlier inhabitants fled to the coast. Others fled to the islands, and the mountains, some even to southern Italy and Sicily. Thus, the Greek element was reinforced on the coastal rim, recreating an earlier pattern: Greek coast versus "barbaric" interior.

Eventually, the Greek speakers of Moesia and Thrace and Latin speakers in Illyria, both precariously clinging to the narrow strip of the coast, were assimilated. But in Greece and Albania the non-Slav languages proved to be more resilient. This is all the more amazing since, according to Patriarch Nicholas III (1084–1111), "for two hundred and eighteen years not a single Roman [Byzantine] set foot in Peloponnesus" (Conte 1995, 33, n.46). And Bishop Willibald, on a voyage to the Holy Land in 723–728, noted that Monemvasia was in Slav territory. In Corinth, Byzantine coins disappeared from the end of the sixth until the beginning of the ninth century. They reappeared only when the Byzantine victory at Patras in 805 reestablished imperial control over the area (36). (Unexpectedly, modern Greek includes only 300 Slav words [34], although Vasmer found 429 Slav names in Greek toponymy [35].)

It was Constantine VI who brought the Slavs of Macedonia and Greece to heel in 783. His successor, Empress Irene, crushed a Slav revolt in Greece. An unsuccessful Slav siege of Patras in 805 was the last attempt to resist the Greeks. The reimposition of the Byzantine rule in the early ninth century was decisive in the re-Hellenization of Greece, although some Slavic dialects survived until the fifteenth century (Gimbutas 1971, 109; Bon 1951; Charanis 1950 and 1952; Setton 1950 and 1952, in Dvornik 1956, 117, n.1). (The reimposition of the Byzantine rule may account for the re-Hellenization of Greece, but it does not explain the survival of Albanian. This language may have survived thanks to the isolation of its population protected by mountains, forests, lack of urban centers, and the peculiar clan structure that made assimilation difficult.)

In the west, Slav migration came from the south, not directly from the east. Here, the point of departure was the destruction of the Gepids in 567 and the subsequent emigration of the Langobards. Pannonia was emptied, and

Avars and Slavs could migrate up the Danube and then, via Moravia and Bohemia, down the Elbe deep into Germany. However, Bialeková (1962) found the earliest Slav graves in western Slovakia going back to about 500 (Gimbutas 1971, 118). If so, some Slavs may have preceded the Avars and could have come from the north, from across the northern Carpathians.

There is also a curious passage in Procopius, who wrote that the Heruli, having been defeated by the Lombards, decided to return to their ancestral homeland in Denmark and were given free passage by the Slavs through their territory in 508–514. They probably crossed Moravia and moved on to the Vistula (Procopius; Vasiliev 1950, in Dvornik 1956, 33–34, n.1).

It is possible that some Slavs had already moved west and were encountered by Avars and their Slav allies when they attacked Franks in 561–62 and 566–67 and invaded Thuringia in 595 (60). By the early seventh century, Slavs were already settled on the Baltic. Theophilactus Simokattes mentioned three wandering Slav musicians who came (they said) from the coast of the Western Ocean (the Baltic Sea) (Gimbutas 1971, 107–08).

In 623, under the leadership of a Frankish merchant (or nobleman) Samo, the Slavs shook off the Avar overlordship, creating the first proto-state. However, it fell apart after Samo's death in 658/59 (104; Dvornik 1956, 61).

Byzantines and Franks may have played a role in both creating and destroying Samo's state. In the early seventh century both were threatened by the Avars. It is known that Dagobert, king of the Franks (628–38), and Emperor Heraclius (610–41) exchanged embassies (Dvornik 1956, 62) and may have instigated the Slav revolt.

Later, pressure from the Franks may have prompted Serbs and Croats to look for a new home. When Heraclius offered them land in the Balkans, in exchange for assistance against the Avars, they agreed. With Byzantine help, Croats and Serbs evicted the Avars from Dalmatia, Illyria, and the Sava-Drava mesopotamia and settled in the Balkans.

Of course, not all Serbs and Croats moved south. Some Croats remained in Bohemia, southern Poland (around Cracow), and eastern Galicia, where they were mentioned in the tenth century by the Russian Primary Chronicle (63). They were eventually absorbed by the surrounding Slav population. The Serbs, however, found themselves among Germans, and their assimilation proceeded much more slowly. Some (now known as Sorbs), still remain.

Archeological sites in the middle Danubian area show a smooth transition from the Avar period to the Moravian Empire in the ninth century (Gimbutas 1971, 121), suggesting a gradual assimilation of non-Slav elements by Slavs (a notion generally supported by Czech scholars but rejected—for some reason—by many Hungarians). Funeral gifts of meat and eggs found in the graves, a Slav custom known from the Middle Ages, also points to Slavs, although they were clearly exposed to strong Avar, Byzantine, and Germanic influences (122).

The Slavicization, after the initial settlement, was mostly peaceful. Evidence to that effect comes from a former Germanic settlement at Březno, northwest of Prague. Here, houses and pottery of Slav and Germanic type were found in the same layer. The settlement appears to have been purely Germanic until the arrival of the Slavs some time in the first half of the sixth century (Pleinerová). The presence of Slavic and Germanic elements indicates that at least some Germans remained and continued to live and farm until assimilated by their Slav neighbors (122–23).

Slavs entered central Germany by way of the Elbe valley soon after they occupied Bohemia. They probably followed in the Avar footsteps shortly after their raid in the Elbe-Saale area in 565–66 (124). Archeologically, the early Slav complex in central Germany is a distinct, "totally foreign," element that is impossible to confuse with Merovingian materials (125).

Documentary evidence from contemporary German writers confirms their presence. Fredegar, writing in 630, placed them (the Sorbs) east of the Thuringians. And Einhard in *Annales Regni Francorum* mentioned "Sorabi" in 782 and 806, "qui campos inter Albim et Salam interiacentes incolunt" (who inhabit the plains between the Elbe and the Saale) and elsewhere "qui sedent super Albim fluvium" (who live along the river Elbe) (126).

Toponymy shows that Slav settlement reached Erfurt, Weimar, and Hanover (Ilmenau) (127, n.53). In the eighth century, Slavs spread to western Mecklenburg and eastern Holstein. Only the expansion of the Frankish Empire into Lower Saxony stopped the Slavic *drang nach westen:* Charlemagne established a defensive *limes Sorabicus* in 805 (Conte 1995, 22). By then, the Slavs were within 50 kilometers of Hamburg, where a few Polabian villages survived until 1798 (Musset 1965, II, 81).

In Germany, Slav migration led to the formation of five large Slavic groups: (1) Sorbian on the Saale-Elbe; (2) Obodritian in western Mecklenburg and eastern Holstein; (3) Vilzian (Vedletian) in Mecklenburg; (4) the Sprevane on the Havel and Spree; and (5) Lusatian on the Oder, with relatives in western Poland (Gimbutas 1971, 129). But their "stay" was relatively short.

In the winter of 928, Henry I crossed the Elbe in a first major German drive against the Slavs. He had already dealt with the Magyars, and now the Havelians, Veletians, Obodrites, and Sorbs between the Saale and the Elbe submitted. The Havelians' main town, Brunabor, became Brandenburg; Meissen was founded on the site of Jahna, the capital of Daleminci (Dvornik 1956, 107). Henry's son Otto I (936–73) further integrated the eastern territories by building castles and creating bishoprics (Havelberg, Brandenburg, Meissen, etc.).

However, when his successor Otto II died fighting Arabs in Calabria in 983, Slavs on the Elbe, Oder, and Baltic revolted and burned down German castles and towns, including Havelberg, Brandenburg, and Hamburg. Germans retained only Holstein (112–13). It took another crusade, preached by Bernard of Clairvaux in March 1147 (Conte 1995, 40), to launch another German reconquest.

German drive east did not stop on the Oder. It came to a halt in Russia in 1242, in Poland in 1410, and again in Russia in 1943. Throughout the centuries, German migration east, assimilation, and education have thoroughly Germanized large areas inhabited by western Slavs. Their descendants, now turned German, continued to fight their Slav neighbors in wars that frequently punctuated the uneasy Slav-German coexistence ever since.

Compared to Slav migrations south and west, migrations north and east came late.

Archeological materials show that the Dregovichi appeared north of the Pripiat' (west Belarus) only in the ninth and tenth centuries (Sedov 1966, in Gimbutas 1971, 93, n.18). The same time frame holds for Slav artifacts in east Belarus along the Sozh', the Iput', and the Beseda settled by the Radimichi. Nor does the area contain ancient Slav onomastics (Sedov 1966, in Gimbutas 1971, 93, n.17).

In the region of Smolensk, later settled by the Krivichi, the earliest Slav sites appeared in the eighth century. In the eleventh and twelfth centuries the Krivichi are attested in a large area between the upper Neman in the west and Kostroma in the east, and from Lake Peipus in the north to the Desna in the south.

Baltic and Finno-Ugric substrata played an important role in the formation of the Krivichi. The Baltic population slowly merged with Slavic newcomers, but Baltic dress, jewelry, and funeral rites lingered on in the upper Dnieper region into the eleventh century. And Baltic dialects in Belarus survived until at least the fourteenth century (Zinkjavicius and Gaucas 1985, in Dolukhanov 1996, 170). Even the "Goliad'" (Galindians) mentioned in the Primary Russian Chronicle, who lived in the upper Oka basin southwest of Moscow, remained an identifiable entity until the twelfth century (Gimbutas 1971, 97).

Why did the Slavs expand north when they did? One reason, of course, was pressure from the nomads, especially the Khazars, who established their overlordship over some Slavic tribes in the eighth century. Another reason is the closing of the south and west: the reemergence of the Byzantine power by 800 and the establishment of *limes Sorabicus* by Charlemagne. In fact, the Byzantine victory at Patras and the building of *limes* occurred in the same year, 805. That is why the Slav expansion up the Dnieper did not get going until the ninth century. The fact that dialects of the Pskov and Novgorod area contain Lechitic (Polish) elements (97) indicates that some of the early migrants to this area came from Poland, most likely because the increasing pressure from the west caused a reflux of Slavs east.

However, this sequence is not without problems. The most salient is the fact that the Krivichi are associated with the long barrows type of burial (94). Long barrows are found in the catchment of Lake Peipus and along the Velikaia River that flows into it from the south (Dolukhanov 1996, 167). Another type of burial also found in the area of early Slav settlement is known as "conic barrows" (*sopki* in Russian). The problem is that both these burials appear in northwest Russia already in the sixth century (168). Either these burials predate the Slavs or, perhaps, Slav migration started earlier, at about the same time as Slav migration south and west.

Dolukhanov and E. N. Nosov (1985) conducted a survey that found that the two types are located on different soils. Long barrows are concentrated on undulated fluvio-glacial plains covered with sandy soils and pine forests while conic barrows are located on the fringes of end-morainic hills, with predominantly clay soils covered, until recently, with mixed forests (Dolukhanov 1996, 168).

According to Dolukhanov and Nosov, the "long barrow" populations practiced swidden agriculture on soils that produced high yields but unpredictable harvests; the economy of the "conic barrows" population was based on intensive plough-type agriculture with a forest-fallow field system. The populations closely interacted with each other and with the agricultural communities further south, where many elements of their agricultural technology had originated.

Nosov (1981c) has shown that in several regions of the northwest, particularly in the Volkhov catchment, long barrows had a long history of uninterrupted local development. And this may be the clue to ethnic processes that occurred in this area. Dolukhanov believes that Slavicization in the area was a two-track process. The slow ("long barrows") track implies egalitarian units practicing swidden agriculture. The fast ("conic") track developed on more fertile but heavy soils. Their cultivation required a more advanced equipment and complex social organization of the chiefdom kind. In the two cases we are dealing with similar substrata differently affected by socioeconomic change and differently integrated in the new network (169).

Dolukhanov believes that the entire process of Slavic dispersion involved an expansion of a socioeconomic network based on productive agriculture, gradually incorporating and assimilating various ethnic groups. That Slavic language functioned as a common communication medium indicates that it was the language of chiefdoms (170).

But, if the long barrows type shows a long and uninterrupted line of local development, then it stands to reason that it was originally non-Slav. It was at a disadvantage vis-à-vis the more stratified "conic" type. Chiefdoms had an advantage over more egalitarian societies because they could better organize and concentrate manpower. They also produced higher yields. This was probably the Slav element. The major problem left unresolved by this paradigm is the early sixth century appearance of both types in the north. It contradicts all other evidence that precludes the appearance of Slavs north of the Pripiat' before the eighth century.

The ethnogenesis of the Slavs was a complex process that involved Scythian, Zarubintsy, and Cherniakhovo influences on at least two groups of Indo-European population living in the middle Dnieper; southeast Poland; and the area in-between, along the Pripiat' and the Bug.

The evolution and differentiation of the Proto-Slav population was a slow process that lasted more than a thousand years and concluded only toward the beginning of our era. Physical anthropology shows that there was a considerable admixture from several adjacent ethnic groups.

The Proto-Slav was a sedentary population engaged in agriculture. Perhaps, this fact accounts for the slow pace of cultural change, despite close contacts with Greek colonies in the Pontic area and Roman provinces in the Balkans. Another factor may have been Scythian overlordship that may have slowed down the pace of development. For early Slavs, the way south was blocked by the nomads and later Goths, while the west was closed off by Germanic tribes.

Ironically, it was the nomads, first the Huns and then the Avars, who set in motion the earliest Slav migrations. The direction of nomadic raids, into the rich regions of developed civilization, determined the direction of the initial Slav displacement: south. And the outflow of the Germanic population west depopulated vast areas of eastern Europe and created favorable preconditions for Slav colonization in central Europe. Here, the decisive event was the destruction of the Gepids and the emigration of the Lombards from Pannonia that opened the way for the Avars and their Slav allies deep into central Germany (although it is possible that some Slavs had preceded them there).

But there were also unforeseen circumstances best explained by chance: when Byzantium needed allies in a struggle against the Avars it invited Serbs and Croats to move to the Balkans.

With continuous pressure from the Khazars and the closure of the west (by Charlemagne) and southwest (Byzantium)—by coincidence, it happened the same year, in 805—the upper Dnieper valley remained the only venue for Slav outflow. Starting from the ninth century, Slavs migrated north and then northeast, slowly assimilating the Baltic and Finno-Ugric substratum. Slav chiefdoms were better organized and possessed better implements than the indigenous populations. Hence, they succeeded in absorbing their weaker neighbors. In the process, they also laid the demographic foundations for the emergence of an east Slav state in the valley of the Dnieper. But this development also belongs to the history of the Vikings.

CHAPTER 9

The Vikings

The Viking period spans roughly four centuries, from 700 to 1100.

Its similarity and parallels with the Völkerwanderung is striking. "Historians have long debated whether we should see more than superficial resemblances between the late and early manifestations of northern unrest," wrote Gwyn Jones, " . . . but though we shall be wise to reserve the word 'Viking' for its agreed post-780 context, there are convincing reasons for seeing northern history, however diversified, as a unity, and the northern excursus as a continuing rather than a fortuitously repetitive or coincidental process" (Jones 1968, 3).

The hiatus of some two hundred years separating Germanic from Viking migrations is the main reason that the question of (dis)continuity arises. Jones explains the break by the "unrelenting struggles for regional and national power both within and between the Scandinavian countries during this time, the easing of their population and land problems brought about by the Great Migrations, and their preoccupation with the Baltic lands and the peoples east and north of them" (182–83). His opinion is shared by many scholars. For example, Holger Arbman believed that "a closer study of the archaeological material shows that a fundamental continuity underlies it" (Arbman 1961, 27).

One of the facets of this continuity was the existence of close ties with the Mediterranean. Already in the second millennium B.C. the so-called Amber Way linked the Baltic with the eastern Mediterranean. A thousand years later there are indications that the Roman fleet may have reached northern Jutland (the "Cimbrian promontory" [Derry 1979, 9]) in A.D. 5 on a reconnaissance mission (Wilson 1970, 13–14). But Romans never tried to conquer the inhospitable northern "wastelands." Nevertheless, numerous items of Roman manufacture found in Scandinavian graves— bronze and silver vessels, glass bowls, jewelry, pottery, weapons (17–18; Sawyer 1982, 65)—testify to the large volume of trade. Already in Hadrian's time (A.D. 76–138), Roman coins could be found in Finland

(Derry 1979, 10). For their part, Scandinavians dealt in amber, furs, and slaves. Amber was in vogue in Rome and, on occasion, was imported in such quantities that it flooded the market (Pliny, Nat. Hist. Xxx.vii.41, in Sawyer 1982, 66). So pervasive was the Roman influence in Scandinavia that the first four centuries of our era in Scandinavian history are known as the "Roman Iron Age."

Initially, trade routes followed major river valleys. One went from Carnuntum on the Danube to (Marcomannic) Bohemia, from which point it split in three to follow the Elbe, the Oder, and the Vistula (Wilson 1970, 18). After the Marcomannic wars this route was blocked and was replaced by another one, down the Rhine and up the Atlantic coast to Jutland (Derry 1979, 10). Frisia's strategic location turned its ports into the lynchpin of the trade network connecting Scandinavia with the Mediterranean.

Trade continued even after the collapse of the empire, especially between Frisia and Jutland. It alerted Scandinavians of Frisia's riches. Already circa 565, Venantius Fortunatus, bishop of Poitier (530–609), mentioned a Geat fleet defeated off the coast of Frisia (Jones 1968, 42).

By the eighth century, Scandinavians learned the art of making masts and sails. They could now venture far and wide across the open sea. This technological achievement, probably more than anything else, inaugurated the beginnings of the Viking Age. In a sense, the Viking Age was a maritime Great Migration.

Ties with eastern Europe developed as early as those with the Mediterranean (if we count the early Amber Way). Various Scandinavian artifacts from the Swedish Middle Bronze Age (1100–700 B.C.) found on the lower Oka and axes of the Mälär type scattered in Finland, along the east Baltic coast, north Russia, and Belarus testify to early trade from the beginning of the first millennium B.C. The fact that they were widely scattered and are small in number indicates that this was not a migration (Sulimirski 1970, 331, n.21). Only in Courland (Latvia) do we find traces of a Late Bronze Age Scandinavian colony originating in Gotland (331, nn.18 and 19). Another indication is that pottery excavated in contemporary cemeteries was locally produced.

Although it is possible that these artifacts spread through a chain exchange, traded from tribe to tribe, Sulimirski believed that they were carried by traders. These early Scandinavian merchants or adventurers penetrated as far as the mouth of the Kama. Their colonies near Kazan' and on the Lower Oka survived for about two centuries until they were absorbed by the local population (331).

Why did the Scandinavians venture east? Sulimirski believed that, like their Mediterranean counterparts, they were looking for metals. Bronze hoards hidden in central Europe at this time hint at a major invasion that had disrupted older trade routes between Scandinavia and the eastern Mediterranean (the Amber Way). Scandinavians lost their supply of raw materials.

But they also ventured west, to the British Isles, where they were probably looking for tin. In fact, Scandinavia seems to have developed into a focal point of a vast network of indirect trade between Britain and eastern Europe. At least, some bronze objects (e.g., socketed spears and lance-heads) from Ukraine and Britain display striking stylistic similarities. They appeared almost simultaneously, around 1000–800 B.C. in Ukraine (and as far east as the Urals) and about 800 B.C. in Britain. They were probably transmitted by Scandinavians (334).

Scandinavian expansion of the early first millennium B.C. established patterns that would be replayed by their Viking descendants almost two thousand years later.

Why did they stop? Probably because they could reestablish their contacts with central and Mediterranean Europe and expand south where trade and settlement were much more lucrative because they involved areas of high civilization.

Archeological material indicates that ventures east resumed in the middle of the seventh century.

The earliest burials date from circa 650 (Jones 1968, 243). Weapons and brooches of Gotland design dating from 650–800 were found in cemeteries at Grobin near Liepaja (Latvia); Apulia (Apuole, Lithuania); and Truso (Elbląg, Poland) (Arbman 1961, 28). At Grobin, there were three distinct cemeteries: one, of "Swedish" provenance, contained mostly men of warrior age, with very few women; another one had merchants from Gotland, with quite a few women; and the third one was local, with the ratio of the sexes evenly balanced. A similar distribution can be observed in Apulia.

According to Vernadsky, the Vikings reached the mouth of the Daugava sometime before 700 (Vernadsky 1943, 266, in Davidson 1976, 26) but established their overlordship only in the next century. The eighth century saw the rise of a powerful kingdom in central Sweden based on Uppsala. Although it could expand in any direction, its main thrust was directed east, to Finland, Gotland, and the east Baltic littoral. The *Ynglinga Saga* describes raids into Estonia (Jones 1968, 241). And Rimbert's *Vita Anskarii* (circa 870) tells us how sometime around 850, the Chori (Courlanders) refused to continue paying tribute to their Scandinavian overlords. They defeated a "Danish" punitive expedition but could not repulse the "Swedish" king Olaf of Uppsala. About 855, after he had captured Seeburg (Grobin?) and besieged Apulia, the payment of tribute was resumed (Davidson 1976, 22; Jones 1968, 242–43).

While the "Danes" and the "Swedes" concentrated on the east Baltic littoral, "Norwegians" followed the coastline north into today's Finnmark and

Karelia and on to the lands along the White Sea known as "Bjarmaland" (Davidson 1976, 32), where tribute was also occasionally imposed.

The stabilization in western Europe under the Franks probably increased the demand for amber, furs, and slaves (Ozols 1976; Sawyer 1982, 75, 122). It sent Scandinavians across the sea looking for tribute. The remains of a large farm on Helgon in Lake Malaren, about 12 miles from Stockholm, indicate that its merchant-cum-farmer owners were in close contact with western Europe already in the eighth century (Arbman 1961, 27).

Once they entered the river system of the Russian plain, Scandinavians could sooner or later reach the Black and the Caspian Seas, Constantinople, and the Muslim lands. In Russia, the oldest Scandinavian settlement was Aldeigjuborg, some seven or eight miles up the Volkhov from Lake Ladoga. From here, one route led south to the Dnieper, another one went east and eventually reached the Volga.

The earliest inhabitants at the site were probably Finns, although Scandinavian artifacts were found at the lowest level (Davidson 1976, 46). Scandinavian settlers stayed in the area for some two hundred years, from the early ninth to the early eleventh century (Arbman 1961, 93) but were eventually assimilated by Slavs (Jones 1968, 250–51). The same process occurred in Gnezdovo, near Smolensk, at an early settlement dominated by warriors of Scandinavian descent (Sawyer 1972, 62–63).

From Aldeigjuborg, Scandinavians spread south and built a new city of Novgorod, at the point where the Volkhov flows out of Lake Ilmen'. The area became the heartland of the "land of the Rus." Most western scholars trace the origin of the name from "Ruotsi," Finnish for Swedes, derived from Old Norse "rothr," "row" (probably from today's Roslagen, a coastal region where the earliest Swedish adventurers originated). The term applied only to "Swedes" in Russia, never to "Swedes" in Sweden. (Russian "Varyag," from Old Norse "Vaeringi," akin to "Viking," probably derives from Old Norse "varar," [pledge, oath, guarantee] and refers to confederates in a war band (Jones 1968, 246–47).

Many Russian scholars tried to link "Rus'" with River Ros', a tributary of the Dnieper, or the "Rosomanni" (Roxolani?) mentioned by Jordanes (Davidson 1976, 60). But other evidence supports the Swedish origin of the Rus. One is a mention in the Annales Bertiniani in the year 839 of several men who came to the court of Louis the Pious at Ingelheim with the Byzantine embassy sent by Emperor Theophilus. Asked about their origin, they said they were Rus (*qui se, id est gentem suam, Rhos vocari dicebant*). Further inquiry revealed that they were ethnically "Swedish" (*comperit eos gentis esse Sueonum*) but came from Russia (Diaconus 1883, 19–20; Davidson 1976, 57; Jones 1968, 249–50). They were afraid to retrace their way across the Black Sea and the Dnieper because nomads had cut the route across the Pontic steppe.

Another testimony comes from Lui(d)tprand, the bishop of Cremona (died in 975), who mentioned "the Rus, whom we otherwise call Normans" (*Rusios quos alio nos nomine Nordmannos appellamus*) (1915, I. II, in Jones 1968, 254). And an Arab writer, Al-Ya'kubi, who died at the end of the ninth century, identified the Vikings who attacked Seville in 843–44 as "pagans who are called Rus" (Birkeland 1954, 13, in Davidson 1976, 59, n.2).

Finally, the Russian Primary Chronicle mentions an embassy sent to the Varangians: "They were called Rus as others are called *Svie,* others *Nurmane,* others *Angliane,* others *Gote*" (i.e., Swedes, Normans, English/Angles, Goths) (Jones 1968, 245, n.1).

According to the chronicle, a twelfth-century compilation based on eleventh-century documents (Cross and Sherbowitz-Wetzor 1953, in Sawyer 1972, 44, n.49), the Variags came to "Russia" in 859. But this date is much too late, since "Swedes" from "Russia" were in Ingelheim in 839. Numismatic and archeological materials point to the beginning of the ninth century (44–45).

Although the date may be incorrect, the story itself is probably not. The Vikings repeated the pattern they had followed in the Baltic and Finland, building small strongholds from where they could collect tribute. (The process is described in the *Egils Saga* [Davidson 1976, 51].)

At first, the local tribes rebelled and expelled the Vikings. But the strife that ensued supposedly convinced the Slavs to recall them. The Scandinavians were only too happy to oblige. Or, equally possible, the Vikings may have reimposed their rule by force, as they had done in Courland, but the author(s) of the chronicle did not want to deny legitimacy to the founders of the ruling dynasty.

From Novgorod, they reached the Dnieper valley and eventually arrived in Kiev, then a small settlement of the Slavic Poliane that was used as a tribute collection center by the Khazars. (The name seems to be of Khazar derivation, "Kiy-ev" meaning "river settlement" in Turkic). The tax was one squirrel and one beaver skin per household (63).

The Varangians expelled the Khazars and established their rule. Although tradition preserved the names of the Scandinavian adventurers (as in Novgorod), the names cannot be verified. However, there are some indications that, while the first batch was "Swedish," the second came from Halogaland in today's Norway (75).

For a while, conditions in Kiev were unsettled as Varangians fought Khazars, each other, and Slavs. They were also close to the steppe, with its dangerous nomads. Few in numbers and isolated, the Varangians of Kiev needed support from their cousins in Novgorod. Soon, the Varangians of Novgorod absorbed those of Kiev and in the process laid the foundations of a new state in the valley of the Dnieper. The Russian Primary Chronicle preserved this event in an apocryphal story in which Rurik's kinsman Oleg/Helgi kills the first Scandinavian rulers Askold and Dir and establishes himself as a ruler in Kiev. The chronicle also said that his followers, Varangians, Slavs, and others, were known collectively as "Rus" (123).

Thus, the "Russian" state coalesced from two centers, one in the north, with a largely Finno-Ugric population (the Chud', the Meria, the Ves'), the other one in the south, where the population was Slav (Poliane, Severiane, Vyatichi) (Jones 1968, 245). This duality was reflected in its dual orientation, toward the Baltic and Scandinavia in the north, toward the Black Sea and Constantinople in the south.

The importance of the southern connection (with areas of high civilization) determined the choice of Kiev as the capital. According to the Nestorian Chronicle, it happened in 882 (Arbman 1961, 98).

The assimilation of the Scandinavian element was fairly slow. Among 14 people who comprised the embassy sent to Byzantium in 912, most had Norse names, a few Finnish, but none Slav (101–102). Only in 942, more than a hundred years after Scandinavians had appeared in Russia, was a child born to the ruling family given a Slav name (Sviatoslav, son of Igor [Ingvar] and Olga [Helga]); at the time, Igor was 75, and Olga was 60. It looks like part of their family tree is missing (102–103).

By the time of Sviatoslav's death in 971 (972 according to Jones 1968, 261), the ruling family was beginning to intermarry with prominent Slavs: Vladimir's mother was of the Drevliane descent and had been in charge of Olga's household (her mother-in-law considered this marriage a mésalliance). Her brother Dobrynia was an advisor to Vladimir (Davidson 1976, 148).

Despite assimilation and intermarriage, the Kievan ruling family continued to maintain close contacts with the royal families of Sweden and Norway. Yaroslav the Wise (1019–54) married Ingigerd, daughter of Olaf of Sweden (164); his daughter Elizabeth was married to Harald Hardrada of Norway (Jones 1968, 263). And Scandinavians who had lost in power struggles back home often found refuge in Rus': Magnus Olafsson, Olaf Haraldson, and Harald Hardrada from Norway; and many others (263).

Jones believes that by the time of Yaroslav, the Kievan state had lost its Varangian character: "There had been a steady process of assimilation to the native population for almost two hundred years: concubinage, intermarriage, a change of language and religion, and the adoption of Slavonic customs had quietly eroded the Norseness of the Rus, and the massive influence of Byzantium carried the process ever farther" (264). The assimilation of the alien elite was accompanied by an increase in the power of the Slavs. Strapped for money and manpower, Varangians conceded their Slav subjects the right to pay for the troops and even raise their own armies.

The adoption of Christianity in 988 was a decisive break between Sweden, which was still heathen, and Greater Sweden (Russia) (266).

The takeover of Russia allowed Scandinavians to establish close commercial ties with Byzantium, the Khazars, and the Muslim world.

Muslim merchants established trade with "Russia" toward the end of the eighth century (Sawyer 1982, 2). Their main trade route went up the Volga to Bulgar, which served as the main entrepot. There, by the middle of the ninth century, they met their Scandinavian counterparts, creating a trade network that linked Scandinavia with the Middle East.

Trade made Varangians aware of the riches of the Muslim lands. And trade was soon followed by war.

The first raids were launched some time in 864–884 while they were still trying to establish a base in Kiev (Ibn Isfandiyar, 1905, 199, in Davidson 1976, 126).

In 910–12, a fleet of 16 ships crossed the Caspian and attacked Abasgun (Al-Mas'udi, in Arbman 1961, 94–95; Davidson 1976, 126–28). Later in 912, five hundred ships (clearly an exaggeration) sacked Baku and sailed up the Kura deep into Muslim territory (Arbman 1961, 95; Davidson 1976, 127–28; Jones 1968, 260–61). Yet another great raid occurred in 943 (Ibn Muskawaych, in Arbman 1961, 95; Davidson 1976, 126).

To reach the rich Muslim lands across the Caspian, Varangians had to reach an agreement with the Khazars who controlled the lower Volga. Indeed, they did, in 912, and shared the booty. But the Muslims applied pressure on the Khazars, and the Varangians found their way blocked, not only to the Muslim world but also to Byzantium since the Khazars also controlled the Dnieper. As a result, the fight against the Khazars became the cornerstone of Scandinavian policy in "Russia."

In this they succeeded. The Khazars were first expelled from the Dnieper valley in 883–85, and then, in about 965–68, Sviatoslav destroyed Khazaria and its capital Itil' (Davidson 1976, 112). A successor state may have survived in the Crimea but was subdued by the Byzantines in 1016.

The destruction of the Khazar state carried a steep price: it opened the Pontic steppe to the nomads. Already in 967, while Sviatoslav was in the process of conquering northeast Bulgaria, the Pechenegs attacked Kiev. He had to abandon Bulgaria and, eventually, the long-range plans of transferring his capital to Pereiaslavets (140–42). (How different the history of Russia and the Balkans would have been if he had!)

As the Pechenegs gained supremacy in the Pontic steppes, they destroyed any chance that Kievan Russia may have had of reaching the sea. And after 1060, as nomadic incursions into Kievan territory intensified, Russia was forced to adopt a defensive posture.

But neither the Khazars nor the Pechenegs could completely cut off the Varangians from Byzantium. Constantinople quickly became—and remained—the focal point of the Scandinavian trade network in eastern Europe.

The reference to Swedes from Russia in Annales Bertiniani in 839 also attests to their presence in Constantinople. But it is obvious that this was not the first time that they had reached the city. When they established their base at Kiev, they could organize annual expeditions to the Byzantine capital (75). (An account of a journey from Kiev to Constantinople can be found in *De Administrando Imperio*, a book written by emperor Constantine Porphyrogenitus (912–59) for the edification of his son and probably compiled about 944 [Moravcsik and Jenkins 1949, in Davidson 1976, 81].)

As had happened elsewhere, trade led to war. According to the Brussels Chronicle (probably compiled in the eleventh century), the first Varangian attack occurred on June 18, 860, when two hundred Rus ships tried to capture the city. (The Russian Primary Chronicle put the number of ships at two thousand.) (120–21). At the time, the Byzantine fleet was engaged in fighting the Arabs further east, and the city defenses were denuded. The Brussels Chronicle is corroborated by two sermons preached by Patriarch Photius at Hagia Sophia, one when the assault was in progress, the second one shortly thereafter, in gratitude for the deliverance (Mango 1958, 74ff, in Davidson 1976, 118). The attack failed, and the Vikings left on June 25 (Gregoire and Orgels 1954, 141ff, in Davidson 1976, 122), after pillaging nearby islands and the shores of the Sea of Marmora (118).

The next raid, in 907, by Oleg, is not corroborated by the Byzantine sources (123), and its veracity has often been questioned. But there are no doubts concerning the assault led by Igor in 941. It failed because "Russian" ships were destroyed by Greek fire (130–31; Jones 1968, 256). However, the Russian Primary Chronicle says that Igor returned three years later with another fleet and was paid tribute (Davidson 1976, 132). The conflict was settled by the treaty of 945 (Jones 1968, 259–60).

The last major Rus raid on Miklagard, also unsuccessful, took place in 1043 and is corroborated by Psellus (Psellus VI, 91, 199ff, in Davidson 1976, 170).

Scandinavians also served the empire in the so-called Varangian Guard. The tradition goes back to the Roman imperial practice of hiring barbarians for the army and administration. By the time of Constantine the Great it was well established. Constantine himself showered honors on the Cornuti who had taken part in the Battle of the Milvian Bridge in 312 (170).

The treaty of 911 (between the Rus and Byzantium) recognized their right to serve in the imperial forces. At first, they were scattered throughout, but in 988, at the time of Vladimir's conversion and marriage to a Byzantine princess, six thousand "Scythians" joined the army, and Emperor Basil II decided to assign them to a separate Varangian unit (Dolger 1924, I, 771, 99, in Davidson 1976, 179).

Among those serving in the Varangian Guard, Swedes predominated, followed by Norwegians, Danes, and a few Icelanders, although, according to Saxo, the Danish element predominated at the beginning of the twelfth century (181). In the provinces of Uppland and Södermanland, numerous memorial stones commemorate overseas ventures by local men. In Uppland, 42 stones record journeys east, 11 west, and 15 are indeterminate (236).

The Varangian Guard remained predominantly Scandinavian until the arrival of large numbers of Englishmen and English-born Danes in the aftermath of the Norman conquest of England. Eventually, they developed into a sort of a praetorian guard and played an important role in Byzantine internal affairs. They also fought external enemies of the empire: the Saracens in 1034 and Iverians in 998–1122 (Davidson 1976, 241) and even Normans of southern Italy.

The guard existed until the fall of Constantinople in 1204 (Davidson 1976, 180).

In the West, the trade between Scandinavia and western Europe, by way of Frisia, continued at a much reduced rate during the sixth and seventh centuries. But close contacts were maintained. So, it is not surprising that the first Christian mission to Denmark came from Utrecht (Willibrord, in about 700) (Arbman 1961, 74). (Derry dates it in the 720s [Derry 1979, 15].)

The Viking raids started about a hundred years later. Some scholars believe that they were provoked by pressure from the Franks; others—like Johannes Brondsted—fail to find adequate proof (Brondsted 1965, 25, in Jones 1968, 199). However, a closer look at the history of the Frank expansion toward the northeast suggests that this may be the case indeed.

Charlemagne's wars against the Saxons, which started in 772 and continued for the next 30 years, brought the Franks into the Danish "neighborhood." The wars grew more and more brutal, as Saxon resistance and Frankish suppression fed on each other.

The Danes grew increasingly apprehensive since Lower Saxony was right on their doorstep. It was clear that they would be next. They probably helped the Saxons. And when Saxon chief Widukind fled to Denmark in 777 he was given refuge at the court of King Sigfred.

Naturally, Charlemagne sought an alliance with the Slav Obodrichi (Abodrites), who lived east of the Saxons and south of the Danes. He encouraged them to move into east Holstein, which, among other things, cut Scandinavian trade links with central Europe.

King Sigfred died in 800 and was succeeded by a more aggressive king Godfred (Gottfrid) (Jones 1968, 98). Godfred fortified his southern frontier with a rampart (Arbman 1961, 75) and then, in 804, made a show of force with his fleet and army. In 808 he "dealt" with the Abodrites, sacking their main commercial center (Reric) and forcibly relocating its merchants to Danish Hedeby (Jones 1968, 98). And then he chose a good time for a counterattack against the Franks when Charlemagne was "busy" in Italy and Spain. In 810, he raided Frisia with 200 ships and demanded 100 pounds of silver in tribute (Arbman 1961, 75). (Charlemagne saw it coming, for he had positioned his fleets at the estuaries of the Loire and the Garonne; then, after the attack on Frisia in 810, he built new fleets and positioned them in Ghent and Boulogne [Sawyer 1982, 78].)

The next year, Franks and Danes reached an agreement, but it was short-lived. In 815, the Franks launched an expedition against Denmark (53). The Danes descended upon Flanders in 820 (Arbman 1961, 75). And the cycle of move and countermove was on. Or so it seemed.

In the fall of 833, Emperor Louis the Pious was deposed by his sons, in-augurating a long period of instability in the Frankish Empire (Sawyer 1982, 81). The Danes did not miss their chance. In the summer of 834 they at-tacked Dorestad, a major trade center on the Rhine, some 80 kilometers in-land. They returned in 835 and 836, and exacted tribute in 837. Three more assaults were visited upon Dorestad until the river changed its course in 863 and in the process destroyed the unfortunate city (St. Bertin, in Sawyer 1971, 140).

In 841, the Vikings sailed up the Seine and plundered Rouen; they also sacked Quentowic, a major port in the English Channel (where some build-ings were spared in return for payment) (Sawyer 1982, 85). The penetration of the Loire valley proceeded in several stages. In 843, Nantes was brutally sacked on St. John's Day (June 24) (Arbman 1961, 78; 842 according to Jones 1968, 211). In 853 they reached Tours. The next year they reached Blois but were beaten back at Orléans. But in 856, Orléans too was captured and sacked. In 865 they penetrated as far as Fleury and were undisputed masters of the river from source to mouth (Sawyer 1982, 86).

An important milestone was reached in 845 when Vikings plundered Paris on Easter Sunday (March 28, 845). They left after Charles the Bald paid 7,000 pounds of silver (Jones 1968, 212). Paris was plundered again in 856 and 857 (Arbman 1961, 80–81), but successfully defended itself in the siege of 885–86 (Sawyer 1971, 210).

Another important milestone was reached in 851, when they wintered in the valley of the Seine for the first time (86).

Between 836 and 876 the lands of the Franks were attacked every year save one (Annales Bertiniani, in Sawyer 1971, 2, n.5). Altogether, the Franks paid 13 danegelds; the amount of 7 that we know amounts to 40,000 pounds of silver, plus, on occasion, meat and drink for the raiders (Jones 1968, 213).

For a couple of years the Vikings were "busy" in England, but events in England (Guthrum's defeat in Wessex in 878 and the delimitation of Danelaw in England in 879), as well as events in France (where the death of Charles the Bald in 877, followed by his son's death in 879, inaugurated a new period of strife), made them switch back to France. The second wave of Viking depredations concentrated on the Atlantic coast between the Seine and the Rhine and crested in 879–92 (Arbman 1961, 80–81). They sailed up every major river—the Scheldt, the Meuse, the Somme, the Marne, the Seine, the Loire—and attacked virtually every major town: Cologne, Aachen, Trier, Liège, Rouen, Paris. Only Arnulf's victory in the battle of the Dyle in 891 (Sawyer 1971, 210) forced the Danes to turn to England once again.

However, the Viking threat remained. The problem was "solved" in 911 when Rouen and the lower Seine were granted to a Viking leader named Rollo. This was the beginning of Normandy which barred other Vikings from the valley of the Seine and protected the capital and its environs from their depredations.

Already by the end of the tenth century, these "renegade" Vikings were assimilated (3). It was as carriers of the French language and culture that they descended upon England in 1066.

The East Franks (later Germany) were less exposed than their western con-frères. Hamburg was destroyed by Danish king Hork in 845 (Sawyer 1982, 87), and the great raid up the Rhine in 882 reached Cologne and Trier (91). But altogether, in 845–80, there were only three raids on Germany (excluding Frisia). This was the result of the wise policy of elder Lothar, who granted the island of Walcheren at the mouth of the Scheldt to the exiled Danish leader Harald (87). Another piece of land, at the mouth of the Rhine, was awarded to Roric. And in 882 this territory was given to yet another Dane, Godfred (98). These grants, later duplicated in Normandy, were very effective in preventing major raids on Germany.

Another reason could be that Germany was still much poorer than the former Roman provinces farther west. There was simply less loot. And also, they were very close to Denmark. As a matter of fact, the Vikings were no match for a well-organized force. When Harald Bluetooth of Denmark ravaged Holstein upon the death of Otto I, his successor, Otto II, broke through Danevirke and pursued the Danes deep into Jutland. There, he built a fortress and imposed his terms of peace (Jones 1968, 129). Next time the Vikings knew better.

In England, raids began even earlier than on the continent. They were announced by attacks in Wessex in 789 (Sawyer 1971, 17–18), on Lindisfarne in 793, and on Jarrow in 794 (1). This indicates that raids across the sea were a continuation of the earlier Scandinavian expansion across the Atlantic islands and, until the mid-830s, were not linked with the Viking depredations on the continent.

From 835, England was subjected to annual attacks. (Annual raids on France started a year later.) Here, Viking success came earlier and with more lasting consequences than on the continent. In 842 the Vikings captured London and slaughtered many of its inhabitants (Jones 1968, 210). (Paris was plundered in 845.) London was attacked again in 871 (Arbman 1961, 60). In 851, the Vikings wintered in England for the first time (again as in France). The first Danegeld (tribute) was collected in Kent, in 865 (Wilson 1970, 71).

For about 30 years Viking operations in England and France show a remarkable parallelism. By 866, however, the Frankish heartland was enclosed by strongholds sufficient to offer reasonable protection, or at least to make the price of assault prohibitively expensive. As a result, the Vikings concentrated their efforts on an easier target—England. First, they captured York, which became the center of Scandinavian activity on the island. In 869, they occupied East Anglia. In 870, the Danes under Halfdan tried their luck against Wessex and took Reading (Jones 1968, 220). But, as its resistance stiffened, the Danes settled for a truce and turned their attention to Mercia, which collapsed in 874.

The second Danish attack on Wessex, in 878, under Guthrum, was also defeated. The extent of defeat is shown by Guthrum's baptism and the recovery of London by Alfred of Wessex (Alfred the Great). But neither Alfred nor Guthrum was strong enough to finish off his opponent. They were forced to divide England, the division later acknowledged by the treaty of 886 (Sawyer 1972, 151) and confirmed by the failure of a new Viking offensive in 892–96 (Jones 1968, 226).

The treaty of 886 had far-reaching consequences for England. Alfred, in effect, became king of all England outside Danelaw. Inadvertently, the Viking invasions promoted the unification of England.

They also brought Scandinavian settlers. In 876, Halfdan decided that the time was ripe to consolidate his conquests and distributed land in Northumbria among his followers. This was the beginning of the Danish settlement (of which there were two kinds: military and agricultural. We should note that, for the most part, neither one dispossessed the earlier inhabitants [221]). Between 876 and 880, Danes began to settle in Lincoln, York, Nottingham, Derby, and Cambridge. The settlement was strengthened when a new group of Scandinavian settlers arrived in 896 (Sawyer 1971, 173). It is interesting that Norwegians, always starved for land back home, started to farm in the earliest phase of the settlement. The Danes who had plenty joined them two generations later (Jones 1968, 212).

Scandinavian settlement was densest in Lincoln-, Nottingham-, Leicester-, and Yorkshire, where the transfer of land was carried out in accordance with Scandinavian practice (Sawyer 1971, 153, n.12). In the East Riding of Yorkshire, 40 percent of the place names recorded in Domesday Book are of Scandinavian origin; in the North Riding, 38 percent; in the West Riding only between 13 and 19 percent (Wilson 1970, 73–74). In the eleventh century, about half the population of Lincolnshire was of Scandinavian descent (Sawyer 1971, 8, n.18). Lincolnshire Assize Rolls for 1202 contain 215 Scandinavian names, compared to 194 English ones (156, n.19).

Ironically, Scandinavian (and English) names started to decrease after the Norman conquest. Liber Vitae of Thorney Abbey shows that between 1070 and 1200, Scandinavian names declined from 10 to 1, and English ones from 45 to 4, while the incidence of Continental (mostly French) names increased from 45 to 95 (Sawyer 1971, 156–57). Needless to say, names do not always reflect ethnic origin. One should also bear in mind that Scandinavian names are few in those areas of Danelaw that were recovered soon after 900. Even in the main areas, Scandinavian settlement was patchy. Its density depended on many factors. For example, archbishops who cooperated with the Vikings were in a better position to retain their estates and thus had fewer settlers. Also, different types of estates had different life spans in different parts of the country. They acquired and retained Scandinavian names at different rates (Sawyer 1982, 105–06). Finally, change in ownership (and thus in names) could also reflect the fragmentation of estates rather than settlement (103–04). With all these objections, it is still evident that Scandinavian influence in many areas of the Danelaw survived well into the twelfth and even thirteenth centuries.

Victories by Alfred the Great in the later 870s coincided with renewed internal strife in France. Once again, the Vikings chose an easier target. For a dozen years they ravaged France until new defeats redirected them back to England in 892. But this time they faced a united England and were decisively beaten in 896 (Sawyer 1982, 4).

A relatively short status quo was breached by an attack from Northumbria in 910 (Jones 1968, 223). The English counterattacked, and by 918, Alfred's successor, Edward the Elder, reconquered Danelaw south of the Humber (Arbman 1961, 63).

Starting in the 930s, there was a lull in attacks on England. At the same time, a general decay in the Danelaw led to an increasing involvement by Norwegians from Ireland in its internal affairs. In 940, Olaf of Dublin took over Leicester, Derby, Nottingham, and Lincoln. But Olaf soon died and his successor lost these areas to the English in 942. Of all their earlier conquests, the Vikings retained only York. But even York, by then a Hiberno-Norse polity, was rent by endless internecine squabbles that led to the collapse of the kingdom (Jones 1968, 238–40). In 954, Erik Blood-Axe, its last Scandinavian king, was deposed, and the kingdom attached to England (Sawyer 1971, 151).

This seemed to be the end of the Scandinavian involvement in England. But not quite. The relative lull in the raids on England came to an end in 980. The renewed assault was caused by the interruption in supplies of Kufic silver into Scandinavia (6) (of which more later). England was a wealthy country and could make up for the loss.

But Vikings now faced a united England, not a congery of seven kingdoms. By then mutual hatred was such that Danes were massacred (on king Ethelred's orders) on St. Brice's day (November 13) in 1002 (Arbman 1961, 65–66).

The massacre failed to eliminate the Danish threat. Danes conquered England—all of it—in 1016 and installed a Danish dynasty. But Danish hold on England once again proved ephemeral. In 1042 the old Anglo-Saxon dynasty was restored. The death of Harald Hardrada in 1066 at Stamford Bridge was a decisive blow to Scandinavian claims on England. But, inadvertently, Harald's failed attempt at reconquest helped his Norman cousins. In a sense, the Vikings ultimately won.

In the north Atlantic islands the Vikings had been preceded by Celts. According to the Irish monk Dicuil (*Liber de Mensuras Orbis Terrae,* written in 825), hermits and monks had been living in the northern isles for a hundred years before the arrival of the Vikings (Jones 1968, 269).

The monks settled on the Faeroes soon after 700 and abandoned them in about 800 because of the Viking depredations (Derry 1979, 31; Jones 1968, 270). Indeed, the Faeroes, located some 200 miles from the Shetlands and 240 miles from Iceland, were a convenient base for raids norths and south (Jones 1968, 272).

The Vikings reached the Shetlands in the first half of the ninth century (Arbman 1961, 55). Here, they encountered a small population that could be displaced and assimilated unlike densely settled England. That is why geographical nomenclature in the Shetlands and Orkneys is predominantly Scandinavian. (A few of the islands—Unst, Fetlar, Yell—kept pre-Scandinavian names [Stewart 1965, 248, in Sawyer 1982, 100].) The islanders also adopted a Scandinavian dialect ("Norn"), which survived until the eighteenth century when it was replaced by Anglo-Scots. In Outer Hebrides, Scandinavian speech gave way to Gaelic in the sixteenth century (Oftedal 1962, in Sawyer 1982).

The displacement of Celtic inhabitants was not uniform. On the island of Lewis, 99 of 126 village names are Scandinavian, and another 11 are partly Scandinavian (Oftedal 1954, 363–408), which suggests a high rate of displacement. In Inner Hebrides, the share of Scandinavian place names decreases from north to south, from 66 percent of pure Norse in the northeast Skye to only a few in Arran (Gordon 1963, 82; Oftedal 1953, 107).

In Iceland, four Roman coins from the late third century testify to the presence (or a visit?) of people from Scotland in about 300. The Caledonians didn't stay because the monks who reached Iceland in the 790s (Jones 1968, 272) found it empty. Their arrival coincided with the abandonment of the Faeroes. It is more than likely that the monks who came to Iceland were refugees from the Faeroes.

Thus, by the time Gardar the Swede and Naddod the Norwegian came upon Iceland in the 860s (Wilson 1970, 77), there were already Irish monks/hermits living there (Ari the Wise (1067–1148) (Arbman 1961, 106–107)). The fact that the monks could maintain their presence for about 70 years indicates the existence of permanent communications with the wider world, probably Ireland.

The "discovery" of Iceland was a spin-off from an earlier settlement on the Atlantic islands. Gardar was blown off course when he was heading to the Hebrides, while Naddod lived in the Faeroes and was on his way to Norway. That is where most settlers came from, but many arrived from the Scottish islands, Ireland, the Isle of Man, and the Faeroes (Derry 1979, 32). In fact, founders of many great Icelandic families came from the Hebrides (Arbman 1961, 55). Others originated in areas of Scandinavian settlement in the British Isles (Palsson 1952, 53; Dahl 1970, 60, in Sawyer 1982, 108); many of these brought their Irish wives and slaves with them (Sawyer 1972, 207, n.13). It has been estimated that about one-seventh of the original settlers had a Celtic connection, that is, they were either Vikings who came from Celtic areas conquered by the Norsemen or were their Irish wives or slaves (Jones 1968, 279).

But it is unlikely that the settlement in Iceland would have succeeded without a major influx from Norway. The main push factor was probably the consolidation of royal power by Harald Harfagri: after the battle at Hafrsfiord, those who could not or would not accept a strong royal authority left the country. And, significantly, the new country was a republic.

Permanent settlement started in or around 874 (Derry 1979, 32). The first planned expedition, by Floki Vilgerdharson, came from Rogaland in two ships (by way of the Shetlands and the Faroe). The first wave lasted till 930, by which time the population reached 20,000 (Derry 1979, 33). By the middle of the tenth century 50,000–60,000 people lived in Iceland (Wilson 1970, 78). And by the end of the eleventh, the total population was estimated at 80,000 (Steffensen 1968, in Sawyer 1982, 59).

Iceland, of course, served as a base for further exploration in the north Atlantic. Greenland was first sighted by Gunnbjorn Ulf-Krakason circa 930

(Wilson 1970, 80) and settled by Erik the Red in 985 or 986 (only 14 of the 25 ships reached their destination [Arbman 1961, 110]). The colony in Greenland, starting with some 450 people, grew into two major areas of settlement, with 190 farms in the east and 90 farms in the west. Their total population probably reached 3,000 (Derry 1979, 33). The colony supported 16 churches, a monastery, a nunnery, and a cathedral at Gardar (Jones 1968, 293, n.1).

Once they were established in Greenland, the Vikings could not fail to reach North America. Bjarni Herjolfsson was the first Norseman to sight the new continent in about 985 (Wilson 1970, 82). Some 15 years later, Erik's son Leif Eriksson reached Markland, a wooded coastal region somewhere in Labrador. Further south lay Vinland, where explorers found corn and even grapes. They found it enticing but were too few to overcome the hostility of local inhabitants. Fights over women among the Norse didn't help either. Three years later the camp was evacuated, and by 1020 voyages to America stopped (Jones 1968, 303). Still, Adam of Bremen knew about Vinland in the 1070s (Derry 1979, 34), and annals in Iceland mention Markland as late as 1347 (Wilson 1970, 85). If there were any doubts that the Vikings reached America, they were dispelled by the discovery of a Norse site at L'Anse aux Meadows in Newfoundland (Ingstad 1970; Schonback 1974 and 1976, in Sawyer 1982, 1).

There are two more regions, important for the history of Viking expansion, but peripheral for the purposes of this book: Ireland and Iberia. We'll sketch both in very broad outline.

Raids on Ireland started almost simultaneously with raids on England: the first one occurred at Lambay north of Dublin in 795. But here Norwegians came first (in England it was Danes) (Jones 1968, 208–10), probably because they reached Ireland from the north, via the Scottish islands. For example, the Vikings who raided Ulster in 811 and 837 came from the Hebrides (Sawyer 1982, 81). (It also worked the other way: in 839, 865–70 [Jones 1968, 208], 892, 900, and 904 [Arbman 1961, 54], they raided Scotland from Ireland.)

At the time, Ireland was a rural society where monasteries were the main repository of wealth. (In fact, the first towns were founded by the Vikings. Dublin, founded in 836, was the first one [Arbman 1961, 68].) That is why churches and monasteries became the prime target. The Annals of Ulster report 8 attacks on churches in the 820s, 25 in the 830s, and 10 in the 840s (Sawyer 1982, 84). The most famous was the capture of Armagh, a holy place and a leading ecclesiastical center in Ireland, by Norwegian Turgeis shortly before 840 (Jones 1968, 204–05). After that the church must have found other "storage facilities" for its valuables because the attacks decreased to 2 or less between 850 and 920 (Sawyer 1982, 84).

Viking penetration was facilitated by the political disunity on the island. However, there was no unity among the Vikings either. Danes fought Norwegians and each other. Dublin was attacked in 849, and in 866 all Viking strongholds on the northern coast were destroyed.

Soon, a new category of people was added to the Irish melting pot: the Gall-Gaedhill, or Foreign Gaels. They were people of mixed antecedents; many among them were heathen. By 850, their numbers increased and so did their importance (Jones 1968, 206).

Toward 900 the Vikings in Dublin were so weakened that the Irish managed to take the city in 902 (Sawyer 1982, 85). (Arbman puts the date at 901 [Arbman 1961, 70]). But the Vikings rallied and recaptured it in 914 (Jones 1968, 397); in the next three years they even reimposed their rule on the entire island and held it until 980 (Arbman 1961, 70).

Despite this temporary success, the Vikings gradually lost their preeminence in Irish affairs, if not by the mid-tenth century, as Sawyer believes (1982, 93), then definitely toward the end.

As in England, the wars against the Vikings played an important role in Ireland's unification. In 1002, Brian Boru united the island for the first time in its history. The Irish ascendancy was confirmed by the great Irish victory at Clontarf on Good Friday in 1014 (Arbman 1961, 72). (Although it was later reinterpreted as a fight against the Vikings [Sawyer 1982, 22], the battle was fought by Munster against Leinster. Both recruited Norsemen from all over Britain.) Despite their eclipse, Viking strongholds and enclaves survived until the arrival of the English in the 1160s and 1170s (Jones 1968, 397).

Among Viking foundations we must also mention the Isle of Man. It was first raided in 798 (Arbman 1961, 56), but the kingdom was not established until 1066 (by Godfred Crovan, who had fought at Stamford Bridge). Its kings acknowledged Norwegian suzerainty although Norwegian kings had little real authority there. At its height, its rule spread as far as the Hebrides. The kingdom was transferred to Scotland by the treaty of Perth in 1266 (Sawyer 1982, 111–12), at the time of the final eclipse of the Viking world: Greenland surrendered its independence to Norway in 1261 (Jones 1968, 293), as did Iceland in 1262–64 (Wilson 1970, 79). Only the Orkneys and Shetlands remained. They were ceded to Scotland in 1472 (Sawyer 1971, 217).

In Iberia, the Vikings appeared at the same time as they appeared in England and Ireland. In 795 they fought against the Moors with Alphonso II, and in

799 they raided the coast of Aquitaine nearby. There are some disputes as to the veracity of the sources on which accounts of these raids are based.

The first attack that is beyond dispute is the 844 assault on Seville (Arbman 1961, 85). (Jones dates it at 845 [Jones 1968, 214].) The assailants took the city, but the citadel held out. Soon, the Moors rallied and counter-attacked. Many Vikings were captured and hanged. Before long, the tables were turned: the Vikings were besieged on their island base at the mouth of the Guadalquivir and had to release prisoners in exchange for food. The next year Abd-al-Rahman II sent an embassy to the king of the "Majus," but we don't know whether it was Denmark or Norway, or whether the embassy succeeded (214–15).

In 859 they raided Algeciras, harried the coast of North Africa, where they captured "blue" and "black" men; then spent the winter months in Ca-margue, raiding up the Rhône to Nîmes, Arles, and Valence.

The following year they attacked Pisa, sacked a small fishing port at the mouth of the Tiber that they mistook for Rome, and, by some accounts, showed up in Alexandria.

In 861 they once again entered the Mediterranean but lost 40 of 62 ships in a battle with the Saracens. They did not return—evidently, they found their match—but they continued to raid Iberia's northern coast, where even Santiago de Compostela did not escape them (Arbman 1961, 85–87; Jones 1968, 216–18). But compared to so many other areas, Iberia and the Mediterranean had escaped the Viking scourge.

Trade and the desire for profit was probably the main driving force of Scandinavian expansion during the Viking period. The eighth century witnessed a great upsurge in trade in both directions.

Toward the end of the century, Muslim merchants penetrated far up the Volga in search of northern products. Scandinavian traders met them half way. This, incidentally, offers a clue as to why earlier Scandinavian ventures in the seventh century B.C. came to naught: there were no trading partners coming from the south. Scandinavians reached the mouth of the Kama, where it joins the Volga, and stopped there, probably because Persian and Assyrian merchants did not venture so far north at that time. And the Scandinavians did not go far enough south.

The eighth century also witnessed an increase in imports from Europe: glass, pottery, millstones, coins (Sawyer 1982, 72–73). As we know, trade with the West had long antecedents, going back to pre-Roman times. The collapse of the Roman Empire reduced the grade flow but did not bring it to a complete halt. It started to revive in the seventh and eighth centuries with the stabilization of Frankish power. Frisia continued to be the lynchpin of this trade route (2), with Dorestad developing into the main entrepot of a far-flung trade network encompassing Rhineland, England, the Frankish domain, and Scandinavia (70).

With trade going in both directions, Scandinavia found itself at the center of the east-west trade. Hedeby, at the base of the Jutland peninsula, was in a perfect location and quickly turned into the largest and best known of Scandinavian markets. It got a major boost in 808 when Godfred forcibly transferred merchants from Reric to Sliastorp, close to Hedeby (Sawyer 1971, 186). The transfer eliminated a major competitor and established Hedeby as the hub of the east-west trade. (It remained so until its destruction by Harald Sigurdson of Norway in 1050 [Davidson 1976, 68].) The transfer also shows that Godfred knew the layout of trade routes and understood their importance.

Another major center, Birka, developed in Sweden, on an island in Lake Mälär. It appeared some time between 780 and 830 (Sawyer 1972, 184; Davidson 1976, 70) and flourished until 960–70, that is, until the destruction of Khazaria by Sviatoslav, which brought trade along the Volga to a standstill. (Another possible reason is the rise of the Scandinavian land mass, which lowered the sea level and made southern approaches to Birka impassible.) Its inhabitants abandoned Birka and probably moved to Sigtuna, further north (Davidson 1970, 70).

Smaller trade centers sprang up in Norway and southern Baltic. Kaupang, on the west shore of the Oslo fjord, flourished from the ninth until the early tenth century, when the lowering of the sea level in the channel made it unreachable (71). Other markets were located at Truso (today's Elbląg, in northeast Poland) and the island of Gotland, which eventually became a major Hansa hub during the Middle Ages.

Aldeigjuborg (Staraia Ladoga) was the eastern terminus of Scandinavian trade posts in the Baltic and, at the same time, a gateway to the east. It was there that the earliest dirham hoard was found. It consisted of coins minted between 749 and 787. Early hoards found in "Russia" indicate Iranian provenance, the coins having been taken by Muslim merchants to Khazar markets on the Volga (Sawyer 1982, 120).

The discovery of large silver deposits in today's Afghanistan at the end of the ninth century allowed the Samanid rulers to start minting silver coins on as large a scale. These coins, minted at Bukhara, Samarkand, and elsewhere from 893, reached "Russia" by about 910 (Sawyer 1982, 120). Soon the Samanid silver appeared in Bulghar, where Varangians traded with Muslims (unlike the Khazars, the Bulghars did not encourage through-traffic [126]) and then in Scandinavia.

The inflow of dirhams to Scandinavia increased after 850, but was still on a relatively small scale (123–24). It stopped completely after 965 but resumed after 983 (Sawyer 1982, 124). And when it did, it came from a different region, from Syria and Mesopotamia. This silver reached Scandinavia via Poland, not Russia. But this silver also dried up; the last coins found in Norway and Denmark date from 1012–13 (Sawyer 1971, 116).

With very little silver coming from the east, Scandinavians turned west. Almost all of the 50,000 English coins found in Scandinavia date from 980–1051 (Sawyer 1982, 127) even though the Vikings had been "at work" in western Europe since at least 800.

Most of these coins were extorted: in 991, for example, 93 ships raided southeast England and extorted 10,000 pounds worth of silver. Another fleet, in 994, was paid 16,000 pounds (145). As the victims recruited Vikings to fight against other Vikings, a veritable protection racket developed. In 1012, Thorkell the Tall was paid 48,000 pounds for protecting London (146). With the imposition of Danish rule in 1016, extortion turned into tribute. But even the Anglo-Saxon dynasty that regained power in 1042 retained a Viking fleet. It was disbanded only in 1051 by Edward the Confessor. With this, the flow of English silver to Scandinavia came to a halt (147). (For comparison, Charles the Bald paid 7,000 pounds in 845 to induce Vikings to leave the Seine valley; the total Frankish payments for the period amounted to 685 pounds in gold and 43,000 pounds in silver [Sawyer 1971, 99].)

Altogether, in the ninth and tenth centuries, some 62,000 Kufic (Islamic), 70,000 German, and 40,000 English coins reached Scandinavia (Sawyer 1972, 88). (In Sawyer 1982, 127, the author mentions 50,000 English coins, but that number probably includes those from the eleventh century as well.) But, like their Kufic counterparts, relatively few English coins show up in hoards found in Norway (3,000 coins) or Denmark (5,300), compared to 30,000 English coins in Sweden (Wilson 1970, 101–102). The "Swedes," unlike their "Danish" and "Norwegian" cousins, did not spend their money on the spot.

The pattern is very clear in Gotland: before 950, hoards were almost exclusively Kufic. Those from 990–1020 are 40 percent German and 10 percent English, and in the next 30 years, the proportion of Kufic coins declined to 5 percent while the share of German ones increased to 56 percent and English to 30 percent (Sawyer 1971, 117).

One of the most fascinating aspects of the Viking expansion was the great diversity of conditions that they encountered. The Vikings came into contact with all three types of society: the high civilizations of Europe, Byzantium, and the Middle East; the nomads (Khazars and Pechenegs); and "forest" tribes, such as the Slavs, Balts, and Finns of eastern Europe and even America. In their peregrinations they encountered densely settled areas, as well as uninhabited territories, rich lands, poor lands, northern and southern climes, and so on. The diversity of conditions and systems that they encountered makes them a veritable laboratory of migratory possibilities and interactions.

Their settlement patterns can be subdivided into several categories: Where they came across uninhabited land (Iceland, Greenland, the Faeroes) or where the population was small and vulnerable (Shetlands and Hebrides), the Vikings settled the land recreating their distinct type of civilization.

In areas inhabited by other "forest" tribes, the Vikings created new states where they either evolved into an elite that gradually assimilated (Rus') or created small enclaves that competed against "native" polities and also gradually assimilated, as in Ireland.

Where stronger entities were encountered (England, France, the Holy Roman Empire), the Vikings either carved themselves a good chunk of real estate (Danelaw) or acquired a province that gave them a new base (Normandy).

When the enemy proved invincible, as was the case with Byzantium, the Vikings hired themselves as soldiers of fortune, usually ending up in elite units that evolved into a praetorian guard. Only in the Muslim world, whether in Iberia or around the Caspian, was the rejection complete and mutual.

In their limited encounters with the nomads, Vikings proved to be no exception: they could destroy sedentarized polities like that of the Khazars, but were powerless against "true" nomads like the Pechenegs. Of course, in their encounters with both, the Vikings were no longer the Vikings but a polity based on agriculture whose elite retained some tradition of long-distance adventure and conquest.

If anything, the Vikings were the nomads of the sea. If "pure" Vikings had encountered "pure" nomads, it probably would have turned out to be a no-contest: nomads did not have a concentration of wealth that would have allowed the Vikings opportunities for harvesting it, as they did in cities in western Europe or monasteries in pre-urban Ireland. And nomads' mobility would have precluded the imposition of taxes, as was possible in the Dnieper valley. For their part, the Vikings would have been invulnerable to nomads. These two elements could meet but could not mix.

The pattern of Scandinavian penetration in eastern Europe during the Bronze Age strikingly resembles later Scandinavian ventures of the Viking Age. It is unlikely that the earlier activity had established patterns that reappeared 1,500 years later. The similarities, despite enormous differences in political, economic, and social conditions, both in Scandinavia and eastern Europe, in which migratory movements were played out, imply the presence of fundamental factors. The question is: what were they?

One of the constants, undoubtedly, was trade. At a surprisingly early age, it created large networks that linked far-flung countries. Scandinavia of

1000 B.C. is a good example: it was, if one follows Sulimirski, a linchpin of two vast trade networks, one linking it to Britain, the other to Ukraine. Trade facilitated the creation of industry and wealth, which attracted neighbors' beady eyes. But it was not just neighbors. Trade spread knowledge of distant places far and wide. It prepared grounds for raids and/or migration. In short, trade was a catalyst.

But not everyone who traded raided and migrated. In that respect, the Vikings were quite exceptional. Why did they stubbornly venture overseas?

Traditionally, two types of explanation have been offered: economic, based on the assessment of the push/pull factors, and socio-psychological. (We should note that they are not mutually exclusive.)

The economic explanations usually point to overpopulation caused by polygamy among chieftains. According to Adam of Bremen, every wealthy Swede had two or three wives; the rich and the high-born set themselves no limit (Jones 1968, 196–97). Erik Blood-Axe, for example, had eight sons, his father Harald at least nine (198). And they all had to make a living.

Feeding a rapidly expanding population in a preindustrial society presented a problem because the region was poor in agricultural land. Even today, all Scandinavian countries, except Denmark, have a shortage of arable land. It amounts to only 9 percent in Finland, 8 percent in Sweden, 2.8 percent in Norway, and 1 percent in Iceland (Derry 1979, 2, n.1), not to mention a short growing season. Thus, many Scandinavians probably needed land. Archeology seems to confirm that: "In the eastern parts of Norway, the early Viking period is marked by a significant growth of the settled area, but in the west, where the reserves of exploitable land were more limited, the path across the sea to new and often underpopulated land must have seemed attractive" (Sawyer 1971, 208).

And yet, this cannot be the whole story. For one thing, Danes were as avid raiders as other Scandinavians even though there was no shortage of arable land in Denmark. All it did was to delay Danish settlement by a generation or two. (It is interesting that in Britain, Norwegians chose poorer agricultural areas because they resembled the habitat they were familiar with. For the same reason, Danes settled in fertile lowland regions. In other words, people who needed land the most chose the least promising areas while those who needed it least chose the best. So much for economic rationale!)

Finally, fast proliferation among Scandinavian elites, especially the number of adult sons, may explain the interminable feuds within early Scandinavian society and raids overseas, since losers sought their fortunes elsewhere. But even the most prolific chiefs could not create a wide demographic base for a permanent settlement and expansion overseas. If early Scandinavian societies suffered from relative overpopulation, they were still numerically insignificant when compared with many other populations.

Many scholars look for other explanations. Derry, for example, believed that there was no scarcity of land, except in some areas of western Norway. Rather, it was their passion for adventure and the pursuit of wealth and glory, as attested by the sagas, that sent Scandinavian warriors all over the world (Derry 1979, 17). "To go viking was a trade or profession, a means to the good life, or at least to a living. Its three main elements, trade, piracy, and land-taking, often closely blended, had been northern activities long before the Viking Age, and would long outlast it" (Jones 1968, 3). Once the process got started, it had a momentum of its own (200).

Ultimately, it was the heroic ideal of a successful warrior and ambition, the desire for wealth and glory in a society that highly valued both, that sent generations of northerners in all directions.

They had access to virtually inexhaustible supplies of furs and slaves, two commodities highly prized by Europeans and Muslims, but did not disdain any saleable commodity: grain, fish, timber, hides, salt, wine, glass, glue, horses and cattle, white bears and falcons, walrus ivory and seal oil, honey, wax, malt, silks and woollens, amber and hazel nuts, soapstone dishes and basalt millstones, wrought weapons, ornaments, and silver (3). The Vikings were courageous, flexible, and entrepreneurial—natural capitalists and captains of industry long before the advent of capitalism.

It seems that both sets of explanation are valid, although not to the same degree.

The continuity of periodic expansion of Scandinavian populations across the sea points to underlying factors among which trade and relative over-population are probably the most fundamental ones. But social factors, such as the existence of warrior elites, and competition for wealth and glory, both valuable social commodities, also played an important role. Ultimately, one cannot agree with Sir Thomas Kendrick that "[it is] impossible to explain in final and satisfactory terms the huge outpouring of the northern peoples that is known as the Viking expansion. . . . It may well be that overpopulation, lack of land, and political grievances were the most urgent motives, yet . . . it must be conceded that neither severally nor together do they seem sufficient to explain migrations so considerable and so long-sustained" (Kendrick 1930, in Sawyer 1971, 202). We do know what the push factors were. It is assigning each one an appropriate weight that is next to impossible.

One more aspect of the Viking expansion is worth mentioning: its global character. The Vikings knew where the opportunities lay and how to exploit them. Their raids on France and England developed in close conjunction with each other. The parallels are evident: both ventures turned into annual expeditions within one year of each other, Paris and London were attacked within two years, and so on. Thus, it is not surprising that the erection of defensive fortifications in France, which increased costs of raiding, redirected the Vikings toward England, just as the English success under Alfred the Great sent them back to France.

The close interconnection between raids east and west is even more astonishing. Access to Kufic silver made western Europe less attractive, hence the lull of 930–980. Conversely, when supplies of Kufic silver dried up after 965, the Vikings "returned" to the west, particularly England, in what came to be known as the second Viking age.

We should not overlook the principle of reciprocity in the development of Viking expansionism. It was their encounter with Muslim traders in the eighth century that determined their success in establishing contacts with the Middle East. Conversely, the earlier Viking attempt in the eighth and seventh centuries B.C. came to naught because the Scandinavians reached the confluence of the Kama and the Volga and came to a halt, probably unaware that the Volga would lead them to Persia and Assyria.

Several centuries of trade with the Romans conditioned them to trade with the West. This trade did not come to a halt with the collapse of the Roman Empire, although it continued at a much reduced volume. Germanic migrations may have enhanced it: excavations at Sutton Hoo prove beyond any doubt that there were close ties between East Anglia and the Svears in the sixth century. Yet, the first ventures overseas were directed east, not west. Why?

The likeliest explanation is that the massive outflow of Germanic tribes from today's Denmark and Schleswig to England denuded these areas for a few hundred years. Conversely, in the eighth century, a strong "Swedish" kingdom centered on Uppland was ready for expansion overseas. This kingdom faced east, to Gotland and across the Baltic. The Ynglinga Saga describes the first pre-Viking raids into Estonia (Jones 1968, 241). Eventually, these "eastern" Vikings would reach the rivers of the Russian plain and on, via the Dnieper and the Volga, to the Black and the Caspian Sea.

Finally, there are factors that are often underplayed in accounts of Scandinavian expansion.

One is perfecting the art of making masts and sails that enable Scandinavians to venture into the open sea. Could this account for the simultaneity of their appearance everywhere in the west?

Another one is the role of climate and their inability to deal with climatic change. Thus, their success in settling northern islands was partly determined by the relatively high temperatures of the "Little Climatic Optimum" in 1000–1200 (Dolukhanov 1996, 146). But after 1200 the climate grew colder and by the mid-fifteenth century it was very cold indeed (Jones 1968, 307). Ice made northern sea routes more dangerous. At the same time, Northerners faced economic ruin as furs from Russia and cloth from England and the Low Countries successfully competed against Greenland's woolens while walrus tusks could not compete with elephant tusks (308). Cut off from Europe, economically enfeebled, and culturally inflexible, the descendants of the Vikings could not compete against the Inuit. By about 1340 they reached the Western Settlement and a little later took it over (308). The Middle Settlement held on till about 1380 (Jones 1968, 309). The Eastern Settlement survived till about 1500. The colonies in Greenland were doomed due to the isolation from Europe, neglect by Norway, lack of trade and new blood, worsening climatic conditions, and encroaching Inuit (311).

The mode of Scandinavian expansion was not a constant. In the early phase, most Vikings wanted to establish a base in the west from where they could raid and plunder. A sizable minority wanted land. Relatively few of these adventurers returned home. In the second phase, after the Kufic silver had dried up, most warriors accumulated wealth and returned home (Sawyer 1982, 215).

Scandinavian settlers in the northern isles could not count on much help from the mother country. The Black Death arrived in Norway in 1349 and killed one-third of the population. And Hansa had a stranglehold on its trade.

Despite four centuries of frenetic activity, east and west, north and south, the Vikings left relatively few traces. Even in England, where they once ruled and settled half the country, only crosses, place names, and a few hundred loan words remind one of their presence. Most Danes who settled in England at the end of the ninth century were a comparatively small group of warriors who had made themselves rich by plunder and hoped to continue (Sawyer 1971, 209). One encounters a similar lack of artifacts in the east. When the Vikings needed a house, they either took one over or hired local labor, who built in the local tradition. The Vikings were practical, traveled light, adapted easily. They took concubines and intermarried. As they were few in numbers, they could not implant their way of life. The first generation might leave clear material evidence in their graves, but two or three generations down the road they would be thoroughly assimilated (Davidson 1976, 79).

Once Scandinavia was incorporated into the European system, sustained raiding became impossible. As there were no new lands to conquer (and Finland, evidently, held no attraction until its conquest by Sweden in the thirteenth century), the younger sons of the aristocracy had to turn to farming or even sell their labor. The once-esteemed profession of piracy offered few openings and even fewer opportunities. And at home, the seizure of cattle, food, or booty was banned (Jones 1968, 392).

By the end of the eleventh century, the Vikings had become an anachronism. After four centuries of expansion, the Scandinavian peoples were still confined, except for the addition of Iceland and Faeroes, to their original habitat. Jones enumerates the following reasons: 1) constant internecine struggles; 2) inability to impose their political, social, and cultural systems; 3) adversaries who were in the long run wealthier and stronger; and 4) lack of manpower (393).

In England, the death of Harald Hardrada in 1066 is taken to mark the end of the Viking Age, but a better end is the failure of the Danish invasion planned by St. Cnut in 1085 (Sawyer 1982, 217). Or maybe it is the death of Norwegian king Magnus, who was killed in Ulster in 1102. In any case, the Viking Age was "killed" by centralization, urbanization, stratification, and the conversion to Christianity (6).

Before their integration into the European state system (approximately in the tenth century), the forest tribes of eastern Europe had to deal with three kinds of adversary: developed civilizations represented by empires and states, nomads, and other forest tribes.

Among these three, areas of high civilization were the most attractive (for nomads as well) for the simple reason that they accumulated more wealth, and the wealth was easier to skim because it was concentrated in urban centers. (Early Ireland is an example of a pre-urban civilization in which wealth was deposited in monasteries. In this it was not unique: temples and various religious institutions were repositories of wealth in many civilizations, e.g., ancient Egypt and Mesoamerica, among many others.)

The forest tribes tried to either appropriate this wealth or settle in these areas, often both. Those tribes that could not fight their way in or gain entrance through negotiation gravitated toward the (fortified) frontier that became a zone of ethnic and cultural intermixing. Eventually, this zone developed into a hybrid civilization distinct from areas of high civilization further "inland" or the forest tribes far from the zone of contact.

Proximity to developed civilization led to a differentiation among the forest tribes. As a rule, the closer they were to the frontier with high civilization, the wealthier they were, the more complex their political and economic structures. The "country bumpkin" cousins from far afield, living in the mountains or dense forests, and less favored geographically, cast a covetous glance at their richer cousins at the zone of contact.

Often, the tribes at the frontier played the role of the middleman, mostly in two spheres, economic and cultural, transmitting their version of high culture through trade.

Trade between areas of high civilization and forest tribes developed early and reached far, so that even distant Scandinavia was well acquainted with Roman merchandise. Trade spread knowledge about distant lands and their fabulous wealth. It made people in the most distant, god-forsaken hamlet aware of the possibility of loot and plunder. In a sense, trade facilitated raiding and invasions.

Culturally, the contact was an instrument of decomposition of tribal society. This was especially so after the adoption of Christianity. The polytheism of the advanced civilizations of Antiquity was on a par with the polytheism of the forest tribes. For all the external dissimilarities, its function was not radically different. Any god of thunder could be translated into Zeus. Monotheism made such translation impossible. It turned the imposition of Christianity into a cultural divide, producing strong reactions in virtually every society, from Thervingi to Scandinavians in Rus' (and, as we will see, nomads, such as Bulghars).

Ultimately, all forms of economic and cultural contact promoted by trade and the hybridization at the frontier led to the decomposition of the tribal society in areas adjacent to the frontier and the integration of these regions into areas of advanced civilization. The integration could be achieved either through occupation and incorporation into the empire (Gaul, Slavs of east Germany) or by creation of new states (Galatia, Rus', Iceland) and/or marches (Poland, Bohemia, Normandy, although, strictly speaking, none of these was a march akin to Brandenburg) that could either be later incorporated/reabsorbed into the empire/state (Galatia, Normandy, Iceland) or integrated into the European state system (Poland, Bohemia).

If high civilization attracted, nomads repelled. They were dangerous, unpredictable, and, to the forest tribes, invincible. Inadvertently, nomads played a key role in spreading the forest tribes. This could be achieved in two ways: nomads either destroyed the polities that lay in their path, sending thousands of refugees to flight (Huns and Goths), or imposed their supremacy by turning forest tribes into (un)willing allies and, inadvertently, launching massive migrations (Avars and Slavs). Either way, they played a creative/destructive role that helped destroy the Roman Empire and changed the ethnic composition of vast areas.

Other forest tribes could also play a creative/destructive role vis-à-vis other forest tribes (ancient Germans and Celts, medieval Germans and Slavs). This duality is characteristic of the interaction between high civilizations, forest tribes, and nomads that found expression in migration.

Two major factors seem to have determined migratory patterns of the forest tribes: population pressures and the attraction of advanced civilizations. The fact that both groups expanded in all directions and not just toward developed civilization, suggests that there were internal reasons for out-migration. The most plausible reason is relative overpopulation, although the degree is hard to ascertain. Even in Scandinavia only parts of west Norway experienced genuine overpopulation. It is even harder to prove for Celts, Germans, and Slavs, whose habitat was much more generous.

Social factors, like polygamy, are unlikely to have played a significant role since it was limited to the elites. But the fame and example of successful warriors, especially in Scandinavia, and the desire to "strike it rich" in the fabulous South—the image of Rome, and later Constantinople, as an El Dorado—were certainly powerful enough to attract swarms of young warriors and later mass migration.

One of the most interesting aspects of forest tribe migrations was the "portability" of their states (actually, they were repeatedly recreated). This feature particularly applied to early Germans. The Goths, for example, created a primitive early state in south Baltic, and recreated it in the Pontic steppes, then again in Gaul, and again in Iberia (Visigoths) and Italy (Ostrogoths).

If areas of high civilization attracted like a magnet, geography played an important role. This is particularly true of the river systems, since rivers served as convenient thoroughfares for penetration. This was true for Celts (down the Rhône and the Danube), Slavs, and Scandinavians, although somewhat less so for Germans.

Another determinant was the geopolitical situation: when Rome blocked the Celts from the south, there was a reflux north, soon blocked by Germans; when the Balkans and the West were closed to Slavs, they could go only north.

The stage of imperial trajectory was also an important factor: in the West, Germans "contacted" Rome at the time of its still aggressive expansion, hence a strong counteroffensive. By the time Goths reached the northern Black Sea littoral, Rome had become a status quo power, hence no offensive as in Germany.

The global, or at least continental, scale of early migrations is their outstanding feature. All forest tribes migrated across the European continent.

Economic considerations were implicit in the attraction of the areas of high civilization. This is particularly clear in the case of Scandinavians: Kufic silver redirected them east; when the flow stopped, they returned to the west. But sometimes, economy did not work: Norwegians who experienced a shortage of arable land settled on poor soils in England because they were familiar with this kind of soil, while the Danes, who had enough fertile land, chose the good land.

Finally, we should not leave out the socio-psychological aspect: the ideal of a heroic warrior who comes home with gold and glory—a decisive factor in promoting Scandinavian expansion.

Perhaps, the most outstanding feature of "forest" migrations was their continuity. This is particularly true of Germanic and Scandinavian movements. The continuity manifested itself in two ways: first, already the initial Germanic invasion of western Europe at the end of the second century B.C.

shows basic traits of subsequent Germanic migrations: continental scope (from Jutland to Bohemia to the upper Danube to Gaul to Spain back to Gaul, then Italy); mass movement; the ability to stay together for long periods of time (good organization); warriors' being followed by families. And second, Scandinavians twice ventured into eastern Europe while ancient Germans kept migrating throughout their entire history, and, if we add medieval migrations and emigration overseas in the last three centuries, they have never stopped. Clearly, there must be some deep fundamental reasons.

PART III

Nomadic Migrations
Nomads and Their Origins

In this book, the term "nomad" refers only to "predatory pastoralists." The reason? Only this category was engaged in a more or less constant interaction with areas of high civilization and the forest tribes in the Eurasian steppe and adjacent areas. Among mobile groups only they fit within the framework of this book.

Anatoly Khazanov defines pastoral nomadism as "a distinct form of food-producing economy in which extensive mobile pastoralism is the predominant activity, and in which the majority of the population is drawn into periodic pastoral migrations" (Khazanov 1994, 17). In these societies (1) pastoralism is the main form of economic activity; (2) herds graze free-range without stables, year-round; (3) seasonal mobility is contained within a specific grazing territory (this particular characteristic does not apply to nomads of Sahara); (4) the entire population is mobile; and (5) production is geared to subsistence (16).

In principle, pastoralism does not preclude agriculture, and some scholars even include populations for whom herding is secondary. They call these populations "semi-sedentary" (Forde 1963, 404, in Khazanov 1994, 21), distinguishing them from semi-nomadic (for whom herding is primary). The term "herdsman husbandry" is used when only a part, often significant, of the population is engaged in cattle breeding. For the purposes of this book such distinctions are not very important, although we should keep in mind that pastoralism is a continuum.

Nomadism lies at one end of this continuum. It implies no or little dependence on agriculture and a predatory stance vis-à-vis sedentary neighbors.

This is what distinguishes a nomad from a herder. If the herder is a pastoralist who lives off his flocks, a nomad is a predatory pastoralist.

Nomadism leaves little scope for specialization and the development of complex economy (Khazanov 1994, 70). Population size is limited by the carrying capacity of the pastures in the least productive period of the year (Barth 1959–60, 8, in Khazanov 1994, 70–71). As a mode of production, it is very conservative and prone to stagnation. According to some calculations, the number of livestock per person among the Mongols in 1918 was lower than that for the Hsiung-nu two thousand years earlier, 19 and 17.8, respectively (Egami 1956; Taskin 1968a, 41ff, in Khazanov 1994, 71).

In terms of distance, pastoral migrations range from as little as 20–30 kilometers among some Turkmen (Orazov 1975, 216–17), to 150 kilometers among the Mongols of Inner Mongolia (Lattimore 1967, 73, n.21), to 600 kilometers in the Gobi desert of Outer Mongolia (Graivoronsky 1979, 49), and up to 1,000–1,500 kilometers among some Kazaks (Narody Srednei Azii 1963, 354) (all in Khazanov 1994, 52). The greater the distances covered in annual transhumance, the easier it was to "slide" into large-scale migrations.

Nomadism originated in areas where cattle breeding offered comparative advantages over agriculture. In Antiquity, harvests in the Crimea, one of the most fertile areas in the Eurasian steppe, yielded only 30-fold, compared with Mesopotamia's three hundred-fold (Strabo VII.4.6, in Khazanov 1994, 69). Even nowadays, in many areas where pastoralism predominates, it is less labor intensive and two and a half times more profitable than cotton growing (Fedorovich 1973, 218, in Khazanov 1994, 69).

Since man cannot live by meat alone, nomads have to get grain somehow. They can either trade or raid, but in either case they are dependent on the agriculturalist. In a sense, they are parasitic. That is why Kroeber said that nomadism is not a culture but a half-culture or part-culture, which depends on sedentary neighbors (Kroeber 1948, 278).

There were several factors that favored the transition to nomadism. Climate was probably one of them. It turned increasingly arid from the third millennium B.C. A short wet period in the middle of the second millennium B.C. was followed by another dry spell in 1200–500 B.C. Almost all paleoclimatologists accept that the second millennium B.C. was characterized by a dry climate that was at its driest at 1000 B.C. (Riabtseva 1970, 117; Sinitsyn 1967, 150; Butzer and Twidale 1966, 135; and others). Their data are confirmed by archeology (Vinogradov and Mamedov 1975, 251; Piperino and Tosi 1975, 186) (both in Khazanov 1994, 95).

Opinions regarding the role of climate differ. One school believes that during increased aridity, the steppe and semidesert could be used more effectively as pasture for livestock (Basilov 5, in Basilov 1989). Another holds that the gradual change from the dry sub-boreal of the earlier period to the damp sub-Atlantic turned the steppe into rich grasslands that could provide pasturage for larger herds (Sulimirski 1970, 337). This factor, and the increased use of the horse, made the development of migratory steppe pastoralism possible.

Although important, the dry climate was probably the final stimulus. The transition to full nomadism coincided with the emergence of sedentary states in the Mediterranean, the Black Sea, and Middle Asia. To the nomads, these states, with their great accumulation of wealth, were an enticing target. They greatly contributed to the appearance of predatory nomadism.

The transition itself was a gradual process that took several thousand years. In Khazanov's view, it was made possible by the emergence of two modes of production during the Neolithic revolution—cultivation and animal husbandry. Only sedentary groups with vegetable food surpluses could domesticate animals (Khazanov 1994, 89).

The domestication of cattle and even horses started very early, in the fifth and fourth millennia B.C. in the southern part of eastern Europe (Tsalkin 1970, 265, in Khazanov 1994, 91) and no later than the fourth millennium B.C. in south Russia (Khazanov 1994, 91). By 3000 B.C., pastoralism was predominant between the Volga and the Urals (Zbenovich 1974, 112–14; Merpert 1974, 102–12, in Khazanov 1994, 91). But these early pastoralists were no nomads (91).

The mobility of early pastoralists facilitated their migrations in the fourth, third, and second millennia B.C. (93). The reasons were probably the same as in later migrations: population increase, exhaustion of pastures, the attraction of more advanced agricultural cultures and civilizations. But these early migrations were gradual and proceeded slowly, especially when compared to later ones (Scythians or Mongols) (94).

According to Khazanov, the horse was saddled no later than the first half of the second millennium B.C., and the wheeled draft transport was borrowed from the Near East still earlier (Khazanov 119, in Weissleder 1978). These and other technological preconditions for pastoral nomadism appeared in the European and Kazak steppes by the middle of the second millennium B.C. But the final transformation occurred only after 1000 B.C., when agricultural settlements were abandoned, and the authors of Antiquity started calling steppe people "drinkers of milk" and "milkers of mares." In other words, the transition was not completed for about five hundred years. Explanations can be sought either in natural (Khazanov) or cultural (Lattimore) stimuli, but most are a matter of conjecture.

Nomadization is not a one-way street. It could be—and was—reversed many times. But since sedentarization affected mostly people who had come from the steppe, in areas that were located in a "bad" neighborhood, it was often interrupted. Thus, sedentarization of the Scythians was cut short by the Sarmatians. The Huns and the Avars also began to sedentarize, and this may have contributed to their destruction. The Khazars settled down between the eighth and tenth centuries and were defeated as a sedentary power by the Rus. Hungarians and Bulghars sedentarized as well, but were integrated into the system of European states. In this case, sedentarization was the key to success, although both polities paid the price when confronted by Mongols and Turks.

Some scholars (Burnham 1979 and Irons 1979, in Barfield 1989, 7, nn.9 and 10) argue that high mobility and low population densities slowed down or even prevented the development of hierarchies in nomadic societies. These factors rendered the appearance of state among nomadic pastoralists difficult: it developed when they were forced to deal with sedentary states on a continual basis (Barfield 1989, 7). In inner Asia, the impetus for nomadic state formation was provided by the interaction with China.

Structurally, nomadic states display an interesting duality. In their internal structure, they were federal, and their mode of operation was consultative. Externally, however, they acted as autocratic "imperial confederacies" (8).

Administratively, they had a three-level hierarchy: at the top was the emperor and his court; the middle level was composed of imperial governors who provided the link between the emperor and the tribes within the empire; and at the tribal level, local leaders were retained and incorporated in the overall structure. Thus, the tribal structure was intact. And when the system collapsed, local tribal leaders regained their autonomy, and the steppe reverted to anarchy (8). Tribes and clans were the building blocks of nomadic society. Unless their members had been physically annihilated, they were indestructible. The structure accounted for the inherent instability of nomadic confederations and the ease with which they were destroyed and reconstituted. But it also made them (the confederations) flexible and, without external interference, ineradicable.

The period of 2000 to 1400/1300 B.C. in eastern Europe saw the expansion of the central European Corded Ware/Battle Ax people, as well as the Globular Amphorae culture (Sulimirski 1970, 244). The Corded Ware culture first expanded in Lower Saxony (the Single-grave culture) during 2200–2100 B.C. (154), but later the main direction of expansion was east. In today's Poland, it contributed important constitutive elements to the Trzciniec and, further east, the Komarów cultures. In general, until about 1200 B.C., large areas of eastern Europe were taken over by cultures of central European origin (148–49, 240).

Around the thirteenth century B.C., the easterly direction was reversed.

The Minusinsk valley on the Yenisey River, in west Siberia, had long been a boundary between Europoid and Mongoloid populations. In the thirteenth century B.C., the (Mongoloid) people of a local branch of the Karasuk culture overwhelmed the (Europoid) people of a local branch of the Andronovo culture.

The Karasuk originated somewhere in the eastern foothills of the Tien-Shan mountains in northwest China (Chlenova 1964, in Sulimirski 1970, 308, n.69). They shared numerous traits with the people of Ferghana and Pamir and maintained close relations with Baikal, Mongolia, and northern China (307). Their economy was based on animal husbandry and showed signs of pastoralism, including seasonal migration. Another indication of the nomadic lifestyle is that no permanent settlements have been found. Skilled smiths, the Karasuk were well armed (307).

The movement of the Karasuk set in motion a chain of migrations. It was a pattern that would be reproduced again and again in the next three thousand years, with migratory pressures originating deep in central Asia spreading west in a domino effect.

Their immediate neighbors to the west, the people of the Andronovo culture, bore the brunt of the Karasuk expansion. Originally (in the eighteenth and seventeenth centuries B.C.) an assemblage of several distinct foci in northern Kazakstan, on the Yenisey, and the upper Irtysh, the Andronovo culture by the thirteenth century B.C. had spread over a huge area from the river Ural to the Altai mountains and the Yenisey valley, a distance of some 1,700 miles (261, 265). We should note that they were the first people who used horses for transportation (266).

Despite their precocious nomadism, the Andronovites were no match for the Karasuk. Those who stayed were subdued and gradually absorbed by the invaders. The rest spread in several directions, displacing their neighbors (305). Most of the refugees fled west. Others went south, later evolving into Sacians (Sacae); still others made their way north (ancestors of the Eastern Scythians (309).

The domino west of Andronovo was the people of the Srub ("timber-grave") culture. They had been influenced by the Andronovites and were also beginning a transition to nomadism (257–58). Some Srubnians stayed and mingled with the incoming Andronovians. By the seventh century B.C., the blend of the two cultures produced the Sauromatian (later Sarmatian) tribes in the territory between the lower Volga and western Siberia (339, n.32). Others fled north, west, and south, where they displaced several cultures, including foci of the Catacomb culture. Those who advanced west, toward the Carpathians, caused a considerable upheaval, judging by the number of bronze hoards and swords found in the area dating from

1250–1200 B.C. As a result of the invasion, centers of bronze industry in Transylvania and Hungary were destroyed (340–41). The upheaval was strong enough to interrupt Pontic ties with Troy and the Myceneans, as well as the trade between North Caucasus and eastern Europe (260).

By the beginning of our era, the Europoid populations had abandoned Siberia to the peoples of Turkic and Mongol origin. The Sarmatian-Alan tribes were the last Europoids (and Indo-European speakers) to linger in the westernmost part of the Siberian steppe country, but even they had to retreat, in the third or fourth centuries, before Turkic Huns (among whom the Mongoloid element was predominant) (308).

Migrations of the thirteenth century B.C. demonstrate a pattern of subsequent population movements in the Eurasian steppe: the chain migration of the nomadic people from central Asia to the west. The nomadism, developed by the Andronovites, had momentous consequences for the history of Eurasia. It led to the development of a new, mobile civilization that became an adversary of the sedentary civilizations of Europe and China. The interaction of the two types of civilization can be regarded as the leitmotif of Eurasian history.

Thus, the first period of the nomadic expansion, the "expulsion" of Europoids from Siberia, took place in thirteenth century B.C. through the fourth century A.D., a time span of some 1700 years. It can be subdivided into three sub-periods, the Cimmerian (thirteenth to eighth centuries B.C.), the Scythian (eighth to third centuries B.C.), and the Sarmatian (third century B.C. to third century A.D.), based on the dominant cultures in the Pontic steppe.

At the beginning of the Cimmerian age, while the Srubnians were advancing across the Pontic steppes, a parallel migration proceeded in the forest zone to the north where tribes of the Finno-Ugric stock spread over today's Russia and reached the Baltic coast (389). This movement, carried out by a non-nomadic population, undermines the argument that the migration in the steppe zone was a consequence of nomadism.

Cimmerians present a very confusing picture. At first glance, Cimmerians can be equated with the Catacomb culture. The expulsion of the Issedones by the Arimaspians described by Aristeas of Proconnesus fits in well with the archeological evidence. It probably reflects the upheaval of the thirteenth and twelfth centuries (313). Herodotus also lends weight to this chronology. He says that the Scythians had originally dwelt in Asia. Repeatedly harassed by their eastern neighbors the Massagetae, they crossed the Volga and invaded Cimmerian territory. For whatever reason, Cimmerians chose not to fight and abandoned their country. The sudden displacement of the Catacomb by the Srubnian culture in the Don-Donets area in the thirteenth century neatly fits in with this version. The fact that the Srubnian culture expanded from across the Volga lends further credibility to his account (395).

However, when they next reappear on the scene, in the eighth century B.C., the Cimmerians are a major force that threatens the Near East from across the Caucasian mountains. In 714 B.C. they attacked Urartu. In 705 B.C., defeated by Sargon II, they fell on Cappadocia. In 696–95 B.C. they defeated Midas and conquered Phrygia. In 679 B.C., they appeared on the Assyrian border but were driven off by Esarhaddon. In 652 B.C. they took Sardis, the capital of Lydia. Finally, in 637 or 626 B.C., they were routed by the Lydians and disappeared from history (396).

It is clear that these later Cimmerians ("gamirru" in Assyrian) are unlikely to be the same people as the bearers of the Catacomb culture. After its defeat in the thirteenth century, the Catacomb culture collapsed; its remnants were ejected from the steppe country. Small, insignificant groups that may have survived in the Crimea and northwest Caucasus until the eighth century B.C. (397, n.6) could not have posed a threat to powerful Assyria. This is an enigma. Perhaps, only the name was "transferred." Similarly, Prussians annihilated in the twelfth and thirteenth centuries reappeared at the gates of Paris in 1870.

Mobility was a major factor in assuring the success of nomadic peoples. It gave the nomad the ability to strike unexpectedly and from far away, making conquest easier, resistance more difficult. Other factors include: (1) the development of nomad pastoralism; (2) the change to a militarized way of life that involved early training in warfare and spending most of adult male life fighting and skirmishing; (3) the development of a special tactic: assaulting the enemy with large groups of mounted bowmen who were consummate horsemen and had perfected the art of shooting from the gallop. This tactic, characteristic of the Scythians in the second half of the first millennium B.C., developed in the Eurasian steppe well before the Scythian advance into eastern Europe; and (4) the growth of the bronze industry in western Siberia based on rich local deposits of copper and tin. It provided the peoples of Siberia with very effective weapons. The "Europeans" had no proper organization or adequate arms to resist the nomadic invaders (394).

CHAPTER 10

Horses and Gold:
The Scythians of the Eurasian Steppes

Rebecca W. Wendelken

For 28 years the Scythians were masters over Asia, and all was wasted by their violence and pride, for apart from their exacting of tribute, which they laid upon each man, they rode around and plundered whatsoever it was that anyone possessed.[1]

Beginning in the seventh century B.C., a people known to us as the Scythians ranged over Eurasia from the Black Sea to the borders of China. They were one of numerous eastern nomadic groups that swept over Europe between the first millennium B.C. and the middle of the second millennium A.D. The east-to-west movement of these nomadic military societies changed the character of the population in Europe and Asia both by displacing indigenous peoples and by transmitting a new culture. By the third century A.D. the Scythians had passed from the historical scene, but their art and culture left a lasting legacy. Little was known about them outside of contemporary writings until the late eighteenth century, when an intense scientific interest in ancient cultures began to develop. Earlier Russian engineers and explorers had collected objects from Scythian graves, but these discoveries were not widely disseminated. It was not until the early twentieth century that the world became aware of the richness of Scythian culture, when finds from the Altai Mountains were published.

The nomadic invasions, of which the Scythians were a part, were greatly aided by the geography of Eurasia. Stretching from the northern European plain to the borders of China, the steppes form a single geographic unit of natural grassland. Although the European and Asian sections are nearly divided by the Ural mountains, continuity is evidenced by the presence of much of the same flora and fauna on both sides of the Ural range. In Asia, the Pamir, the Tien Shan, and the Altai Mountains break up the vast expanse of the steppes. But major passes, particularly the Zungharian and the Ferghana, allow relatively free access between the two sections. Of the two, the European region was more lush and fertile, although the climate during the first millennium B.C. was colder and wetter than today.[2] The European steppes were also transversed by many rivers. The annual floods of the Volga, the Don and Donets, the Dnieper, the Bug, and the Dniester brought fertile soils, which produced rich grasslands. However, despite their number, the rivers did not greatly inhibit the movement of peoples. Geographically, the only major differences between the times of the Scythians and today is that the Caspian Sea was much larger then, and the Oxus River, now called the Syr Darya, emptied directly into it.

The Origin of the Scythians

Who exactly were the Scythians? The answer is not always clear cut. The true Scythians were an Indo-European people, who spoke a language from the Iranian family. Groups of Scythians were found from the Black Sea to the Altai mountains, and were generally divided into the European or "Pontic" Scythians and groups in the Eurasian steppes, often termed the "Oriental" Scythians. Because they had no written language of their own, our information about the Scythians comes from two main sources. The first is contemporary writings. These were generally produced by literate peoples who were neighbors, allies, or victims of the Scythian hordes. The greatest body of these comes from Greece and deals with the Pontic Scythians who lived on the shores of the Black Sea. As one moves east the written record diminishes dramatically and what remains is muddled and confused, at times taking on the quality of myth or legend.[3] The second source of information is the rich burial remains of the Scythian nobility. Archeological evidence is more wide ranging than the written sources, but nonetheless is primarily concentrated in two areas, the Pontic steppes and the Altai. Physical evidence from the numerous archeological sights shows that the Scythians were a racially mixed group. Caucasoid types are found more frequently in Europe and the Central Asian steppes, while Mongoloid types are more common in the east. This situation probably represents the effects of intermarriage or at least close personal contact between the Scythians and their neighbors.

The history of the Scythians is sometimes confused because groups fitting the modern description of "Scythian" were known by different names to different peoples. To the Greeks, they were the Scythai, the origin of our term "Scythian"; to the Assyrians they were the Askkuz, the Ashguzai, or the Ishkuzai; and the Persians and Indians called them the Saka.[4] It is probable that as the fame of the Scythians spread, their name was applied to groups of nomadic cavalry in general, much the same as the name "Hun" was attached to totally unrelated people in different time periods.[5] Also, while the Scythians were typical of the pre-Hunnic, Iranian-speaking nomads, there were other major groups in this category. The first were the Cimmerians, who were driven out of the Black Sea area around the end of the eighth century B.C. by the Scythians themselves.

The Cimmerians were mentioned in Homer's *Odyssey* (XI, 13–19), as well as in Assyrian sources, and are thought to have been culturally indistinguishable from the Scythians. They even used the same unique type of arrowheads, especially adapted for the light bows of mounted archers.[6] The second related groups were the Sarmatians, the eastern neighbors of the Scythians. Like the Scythians, the Sarmatians were nomadic and ranged widely. One offshoot of late Sarmatian culture, the Alans, pushed as far west as the coast of Brittany.[7] The Sarmatians will be discussed later in terms of their relationships with the Scythians and the distinctions between their cultures.

Besides the Cimmerians and Sarmatians there were a large number of groups who embraced a Scythian-type lifestyle and culture, but who did not belong to the Iranian language group. These have also frequently been subsumed under the general heading of "Scythian" for two reasons. First, contemporary authors often did not distinguish between peoples based on languages, but rather on their outward appearance or culture.[8] Second, their material culture is often so close to that of the Scythians that even modern scholars are sometimes at a loss to make the distinction. Herodotus describes some of these groups, including the intriguing "Baldies." These Scythian-like people were born hairless and lived primarily on the fruit of the "ponticum," a plant that provided both food and drink.[9] Who they actually were and whether they were really Scythians is not known. Another example is that of the Saka. There is some question about whether these Oriental Scythians can even be called "Scythian" at all.[10] As far as the Pontic steppes there were a number of peoples who appear to have shared a common culture and, sometimes, language. What Greek writers called "Scythians" may have been a culture rather than a distinct people. Indeed, for these and other reasons it has been suggested that perhaps Scythia, when discussing the Pontic steppes, should be considered a political rather than an ethnic unit.[11]

Herodotus sets the political geographic stage by identifying some of the nations that bordered on Scythian territory. Some of the more important include the Sauromatians, who Herodotus said lived to the east of the Royal Scythians in the Volga basin southeast of the Urals, and spoke an "impure" form of the Scythian language.[12] These people are believed to have been the ancestors of the Sarmatians, the nomadic wave that followed the Scythians. Another neighbor, the Maeotians, inhabited the region of the northern Caucasus, while the Salus, like the Massagetae, were located in the Central Asian steppes.[13]

As is true with many nomadic peoples, the origin of the Scythians is lost in the mists of time. It became a matter of speculation, especially after they came into contact with the more civilized cultures of the Near East and Mediterranean. The Greek historian Herodotus, writing in the fifth century B.C., provides two different contemporary stories on the genesis of the Scythian people. He said that they themselves claim to be the youngest of all nations and the product of a union between Targitaus, a son of Zeus, and a river goddess. The second story comes from the Pontic Greeks, who said the Scythians were born when Heracles cohabited with a viper-maiden, a woman half-human and half-serpent. Herodotus himself believed the Scythians originally lived in Asia and were forced out by another group, the Massagetae. The fleeing Scythians moved westward, eventually settling in the region called Cimmeria, located in modern southern Russia.[14] Herodotus also speculated on the origins of the Sarmatians. These people, he believed, were the result of a union between unmarried Scythians and Amazons.[15] Most modern historians and archeologists agree that both the Scythians and the Sarmatians came from the eastern steppes, either from Central Asia or from Turkestan and western Siberia. It is certain that, whatever their origin, these peoples "hovered at the entire northern frontier of the established civilizations of Greece and Central Asia" during the entire first millennium B.C.[16]

Scythian Lifestyle and Culture

Scythian lifestyle and culture is often compared to that of the Turko-Mongol Hunnic tribes that lived further to the east, along the Chinese border. It is possible that Scythian or Scythian-like groups in the region of the Ferghana Valley, known to the Chinese as the Yueh-chih, transmitted their culture to the Huns. Both the Scythians and the Turko-Mongols were migratory; used mounted archers for warfare; wore trousers and boots (unlike the Chinese and Greeks, who wore robes); used iron technology; and employed the stirrup. The latter helps account for their renowned skills as horsemen. But whether the similarities developed independently because the two groups lived under similar situations or were the result of actual close contact is not known for sure. It appears from the archeological record that the Scythians may have developed their iron culture during their migration across Eurasia. This gives weight to the independent-development theory.[17]

Where and how a distinctive Scythian culture developed is not clear. One theory speculates that the Scythians descended from the Srubnians. These people migrated in several waves from the Volga-Ural steppes to the northern Black Sea region between the middle of the second millennium B.C. and the end of the seventh century B.C. The Cimmerians who originally inhabited this region were either assimilated or driven out by the Srubnians, and the result was the creation of a distinct Scythian culture.[18] Another possibility, backed by some archeological evidence, is that some of the Srubnians crossed the Caucasus and traveled along the coast of the Caspian Sea. In this region (now modern Azerbaijan), the Srubnians came into contact with the Urartians and other tribes with more advanced cultures. By adopting and adapting new ideas from these groups, the Srubnians developed a unique new Scythian culture that retained a strong Andronovo Siberian element.[19] A third, less convincing theory is that the Scythians were autochthonous to the Black Sea coastal region, and that their culture spread both east and west from this location.[20]

The Indo-European Scythians were nomadic pastoralists. This type of economic system has an economy based on animal husbandry sustained by periodic pastoral migration.[21] Nomadic migration can be described as "fixed" or "tied," following a well-worn migratory track, rather like a comet. It could also be "untied," with an unstructured pattern of wandering.[22] The type of migration used was determined by the conditions of a particular location. The Scythians' movement from Asia to Europe appears to have been "untied," while their migration, once they arrived in the Pontic steppes, appears to have been "fixed." The Oriental Scythians are known to have used both forms of migration depending on the climate and local conditions. Nomadism was deeply entrenched and appears to have formed a major part of Scythian identity. Scythians who could no longer afford the herds and could not readily move from place to place were said to be viewed as "dishonorable people . . . of the lowest provenance."[23] The distaste for the settled life was so strong among Scythian nobility that they remained nomadic until Scythia's exit from the historical scene in the third century A.D.

Herodotus believed that the Scythians' nomadic nature was one of the reasons they were so invincible:

For the Scythian nation has made the most clever discovery among all the people we know, and of the one thing that is greatest in human affairs—though for the rest I do not admire them much. This greatest thing that they have discovered is how no invader who comes against them can ever escape and how none can catch them if they do not wish to be caught. For this people has no cities or settled forts; they carry their houses with them and shoot with bows from horseback; they live off herds of cattle, not from tillage, and their dwellings are on their wagons. How can they fail to be invincible and inaccessible to others?[24]

The mobile dwellings described by Herodotus are believed to have been similar to the felt yurts found in some areas of Mongolia and Central Asia today. Clay models found in tombs, as well as Chinese depictions of later nomads, show these dome-shaped houses mounted on wheeled carts. These carts were also used to transport the women and children on their long journeys. It is not known if the dwellings were removed from the carts when the Scythians camped for an extended period of time, or whether the structures were permanently attached.

As discussed earlier, the greatest body of information on the Pontic Scythians is from the works of Herodotus. Although he does exaggerate at times, his descriptions have, for the most part, been substantiated by archeologists. Herodotus recognized several distinct Scythian groups, at least two of which were purely nomadic. The Royal Scythians, who called themselves the Skolotoi, were dominant in the Black Sea region from the Bug to the east and south as far as the Don. Herodotus described them as "the best" of the Scythians and the group with the highest population.[25] Although the office of king was apparently hereditary, it's holder did not have unlimited power. His actions were subject to approval by an assembly of warriors. Like many early kings, he was not only a war leader, but also served as an intermediary between the people and their gods.[26] The king of the Royal Scythians was recognized by the other Scythian groups in the Black Sea region. Subject peoples paid tribute to the Royal Scythians and were required to provided servants for the king and tribal aristocracy. West of the Dnieper and around the Sea of Azov lived a second group of purely nomadic Scythians that Herodotus called the Nomad Scythians. These people, like the Royal Scythians, he said, "neither plow nor sow."[27]

Despite an apparent aversion to settlement on the part of some Scythians, many others eventually settled to a greater or lesser degree. In the Pontic steppes they may have been influenced by Greek practices, since intermarriage between the two groups was "not at all uncommon."[28] Agriculture, requiring at least some measure of settlement, developed in the lands along the Black Sea, as well as along the river valleys. Herodotus relates that along one unidentifiable river, probably located in modern Bulgaria, Scythians worked the land along the banks for a distance of ten days' journey.[29] Semi-settled groups in the Pontic region were the Callipidae, or "Greek Scythians," and the Alizones, thought to have been a mixture of Iranian and Thracian peoples. Both were both seminomadic and supplemented their diet by farming.[30] They grew crops such as grain, onions, garlic, lentils, and millet. It is even possible that the Callipidae were not true

Scythians but rather one of the Scythian-like groups, or perhaps Thracians under Scythian overlordship.[31] Another group called the "plowing Scythians" lived in the area of the forest steppe between the Dnieper and the Bug.[32] There is some question about another group that Herodotus called the "agricultural" Scythians or the "Georgi." He said they were located in the lower Dnieper area, but there is no archeological evidence to support this. One recent theory argues that the term "georgi" should actually be translated as "esteeming livestock" not agricultural. If this is true, then they could have been either nomadic or seminomadic.[33] Although Herodotus said there were no Scythian fortified settlements, a few have been located. One trading post, Kamenskoye, located near the Dnieper, shows definite signs of fortification, and in Pontic Scythia defensive structures, including ditches and dikes, have been identified dating from as early as the fifth century B.C.[34]

The economy of the nomadic and semi-settled Scythians was directly tied to their herds, which consisted primarily of sheep, goats, and horses. For steppe nomadic groups, sheep were vitally important. Hardy and well adapted to steppe conditions, they were useful both for food and for their wool, which could be turned into carpets or cloth. Felt, a non-woven fabric made of wool, was especially important. This thick water-resistant material was used to make the covers for their mobile dwellings.

Another animal particularly important for the Scythian economy, and especially for their culture, was the horse. It was an identifying factor of Scythian life. The horse was domesticated somewhere around 1500 B.C. in the Russian steppes and was crucial for the spread of the Scythians and other steppe nomads. The horses found in Scythian tombs were geldings, but some contemporary writers said that the Scythians rode mares into battle because mares "can urinate while galloping" and stallions and geldings cannot.[35] The tomb horses were small by modern standards. The largest had a height of around 59 inches at the withers, but despite that, they were taller than other contemporary horses in Europe. The finest of the Scythians' mounts resembled today's Arab breeds. It is known that Scythians in the Altai preferred reddish-brown horses, riding only bays or chestnuts with no white markings.[36]

Horses, like sheep, were multipurpose animals. Hides were made into leather, and horseflesh also was eaten. But the records, both archeological and those written by authors of Antiquity, most frequently indicate that horses were used as dairy animals. Horse milk, especially when fermented into a drink known in Central Asia today as *kumiss,* is highly nutritious. It is the only animal milk known to contain high amounts of vitamin C. This allowed nomads to rely almost entirely on a meat and dairy diet without falling victim to diseases such as scurvy. Mares' milk and sheep's milk were also made into other products, including cheese, which was often dried for use on long journeys. Small balls of this dried cheese called *kurt* are still a favorite snack food in Central Asia and the Balkans.

Besides their herds, another important part of the Scythian economy was trade. Unlike most agriculture, trade was not considered demeaning, and it is fairly certain that, like many nomadic peoples, Scythians traded to acquire necessities and luxuries they could not produce themselves.[37] Scythian grain, as well as salt, fish, honey, meat, milk, hides, furs, and slaves, was exchanged for goods from the Greek city-states.[38] It appears that the one form of agriculture that was not looked down on was growing grain for trade.[39] Trade may also have affected the herd composition for some Scythian groups. Cattle or cows are not particularly suited to nomadic life in the steppes, where the winters can be quite harsh. The nomadic Kazaks of Central Asia, for example, did not begin to switch the bulk of their herds from sheep to cattle until they came into contact with Russian markets in the nineteenth century. It is possible that Pontic Scythians may have made the same type of change in response to Greek market pressure.

Scythian trade was wide ranging. Herodotus said the Scythians brought Greek goods to the very foothills of the Urals, and that they had to employ seven different interpreters in order to communicate with the wide variety of peoples who lived along the route.[40] The city of Olbia on the Black Sea was connected by a vital commercial network to the Urals and beyond. Both manufactured goods from Greece, and items from the middle Volga and western Siberia have been found all along this route.[41] One measure of the extent of trading is the large amount of gold found in Scythian tombs in Ukraine. There are no gold deposits in that region, so all the gold from the tombs had to be imported. It could only have come from three places: Transylvania, a known source of gold since ancient times; the Caucasus, known as the "Land of the Golden Fleece"; or Kazakstan or the Altai.[42]

The Oriental Scythians

Because of a scarcity of written records, far less is known about the social hierarchy, tribal designations, and territorial range of the Oriental Scythians. These groups, sometimes called the "Saka," were divided into several large tribes and were, like the European Scythians, Indo-Europeans. It is currently believed these Oriental Scythians were primarily nomadic. However, it is possible that they may have engaged in agricultural activity in some areas, especially in the river valleys along the Syr and Amu Darya. As the European Scythians were affected by Greek culture, so those of the east came under strong Chinese influence. Trade with China is evidenced by the remains of Chinese textiles and other products in Scythian tombs, and the locally produced items often merged Chinese motifs with the Scythian styles.

The Cultural Record from Scythian Tombs

In the absence of written sources, art and ornamental motifs found in Scythian burial mounds, or *kurgans,* can be used to help trace their migrations across the steppes. Their burials, especially for nobles, were quite elaborate. The male warriors were buried with their weapons and armor as befitted their rank. Noble burials contained richly decorated armor, helmets, bows with quivers of arrows, many spears, and, especially during the early period, a quantity of horses.[43] A common warrior might be buried with a bow, some arrows, and perhaps a spear or spear and javelin. Wives or concubines might also be interred with the males and were often provided with personal possessions and household goods. Sarmatian women were buried with weapons and armor of their own. This is one of the distinctions between the Scythian and the Sarmatian cultures. Scythian women are believed to have led a life of retirement and seclusion while Sarmatian women fought, rode, and hunted together with the men. Once the Sarmatian female had killed an enemy in battle, she could marry, thereafter devoting herself to domestic affairs.[44] It is possible, since the evidence is rather sparse, that only Scythian women in the Pontic region were confined to the home. This may represent the influence and adoption of Greek customs.

The kurgans of the Scythians and Sarmatians were first opened by gold-seekers. In many cases the entries took place not long after the tombs were completed. By the seventeenth century the tombs were still yielding gold. Objects found there by Russian peasants were either melted down or sold on the open market. A few made their way to the *kunstkammer* of Peter the Great in Petersburg. He was so intrigued by these objects that he instructed the governor of Siberia to confiscate all future finds. He also issued an imperial decree that established a system of protection for antiquities, one of the first of its kind in the world. During the next year, the governor of Siberia was able to collect nearly 53 pounds of gold artifacts, which were shipped on to St. Petersburg.[45]

In the eighteenth and nineteenth centuries, Russian engineers and explorers, such as P. Frolov, collected objects from Scythian graves, but these discoveries were not widely disseminated. V. V. Radlov exhumed two large kurgans in the Altai in the 1860s and was amazed by their high state of preservation. However, what made the Scythians world famous was the excavations by S. I. Rudenko. He examined five *kurgans* at Pazyryk in the upper Altai mountains between 1929 and 1949. These tombs, dramatically preserved by a thick layer of ice, provided a wealth of information on Scythian culture. Although grave robbers had removed most of the gold and silver objects, these tombs, dating from about 340 B.C., contained large quantities of material possessions, including leather, clothing, wooden implements, and textiles. Because the tombs had been completely frozen since shortly after their internment, the contents of the tombs were completely preserved. One find, the famous Pazyryk carpet, is the oldest known knotted carpet in the world. It is believed to have been made in Persia, and probably made its way to the Altai as a trade item. Other textiles found in the tomb were produced in China, further evidence of the widespread trade.

Besides the grave goods, the ice also preserved complete bodies. The tombs contained both male and female bodies, and both sexes were tattooed with fantastic beasts—a sign of high social position among many barbarian tribes. Each kurgan also contained numerous horses, primarily geldings from 2 to 20 years old. The graves also provided information on other forms of transportation. Wagons with solid wheels sawn from tree trunks were included. Each wheel had a hole cut in the middle to receive an axle. These were the ox-drawn wagons known as *kibitka,* used to transport their portable dwellings as well as women and children.[46]

Household goods, horse trappings, and the small bits of jewelry were all highly decorated, showing a variety of techniques and applications. The most important motifs are the uniquely stylized animal forms. Scythian artisans depicted animals common to their homeland, including birds, elk, deer and wild goats, and large carnivores such as panthers. Scythian depictions of animals were stylized, redefined, and molded into ornamental figures. The most common and distinctive Scythian motif is of a beast lying on its back; beasts are shown in a number of different postures—walking, lying down, or curled up.[47] The animal is twisted so that the hind legs point upward while the forelegs point down, as though its back were broken. This particular motif and the Scythians' animal-style in general probably developed in the ancient Middle East on the periphery of Assyria. From there it traveled to the northern Black Sea region, where Scythian artifacts began to appear in the second half of the seventh century B.C.[48] Its highest development in Ukraine was between 350 and 250 B.C., the time when the royal kurgans on the lower Dniester were constructed. Animal-style motifs have also been found as far east as the Ordos region of Mongolia and northern China.[49] In the west, Scythian-influenced objects were found in a late-fourth-century B.C. grave at Vix in the Côte d'Or, France. This burial, identified as belonging to a Celtic "princess," contains a mixture of both Celtic and Scythian styles. The woman interred there may have been a member of Scytho-Sarmatian nobility who married a Celtic rex, or perhaps she simply belonged to a group of rich traders.[50] It is interesting that although Scythian-style artifacts are found all over Eurasia at this time, they are curiously missing from the Aral and Caspian Sea regions. Was the environment unfavorable for the preservation of remains; has the area been inadequately explored; or were there simply no Scythians there, and if not, why not?[51]

The Scythian Migrations

Contemporary writings and art styles can help track the Scythians across the steppes, but it is not known for certain what triggered the Scythians' migrations. Perhaps it was external pressures that pushed the Scythians westward. One theory speculates that there was a major ethnic and cultural migration from west to east in the ninth and eighth centuries B.C. Thracian, Caucasian, and possibly even Germanic peoples crossed the Central Asian steppes and moved into the reaches of eastern Asia. A similar movement, occurring between 1250 and 1100 B.C., has been documented by J. Wiesner.[52] Such an incursion may have broken the existing balance of power in the steppe. The Scythian tribes, pressed against stronger neighbors and unable to move any further to the east, flowed around the invaders, moving to either the northwest or the southwest.[53] Another possibility is that the external pressure originated in the east. In China, in the ninth century B.C., the emperor Suan (827–781 B.C.) launched a punitive expedition against the wild Hsiung-nu tribesmen, thought by many to be the forerunners of the Huns. He forced the Hsiung-nu to the west, beyond the Chinese frontier. It is possible that this action created a sort of domino effect as tribes displaced each other towards the west. In this scenario, which is supported by Herodotus, the eastern tribes displaced the Massagetae, who lived north of the Oxus River. They in turn attacked the Scythians, and the displaced Scythians invaded the lands of the Cimmerians, who lived on their western borders.[54] The problem with these theories is that archeological evidence can be found to support either one. Another possibility is that there was a period of extreme drought around 800 B.C. The Scythians and their herds may have begun moving west in search of water and pastures, or they may have needed to be closer to markets as part of their trading ventures.[55]

A second group of theories on the genesis of the Scythian migration emphasizes internal pressures. One possibility is that there was a collapse of Bronze Age aristocracy in the steppes that created confusion and conflict. This resulted in a migration.[56] Another popular model, especially in the former Soviet Union, suggested that as the steppe economy developed, larger and more complex economic units were created. As the number of settlements and size of herds increased, migration was a way to relieve the population and economic pressures.[57]

Whatever triggered the Scythian migration, their movement across the steppes was probably slow, with an intervening period of social and economic upheaval. This contradicts Herodotus, who said that the Scythian invasions occurred very suddenly.[58] We know that the Scythians began to arrive in the Pontic steppes between 750 and 700 B.C. The indigenous Cimmerians, who used exclusively infantry units, proved no match for the equestrian Scythians. Those who resisted were either wiped out, taken as slaves, or more likely absorbed into the Scythian population, due to the closeness of their cultures. Groups of Cimmerians who chose to flee moved westward, settling in what is now Hungary or in Thrace.[59] Another group fled into Asia Minor. The pursuing Scythians allegedly lost their way. Instead of following the Cimmerians, they took a wrong turn and traveled along the Caspian Sea. They ended up in Persia. But another group did arrive in Asia Minor, where they are said to have ruled for 28 years.[60]

Migration and War

The Scythians' migration and wars are closely interwoven. Like most nomads, the Scythians generally appear in historic documents only when they have political importance—when they are attacking or being attacked. These writings address primarily armament or tactics.[61] For this reason our information about Scythian military organization and tactics is more detailed than our knowledge of their lifestyle.

Scythian tactics owed much to their mobility and use of evasion. Scythian forces had to be able to compete successfully against both cavalry and infantry units and to fight on horseback or on foot.[62] Cernenko describes the tactics of the Scythian armies:

> The bulk of the cavalry was probably made up of lightly armed warriors, protected by no more than fur or hide jackets or headgear. The shock force of the Scythian host was the professional, heavily armed cavalry commanded by local princes. Both horses and riders were well protected. They fought in formation, under discipline, and brought to the battlefield considerable experience of warfare. The engagement opened with a shower of arrows and sling-stones, followed at closer range by darts and javelins. The heavy cavalry then charged in close formation, delivering the main blow to the centre [sic] of the enemy's array. They were certainly capable of manoeuvre [sic] in battle, breaking through the enemy ranks, regrouping in the thick of action, and changing direction to strike at the right place at the right time. When the enemy had been broken, the lightly armed mass of the Scythian horse closed in to finish them off.[63]

Once the golden-clad Scythians on their red horses began to contact civilized groups in the Middle East and the Black Sea region, we are better able to trace some of their movements. Ancient Greek authors, and also contemporary writings from Urartu and Assyria, mention the Scythians.[64] In the mid-seventh century, the Scythians were also influential in Media, a mountainous country lying to the southwest of the Caspian Sea. So powerful were they that the Assyrian king Esarhaddon asked the god Shamash if the Scythians would remain friendly if the king offered them his daughter in marriage.[65] He did, but they didn't. In 612 B.C., the Scythians united with their former enemies, the Medes, against Assyria. The combined forces captured the Assyrian capital of Nineveh and destroyed the Assyrian Empire.

The Scythian war bands ranged over a wide area, and Herodotus says that they "subdued and occupied nearly all of the upper lands of Asia," by which he appears to mean Asia Minor.[66] They were active as far to the south as Egypt, where, during the late seventh century B.C., the Scythian king Madyes led a military expedition. To propitiate their gods and render their slain enemies' spirits helpless, the Scythians sacrificed one captive out of every hundred: "They pour wine on the men's heads and cut their throats into a bucket. This they then carry up on to the pile of firewood and pour the blood on the sword. The carrying-aloft is the work of some of the sacrificers, while others, below, cut off the right arms of all the slaughtered men and, hands and all, throw them into the air. Afterwards they finish the sacrifice with the rest of the victims and then go away. The arm lies where it has fallen, and the rest of the dead body apart from it."[67]

This type of scare tactics prompted one Egyptian Pharaoh in the fifth century to pay a heavy tribute to the Scythians to protect his country from an even more costly invasion.

The Medes/Scythian cooperation did not last long. Shortly after their success against the Assyrians, the Medes drove the Scythians north over the Caucasus Mountains. Herodotus has a story about the situation surrounding the Scythians' flight. The Median king Kyaxares invited all the Scythian commanders to a feast and then killed them during a drinking bout. Many historians accept this story as plausible.[68] It is possible that after such a blow the remaining Scythian army may well have retreated to southern Russia. There they concentrated in the Black Sea region, between the arc of Greek coastal cities and the edge of the forest steppes.[69]

Persia, which replaced Assyria, Babylonia, and Media as the major power in western Asia, also had a close relationship with the Scythians. The Scythians supplied the Persians with much of the gold on which their power depended.[70] Between 514 and 512, the Persian ruler Darius attempted to Persianize the periphery of his kingdom. His campaign appears to have been partially successful against the Sakas of Central Asia, but far less so against the Pontic Scythians. Darius attacked the Pontic Scythians via Bessarabia, but nearly succumbed to the nomadic tactic of luring the enemy deep into one's own territory and then vanishing. Darius followed them as far as the Don River before he finally gave up. His return to Persia was very difficult as the Scythians had fouled the wells and springs and burnt fodder. Because Darius failed, these Scythians "escaped Persian influence and remained in peaceful possession of southern Russia for another three centuries" (Grousset 1970, 9). Persia, instead, set its sites on Greece, while the Scythians launched an expedition against the city of Chersonesus on the Black Sea.

In the mid-fifth century B.C., during the reign of the Scythian king Scyles, Herodotus visited the trading colony at Olbia and recorded his famous descriptions of Scythian life. Olbia was, at that time, undergoing a massive expansion and had become "the pivot of trade and traffic with the peoples of the steppes."[71] However, the Scythian hegemony was not to last. By 350 B.C., the Sarmatians, a nomadic confederation of tribes, began to expand into Scythian territory.[72] These Indo-European newcomers crossed the Volga in the fourth and third centuries B.C. and began to move into the northern Caucasus and Scythia. The Scythians proved no match for the Sarmatians' heavily armored cavalry and their long swords. The Scythians and Sarmatians were so closely related in terms of culture that they are sometimes difficult to distinguish from each other. Both had a huge, nomadic, and politically loose federation of tribes each ruled by a king or prince. Both buried their dead in kurgans with a wide variety of grave goods. Perhaps the similarities account for the fact that the Sarmatians made no stylistic changes in the region's culture. Many more changes would be made by the Huns, who came later.[73]

Driven westward, Athaes, the Scythian king, centered his power on the left bank of the Danube on land seized from a Thracian tribe called the Getae. He established what may well have been the first nomadic state in history.[74] Scythian settlements were also built on the west bank of the Danube delta, in present day Dobrudja. With his position secure, at least in his own mind, Athaes even had his own coins struck in one of the towns of the western Pontic area.[75] In 339 B.C., at the age of 90, Atheas was killed in Romania fighting against the Macedonian forces of Philip II. The entire Scythian encampment with about 20,000 women and children was captured and resettled to the south in an area the Romans later called "Scythia Minor."[76] This point has traditionally been seen as the end of Scythian presence in Europe. However, recent archeological evidence has shown that some Scythians continued to rule in the northern Pontic steppes even after their defeat by Philip. These groups, with the exception of some of the nobles, gradually adopted agriculture like the people around them.[77]

The remaining Scythians in the southern Pontic region gradually withdrew from the banks of the Danube into the Crimea. With their territory rapidly shrinking, they sought to gain control of Greek coastal cities so that they could continue their profitable foreign trade. Some cities, like Olbia, fell. Others, for example the city of Chersonesus, turned to powerful foreigners like King Mithridates Eupator of Pontus for assistance. Mithridates, eager to expand his empire, attacked the Scythians, finally defeating them in 106 B.C. As they had in the past, the Scythians allied, or were forced to ally, with former enemies (Mithridates), this time against Rome. The Romans, however, were triumphant and succeeded in establishing a protectorate over the Pontic steppes, but made no attempt to bring the region under a more active policy.[78]

In the first century A.D., the Scythians once again pressed the city of Terseness. This time the city requested aid from the region's current power, the Romans. The Roman general Platius Silvanus broke the Scythian siege in A.D. 63.[79] A small Scythian kingdom continued in the region until the mid-third century A.D., when it was crushed by the Gothic invasions. The remaining Scythians were assimilated into the Gothic population and lost their "ethnic identity."[80] How and when the end came for the Scythian groups in the Russian steppes and for those called the "Oriental Scythians" is not known. Quite probably they too were absorbed into the local populations or swept away during subsequent waves of invaders.

Although the Scythians were no more, their name did not die with them. The image of the Scythians as a strong, nomadic warrior culture was so strong that the area they dominated was still known as "greater Scythia" a thousand years later. So powerful was their memory that many diverse nations as far removed from one another as Russia and Ireland have, at one time or another, claimed the Scythians as ancestors. An attempt to tap into the legacy of the Scythians has become a strong part of the development of a national identity in the Republic of Kazakstan. In the former capital of Almaty, a monument to those who died in the 1989 riots features Scythian motifs, including a huge statue of the so-called Golden Man of Issyk. This Golden Man, named for his clothing that was richly decorated with gold plaques, was found some 31 miles east of Almaty in 1969. This fifth-century burial was thought to have been the remains of the burial of a young Saka chief, but whether he was really a Scythian or not is still questionable. As for the Kazaks, they are descended from Turkic, not Indo-European groups.

Although they did not build cities, roads, or monuments, the Scythians have nonetheless left their mark on world history. Besides their rich tombs, the Scythians left a legacy in place names across Eurasia, especially geographic labels such as the names of mountains and rivers. Their involvement in trade has given names to many common material goods in Eurasia, and it is probable that they introduced a system of weights and measures based on Near Eastern models into the Pontic steppes. And, perhaps most importantly, their culture and art influenced many divergent groups, forming a legacy for the peoples of the future.

Notes

1. Herodotus, *The Histories* (New York: Penguin, 1972), I. 106.
2. T. Sulimirski, *The Sarmatians* (New York: Praeger, 1970), 150.
3. M. I. Artamonov, "Frozen Tombs of the Scythians," *Scientific American* 212, no. 5 (May 1965): 101.
4. Réné Grousset, *The Empire of the Steppes: A History of Central Asia* (New Brunswick, NJ: Rutgers University Press, 1970), 6.
5. A. I. Melyukova, "The Scythians and Sarmatians," in *The Cambridge History of Inner Asia.*, ed. Denis Sinor (Cambridge: Cambridge University Press, 1990), 98.
6. These bronze arrowheads were "trilobate or of the solid pyramidal type and often barbed." Ibid., 94.
7. Sulimirski, *The Sarmatians,* 142, 185, 188.
8. Anatoly M. Khazanov, *Nomads and the Outside World,* 2d ed (Madison: University of Wisconsin Press, 1984), 8.
9. Herodotus, *The Histories,* IV, 23.
10. Artamonov, "Frozen Tombs of the Scythians," 101.
11. Melyukova, "The Scythians and Sarmatians," 102–03.
12. Herodotus, *The Histories,* IV, 17–20; T. Sulimirski, "The Scyths," in *Cambridge History of Iran,* Volume II (Cambridge: Cambridge University Press, 1985), 153.
13. Herodotus, *The Histories,* IV, 17–20.
14. Ibid., 17–20.
15. Ibid., 100–17.
16. Artamonov, "Frozen Tombs of the Scythians," 101.
17. Grousset, *The Empire of the Steppes: A History of Central Asia,* 8, 11.
18. A. I. Terenozhkin, *Kimmeriicy* (Kiev: Naukova dumka, 1971), 183, 208; Grousset, *The Empire of the Steppes: A History of Central Asia,* 6; Melyukova, "The Scythians and Sarmatians," 98–99.
19. Sulimirski, "The Scyths," 169.
20. I. I. Artëmenko, "Archaeological Research in the Ukrainian SSR," *Soviet Anthropology and Archaeology* XVIII, no. 3 (1979–80): 51.
21. Khazanov, *Nomads and the Outside World,* 7.
22. Roger Cribb, *Nomads in Archaeology* (Cambridge: Cambridge University Press, 1991), 16–18.
23. Khazanov, *Nomads and the Outside World,* 83.
24. Herodotus, *The Histories,* IV, 46.
25. Ibid., 20.
26. Khazanov, *Nomads and the Outside World,* 168.
27. Herodotus, *The Histories,* IV, 9.
28. Renate Rolle, *The World of the Scythians* (London: Batsford, 1989), 12.
29. Herodotus, *The Histories,* IV, 53.
30. Ibid., 17.
31. Sulimirski, "The Scyths," 182.
32. Melyukova, "The Scythians and Sarmatians," 102–03.

33. Ibid., 98; V. I. Abaev, "Diskussionye Problemy Otechestvennoji Skifologii," *Narody Azii i Afriki,* no. 5 (1980): 23–25.

34. Ann Farkas, "Introduction," in *From the Land of the Scythians* (New York: Metropolitan Museum of Art, n.d.), 20–21.

35. Rolle, *The World of the Scythians,* 101.

36. Ibid., 101–03, 109.

37. Cribb, *Nomads in Archaeology,* 13.

38. Tamara Talbot Rice, *The Scythians* (New York: Praeger, 1957), 51.

39. Herodotus, *The Histories,* IV, 17; *Herodotus: The History,* tr. David Grene (Chicago: University of Chicago Press, 1987), fn. 10, pg. 286.

40. Ibid., 24.

41. Sulimirski, "The Scyths," 180–81; Rolle, *The World of the Scythians,* 14.

42. Rolle, *The World of the Scythians,* 53.

43. E.V. Cernenko, *The Scythians: 700–300 B.C.* (London: Osprey, 1983), 5.

44. Rice, *The Scythians,* 48.

45. Karl Jettmar, *Art of the Steppes* (New York: Greystone, 1964), 11.

46. Georges Charrière, *Scythian Art: Crafts of the Early Nomads* (New York: Alpine Fine Arts Collection, Ltd., 1979), 9–10.

47. Farkas, "Introduction," 9; M. I. Artamonov, "The Origin of Scythian Art," *Soviet Anthropology and Archaeology* IX, no. 1 (Summer 1970): 52.

48. Melyukova, "The Scythians and Sarmatians," 99.

49. Khazanov, *Nomads and the Outside World,* 96.

50. J. Rosen-Przeworska, "Ethnology and Archaeology in Foreign Areas," *Sovetskaia arkheologiia,* no. 3 (1963): 26.

51. Jettmar, *Art of the Steppes,* 222.

52. J. Weisner, "Eurasische Kunst in Steppenraum und Waldgebiet," in *Illustrierte Weltkunstgeschichte,* ed. E. Th. Timli (Zurich: K. Fischer, 1959), passim.

53. R. Heine-Geldern, "Das Tocharerproblem und die Pontische Wanderung," *Saeculum* II, no. 2 (1951): 230; Jettmar, *Art of the Steppes,* 231.

54. Rice, *The Scythians,* 43.

55. Khazanov, *Nomads and the Outside World,* 206; Rice, *The Scythians,* 43.

56. Jettmar, *Art of the Steppes,* 227.

57. Ibid., 225.

58. Ibid., 225–26; Richard P. Vaggione, "Over All Asia? The Extent of the Scythian Domination in Herodotus," *Journal of Biblical Literature* 92 (1973): 530.

59. Grousset, *The Empire of the Steppes: A History of Central Asia,* 6–8.

60. Jettmar, *Art of the Steppes,* 24.

61. Cribb, *Nomads in Archaeology,* 12.

62. By the late fourth century, the Scythian infantry is known to have outnumbered the cavalry by two to one. Cernenko, *The Scythians: 700–300 B.C.,* 20.

63. Ibid., 20.

64. Farkas, "Introduction," 15.

65. Ibid., 16.

66. Herodotus, *The Histories,* VII, 20; Vaggione, "Over All Asia? The Extent of the Scythian Domination in Herodotus," 530.

67. *Herodotus: The History,* tr. David Grene, Book 4.62.

68. Jettmar, *Art of the Steppes,* 25; Melyukova, "The Scythians and Sarmatians," 22.

69. Jettmar, *Art of the Steppes,* 25.

70. William Culican, *The Medes and the Persians* (New York: Praeger, 1965), 136.

71. Rolle, *The World of the Scythians,* 13–14.

72. Evgenii I. Lubo-Lesnichenko, "The Huns, Third Century B.C. to Sixth Century A.D.," in *Nomads of Eurasia,* ed. Vladimir N. Basilov (Seattle: University of Washington Press, 1989), 41.

73. Lubo-Lesnichenko, "The Huns, Third Century B.C. to Sixth Century A.D.," 41–53.

74. Larisa R. Pavlinskaya, "The Scythians and Sakians, Eighth to Third Centuries B.C.," in *Nomads of Eurasia,* ed. Vladimir N. Basilov (Seattle: University of Washington Press, 1989), 27.

75. Melyukova, "The Scythians and Sarmatians," 106.

76. Sulimirski, "The Scyths," 198.

77. Jan and Sergei Skoryi Chochorowski, "Prince of the Great Kurgan," *Archaeology,* September/October 1997, 32.

78. Jettmar, *Art of the Steppes,* 26.

79. Melyukova, "The Scythians and Sarmatians," 108.

80. Ibid., 108.

CHAPTER 11

The Last of the Iranians

The Sarmatians

Sarmatians were the last wave of Iranian-speaking nomads to reach Europe.

In the sixth to fourth centuries B.C., early Sarmatians, then known as Sauromatae, could be found east of the Scythians. Herodotus placed them "fifteen days journey northward from the northern tip of Lake Maeotis" (Herodotus, IV, 21, in Melyukova 110, in Sinor 1990).

Archeological evidence locates them in two areas: between the lower Volga and the Don and in the Samara-Ural region. Thus, it seems that Herodotus knew only the western branch. But this is hardly surprising since their territory stretched some 550 to 600 kilometers east (110).

Like their Scythian cousins, the Sauromatae were descendants of the Srubnians. But they were the Srubnians who stayed put and acknowledged the overlordship of their Andronovo neighbors (111). It is interesting that by the middle of the first millennium B.C. the Sauromatae in the Urals area were more advanced than their western compatriots. They were wealthier, probably because of the rich metal deposits in the region, and their warrior aristocracy was stronger. It is here, in the wealthy east, with its strong warrior elite, that the nucleus of the Sarmatian people first emerged.

Sarmatian trek west started no later than the end of the fifth century B.C., when some of the Sauromatae crossed the Don, which had long served as the boundary between them and the Scythians. They settled around Lake Maeotis, in close proximity to the Royal Scythians and the Maeotians. (It looks like their relations with the Scythians continued to be friendly. They had even helped them beat off the Persians [111].)

By the fourth century B.C., the Sauromatian ethny had split into Sauromatae (west) and Sarmatians proper. It is these Sarmatians, from the Urals, that launched the "Sarmatian" migrations.

Their main migration occurred in the fourth and third centuries B.C., when the now-distinct Sarmatians crossed the Volga and conquered their

Sauromatae cousins. As a result, new tribal federations that we can identify from writers of Antiquity coalesced: the Alans, the Iazyges, the Roxolani, and the like (112). These federations, reinforced by their Sauromatian cousins, burst into the Scythian Pontic steppe in the third century B.C. and "turned the greater part of the country into a desert" (Diodorus Siculus, *Bibliotheca,* II, 43.3, in Melyukova 113, in Sinor 1990).

Strabo, writing in the second century B.C., placed the Iazyges between the Don and the Dnieper. By the time of Ovid (beginning of the first century A.D.), they had reached the right bank of the Danube. And Pliny, half a century later, located them in the Tisza valley. The Roxolani followed in the Iazyges' footsteps (113).

Other Sarmatians went south, toward the foothills of the Caucasus. Here, the Aorsi and the Siraces battled each other, sometimes alone, on other occasions in alliance with Mithridates or the Romans (113).

Sarmatians remained supreme in the Pontic steppe until the arrival of the Goths in the third century A.D. Somehow, they seem to have established a modus vivendi with the new arrivals and became one of the constituent elements in the composite Cherniakhovo culture.

Archeologically, the late Sarmatian presence is attested over a vast area from Hungary/Romania in the west to the Volga and beyond in the east. In the north, they had expanded deep into the forest-steppe zone, reaching today's Poltava and Orel (114).

While Sarmatians in the Pontic steppe and on the Volga remained nomadic, those in the north Caucasus sedentarized. Many of the Pontic Sarmatians, not unlike their Scythian predecessors, must have also embraced sedentarization. Eventually, they infiltrated Greek towns, such as Olbia, Panticapaeum, and Tanais, where they could be found at all levels of society, even among the ruling elite (115–16).

The Alans

It will be impossible, within the framework of this book, to trace the history of even major Sarmatian groups. I chose the Alans, among many, because they advanced farthest and played a conspicuous role in the barbaric invasions of Europe.

In the beginning of our era, the Alans lived along the lower Don, which, at the time, was regarded as the border between Asia and Europe (113).

It was at this time that the Alans were first mentioned in the West, in Seneca's play *Thyestes,* probably written in the 30s of the first century A.D., or slightly earlier (Bachrach 1973, 3). We next encounter them in Lucan's *Civil Wars,* an epic poem written in the early 60s of the first century A.D. (4). And then we learn from Josephus, in *Jewish Antiquities,* that Tiberius, sometime around A.D. 35, asked Iverians (ancestors of today's Georgians) and Albanians (ancestors of today's Azeris) to help him in a war against the Parthians. Neither did. But they allowed the Alans to pass through their lands to fight the Parthians as allies of Rome (5).

Their alliance with Rome served them well: the defeat inflicted by Rome on the Siraces and their Aorsi allies in A.D. 49, opened the plains of north Caucasus to Alan penetration (in the 50–60s of the first century A.D.). By the second century A.D., they were at the head of a powerful tribal confederation that controlled north Caucasus and the Pontic steppe (Melyukova 113, in Sinor 1990). By this time, their steppe warfare tactics were well known to the Romans and were beginning to influence Roman cavalry doctrine. Arrian (*Contra Alanos,* in Bachrach 1973, 8–9), was the first Roman general to face them, yet he already knew their tactic of feigned retreat. He took vigorous countermeasures, restraining part of the Roman cavalry from pursuit and ordering infantry not to break its phalanx formation regardless of how disorganized the enemy cavalry appeared to be (8–9).

Familiarity with Alan tactics served the Romans well. Already Antonius Pius had to parry their raids into imperial territory (Antonius Pius, V, 5, *Scriptores Historiae Augustae* ["*SHA*"], in Bachrach 1973, 12, n.24). And his successor, Marcus Aurelius, encountered Alans among barbarians who invaded the empire from Illyria to Gaul (Bachrach 1973, 12). They may also have raided Greece in the 240s (along with the Goths?) only to be defeated by Emperor Gordian III on the plains of Philippi (Gordian, III, xxxiv, 4, *SHA,* in Bachrach 1973, 15, n. 30), as well as in northern Italy and Gaul. They were also listed among the captives in the triumph of Aurelian in 273 (Aurelian, XXXIII, 4, 5, *SHA,* in Bachrach 1973, 15, n.32).

But they were not only looters and pillagers. They were also experienced merchants who had established close relations with the Mediterranean world: a Greek monument from Taman' of A.D. 208 praised the chief Alan interpreter (Bachrach 1973, 13).

Alans who had settled within the empire rapidly assimilated. The best known example is Maximinus the Thracian, born of an Alan mother and a Gothic father in northern Thrace. He spoke bad Latin. Yet, despite this handicap, he was able to enter the Roman cavalry and, eventually, became the first barbarian emperor, a striking example of upward mobility in ancient Rome! (13–15)

Alans who remained outside the empire conquered and assimilated people of diverse of origins. They were a cultural entity, and not only a linguistic or ethnic one. However, perhaps because they were more numerous, they managed to absorb other elements almost without a trace. Ammianus Marcellinus wrote that "almost all of the Alans are tall and good looking, their hair is generally blond" (Ammianus Marcellinus, *Res gestae,* XXX, 2, 21, in

Bachrach 1973, 19, n.40). And they were tall: men in the Middle and Late Sarmatian graves in the Volga region reached 182, 185, 187, and 189 centimeters (6'–6'3") (Rykov 1925, 66, and 1926, 103, 117, 123, in Maelchen-Helfen, 1973, 362, n.39).

Alans were the first victims of the Huns when they appeared in the Pontic steppe in the early 370s. Several years of relentless pressure—raiding, burning camps, stealing cattle—shattered their resistance (Bachrach 1973, 26). Some submitted, others fled west. It was only after they had overwhelmed the Alans that the Huns attacked the Goths.

When their resistance crumbled, many Goths fled to the Danube requesting admission into the empire. One of the generals who led the Goths in retreat had an Alan name, Saphrax (Ammianus Marcellinus, XXXI, 3, 1ff, in Bachrach 1973, 27, n.2).

The situation in the Pontic steppe and the Balkans in the 370s was chaotic. There were Alans fighting with the Huns against the Goths and Alans fighting with the Goths against the Huns. Likewise, there were Huns on both sides. When Gothia was overrun, bands of Alans, Goths, and Huns roamed in Thrace and elsewhere. Another group of Alans, in Dacia Ripensis, fought Emperor Gratian, who was heading east to help Valens. Others joined Goths under Fritigern, who was allied with Alatheus and Saphrax. It was their combined forces that inflicted a crushing defeat on Valens near Adrianople in 378 and opened the way to Constantinople (Ammianus Marcellinus, XXXI, 8, 4; 2, 6; 12, 1ff; 16, 3, in Bachrach 1973, 27, n.4). (However, some Alans had been recruited by Gratian and fought on his side. The outcome of the battle was decided by the largely Alan and Gothic cavalry [Ammianus Marcellinus, XXXI, 12, 1ff, in Bachrach 1973, 28, n.6].)

The Alans' main handicap was the absence of a unified political structure. Their lack of cohesion was a major contributing factor in their defeat by the Huns.

Some of the Alans in the steppes between the Don and the Volga retreated into the mountainous regions of the Caucasus. They were an important element in the ethnogenesis of the Ossets, the Kabardians, and some other ethnic groups (Melyukova 113, in Sinor 1990).

Those who found themselves in the Balkans came to play an important part in the affairs of Byzantium. An anti-German mood in Constantinople in the 400s allowed some military commanders to capitalize on their Alan origin. One such was Ardaburius, a general in the East Roman army, who was made consul for 427. His son Aspar was made consul in 434; his grandson, also named Ardaburius, became consul in 447.

Aspar made a brilliant career in the 430s and 440s. Wisely, he refused the throne. Instead, he installed his *domesticus* Marcian, becoming a veritable *éminence grise* behind the imperial throne (Bachrach 1973, 42–44). When Marcian died, Aspar was instrumental in securing the throne for Leo (46).

When the latter was seriously weakened by a defeat inflicted by a Vandal-Alan force in 468, Aspar married another son, Patricius, to Leo's daughter and had him proclaimed Caesar, making him eligible for succession to the imperial throne. But Ardaburius Jr.'s intrigues with the Persians led to a falling-out between Leo and the Alan faction. He had Aspar and Ardaburius murdered. Only Aspar's younger son Hermaneric survived (47–49). (We should note that Aspar's sons had Alan [Ardaburius], Latin [Patricius], and Germanic [Hermaneric] names, probably indicating intermarriage. It is likely that the names had been chosen by Aspar's wives. We should also note that it was half-Latin Patricius who was eligible to marry the emperor's daughter [50]. Another note of interest is that "Aspar" may be a proto-Bulghar name, similar to "Asparuch.")

The Alans who retreated into the Caucasus and those who ended up in Byzantium were only a fraction of the original Alans.

Some Alans who had escaped from the Huns reached Pannonia and settled there as allies of the Vandals who lived there. In the 390s, undoubtedly under increasing pressure from the Huns, they started moving west (Jordanes, XXXI, XXII; Procopius, I, iii, 1; Courtois, 1955, 38–39; all in Bachrach 1973, 51, n.63).

Stilicho (himself part Vandal) had quite a few Alans in his entourage. He gladly settled these Pannonian Alans and Vandals in Noricum and Raetia as Roman allies. But provisions for the new settlers were inadequate, and in the winter of 401 they began to plunder the provinces that they were supposed to defend (Bachrach 1973, 51). Stilicho fought and defeated them, and they fled north and east into Germany (52).

Later, other Alans took part in Stilicho's campaigns against Alaric and were eventually settled in Northern Italy as colonists (34–36). Seven Alan settlements in northern Italy have been identified (40), but many were allowed to settle in cities like Pollentia and Verona (38). Like other immigrants, these Alans adopted Latin customs (*in Latios ritus transistis Alani*) (Claudian, De Con. Hon. IV, II. 485ff, in Bachrach 1973, 35, n.29) and soon became indistinguishable from the local population.

The great exodus of the Barbarian peoples from Pannonia in 406 brought more Alans and Vandals into the empire, this time into Gaul. As elsewhere, Alans fought on both sides: some plundered about two dozen cities in Gaul, from Tournai to Toulouse (52–53), but others chose to become allies.

A large number of Alans and Vandals crossed Gaul and invaded Spain (55). After two years of looting, they reached an agreement with Hispano-Romans. The invaders were now "guests" of Roman landowners entitled to a substantial portion of the income from their estates. In return, they undertook to protect their hosts from outside raiders like themselves. Alans settled in Lusitania and Cartagena; Siling Vandals in Baetica; and Hasding Vandals in Gallaecia (Galicia), among the Suevi.

It was a temporary arrangement. Constantius, the Roman commander in the West, asked his Visigothic "allies" (whom he had recently forced to submit) to subdue the Alans and Vandals in Spain. It took them three years to bring the Silings and the Alans to their knees. But the Vandal king Guntharic must have reached an understanding with Constantius. The Visigoths were recalled, leaving Guntharic as the real victor. In 419 he assumed the title Rex Vandalorum et Alanorum (58). In the subsequent century, as Vandals established a kingdom in North Africa, sacked Rome, and came to dominate the western Mediterranean, Alans followed their allies but retained their distinctive identity (57). Even the adoption of Arian Christianity by both did not promote ethnic merger. Each people kept traditions that made it clearly identifiable to contemporaries (58–59).

It was in Gaul that Alans left most traces.

Sarmatian military colonists (*laeti*) were settled along the Rhine—but not on the frontier—as early as the fourth century. It is more than likely that there were Alans among them. Their colonies extended from Amiens to Rheims, safeguarding the valleys of the Oise, the Aisne, and the Marne. They were positioned to protect important roads and cities, as well as arms depots and manufacturing centers at Amiens, Soissons, and Rheims (Grenier V, 398ff; Stein I, 264; Bachrach 1967, 478; Grohler 1913–35, 7, 295, in Bachrach 1973, 59, n.84).

In 414, Visigoths under Athaulf marched into southern Gaul and took Bordeaux, Narbonne, and Toulouse. This motley force included Alans. Count Paulinus of Pella, an influential Gallo-Roman landowner who was on good terms with the Alan chief, persuaded them to defect, promising land to settle and other inducements. They did and settled between Toulouse and the Mediterranean.

In the 440s, Aetius settled a group of Alans in Orléanais, and another one in Valentinois. Those of Orléanais were supposed to block the *bacaudae* of Armorica and, at the same time, the Visigoths from the south (Bachrach 1973, 63).

The settlement along the Loire (Orléanais) soon came under pressure from the Visigoths. In 452 or 453, they drove Alans across the Loire, but left those north of the river alone (68). (The Loire served as the frontier between the Visigothic and the Frankish spheres of influence.)

It is interesting that Alans entered imperial society at higher levels. Although many Roman landowners in the Orléanais fought the division of land, they could not win. Where Alans were the strongest, they expelled the previous owners and took over their estates. Most soon joined the *potentiores,* the powerful men of late-Roman Gaul.

Assimilation inevitably followed. It was facilitated by their adoption of mainstream Christianity (75), unlike the Visigoths and the Vandals, who chose Arianism (93, n.40). Early in the sixth century, the city of Le Mans had a bishop names Alanus, and a generation later the first of a large number of Breton counts named Alan appeared in a family with distinguished Celtic connections (117). Assimilation was also made easier by their phenotypical heterogeneity that allowed them to blend quickly into the local population (76–77). In Gaul, by the end of the fifth century, contemporaries ceased to refer to the Alans as an identifiable tribal entity. After three generations, they were fully assimilated. Only personal names—Alain, Allan, from Latin Alanus (74)—and a proverb, in Normandy, "cet homme est violent et allain" (*La Grande Encyclopedie* 1886, I, 1118, in Bachrach 1973, 119, n.90) reminds one of their presence.

The only place where they seem to have lingered was Armorica (80). There, the Alan language was still spoken in the sixth century. A few reminders—the cavalry tactics, the cult of St. Alanus, a few personal and place names—lingered till early Middle Ages (106).

Altogether, 11 Alan settlements are known in southwestern Gaul (30); 14 Alan and 8 Sarmatian settlements in northeastern Gaul (61); 9 Alan settlements in Orléanais (62); and 6 Alan settlements around Lake Geneva and Lyons (69).

To sum up, Iranian-speaking nomads in the Pontic and north Caucasian steppes were characterized by disunity. And Alans were more disunited than most, always acting in relatively small groups. That is why, perhaps, they could penetrate the *limes* either by entering imperial military service or by attaching themselves to stronger and more numerous peoples like Vandals and Visigoths. Also, despite their prowess as cavalrymen, they were clumsy and ineffective on foot, as is clear from a comment by Isidore of Seville in the early seventh century (90).

Wherever they settled, the Alans entered society at higher social levels than most other immigrants in late imperial Rome. But their numbers were small and their culture could not compete with the high civilization of contemporary Gaul. Only their horsemanship influenced conceptions of chivalry among the nascent medieval aristocracy as they were being assimilated into Breton society in the early sixth century (87).

However, it is also possible that their input has been largely disregarded because of the difficulty in identifying Alan artifacts. In a period of unrest, dissolution of empire, and mass migration, people mix, adapt, and adopt a bewildering variety of styles, making it difficult to distinguish one group from another (Beninger 1931, 76ff; Polaschek 1932, 239–58; Alfoldi 1932; Maenchen-Helfen 1944–45, 239–41; Thompson 4–6; Werner 15ff; Sulimirski 183ff; Kuznetsov and Pudovin 1961, 79–85; Orosius, *Hist.,* I, 2, on *Alania;* in Bachrach 1973, 52, n.65). But there is no doubt that within two generations the Alans had changed from nomadic warriors to sedentary landholders and members of the upper class (71–73).

CHAPTER 12

The Huns

The argument regarding the origins of the Huns revolves around the question of whether or not they derive from the Hsiung-nu.

The Hsiung-nu were a nomadic people who lived in the steppes north of China. Toward the end of the third century B.C., under the rule of *shan-yu* (commander on horseback) T'ou-man (d. 209 B.C.), they created an empire that reached its high point under his son and successor Mo-tun (208–175 B.C.) (Lubo-Lesnichenko, 43, in Basilov 1989). Later, under shan-yu Chih-Chih (55–34 B.C.), their zone of influence stretched to the lower Volga and the Ural foothills (Pan Ku 1935, 70, in Lubo-Lesnichenko, 47, in Basilov 1989). However, internal strife within the Hsiung-nu confederation was endemic. Eventually, it split into two, North and South. The southern Hsiung-nu fell under Chinese influence and were gradually assimilated (by the fifth century A.D.) (Lubo-Lesnichenko, 53, in Basilov 1989). Their northern cousins, defeated by the Hsien-pi in A.D. 93, withdrew west (53).

The idea that the Huns were or derived from the northern Hsiung-nu was first enunciated by an eminent French orientalist, H. Deguignes, in 1756–58 (Samolin 1957, 143); it was later adopted and popularized by Gibbon (Sinor 1990, 177; Samolin 1957, 143). It was unchallenged until the 1940s (Bernshtam 1926, in Maenchen-Helfen 1973, 367; Gumilëv, in Lubo-Lesnichenko, 42, in Basilov 1989) and is still accepted by some Russian scholars (Lubo-Lesnichenko, 43–52, in Basilov 1989).

Other scholars reject this hypothesis. Maenchen-Helfen, for example, pointed out that it is not supported by either literary or archeological evidence; nor is there any evidence that the Huns and the Hsiung-nu spoke the same language; and their art is fundamentally different (Maenchen-Helfen 1944–45, 243, in Samolin 1957, 143). Nor do we have any conclusive evidence that these tribes had migrated west. Finally, where were these migrants between the flight of the northern Hsiung-nu in the first century A.D. and the appearance of the Huns in Europe in the fourth? (Sinor 1990, 178)

There is another theory advanced by Samolin. He believed that the Hsiung-nu of the later Chinese texts were not the Hsiung-nu of the Han times but rather various Khion groups (Samolin 1957, 148, n.31). These people were known as "Hunna" in India, "Khun" East Turkestan (Samolin 1957, 148, n.34), and "White Huns" in the Byzantine sources (Samolin 1957, 148, n.35). They seem to have been Indo-Europeans, perhaps of Scythian and Issedon origin. Subjected by the Hsiung-nu at an early date, they may have retained the name for prestige. We should note that the onomastics of the Hun ruling house show no traces of Altaic; it may even have been Gothic (Samolin 1957, 148).

Thus, we end up with two possibilities. On the one hand, we have Altaic tribes, probably remnants of the western Hsiung-nu, merged with Uralic tribes in Siberia evolving into the higher stratum of the European Huns. On the other, there are Indo-European nomads or semi-nomads, former vassals of the Hsiung-nu, under general designation of Khion. They took a southern route and came in contact with the Sassanians rather than the Romans (Samolin 1957, 149).

If we turn to the Chinese sources, we find that they consistently identify the Turks as descendants of the Hsiung-nu: "The Ka-ch'e (Turks) were formerly 'Red Ti', and their speech was like that of the Hsiung-nu, but now is a little different" (Samolin 1957, 149, n.41); "the Turks who lived to the right of the Western Lake are a separate branch of the Hsiung-nu" (Samolin 1957, 149, n.43). Hsiung-nu origin was also ascribed to the Uighurs (Samolin 1957, 150, n.45).

Thus, all the tribes derived from the Hsiung-nu are Turkic. There are other affinities between the Hsiung-nu and the Turks, such as slashing one's face in mourning. This was characteristic of other groups as well: the Kutrighurs, who cut their cheeks with daggers (Maenchen-Helfen 1973, 274, n.123); the Turks, who cut off their hair and slashed their ears and cheeks (274, n.124); the Huns; the Magyars; and even the Slavs (275, n.126).

Finally, there is a letter written in Sogdian shortly after 311. Its author, a Sogdian merchant probably living in Su-chou, informs another merchant from Samarkand that the Huns—he spells the name *xwn*—had destroyed the Chinese capital Loyang (Henning 1948, in Sinor 1990, 179). The identity of the *xwn* is not firmly established; Sinor believes that they were southern Hsiung-nu, another proof of the Hun—Hsiung-nu connection. However, we should bear in mind that the Huns were a byword for destructive barbarians, and in this century the name was applied to Germans.

In Europe, the first reliable reference to the Huns (Xounoi) belongs to Ptolemy (Ptolemy, iii.5.10, in Thompson 1996, 25). It suggests that the Huns were known in the Pontic steppe already in the second century A.D.

They are also mentioned by Jordanes: "like a whirlwind of nations the Huns swept across the Alpidzuri, Alcildzuri . . ." (Jordanes, *Getica,* in Maenchen-Helfen 1973, 23). These tribal names are Turkic and, in Maenchen-Helfen's opinion, confirm the existence of Turkic-speaking nomads in the Pontic steppe before the arrival of the Huns.

However, other scholars do not share his opinion because no Roman author mentions them in the next two hundred years (Thompson 1996, 25).

Many, if not most, of the Hunnic tribal names also end in *-cur* and are clearly Turkic. But personal names are a mixed bag: they include Turkic; Germanic or Germanized (e.g., Attila, Bleda, Rua/Ruga); Iranian; and hybrid (Maenchen-Helfen 1973, 441). However, there are no Germanic names among non-Attilanic Huns (442). And the paucity of Iranian names prior to the sixth century shows little interaction with Iranian speakers (Parthians, Sassanian Persians, and others) (443).

Historical records also indicate that the Huns were a mixed population. Among historic characters—but they, inevitably, belong to the upper strata—Balamber married a Gothic princess (364, n.47), Attila's last wife had a Germanic name Ildico, (n.48), and Gepid Mundo was of Attilanic descent (n.49).

Most large cemeteries of the post-Hunnic period in the steppes show a mixture of Europoids and Mongoloids. But it is virtually impossible to ascertain with any degree of certainty the ethnicity of skeletal remains. As Bartucz wrote in 1939, "I don't know of a single skull which could, beyond any doubt, be regarded as Hunnic" (364, n.54). He is right. But no Mongoloid remains have been found east of Vienna before the arrival of the Huns. Conversely, locations and grave goods of Mongoloid burials indicate the time no later than the fifth century. In other words, they are dated within the Hunnic time frame (366).

However, the Hsiung-nu were also a mixed population. Early depictions of the Hsiung-nu show luxuriant beards one does not usually observe on men of the Mongoloid stock (370, n.85). The Mongoloid elements among the Hsiung-nu were considerably strengthened by Chinese renegades (n.87) and POWs. But their raids into oasis cities of Xinjiang probably gave the Hsiung-nu a good number of Europoids (371, n.89). There is a Chinese account of the massacre of the Chieh (Hsiung-nu) soldiers in Chao in A.D. 349 that says that the Chieh were recognized by their high noses and full beards (372, n.94). In fact, Europoids with blue or green eyes and red hair have been living at the eastern edge of the Eurasian steppe since time immemorial. And Genghis Khan and his descendants had blond or reddish hair and deep-blue eyes (374, n.107).

Sometime around A.D. 370, the Alans in the Pontic steppe were overwhelmed by the Huns, as was described earlier.

Soon thereafter, the Huns, together with their (reluctant?) Alan allies, invaded the Ostrogothic kingdom in today's Ukraine. The Goths, under their old king Ermanaric, held out for some time. When it became increasingly clear that victory was impossible, Ermanaric killed himself and was succeeded by his great-nephew Vithimiris (Ammianus xxxi.3.2, in Thompson 1996, 27, n.33). To strengthen his army, Vithimiris hired Hunnic mercenaries. But that did not help either. After a year of desperate resistance and a string of defeats, he was killed in battle and most Ostrogoths surrendered (Ammianus xxxi.3.2, para. 3, and Sozomen l.c., in Thompson 1996, 27, n.34).

Those who did not acknowledged Vithimiris' son Viderichus as heir. But he was still a child, and the actual command was given to Alatheus and Saphrax (Alan name!).

The new commanders were no more successful than their predecessors. Soon they were forced to retreat across the Dniester and ask their Visigothic cousins (under Athanaric) for protection.

By a ruse, the Huns scattered the Visigoths and then inflicted yet another defeat on Alatheus and Saphrax. Athanarich tried to build a defensive wall between the Pruth and the Danube, but it was too late. Panic-stricken Goths began to flee toward the Danube hoping to find safety in the empire (Thompson 1996, 28).

In the fall of 376, some two hundred thousand Goths were allowed to cross the Danube. However, their provisioning was inadequate. Either the Roman administration was overwhelmed by the dimensions of the disaster or, perhaps, the refugees could not resist the temptations offered by the empire. Whatever the reason, they were soon plundering Thrace.

By the fall of 377, the refugees-turned-looters were penned in against Mount Haemus (Judeich 1891, vi, 5, n.1, in Thompson 1996, 29, n.42). In desperation, they sent emissaries to the Huns on the other side of the Danube with stories of the great treasures to be found in the empire.

The Huns and their Alan allies promptly crossed the river, and the Romans had to withdraw. After a year of raiding and looting, on August 9, 378, a combined force of Huns, Goths, and Alans annihilated the army of Emperor Valens on the plains outside Adrianople (Seeck v, 466; Ammianus xxxi.4.6, in Thompson 1996, 29, n.41).

It was a major disaster for the Romans. It may have cost them Pannonia, where traces of Hunnic occupation date from this time (30, n.49). However, it appears that the bulk of the Huns, their demographic center, was still in the east.

In the winter of 395, the Huns swept through Armenia, and on into Cappadocia, Cilicia, and Syria. Soon, crowds of captives and great herds of cattle could be seen along the roads leading to the distant north. Wrote

Jerome: "Behold, the wolves, not of Arabia, but of the North, were let loose upon us last year from the far-off rocks of Caucasus . . ." (Epp. lx. 16, lxxvii. 8, in Thompson 1996, 31, n.58). The Huns also raided in the Balkans, but compared to the campaign in the east, their invasions across the frozen Danube were merely a sideshow. The war continued until the end of 398 (Thompson 1996, 32, n.64).

Seven years passed before the Huns returned to the west in force. This time, they swept across central Europe, sending thousands of barbarians fleeing for their lives into the empire. In the last months of 405, Radagaisus broke into Italy. And on December 31, 406, swarms of Vandals, Suevi, and Alans pierced the frontier and streamed into Gaul (32–33).

This invasion emptied large areas of central Europe of their former, mostly Germanic, inhabitants. One of its ramifications was Alaric's sack of Rome that hastened the collapse of the Western Empire. Another was a more prominent role that the Huns came to play in Roman affairs.

The Huns were useful because they were good soldiers and could be used against other barbarians. Thus, when Alaric's brother-in-law Athaulf appeared south of the Julian Alps in 409, the Romans dispatched 300 Huns against him and, at the cost of 17 dead, disposed of 1,100 invaders (38, n.87). Later in the year, the imperial government brought in another ten thousand Huns from Dalmatia, this time against Alaric, precluding his march on Rome (38, n.88).

From then on, Hun mercenaries were frequently involved in internecine struggles between various Roman factions (e.g., in 412 and 425). Aetius, a patrician who had spent several years among the Huns (as a hostage) and established close ties among the Hun elite, was particularly adept at playing his Hun trump card.

In 437, he used them against the Burgundians. The latter had been settled as *foederati* on the west bank of the Rhine since 413 and were now trying to expand into Upper Belgica. The Huns massacred some twenty thousand Burgundians; survivors were settled in Savoy (72). (The episode served as the basis for the epic of *Die Nibelungen*.) The Huns were also used against the Visigoths; in 439 they even besieged Theodoric's capital Toulouse (76). A treaty that Aetius concluded with Attila's uncle Rua transformed the Huns into an instrument of the Gallo-Roman aristocracy in Gaul (79).

But the Huns were never merely an instrument in Roman hands. They continued to loot and plunder, and attacked whenever it suited their interests. Attacks on the lower Danube resumed in 408, under Uldin (33). And in 420, the Huns took advantage of Constantinople's war with Persia and raided Thrace (35, n.77). We do not know how they were expelled.

The Huns reached the zenith of power under Attila in the 440s. He was preceded by his uncle Rua, who ruled the great Hunnic confederacy in the early 420s. Attila, the son of Rua's brother Mundiuch, took over in 434 (69). At first, he shared power with his brother Bleda. (This seems to have been a custom: Rua had shared power with his brother Octar.) But sometime in 444–46, Attila murdered Bleda and became the sole ruler of the realm (97).

Under Attila, the Hun-Roman relations soured. In 441, the Huns swept through the Balkans sacking Singidunum, Sirmium, and other major towns and fortresses (89). The war resumed in 443 after a short truce. The Huns destroyed Naissus, then Serdica, and finally captured Philippopolis (Thompson 1995/96, 92). Roman resistance crumbled, and the Huns reached Constantinople—but did not attempt to storm the seemingly impregnable city (Thompson 1996, 93).

The emperor (Theodosius) had to beg for peace. Conditions imposed by the Huns were harsh: annual tribute was trebled to 2,100 pounds of gold, arrears (amounting to 6,000 pounds of gold) had to be paid; Hun fugitives had to be surrendered, and the like. The treaty, provisionally signed on August 27, 443, was ratified in the fall of same year (94–95, n.99). The once-mighty empire now had to pay tribute to barbarians!

Despite the tribute, peace was of short duration, because a "continuous intake of plunder was a social necessity for them" (98). The new invasion was precipitated by a destructive earthquake that hit Thrace, Hellespont, and the Cyclades on January 26, 447. Its aftershocks continued for four months (99). In Constantinople, buildings and walls collapsed, thousands died, and plague spread. It was a convenient moment to attack. But within 60 days, when the Huns were already on the way, the old fortifications were rebuilt and a third wall erected (100).

If the capital was safe, the rest of the empire was not. The Romans were routed in a great battle near the river Utus (Vid). Marcianople, the largest city in Thrace, was destroyed. And the Huns, like locusts, spread over Illyricum, Thrace, and Dacia (101). They reached deep into Greece and were stopped only at Thermopylae (102, n.126).

In the next three years Attila was busy fighting the Acatziri, and the Eastern Empire had a brief respite (105–06). But in 448, Attila demanded a strip of land from Singidunum to Novae, 300 miles long and 5 days' journey in depth (100–120 miles) (108). The empire was exhausted and could not resist. In desperation, the rulers in Constantinople decided to have Attila murdered (110–111). The plot, however, went awry. The situation was made even worse by Theodosius's death on July 28, 450. The new emperor, Marcian, refused to continue paying tribute. Perhaps, he could do so because he knew that Attila was about to make a move against Gaul.

In the West, after the massacre of Litorius's Huns at Toulouse in 439, Attila provided no more troops for Aetius (137). Their relations had deteriorated, and in 449, Priscus found West Roman envoys at Attila's court trying to restore them (140).

The new campaign was directed against the Visigoths of Toulouse. For various reasons, Attila did not want to antagonize Rome and made it known that he was coming as an ally of Valentinian III and a "guardian of the Romans' friendship" (144, n.21). An intrigue by Valentinian's sister Honoria added an unexpected twist to the story. Honoria (who lived in Ravenna) had a love affair with the steward who managed her palace. The affair was discovered, and her lover, Eugenius, was executed while she was engaged to senator Herculanus against her will.

In desperation, Honoria appealed to Attila (Grant 1978, 433). She even sent him a ring. (In this, she had a precedent, her mother Placidia's marriage with Athaulf 35 years earlier.)

Attila now had a convenient excuse. He claimed Honoria as his bride and demanded half the Western Empire as dowry (433). Rome refused, ostensibly because the succession passed through the male line.

While Attila was preparing the invasion, Romans found themselves in difficult circumstances. There was famine in Italy and Gaul, and few allies could provide troops. Aetius managed to collect a sizable army, but it was a motley, untested force.

Attila invaded Gaul. On April 7, 451, he sacked Metz, then took the road to Orléans (then ruled by Sangibanus, king of the Alans; he promised to surrender the city to Attila [Thompson 1996, 153, n. 58]).

And that is where Aetius and his Visigothic allies (under Theodoric) met him in battle. It appears that Attila was soundly beaten (on June 14?) and had to retreat. Constantly harassed by Aetius, Attila stopped at the Catalaunian Plains (in today's Champaigne) (154, n.60).

Another battle (on June 20?) was fought. It was bloody but indecisive (154). Theodoric was killed, but the Huns, it seems, suffered heavy losses and retreated behind a circle of wagons.

Now, Aetius did not want to eliminate the Huns completely. He still believed he could use them against the Germans, if need be. Somehow, he convinced his Frankish and Visigothic allies that the campaign was over and allowed Attila to slip away (155–56). Perhaps, he was under the impression that he and Attila had a tacit understanding that Attila would not return.

Imagine his surprise when his former friend invaded Italy the following year! Aetius was totally unprepared.

Aquileia was stormed and sacked. After that, city after city opened the gates (159). Some were destroyed, but some—Mediolanum, Ticinum—were spared (160, n.79). (According to Grant, Mediolanum was sacked [Grant 1978, 433].) Attila wanted to sack Rome, like Alaric, but was reminded that

Alaric died almost immediately thereafter (Thompson 1996, 160, n.81). An embassy sent by Aetius (headed by Pope Leo) met Attila on the banks of the Mincio and managed to dissuade him from marching on Rome. Peace was concluded.

The real reason for Attila's change of heart was probably famine and pestilence in Italy. He simply did not want to endanger his men, especially since he had far-reaching plans in Gaul (161). Whatever the reason, Attila did not advance further, and Italy was saved.

While Attila was in Italy, a Byzantine force under Aetius's namesake crossed the Danube, reached the Hun headquarters, and smashed the Hun force left there (163).

This did not seem to dampen Attila's spirits. When he returned home, he married one more wife, a beautiful Ildico, and died on the wedding night, presumably a happy man (Thompson 1995/96, 164). The reaction of his subjects seems ambiguous: his burial was an occasion for wild revelry where grief mixed with joy (Thompson 1996, 165, n.96).

Upon his death, his numerous sons divided the subject peoples among themselves (land seemed of secondary importance to them), but soon began to quarrel (167).

The struggle for succession—for that is what it was—gave the subject peoples a chance to break free. The Ostrogoths of the Tisza valley were the first to revolt. Their uprising was followed by a great rebellion of various Germanic tribes led by Ardaric, king of the Gepids (and a former confidant of Attila). The Gepids were joined by the Skiri, the Rugii, the Suevi, and the Heruli. Together, they smashed the Huns in a great battle on Lake Nedao in Pannonia, probably in 455.

Hun survivors fled across the Carpathians to the shores of the Black Sea, back to where their ancestors came from 80 years earlier (168). Some of them later returned and attacked the Ostrogoths under Valamer, but suffered another crushing defeat (169). After that, there were only occasional raids by small Hun bands. We also know that some of the Hun survivors were settled in the Eastern Empire by Marcian (170).

With the Huns gone, Constantinople quickly regained some of the lost territories. Whereas none of the bishops of Moesia Inferior had participated in the Council of Chalcedon in 451, by 457 all provinces of the Thracian diocese were again under Roman rule (Maenchen-Helfen 1973, 159). However, no letters were sent to the metropolitan bishops in Dacia Ripensis, Moesia Superior, or Praevalitana (159, n.797). Evidently, there were no bishops in these provinces.

Indeed, the reconquest was patchy: Constantinople lacked adequate resources to reoccupy all areas. Until 457, many regions in Pannonia and even south of the Danube were still outside its reach. They were only reincorporated in 458 (160–61).

By then, the Huns were also anxious to reach an understanding with Constantinople. They could not return to the steppe, which was, as it had always been, the preserve of wild, untamed nomads. Among them the pitiful remnants of the Huns could be no more than "minor robbers and cattle raiders" (Thompson 1996, 176).

In 465 or 466 (Maenchen-Helfen 1973, 165; Thompson places it in 468/69 [Thompson 1996, 172–73]), Attila's son Dengizech and his brother Hernach sent a peace mission to Constantinople. They wanted to trade. But now the tables were turned. Their demands were rejected. Dengizech then invaded the Eastern Empire, and was easily beaten and killed (in 469). His head was cut off and brought to Constantinople, where it was fixed on a pole at Xylokerkos (the Wooden Circus) Gate (173; Maenchen-Helfen 1973, 165–68).

The last raid that we know of, on the lower Danube, about 474, was easily beaten back (Thompson 1996, 173). From then on we find small bands of Huns serving under Goths and in the service of Western Romans (174).

It is hard to be positive about the Huns. Many scholars (e.g., Thompson and Peisker) see them as destructive, predatory nomads devoid of the creative impulse. In Maenchen-Helfen's assessment, "Thompson views the Huns as a howling mass of half-naked savages" (Maenchen-Helfen 1973, 190). Indeed, Thompson calls them a "community of plunderers" (Thompson 1996, 185).

Even their "defender," Maenchen-Helfen, had to acknowledge that "Huns were often nasty in war" (Maenchen-Helfen 1973, 203, n.13). He adds that Germans of the Völkerwanderung period behaved no better. In 406, in Gaul, they killed hermits, burned priests alive, raped nuns, and the like. (n.13). This attempt to excuse, or at least contextualize, Hunnic barbarity by references to German misdeeds may seem rather quaint.

In any case, it was inevitable that nomads (and forest tribes) would be prone to plunder when confronted by the riches of sedentary civilizations, whether Chinese or Mediterranean. The wonder is not that they plundered, but that they could master enough warriors to ravage several empires for an extended period of time. (Albeit Rome was in decline.)

Thompson postulates that the subjugation of agricultural peoples in southern Russia in the 370s brought them from an area with no food surplus to an area where there was plenty. In turn, the food surplus allowed them to increase the number of warriors, which made further conquests possible (Thompson 1996, 68). Thus, he believes that the move into the Pontic steppe was the turning point.

This is debatable. First, the Ostrogoths were the first agricultural people to be conquered by the Huns, *before the latter could have achieved numerical superiority.* Second, it would require at least one generation after the acquisition of adequate food surplus to produce a substantially larger number of warriors. The time span between the appearance of the Huns and the subjugation of the Ostrogoths—a few years at most—was just too short to allow them to increase their numbers substantially.

What is beyond doubt is the fast accumulation of wealth once they could blackmail the Romans: the treaty with Rua concluded in 430 stipulated payments of 350 pounds of gold from the Eastern Empire per annum. The amount was doubled in 435; and after 443, the Eastern Empire had to pay 6,000 pounds in arrears and 2,100 pounds annually (177). Altogether, in the 440s, the Eastern Empire paid the Huns about 13,000 pounds of gold.

However, these amounts are comparable with other extortionary payments made in similar situations. Thus, in 408, Alaric forced the Western Empire to pay 4,000 pounds (Maenchen-Helfen 1973, 180, n.94); that same year, he besieged Rome and was bought off with an additional 5,000 pounds (180, n.95). In 570, Tiberius offered 3,000 pounds to the Lombards to stop raiding Italy (181, n.99). The same year, Avars were paid 1,000 pounds in annual subsidy (181, n.100). In 540, Persians got 5,000 pounds (181, n.102). Even robbers in the Isaurian highlands in 484–492 were paid a yearly "subsidy" of 1,400 pounds (181 n.103).

These "external" payments were in line with the "internal" ones. When Paul, an ex-consul of 498, was in financial trouble, emperor Anastasius helped him out with 2,000 pounds (181, n.106). In 514, Anastasius ransomed Hypatius from Vitalian for 5,000 pounds (181, n.107). In 526 and 527, Emperor Justin sent 4,500 pounds to Antioch when it was heavily damaged by an earthquake (181, n.108). To celebrate his consulship, Justinian spent 4,000 pounds on games and distributions to the populace (181, n.109); in 532, he gave 4,000 pounds for the building of Saint Sophia (n.110).

Substantial as these payments undoubtedly were, they did not come close to bankrupting the Eastern Empire. Its revenue in the fifth century, has been estimated at 270,000 pounds a year, of which 45,000 were spent on the army (182, n.113). Thus, the 6,000 pounds paid to Attila in 447 were little more than 2.2 percent of annual income; the highest annual tribute was about 4.7 percent of what the army required (182). When Leo ascended the throne in 457, he found more than 100,000 pounds of gold in the treasury (182, n.114). (It is a curious fact that Romans cheated the barbarians. A hoard from Kirileny in Moldavia, hidden about A.D. 400, contained a solidus with 3.90 grams of gold, instead of the required 4.54 [183, n.120].)

Ultimately, the predatory behavior of the Huns (and other nomads) can be explained in terms of the great difference in the level of wealth between them and the advanced sedentary civilizations they encountered. It was also the result of their military superiority based on mobility.

In terms of material civilization, the Huns were at the Lower Stage of Pastoralism, as defined in Hobhouse, Wheeler, and Ginsberg (26 et passim, in Thompson 1996, 47). Thomson asserts that their economy could not support them; to survive, they needed an exchange with a sedentary agricultural population (48).

In this they were all too typical. Trade with agriculturalists is essential for the nomads' existence. It was the desire to trade that drew the Huns to the border towns of the Roman Empire (189, n.63). Incidentally, it is a common feature of all nomads that they have virtually no internal trade, while their external trade is quite brisk (190, n.65). One reason is that their economy is not specialized. They produce more or less the same things. Another was the lack of raw materials. This could not have been a long-term impediment, since metals were abundant in the foothills of the southern Urals and elsewhere. But trees were not. Even the Mongols had to import their weapons from China and Khorasan. In normal times, they could make their own bows and arrows, spears and lances, "but as soon as they began to make war on a large scale their slender productive resources failed them and they were forced to rely on other countries for their weapons" (190, n.68). The same goes for early Turks, according to Menander Protector; and Avar ambassadors in Constantinople in 562 tried to buy weapons from imperial factories (190–91, n.70). The same applies to linen and grain.

That is why, whenever they could, East Romans denied nomads the benefits of trade (as in 455/6, when Marcian forbade the export of weapons). (Roman coins in Romania indicate that Huns traded almost exclusively with East, not West Romans [193].) And the closure of market towns to Dengizech was the final blow: no trade and no weapons spelled the end of nomad domination (198–99). Of course, by then the Huns had been greatly weakened. Earlier, East Romans were simply not in a position to impose any restrictions on the Huns. Besides, their mobility allowed them to get weapons elsewhere. So, the ban on exchange could be imposed only on a society already enfeebled. In other words, it could hasten the end, not cause irreparable damage.

At an early stage of the nomadic cycle, virtually all nomads engaged in agriculture. An iron sickle found in a late Sarmatian grave at Kalinovka (on the left bank of the Volga north of Volgograd) (Maenchen-Helfen 1973, 175, n.51) shows that in the first century A.D., Sarmatians grew grain. Similar evidence from Kunya Uaz in Khorezm and on the upper Ob' indicates that in former times the Huns had also tilled the soil (178, n.71). They abandoned it only during the mass migration. Once they conquered large peasant populations, however, they found it more expedient to tax their subjects than to work themselves (177).

This parasitic existence was made possible by their small numbers. According to Peisker, the basic unit of Hun society was one family of 5 or 6 people who lived in one tent. About 6 to 10 tents formed a camp; several camps a clan; several clans a tribe; and several tribes an *il,* or people. An average Hun tribe consisted of some 5,000 people (Thompson 1996, 49). The segmented structure of nomadic society goes a long way toward explaining the ease with which Huns—and other nomads—split into components and changed sides: a treaty made by one tribe was not binding for others. And if tribal leadership was unsuccessful in safeguarding or promoting tribal interests, a clan or several clans could always break away and join another tribe or even the enemy. The military leader retained his position only as long as he was successful (64).

The size of Hunnic armies reflected their low numbers. The average size of an army did not exceed 1,200 warriors (54). Their success was predicated upon their adversaries' limited resources, especially of the later Roman society in full decline. When Honorius employed 10,000 Huns against Alaric, he had to collect grain and livestock from as far as Dalmatia and then have them shipped to Italy (52).

In Thompson's opinion, the Huns did not pose a serious threat to the Romans until they were integrated politically and militarily. As long as tribes and clans sought water and pasture as isolated units, they could not develop sufficient political coherence to threaten the empire as a whole (62). (But they could threaten—and destroy—Alans and Goths!)

This situation changed by 412, when one leading family succeeded in making military leadership hereditary. By the time of Attila (mid-430s), the accumulation of wealth led to social stratification (192). By the time of Priscus's visit in 449, the Huns had become little more than a giant robbers' nest, a parasitic community of marauders. Instead of animals, they herded men: peasants from Syria and Armenia, urban dwellers from the Balkans, and the like (195, 197). Most of their captives were sold for profit, but those who were not, often people with valuable skills, like architects, could eventually buy their freedom and take an honorable place in the Hunnic society. The story of a merchant from Viminacium, a native of Greece, whom Priscus met at Attila's court, provides a good illustration. The man had been captured by the Huns but was allowed to join the army. He fought and acquitted himself well. Eventually, he used his share of the loot to buy his freedom. By the time Priscus met him, he was married to a Hunnic wife and had attained a reasonably good position in the Hun society. It is interesting that in his opinion his present situation compared favorably with his life in the empire (205–06).

As a society, the Huns grew totally dependent on their subject peoples. The growing inequality demanded more and more goods, that is, more and more conquests, than their limited manpower could not assure. Operations in different theaters of war, extending over vast distances, added to their difficulties. Increasingly, they had to retain and rely on non-Hunnic allies (196). Ultimately, it was a case of imperial overreach.

After the disintegration of their empire, the Huns reverted to an earlier, more segmented type of society (201). Peisker pointed out that when a confederacy disintegrates, "the camp, the clans, and in part the tribes also, retain an organic life, and their deep roots survive . . ." (Peisker 334, in Thompson 1996, 202). The clans are the true building blocks of nomadic polities, their atoms. These building blocks enable forceful leaders to create new tribes so that before long the steppe once again swarms with swashbuckling nomads. The Huns failed to reestablish themselves because they were swept aside by an influx of new and powerful nomadic migrants (202).

What was the effect of the Huns on the Roman Empire(s), aside from siphoning substantial wealth?

Many West Romans saw them as a counterbalance against the Visigoths, Burgundians, and other barbarians. Thompson advanced an opinion that the Huns retarded the collapse of the Western Empire by conquering Germans (235). Actually, the Huns sent massive outflows of armed German refugees into the empire in 376 and 405–406, initiating the process of dismemberment. They held them in check only in 435–455, when the Romans, east and west, needed a check against them.

Other suppositions regarding the role of merchants and the ruling elites in both parts of empire are also either contentious or impossible to prove. All one can say is that the effect of the Huns was ambivalent, changed from period to period, and was extraneous to internal developments. But there is no doubt that they caught the empire when it was well past its prime, that they were a great burden on the Roman tax payer and the empire's defensive capabilities, and that they ultimately contributed to Rome's demise. That Constantinople withstood and survived points to the primacy of internal factors.

CHAPTER 13

The Falling Dominoes

The Oghurs and the Bulghars

Already in the second century A.D., Turkic tribes migrated from central Asia to a broad area between the Caspian and the Black Sea (Burmov 1948, 298, in Angelov et al. 1961).

When the Huns arrived in the Pontic steppe, they found at least two tribes whose names indicate Turkic origin: the Alpidzuros and Alcidzuros (Jordanes [Russ. Trans.] 1960, 151, in Golden, 256, in Sinor 1990; Maenchen-Helfen 1973, 23 and 402–403). The Alcidzuros may be related to, or even ancestors of, the Acatziri, who were subdued by Attila. One of Attila's sons, Hernac (the brother of Dengizech), was later listed in the Bulgarian Prince List. It is quite possible that he and his clan joined the tribes that later formed the Bulghar confederation (Golden, 257, in Sinor 1990).

The homeland of the Oghur tribes—the Saraghurs, the Onoghurs, and others—lay in western Siberia and/or the Kazak steppe, in the ancestral lands of the Huns, where they were part of a large Turkic confederation (257).

The Oghurs were pushed west by the defeat inflicted by their eastern neighbors the Sabirs around 463. Four years later, in 467, the Saraghurs smashed the Acatziri, a victory that assured their predominance in the Pontic steppe. And by 480, the Oghurs joined with Hunnic and, possibly, other elements to form a large confederation that came to be known as "Bulghars" or "Bulgars" (Mixed Ones).

In this earliest period of their history, the Bulghars ranged from the Balkans to North Caucasus, raiding the Eastern Empire or fighting on its side as allies and mercenaries (258). Already in 480, Emperor Zenon hired Bulghar mercenaries to fight the Ostrogoths. It did not take them long to find out that the empire was rich and weak. Soon, they were raiding Byzantium.

According to Marcellinus Comes (he calls them "Scythians"), the earliest raids occurred in 493, 499, and 502 (Marcellinus Comes, 94–96, in Runciman 1930, 5, n.2). Despite occasional attacks, the nomads were soon taking part in the internal and external affairs of the empire. In 514, for example, rebel Vitalian employed them against Emperor Anastasius (Malalas, 402, in Runciman 1930, 6, n.2).

Their growing involvement was cut short by the middle of the sixth century, when the Kutrighurs, a closely related tribe on the north shore of the Sea of Azov, blocked their way. The Kutrighurs continued the old pattern, alternating cooperation and confrontation. In 530 they served with Byzantine forces in Italy (Golden, 258, in Sinor 1990). But a few years later they pillaged the empire, as far as Constantinople, Gallipoli, and Greece (Angelov et al. 1961, 53).

But the ascendance of the Kutrighurs did not last long either. The arrival of the Avars destroyed the balance of power in the steppe. The Utrighurs were beaten, Sabirs destroyed, Kutrighurs subjugated (Runciman 1930, 10). Some Bulghars joined (or were made to join) the Avars and took part in their campaigns, including the siege of Constantinople in 626. When the Avars were beaten and fled to Pannonia, many Bulghars followed. There was a strong Bulghar element in the Avar kaghanate. The extent of their involvement in the Avar affairs can be seen in the events of 630–32. That year, the Avar kaghan died, and Bulghars tried to install their own candidate. However, in the struggle that followed, the Avar candidate won. Many Bulghars were killed, others fled, only a few stayed with the Avars. Some nine thousand refugees sought safety in Bavaria, where they were treacherously killed one night (21). Those who stayed in North Caucasus had to submit to the khan of the western Turks, Siljibu (Angelov et al. 1961, 54).

It was the struggle against western Turks that shaped the Bulghar confederation. It was put together by Kubrat (584–642), the chief of the Unogundurs, in the beginning of the seventh century (Golden calls it a state [Golden, 261–62, in Sinor 1990].) The Unogundurs were soon joined by the Kutrighurs, Onoghurs, and others. Its territory was circumscribed by the Kuban', the Dnieper, and the Volga. Kubrat's power was further enhanced when he managed to expel a large group of Avars who still remained in the area.

Relations with Byzantium were mostly friendly. In 634–35, Kubrat allied himself with the empire, accepted baptism (262), and was awarded the title of patrician. But after his death, circa 650, centrifugal tendencies, so common in nomadic states, reasserted themselves, and the alliance gradually disintegrated under pressure from the incoming Khazars (Angelov et al. 1961, 54–55).

Tribes in the east were the first to suffer from the Khazars. Under Kubrat's third son Isperih (Asparuh) (644–701), they went west. About 670, they crossed the Don, the Dnieper, and the Dniester and settled in southern Bessarabia (Anastasoff 1977, 23). From there they raided Byzantium, at a time when it was busy fighting the Arabs (Zlatarski 1918, I, 21; Burmov XLIV, 2, 1–36, in Angelov et al. 1961, 55, n.2).

In about 679, these Bulghars crossed the Danube and conquered Slav tribes living in Thrace. This conquest laid the foundations of Bulgaria, marked by the gradual assimilation of Turkic Bulghars by the Slav majority and the adoption of Orthodox Christianity in 864 (Golden, 262, in Sinor 1990).

Another group, the Kotrags (or Kutrighurs), went up the Volga to the mouth of the Kama, conquered local (mostly Finnic) tribes, and established another Bulgarian state (Volga Bulgaria) that survived until 1236–37, when it was destroyed by the Mongols (242).

Finally, some Bulghars under Kubrat's elder son Batbaian and another leader called Kotragos stayed in place between the Kuban' and the Azov. These had to submit to the Khazars (Angelov et al. 1961, 55, n.2). Some of them were subsequently assimilated, others sought refuge in the Caucasus, where a small group of mountain people, the Balkars, still bears their name.

The Sabirs

If the Oghurs had been displaced by their eastern neighbors the Sabirs, the latter were set in motion by the pressure from their eastern neighbors, the Avars.

The Sabirs probably originated in western Siberia and in the western Tien Shan and the Ili river regions (Gening and Khalikov 1964, 147, in Golden, 257, in Sinor 1990). Like most nomadic people, they were of mixed descent, although Jordanes classified them as one of the two great branches of the Huns (Jordanes 1882, 63, in Dunlop 1954, 27, n.113).

They seem to have followed the defeated Oghurs to the Pontic steppe within two years of their victory (in 463) (Priscus, ed. Bonn, 158, Sinor 1946–47, 1–77, in Dunlop 1954, 27, n.112). But this must have been an avant-garde only because the proto-Bulghar tribal union had coalesced there by 480. It is unlikely it would have survived or even come together in a region dominated by the Sabirs.

According to Golden, the Sabirs had arrived in Pontus by 515 (259, in Sinor 1990), although the exact date is hard to determine. But the Sabirs and the Bulghars must have found some form of coexistence, at least until the arrival of the Avars. All one can say is that the situation on the steppe was extremely fluid. It is possible that the rise of the Kutrighurs in the early sixth century at the expense of their Bulghar cousins was somehow linked with the inflow of the Sabirs. In any case, by 514 they were strong enough to break through the Caspian Gates and invade Cappadocia and Galatia (Theophanes, ed. Bonn, 249, in Dunlop 1954, 27, n.114). The invasion, undoubtedly instigated or at least condoned by Byzantium, established a pattern that characterized the Sabir external policy in the 40 years of their predominance in Pontus: it was predicated upon an alliance with Byzantium, mainly against Sassanian Persia, although they were not incapable of switching sides when this was deemed advantageous.

The Sabir hegemony in the steppe was of brief duration. It was smashed by the Avars in 557 or 558 (Golden, 260, in Sinor 1990). But their remnants lingered until about 576, when they were transplanted south of the Kura by the Byzantines (Menander Prot. 394, in Dunlop 1954, 27, n.115).

Another group must have followed the Bulghars up the Volga. Under the name of Suwar (Sabir/Savir/Savar), they settled in the vicinity of Volga Bulgaria and continued their adversarial relationship. In the tenth century they centered around the town of the same name, Suwar, and had a leader of their own (Ibn Fadlan, 1956, 139, in Golden, 236, n.8, in Sinor 1990; Hudud al-Alam 1970, 162, in Golden, 236, n.9, in Sinor 1990).

Those few who stayed on the steppe were probably absorbed by the Khazars, like other tribes that cease to appear in the sources at about the same time.

The Avars

The Avar migration proceeded in two stages. At first, a defeat by the Chinese in 460 (Pigulevskaia 1941, 51; Czegledy 1954, 11, both in Golden, 258, n.4, in Sinor 1990) propelled them into the lands of the Sabirs.

About a hundred years later, an uprising of their Turkic subjects served as a catalyst for another push west (Dvornik 1956, 36). It is possible that "real" Avars were only a small segment among these migrants. Most may have been a hodge-podge of Uighur, Mongol, and even Manchu clans who had adopted their former masters' name for reasons of prestige. (Golden does not seem to share this opinion.)

Whether "real" or "fake," the Avars in 557 or 558 crossed the lower Volga and swept away the Sabirs, the Oghurs, and the proto-Bulghars who then controlled the area between the Volga and the Don. And then they established contact with Constantinople, which was evidently well known to them.

Byzantium was only too happy to incite them against other nomads who were attacking its possessions south of the Danube, and the Avars were glad to oblige. But they had little respite: their former (Turkic) subjects reached the Pontic steppe, and the Avars had to continue their peregrination. (By this time they included a substantial Kutrighur/Bulghar component [Golden, 260, in Sinor 1990].)

In 561, led by Kaghan Baian (the name seems Bulghar), they approached the Danube and demanded land south of the river. Byzantium refused. The Avars then allied themselves with the Langobards of Pannonia. Together, they conquered and destroyed the Gepid state in Dacia in 567, which gave the Avars control of the Tisza basin, western Romania, Banat, and Bačka (Gimbutas 1971, 101).

Now, the Langobards belatedly realized that they were left alone with the Avars (Dvornik 1956, 37). They decided it was safer to seek a new venue. Their departure for Italy in 568 left the Avars in sole possession of Pannonia and the adjacent lands. They soon spread along the Danube and its tributaries into Moravia, Bohemia, and Germany, as far as the Elbe. But Pannonia remained the center of Avar polity, as it did for other nomads.

At its zenith in the seventh century, Avaria incorporated today's Slovakia, southern Moravia, and eastern Austria. Slavs of Bohemia and northern Moravia, as well as those along the Elbe and in Poland, seem to have entered into an alliance with the Avars of their own will. But those in Wallachia, Noricum, and Illyricum had to acknowledge Avar supremacy. Only the Antes of Bessarabia resisted and were crushed by Kaghan Apsich in 602.

The Avar expansion in the west was checked by the Franks, who fought and stopped them on the Elbe in 561–62 (Dvornik 1956, 38). The Frankish king Siegebert met the second Avar attack in 566. He was defeated and captured in 567 but managed to come to an understanding with his captors. The agreement held until 595, when the Avars attacked again, this time in Thuringia (60).

In the south, their main adversary was Byzantium. During the reign of Maurice (582–602), the frontier still followed the Danube. But it was maintained by expensive tributes to the Avars (Gimbutas 1971, 103).

As allies and junior partners, Slavs were increasingly identified with the Avars in Byzantine eyes. Later Byzantine sources referred to "Slaveni or Avari," and "Slaveni called Avari." Indeed, the Avars were the instrument and the carrier of early Slav migration and colonization. After the capture of Sirmium in 582, Avars and Slavs poured into the Balkans. Latin cities in Illyricum and Greek cities on the Dalmatian coast, and in Epirus, Macedonia, and Thrace suffered destruction. Many were abandoned by their inhabitants, who sought refuge on the islands and high points. The invaders besieged Thessaloniki, the second city of the empire, and by the early 620s threatened the capital, Constantinople. The threat was made ever more serious by an alliance that the Avars attempted to conclude with Byzantium's sworn enemies, the Persians. In response, Emperor Heraclius (610–41) concluded a treaty of friendship with the Frankish king Dagobert (628–38), creating one of the earliest transcontinental systems of alliances (Chronicle of Fredegar, in Dvornik 1956, 62).

Frankish help was instrumental in ensuring the success of the Slav uprising against their Avar overlords. It was led by a Frankish nobleman-turned-merchant, Samo, in 623 (Dvornik 1956, 60). As a result, the Avars lost Bohemia, parts of Moravia, and some other areas (Gimbutas 1971, 104). However, the setback did not stop the Avar assault on Constantinople in 626. Here, they were assisted by the remaining Slav allies. At the same time, Persians attacked from the east. Only the capital's formidable defenses allowed the city to withstand the onslaught.

When the siege failed, it looked as though the adversaries had fought each other to a standstill. In a brilliant move, Heraclius tried to detach more Slavs from the Avars. The Frankish conquest of Thuringia gave him a chance. White Serbs, who now found themselves under Frankish domination, were restless. Heraclius offered to settle them in the Balkans, on land that was nominally Byzantine, but was actually under Avar control. The price? Help fight the Avars. Their task was made easier by the presence of numerous Slavs living in the area since the sixth century (Dvornik 1956, 62–63).

Soon, a good number of Serbs (and Croats) made their way to the Balkans, where they took possession of Dalmatia, then the rest of Illyricum, and finally the mesopotamia between the Sava and the Drava. (It is interesting that Heraclius asked Pope Honorius to send missionaries to the Croats and Serbs. By recognizing Roman jurisdiction over Illyricum (i.e., status quo ante), Heraclius assured himself of Western support. This was another brilliant move on the part of a skillful strategist.)

The setbacks suffered by the Avars encouraged other adversaries. Between 635 and 641, Bulghars under Kubrat drove them to the northeast. And some time later, the Avar hegemony in southern Russia was probably destroyed by a Slav revolt aided by the Khazars; at least, there is no evidence of Avar predominance in that region in the seventh and eighth centuries (64). The only land that the Avars retained was Pannonia (63).

By the middle of the seventh century it looked as though even the heartland of the Avars might crumble. But Byzantine troubles in the east and Frankish preoccupation with Lombards and Saracens gave the Avars some breathing space. More than a hundred years passed till Charlemagne (771–814) and his son Pepin were in a position to take them on. The decisive expedition took place in 796 (Dvornik 1956, 68–69), although some Avars held out until 803/804. After that they fled in all directions. Those who were willing to accept Christianity were settled by the Franks in southern Pannonia (68), where they eventually amalgamated with other ethnic groups.

The destruction of the Avars left a profound impression on contemporaries. The Russian Primary Chronicle even coined an expression, "perished like the Obry (Avars)" (69).

What were the consequences of the Avar "episode"?

On the steppe, they were one of the nomadic groups delivered by the conveyor belt from the borders of China to central Europe. As such, their role was unexceptional.

In Europe, their invasion removed the Bulghar threat from central Europe (190), although it is hard to tell whether they were any better. The assessment "same difference" is probably not far off the mark.

On the other hand, their occupation and devastation of Illyricum, where Latin- and Greek-speaking populations had mingled, destroyed the bridge between the Latin West and the Greek East, facilitating the split of 1054 (it was made easier by the disruption of maritime communications cut by the Arabs) (44). From this point of view, the Avars played a tragic role in the history of Christian civilization.

Also, the devastation by the Huns, the Bulghars, and the Avars prepared the ground for the Slavic "takeover." The nomads' preference for good grazing grounds compelled them to return to the plains after every campaign. Thus, they never colonized the mountainous Balkan peninsula, and the Avars, as Huns and Bulghars before them, were no exception. They all returned to Pannonia, the largest stretch of the plains in central Europe. It was the Slavs who did all the colonizing (Gimbutas 1971, 98).

The Khazars

We know little about the emergence of the Khazars. They seem to have descended from the West Turkic confederation that arose in about 552 and survived until 657–59 when it was defeated by the Chinese (Chavannes 1903, 267–68, in Dunlop 1954, 22).

Some of the earliest references are found in Syriac compilations of 569 (Rubens Duval, in Chavannes 1903, 250, n.4, in Dunlop 1954, 7, n.22). And in 576, Siljibu's son sent a West Turkic force to help their Utighur vassals who were besieging Bosporus (Kerch) (Menander Prot., ed. Bonn, 404; Chavannes 1903, 241, in Dunlop 1954, 25, n.106).

A Byzantine writer, Theophylact Simocatta, mentioned a Turkic embassy that arrived in Constantinople in 598 (ed. Bonn, 282ff, Chavannes, 1903–1904, 246ff, in Dunlop 1954, 5, n.10). By this time, however, relations between the two powers must have been well established because some time around 589 the Persians fought a coalition of West Turks, Khazars, and Byzantines (Dunlop 1954, 26).

After they had chased the Avars from the Pontic steppe, the Turks defeated the Onoghurs and the Alans, and incorporated them, along with the Sabirs and Oghurs, into their empire. These tribes, on the western periphery of the empire, were organized in a vassal union headed by the (West

Turkic) Ashina clan (Hudud al-Alam 1970, 162, in Golden, 263, n.18, in Sinor 1990). It was this unit that evolved into the Khazar kaghanate (Golden, 260, in Sinor 1990).

As an independent force, the Khazars were first mentioned in 627. That year, Emperor Heraclius stopped in Tbilisi en route to invading Persia. There he met Khazars under Ziebel. According to the Byzantine version, Ziebel "loaned" Heraclius 40,000 men and retired to his country (Theophanes, ed. Bonn 485ff; Chavannes 1903, 252ff, in Dunlop 1954, 28, nn.119 and 120).

An Armenian version of the story is more complex. In 625, the Khazars raided Armenia. The next year they came again, but this time, at Tiflis, they met Heraclius. The two armies besieged the city but failed to take it. However, they agreed to join forces again the following year. They exchanged embassies, and in 627 the "king of the North" lent his men to Heraclius. The Byzantine venture in Persia went well. On the way back, in 628, they joined the Khazars who were yet again besieging Tiflis. The siege was unsuccessful, and the invaders withdrew. But in 629 (most likely), the Khazars finally succeeded in capturing the Georgian city, and in 630 launched a major invasion of Armenia, Georgia, and Persia (Moses of Kaghankaytuk, in Dunlop 1954, 28–30, n.121).

In Dunlop's opinion, during the campaigns of 625–30, the Khazars were still under West Turkic suzerainty (Dunlop 1954, 31). But Golden believes that the power of Western Turks was already fading (264, in Sinor 1990), which allowed the Khazars to emerge as an independent actor.

Already at this early stage, the Khazars' external policy was oriented toward Byzantium. Their main competitor at the time was the Onoghur-Bulghar state of Magna Bulgaria, as was described earlier. Wars with the Bulghars continued until the dissolution of Bulgaria in the 670s and the dispersal of the proto-Bulghars north, west, and south. Given the West Turkic connections of the elites in both Khazaria and Magna Bulgaria, it is possible that both were initially vassals of the West Turkic Empire. Perhaps, their struggles reflected internal strife in the parent confederation (Artamonov 1962, 170; Gyorffy 1959, 77–78, both in Golden 265, n.22, in Sinor 1990).

Indeed, by the middle of the century, the struggles within the Turkic confederation were reaching a crescendo. In 652–57, a hundred years after the destruction of their empire, the Uighurs took part in—or may have even led—the destruction of the Western Turks. And another century later the Uighurs took part in the coalition that destroyed the East Turkic power in 742; from then and until 840 they became leaders in the region of the river Orkhon (Dunlop 1954, 36, n.16).

When the Bulghars left, the Khazars occupied their lands; those who remained became their tributaries (Theophanes, ed. Bonn, 544ff, in Dunlop

1954, 42, n.3). By the end of the seventh century Khazar garrisons were firmly planted on the Dnieper and in the Crimea (Dunlop 1954, 45). At the height of their power, the Khazar domains extended from the Dnieper to Khorezm and as far north as Volga Bulgaria. In the south, their border with the Caliphate was well demarcated by the Caucasus. But it was here that they encountered their most determined opponent.

In 642, having conquered Transcaucasia, the Arabs raided Balanjar in Khazaria (Golden, 265, in Sinor 1990). In the next one hundred years they repeatedly tried, but ultimately failed, to reduce Khazaria.

There is a certain parallel with the West, where the Franks stopped the Saracens at roughly the same time. But in the Frankish lands, the issue was decided by the battle of Tours (732). In the east, the struggle was more pro- tracted (Dunlop 1954, 46). And if not for the Khazars, eastern Europe might well have been Islamized, like the Volga Bulgars were later.

On the first occasion, in 642, the Arabs seem to have encountered little resistance and advanced far into Khazaria (50). And in the following years they repeatedly raided Khazar territory (53). However, in the next ten years, the Arabs were busy pacifying Armenia and Azerbaijan and left the Khazars alone.

But in 652, a large Arab force under Abd-al-Rahman Ibn Rabiah entered Khazaria and besieged Balanjar. This time the Arabs were soundly beaten (55–56). Still, as a precaution, the Khazars transferred their capital to the Volga (57, n.75).

While fighting the Bulghars and expanding west, the Khazars had little time for the Arabs (58). But from the early 680s they once again directed their attention south, toward Albania (Azerbaijan) (Moses of Kaghankatuk, II, 36, in Marquart 1903, 114, 302, in Dunlop 1954, 59, n.1; Ibn Fadlan 1939, 106, in Dunlop 1954, 59, n.2).

In 685, the Khazars launched a large-scale invasion south (Stephan Asoghik, in Marquart 1903, 443, in Dunlop 1954, 59, n.7). They overran the entire Transcaucasia, killing the prince of Georgia and a prince of Ar- menia in battle. Yet, they made no attempt to hold the territory south of the mountains. For a while, they occupied Darband, but it was retaken in 713 (Ibn Taghribardi, I, 255, in Dunlop 1954, 60, n.12).

Another invasion, in 717, ended in defeat (Kmośko 1924–25, 361, in Dunlop 1954, 60, n.13), but the next one, in 721–22, was more successful (Tabari, II, 1437; Ya'qubi, II, 378, in Dunlop 1954, 61, n.19).

This pattern of attack and counterattack continued until 730, when the Khazars once again demolished their Arab adversaries, took Ardabil (Dunlop 1954, 69–70) and advanced to the vicinity of Mosul (Ibn al- Athir, in Dunlop 1954, 71, n.62). The Arabs "responded" with another attempt on Darband in 731 (76–79). Their "grande riposte" came in 737 under Marwan, when they defeated the Khazars and chased the Kaghan across the entire country. The Kaghan had to ask for terms (Islam or the sword) and accepted Islam (81–84).

But the Arab victory proved ephemeral. When Marwan withdrew, the Kaghan, now reinstalled in his capital as Marwan's "vassal," soon regained freedom of action (85).

In 740, he converted to Judaism (86). The two events are probably interrelated: the Kaghan wanted to convert to an "established" religion that would not put him under any obligations to either Muslim or Christian religious authorities. Only Judaism offered this choice. (There are other dates for the conversion. Al-Masudi, writing in the tenth century, placed it at the end of the eighth, or the beginning of the ninth century [Al-Masudi 1966–70, 212, in Golden, 266, n.24, in Sinor 1990]). Marquart dated the conversion from 863 (Marquart 1903, 23, in Dunlop 1954, 102, n.55); and Vernadsky from 865 (Vernadsky 1943, 361, in Dunlop 1954, 102, n.56). These later dates are indirectly confirmed by other sources: Abo of Tiflis, writing in 780, and Constantine (Cyril) in 860 were under the impression that the Khazars were pagans (Dunlop 1954, 115). Dunlop concluded that sometime before 730, perhaps as early as 721, leading Khazars may have come under the influence of Judaism. The Byzantines, by their occasional anti-Jewish persecutions, may have contributed to the spread of Judaism in Khazaria. Thus, when Justinian II permitted the Trullan Synod to issue a decree for the "uprooting of Jewish perversity" in 692 (Bury, II, 326–37, 388, in Dunlop 1954, 177, n.23), or when Leo the Isaurian issued a decree, probably in 720, stipulating a compulsory conversion of all Jews to Christianity (Bury, II, 431, in Dunlop 1954, 177, n.24), many Jews escaped to Khazaria. In any case, in 740, the Kaghan accepted modified Judaism, apparently after a religious debate, the date confirmed by ha-Levi in the *Kuzari*. It was only two generations later, circa 800 (which is approximately the date indicated for the conversion by Al-Masudi; Dunlop 1954, 170, n.159), that the Kaghan's descendants accepted rabbinic Judaism (170).

Subsequent dynastic struggles between the Umayyads and the Abbasids diverted the Arabs and probably saved Khazaria (87). And so it came to pass that the boundary of Islam was fixed in the Caucasus.

By 751, Khazaria was again a fully independent player and could offer refuge to Muslim "losers." By 758, Arab governors, at the instruction of the caliph, sought a matrimonial alliance with the Khaghan—clearly, he was a force to be reckoned with (179). Another indication of their strength is that the Khazars continued to raid deep into Muslim territory. The last great raid south that we know of occurred in 799 (Dunlop 1954, 184).

Khazar involvement in Byzantine affairs started even earlier.

In 695, after a reign of ten years, Justinian II was deposed, mutilated, and banished to the Crimea (Theophanes 566 and Nicephorus 44, in Dunlop 1954, 171, n.1). For several years he lived quietly in Chersonesus, then decided to recover the throne. He went to Doros, the capital of Crimean Gothia (then under Khazarian suzerainty), and requested the Kaghan's assistance. To seal the deal, he married the Kaghan's sister (172).

As a result, the Khazars played an important role in subsequent upheavals in the Crimea and Constantinople. In 711, by supporting an insurgent emperor against Justinian (despite marriage to his sister?), the Kaghan was instrumental in installing a new emperor (176). And in 732, Emperor Leo the Isaurian married his son to a Khazar princess, Chichak (renamed Eirene at baptism) (177). This was the same Leo who had forcibly tried to convert Jews 12 years earlier! Clearly, for all participants, reasons of state took precedence over religion.

Byzantine-Khazar cooperation extended to other areas. In 833 (838 according to Golden, 267, in Sinor 1990), Byzantine engineers built a fortress (Sarkel) on the Don at Khazars' request (186). It was probably directed against the new menace, the Magyars. As it happened, the Magyar threat passed.

But the Rus proved to be much more dangerous.

By the middle of the ninth century, they were strong enough to wrest away west Khazar territory with Kiev (in 878, according to Vernadsky 1943, 368, in Dunlop 1954, 238, n.10). Sometime between 864 and 884, the Rus ships reached the Caspian and started raiding. They attacked in 910 (Istakhri, V and VIII, n.82, in Dunlop 1954, 238, n.12), 913, 922, and 943. (These are the "great" raids.) To pass to the Caspian, the Rus needed Khazar permission. They got it, at least on one occasion, for a promise of half the booty (239). Eventually, however, the Khazars denied them passage to the sea for fear that they "would destroy all the country of the Arabs as far as Baghdad" (from the *Reply of Joseph*, in Dunlop 1954, 240). Perhaps, the Volga was closed after the great raid of 943.

Was it this closure that precipitated the Rus invasion and destruction of Khazaria? According to the Russian Primary Chronicle, Sviatoslav defeated the Khazars in 965 and took Sarkel (241). Ibn Hawkal wrote that in 968–69 the Rus destroyed Bulgar, Itil', and Samandar (Ibn Hawqal 1938–39, 15, in Dunlop 1954, 242, n.28).

Some Khazars fled. There are indications that many sought refuge in Shirwan, on the "Naphtha Coast," which had been attacked by the Rus in 913. They later returned to Itil' with the help of Shirwan Shah. (The price for his help: conversion to Islam [Ibn Hawqal 1938–39, 397, in Dunlop 1954, 246].)

But the attempt to rebuild Itil' was unsuccessful, and the town of Saqsin took its place. By the time of Biruni (1048), Itil' lay in ruins (Ibn Fadlan 1939, 206, in Dunlop 1954, 248, n.65). Later, Batu built his capital Saray on its site (Wassaf, cited in Ibn Fadlan 1939, 204, n.1, apparently from Juwayni, I, 222, in Dunlop 1954, 241, n.72).

Was the destruction complete?

Golden writes that Khazaria, greatly reduced, continued to exist as a client of Khorezm; many of its former areas had fallen to surrounding Muslim rulers (Golden, 269, in Sinor 1990). Many earlier scholars reached the same conclusion, but opinions differ as to the location: Graetz believed it was in the Crimea (Graetz, 3d ed, v, 342, in Dunlop 1954, 252, n.90), while Kutschera thought it was somewhere in the Caucasus (Kutschera 1910, in Dunlop 1954, 252). Indeed, some three thousand Khazar households were settled in Qahtan in North Caucasus in 1064 (Golden, 269, in Sinor 1990).

Nor did they disappear from the Rus horizon. The Russian Primary Chronicle says that in 986, Khazar envoys took part in the religious disputation before Vladimir that, supposedly, decided which religion Rus' was to adopt (Dunlop 1954, 250). And in 1016, according to Cedrenus, Byzantium and Rus' joined forces against a Khazar "Georgios Tzule," although he does not specify where (251). Later, a Rus prince named Mstislav Vladimirovich, who had settled in Tmutarakan', recruited his army from Khazar and Kasog (Caucasian) fighters. And a grandson of Yaroslav the Wise, Oleg Sviatoslavich, also led an army made of Cuman and Khazar warriors in 1078, 1079, and 1084 (Bartha 1975, 40, n.115).

Finally, a Hebrew document from the Cairo Genizah refers to a messianic movement in Khazaria in 1096 (Dunlop 1954, 255–56).

Although the Khazar society sedentarized, the strong centrifugal tendencies of its clans and tribes remained. The extreme diversity of its populations and the gap between the elite, a relatively small number of partially Judaized Turks, and the rest of the population contributed to these tendencies; Khazaria also suffered from its limited resource base (224).

Control of major trade routes was the foundation of the Khazar power. Its capital Itil' was an important entrepot; Khazaria's prosperity depended on trade (232) and taxing the subject people (e.g., furs from Slavs). Accounts of Istakhri (932) and Mas'udi (943) depict a flourishing country. At this time, Khazaria was still a major power.

But disruption from within or without could seriously affect the entire organism. Ultimately, Khazaria fell from internal strife (the Kabars), and the pressure of steppe people from the east and Rus' from the north (Golden, 269, in Sinor 1990).

Khazaria was held together by force; once its military power was broken, the economy was bound to collapse. The state was an agglomeration of adjacent territories without natural frontiers; it was far from self-sufficient and incapable of forming a permanently stable political and economic unit. No bond of unity existed (Dunlop 1954, 234–35).

It fell as a sedentary power that was no longer nomadic.

The Hungarians

The Hungarian homeland was located on the left bank of the Volga in the immediate vicinity of Volga Bulgaria (Kuzeev 1974, 413, in Golden, 246, in Sinor 1990). Such precision may seem surprising, but is confirmed both by linguistic analysis and archeological evidence.

Linguistic analysis also shows a significant number of Turkic loan words that entered Hungarian in their original homeland (also known as Magna Hungaria), in the Pontic steppe (in two stages), and, possibly, through the Khabars/Kavars who had been part of the Khazar polity (Czegledy 1976, 82–89, in Golden, 244, n.29, in Sinor 1990). These substantial borrowings suggest an Ugro-Turkic symbiosis that is also reflected in clan and tribal names shared by pre-Conquest Hungarians, Bashkirs, and proto-Bulghars (Golden, 245, in Sinor 1990). In fact, the Hungarian ethnonym derives from Onoghur and was probably adopted at the earliest stage, when Hungarians still lived in Magna Hungaria, because medieval Russian chronicles refer to Hungarians and Finn-Ugors on the Volga as *ugor/iugor* (246).

It is interesting that Muslim sources often call them Basjirt/Bashghird, that is, Bashkir. And the tribal name Szavard (postconquest Zuard) clearly derives from Suwar/Sabir (246). In short, either the early Magyars had Onoghur Turkic antecedents or they came under strong Turkic influence at the dawn of their existence. Some scholars even believe that the Onogur alliance, although culturally Bulgaro-Turkic, was linguistically Finno-Ugric, perhaps with Hungarian numerical majority (Makkai 1940, 9, in Sugar 1990).

Sometime around 800 many Hungarians moved south to the Pontic steppe. (Those who stayed were subsequently assimilated by the Bashkirs.) Golden believes that their migration was connected with the Oghuz-Pecheneg wars (Golden, 247, in Sinor 1990).

The date and direction of their migration have been the subject of much controversy. But the construction of Sarkel suggests that by late 830s they were close to the Don (Nemeth, 1930, 153; Artamonov 1962, 48–49; Moravcsik 1958, 82, in Bartha 1975, 61, n.111). (Sarkel was a link in a chain of at least 12 fortresses built by the Khazars from white limestone along the Don, the Donets, and other rivers [Bartha 1975, 62].)

Another interpretation is also possible. The power structures of early Hungarians follow Khazar models (Golden, 247, in Sinor 1990). This fact suggests that they spent some time under Khazar rule. Perhaps, at an early date, some Hungarians moved to the Pontic steppe, where they had to submit to the Khazars, then the dominant power in the region. If this is true, then the time of their migration to the Pontic steppe has to be moved back.

According to some indications, the Khabars revolted against Khazars in about 780. Dunlop (1954; 115, 144, 148, and 170) and Artamonov (1962, 324–34) link the uprising with the adoption of Judaism by the Khazars, as does Bartha (1975, 63, n.119). The Hungarians may have joined the Khabars in burning Khazar fortifications (Pletniova, MIA, 62, 214; Marquart 1903, 337; Kokovtsev 1932, 117–18, in Bartha 1975, 64, n.124). This would necessitate the erection of new fortifications built of stone, such as Sarkel.

The record of their sojourn in the Pontic steppe is hazy. It is known that Hungarians were semi-nomadic cattle-breeders who frequently raided their (sedentary) Slav neighbors. They also ventured far afield, to the Danube in 839 (Marquart 1903, 30, in Dunlop 1954, 199, n.160) and Germany in 862 (Hincmar of Rheims, I, 50, in Marquart 1903, 33, in Dunlop 1954, 199, n.159). From the raids they brought prisoners, whom they sold to slave merchants in the Crimea.

The reasons for their subsequent move west are also open to interpretation. Bartha believed that they were chased from Levedia (east of the Dnieper) by the Pechenegs in the first quarter of the ninth century (Bartha 1975, 64). Dunlop thought that they were again allied with the Khazars in 840–60 and were pushed into Atelkuzu/Etelköz (west of the Dnieper) by the Pechenegs in 860. The Pechenegs may have cut the Khazars from the Dnieper valley, enabling Variag adventurers to capture Kiev (Dunlop 1954, 199). Bury shared this opinion: he dated the Magyar move to Levedia as of 822–26 (Bury 1912, 491, in Dunlop 1954, 200, n.165). But others (Grégoire 1937, 633, in Dunlop 1954, 201, n.168) contend that the Magyars were displaced only once.

In any case, the Pechenegs played a major role in dislodging the Hungarians. Their original territory was circumscribed by the Khazars to the southwest, Kipchaks (Polovtsy) to the east, and Slavs to the west. It was large, 30 days' journey from every side (Gardezi in Pauler and Szilagyi 1900, 151–52, 159, in Bartha 1975, 60, n.92), and rich: "[Khazars] attack the Pechenegs from year to year," taking cattle and people (Ibn Rusta, n.92).

It was the Khazars who drove the Pechenegs from their homeland (Moravcsik/Jenkins 1962, 143, 146–47, in Bartha 1975, 60, n.93). And the Pechenegs then fell on the Hungarians. This was the domino effect all too familiar to students of nomadic migrations in the steppe. We should note, however, that the direction of the Khazar pressure proceeded from southwest to northeast. One would think that the Pechenegs would retreat north, east, or northeast. But they did not. Like most other nomads they chose to go west, probably because they could not take on their eastern neighbors the Kipchaks.

The circumstances surrounding the expulsion of the Hungarians are far from clear. It could have happened in the 890s or proceeded in two steps, in 889 and 893–95. It is also unclear whether it was a Pecheneg initiative or whether it had been instigated by the Khazars, who may have been trying to preclude another (renewed?) Khabar-Hungarian alliance.

Constantine Porphyrogenitus, in *De Administrando Imperio* in 948(–52), stated that 55 years earlier, that is, in 893, an alliance of the Khazars and the Ghuzz attacked the Pechenegs, evicting them from the territory between the Volga and the Ural rivers (Const. Porphyrogenitus, 37, in Dunlop 1954, 196, n.140). The Pecheneg migration—in 889—is confirmed by Reginald of Prüm (*Reginonis Abbatis Prumiensis Chronicon,* cited in Al-Hudud/Minorsky, 313, n.2, in Dunlop 1954, 196, n.141).

In their new location, west of the Dnieper, the Hungarians found themselves in an uncomfortable proximity to the powerful Bulghars. This probably explains their hasty alliance, also in 893, with the Byzantine emperor Leo the Wise (a major enemy of the Bulghars at this time).

The Bulghars then allied themselves with the Pechenegs, who attacked Hungarians again in 895 and chased them to the Carpathians. Russian chronicles say that Hungarians passed in the vicinity of Kiev, which seems too northern a route. But there was indeed a massive destruction of Slav settlements in the southern zone at the end of the ninth century. It is not clear, however, whether the Pechenegs or the Hungarians—or both?—were the perpetrators (Bartha 1975, 65).

Other versions of these events indicate that in 892, Hungarians fought in alliance with Arnulf, king of the East Franks, against Prince Svatopluk of Greater Moravia. Then they attacked Tsar Symeon of Bulgaria at Byzantine instigation, but were defeated. While the Magyar warriors were away, the Pechenegs swept down on Hungarian settlements along the Dnieper. In the absence of their best warriors, Hungarians could not resist. Led by *kende* Kurszan and *gyula* Árpád, they fled to the Carpathian Basin familiar to them from previous raids (Makkai, 21–22, in Palmenyi 1975).

Whatever the details, the chain of events in the last decade of the ninth century indicates that the Pechenegs and the Bulghars inflicted two disastrous defeats on the Hungarians (Bartha 1975, 83). As a result, all who could fled to the relative safety of the Carpathian basin. But some, inevitably, stayed. Their remnants were found by a Hungarian Dominican friar, Julian, in the first half of the thirteenth century.

What did the refugees find when they crossed the Verecke pass in 896 and reached the valley of the Tisza?

After Charlemagne crushed the Avars in 791–804, there was no effective power in Pannonia. To the north was the first Slav state, Greater Moravia. West of the Danube, Slav dukes ruled a Slovenian principality under German overlordship. Both were under strong German pressure.

The region south and east of the Mureş was controlled by Bulgarians (Makkai, 11, in Sugar 1990). But because of the endless struggles with Byzantium, Bulgaria could not reimpose control in the area between the Mureş and the Danube (Makkai, 22, in Palmenyi 1975). In effect, this area was a no-man's-land. This allowed the Hungarians to "insert" themselves.

Barely had they established themselves in their new abode when the Hungarians attacked their sedentary neighbors. For the next half-century they were busy little beavers, looting and pillaging across Europe. (But they never attacked other nomads, whose tactics were identical. They did join Sviatoslav in his war against Bulgarians in 967. By then, of course, Bulgarians of Bulgaria had completed their transition to sedentary life-style.)

In the initial stage, Hungarians had to secure their new homeland. Although their first raid, in 898, took them to Italy, their early efforts were directed against neighbors: in 902–906 they destroyed Greater Moravia, and in 907 they thoroughly thrashed Bavarians, securing their western border for a hundred years (Makkai, 12, in Sugar 1990).

After 907, with the new Hungary secured, they spread all over Europe: in 915 they reached Bremen, in 924 they crossed the Pyrenees, in 928 they paid a "visit" to Rome, in 937 they were seen at the mouth of the Loire, in 942 they appeared in Moorish Andalusia (13). Some localities suffered twice: Otranto in 922 and 947, Bulgaria in 943 and 961, Constantinople in 934 and 959 (they failed to take the city) (Makkai, 23, in Palmenyi 1975).

Defeats were rare (Merseburg, in 933, was one of the few) (Makkai, 13, in Sugar 1990) until they suffered a crushing defeat at Lechfeld near Augsburg in 955 (14). By then, Hungarians themselves were well advanced in the process of sedentarization. After Lechfeld, the Árpáds realized that their people had no future other than as a sedentary state and a member of Christian Europe. Adoption of Christianity soon followed (15–16).

Even after Lechfeld, Hungarians continued to harry the Balkans. By 970, however, a resurgent Byzantium was able to extend its frontiers back to the Danube (Makkai, 31, in Palmenyi 1975). Thus, the route south was now blocked as well.

The transformation of the Hungarian tribal confederation (it consisted of seven Hungarian tribes, plus the Khabars) into a feudal monarchy should be placed within contemporary context: the rise of Germany under Otto I, the rise of Kievan Rus', the collapse of Khazaria, and the emergence of early feudal states in a wide belt from the Baltic to the Black Sea. Ironically, in view of its own nomadic antecedents, Hungary was now a link in the chain that defended Europe against nomads to the east and demarcated the West from the Orthodox peoples east and south.

How many Hungarians were there at the time of the conquest?

Ibn Rusta and Gardezi based their estimates on Dzaihani that the Hungarians could field 20,000 mounted warriors. With one warrior per four or five families, the estimate of Hungarians in the ninth and tenth centuries would be between 400,000 and 450,000. If we add Slavs and Avars (but there were also Bulghars), the total comes to about 600,000. That translates into three people per square kilometer, similar to the population density of Mongolia in 1924 (Bartha 1975, 110) and Volga Kalmyks in the 1830s (2.5 persons per square kilometer) or approximately eight to seven people per square mile, respectively (111).

Toponymical evidence suggests that early Hungarians occupied open spaces where they could graze their horses. Slavs remained in the forests of the west and southwest and in the forested mountains around the perimeter of the Pannonian plain, where the Hungarians did not start to settle until the middle of the twelfth century (Makkai, 24, in Palmenyi 1975). Slavs who remained on the plain were slowly absorbed by the Magyars.

The Pechenegs

The Pechenegs are first mentioned in the eighth century, in a Tibetan translation of a Uighur report on a war between the Be-cha-nag and the Hor (Bacot 1956, 147; Ligeti 1971, 170–76, both in Golden, 271, n.37, in Sinor 1990). At this time they lived in the middle Syr Darya region and were associated with the Kangar or Kangaras people who had, at some point, joined the Pecheneg tribal union (Golden, 272, in Sinor 1990).

Toward 800 the Oghuz pressure from the east pushed the Pechenegs into the area between the Ural and Volga rivers. Here, they found themselves squeezed between the Khazars and the Oghuz. Tired of ceaseless warfare, they migrated again, pushing Hungarians from Levedia (the Pontic steppe east of the Dnieper) across the river into Etelköz/Atelkuzu in 889. And then, in 893–95, in alliance with Bulgarians, they evicted them again. Thus, by 900, they found themselves masters of the Pontic steppe from the Don to the Danube.

In 915 the Pechenegs were first mentioned in Russian chronicles (273). Five years later, Igor was already fighting them. This campaign inaugurated a long series of small wars, skirmishes, and raids.

Frequent hostilities did not prevent Russian princes from occasionally hiring Pecheneg cavalry. In 944, for example, they were Igor's allies in a war against Byzantium (273). But the Pechenegs also hired themselves out to Poles, Hungarians, and Byzantines alike. It was a Pecheneg prince, acting as an ally of Byzantium, who killed Sviatoslav in 972 (and had a drinking goblet fashioned out of his skull). And after 980, the Pechenegs were frequent participants in Russian internal feuds (274).

As their involvement and familiarity with Rus' deepened, the Pechenegs became a major nuisance. Under Vladimir, Russians started building border fortifications. In 1036, Yaroslav defeated a major Pecheneg attack on Kiev. After that, the Pechenegs seem to have redirected their attention to Byzantium, where the pickings were far richer. They had already raided across the Danube in 1026. And in 1048, they devastated Bulgaria. However, their shift further west was at least partly the result of the mounting pressure from the Oghuz (who were threatened by the Cumans).

Despite mounting hostilities, the Byzantines continued to hire Pecheneg "auxiliaries"—and paid a heavy price when the mercenaries defected to the Seljuks in the decisive battle of Manzikert in 1071, which opened Asia Minor to the Turks.

Alexis Comnene defeated the Pechenegs and the Oghuz in Thrace in 1087. But the following year they penetrated as far as Adrianople. In 1090, they besieged Constantinople, while their Seljuk allies and the fleet of Emir Tzakhas blocked the city from the other side (Bratianu 1969, 162).

The Byzantines had little choice but to fall back on their old policy of striking an alliance with "the enemy of my enemy," in this case, the Cumans. Together, they dealt a crushing blow to the Pechenegs in April 1091, and then again in 1122, when they tried to raid the Balkans. After that, some of the Pechenegs moved to Hungary and Rus, where they were made part of the border guard system (Golden, 275, in Sinor 1990); others joined other Turkic groups and confederations and were eventually assimilated.

The Oghuz

The Oghuz tribal union emerged in the eighth century in a region around the lower Syr Darya and the Aral Sea (275). From very early on they allied themselves with the Khazars against the Pechenegs. As we know, the alliance was victorious but, like all nomad alliances, inherently unstable. In 965, they helped the Rus to destroy Khazaria and, 20 years later, joined them in an attack on the Volga Bulgaria (276).

By 1000, the Oghuz confederation was torn by internal strife, the result of an incomplete conversion to Islam, as some of the Oghuz became Muslim while others remained pagan. These internal dissentions weakened the Oghuz, making resistance against the Cuman migration(s) (starting circa 1017–18) impossible. Some of the Oghuz moved west into the Pontic steppe, pushing the Pechenegs ahead of them; others sought refuge in Muslim areas further south.

Like other nomads who reached the Pontic steppe, the Oghuz did not find peace there. In fact, they found themselves between the Rus and the Cumans, who struck them from two sides in 1054 or 1055 (Golden, 276, in Sinor 1990).

In 1060, the Rus struck again, putting the Oghuz to flight. Untold thousands perished from hunger and cold; thousands more died in an epidemic. By 1064–65, survivors reached the Danube. Beaten back by the Byzantines and, in 1068, the Hungarians, they stayed on the frontier, occasionally raiding, at other times hiring themselves out to the empire. They, along with the Pechenegs, defected to the Seljuks at Manzikert, which probably decided the outcome of the battle.

Other Oghuz found employment as border guards for their old enemy, the Rus. The arrangement that led to the creation of a kind of early Cossackdom, was formalized in 1140. It effectively turned the Chiornyie Klobuki (Black Hoods) into some sort of vassal mercenaries. At this point, the Oghuz leave the stage as independent players.

The Cumans

Cumans have more names than any other people I know. Greek and Latin *Cuman* is derived from Turkic *Quman,* but Muslims call them *Qipchaq;* Russians *Polovtsy* (along with West Slavic *Plauci/Plawci*); Germans *Falones, Phalagi, Valvi;* Armenians *Khartesh;* and Hungarians *Paloc* and *Kun.* This proliferation often resulted from the translation of their original name, which meant "yellow" or "pale-yellow" (277), supplemented by borrowing from neighbors. Thus, Hungarian *Paloc* derives from Slav *Polovets,* while *Kun* is a contraction of *Cuman.*

In the eighth century the Kipchaks were part of the Turkic Empire north of China (278). After the collapse of the Turk Kaghanate, they seem to have migrated from the Altai to the Irtysh-Ishim-Tobol rivers as part of the Kimek tribal confederation, where they gradually established their autonomy (Ibn Khurdadhbih/de Goeje, 31; Hudud al-Alam/Minorsky, 101, both in Golden, 278, n.48, in Sinor 1990).

During the ninth and tenth centuries the Kipchak-Kimeks increasingly encroached upon the Oghuz, pushing them westward. In the process, the confederation became overextended and untenable. As it disintegrated, the Kipchaks split into three major groupings. One group remained in Siberia and later contributed to the ethnogenesis of Siberian Tatars (their name still figures in the clan names of various Altaian Turkic peoples [Golden, 279, in Sinor 1990]). Another group "stopped" in the Syr Darya steppe and later played an important part in the history of Khorezm. The third group reached the Volga-Ural river region (278). It was this group that became the core of the Cumans.

However, the sequence of events is unclear. Al-Marwazi, writing around 1120, says that the Qun came from the northern Chinese borderlands. The pressure from the Khitan and a shortage of grazing land made them move, but they were evicted from their new home by the Qay people. As a result, they fell upon the Shari or Sari people, who fell upon the Turkmen, who fell upon the Oghuz, who fell upon the Pechenegs then living in the Pontic steppe (Al-Marwazi/Minorsky 1942, 18, in Golden, 279, n.49, in Sinor 1990). In short, it was a typical nomadic domino effect.

It is not known who the Qay or the Shari/Sari people were. But the Russian chronicles do mention Kaepichi, "sons of Qay," the Rus version of Qay-oba (279, n.49).

The first stage of this multiple movement started in 1017–18. The Cumans appeared in the Pontic steppe in 1054–55. We are not even sure whether the Cumans were part of the original Kimek tribal union or whether they were outsiders who conquered the Kipchaks (probably the first because the Rus chronicles mention "Yemek Cumans" (Halasi-Kun 1950, I, 52–53, in Golden, 280, n.50, in Sinor 1990). In any case, they defeated the resurgent Kimek confederation and then reorganized it under Kipchak-Cuman overlordship.

Hostilities against Rus began in 1061. They did not augur well for the Slavs: in 1068 the combined forces of the Rus princes were defeated at the river Al'ta (281). But the Cumans lacked cohesion, as each khan retained a high degree of independence, and this lack of central authority probably saved Rus. Soon, the Cuman elites began to intermarry with Rus princes and were increasingly drawn into Rus and Hungarian affairs, mostly inter-princely feuding. Their earliest settlement in Hungary probably dates from this time.

By 1070 they had eliminated the Oghuz as serious competitors (it was at this time that they entered Rus service as Black Hoods) and become masters of the steppe. Indeed, Persians and Russians called it the Cuman steppe (Dasht-i Qipchaq and Polovetskoie Pole, respectively). It was divided into five tribal unions: Central Asia–Kazakstan, Volga-Ural, Don, Dnieper, and Danube (280).

Despite matrimonial alliances and numerous ties, the Cumans increased pressure on Rus' in 1070–1100. The Rus, under Vladimir Monomakh, counterattacked, often successfully: in 1103, 1109, 1111, 1113, and 1116 (Golden, 282, in Sinor 1990). As a result, some Cumans retreated to the Caucasus, where many entered the service of the king of Georgia, while others redirected their attentions to the Balkans and Volga Bulgaria.

But after Vladimir's death in 1125 and the resumption of infighting in Rus after 1128, the Cumans returned. By the late 1160s, Cuman raids were an annual occurrence. A counter-offensive in 1166–69 failed. In the next 50 years, each side was sufficiently divided to give its opponents many chances to interfere. The Rus-Rus and Cuman-Cuman alliances, as well as alliances across ethnic and religious lines, formed and fell apart with kaleidoscopic ease. It is likely that the idea of ethnic unity was alien to the adversaries' way of thinking (283). And the disintegration of Rus' into feudal principalities, as well as the lack of central authority among the Cumans, promoted constant infighting, as when the Cumans helped Riurik Rostislavich to take and sack Kiev in 1202.

The evolving Rus-Cuman "symbiosis" was destroyed by the Mongols.

In 1223, an army under Jebe and Subedei (generals of Genghis Khan) reached Kuban' via Georgia. There, they addressed the Cumans, invoking their Turco-Mongol confraternity. The Cumans abandoned their Alan allies and did nothing while they were pulverized. Then, belatedly, the Cumans realized that they would be next and called upon their Rus allies (at the time, the daughter of the grand khan Koten/Kotian was married to Prince Mstislav of Halich [Bratianu 1969, 199]). Their combined force was beaten on the Kalka in late May 1223. The Cumans were beaten again in 1229–30, and Rus' was invaded and destroyed in 1236–41.

In 1238–39, some Cumans fled to Hungary, where a large Cuman settlement had been in existence for some 150 years; they were eventually Magyarized. The rest were incorporated into the Golden Horde, making the Turkic component preponderant (Golden, 284, in Sinor 1990).

CHAPTER 14

The Mongolian Impact on Eurasia: A Reassessment

Christopher Kaplonski

According to a recent popular book on the Mongols, "The storm that swept across the world during the thirteenth century changed the political boundaries of Asia and Europe, uprooted entire peoples and dispersed them across the continent. It transformed the ethnic character of many regions, while at the same time permanently changing the strength and influence of the three major religions: Islam, Buddhism and Christianity" (Marshall 1993, 15–16).[1] These two sentences sum up the received wisdom on the Mongolian impact on world history. From the European vantage point, an unknown group of nomads appeared from the East and radically changed the face of Eurasian history before disappearing again. One could further argue, and indeed people have, that ultimately the Mongol impact extended to the entire world, including parts unknown in the thirteenth century. Authors on the Mongols are often fond of pointing out that Christopher Columbus set out on his voyages spurred in part by tales of the wealth of the court of the Great (Mongol) Khan reported by Marco Polo (e.g., Marshall 1993, 236; Morgan 1986, 198).

I set out in this chapter largely to argue somewhat against the received wisdom. To anticipate the argument, I argue in short that the Mongolian impact on Eurasia was not as it is normally portrayed. This statement requires elucidation. I am not suggesting that the Mongols were ignored, or ineffective in their military campaigns. Nor am I suggesting that the Mongols had no political or economic impact. The data clearly suggest otherwise.

Rather, what I *am* suggesting is that, in large part as a result of a tradition of indirect and often confederative rule in most of Eurasia, the Mongolian impact was in certain ways not as extreme as people have often assumed and portrayed it. If one puts aside preconceptions of who the Mongols were and what they did, a significantly different picture of the Mongols and their role in Eurasian history emerges. Although they were an unknown group to the Europeans, who clearly did have some unique influences on Eurasian history, I am arguing here that much of the history of the Mongols in Eurasia can be seen as no more or less than another episode in the history of the region (a region parts of which, if the story was told from the Mongolian point of view, weren't even very important).

The "Devil's Horsemen" were only such to those on the receiving end. It should be kept in mind that the histories of the Mongolian invasions we are familiar with were written by the losers. History is not, contrary to the dictum, always written by the victors. This is one of the underlying points of this chapter. In dealing with the impact of the Mongols on Eurasia, we have sought to separate what we see as the actual impact from the imputed one. The latter may make for more exciting reading, but the former is more worthy of our attention.[2]

There is also one other matter that should be taken into account when dealing with the impact of the Mongols. That, simply put, is national pride. I have suggested that in certain ways, the Mongols were unremarkable in their impact. One element that did make them remarkable, at least to later historians, was that they were a foreign ruling class. Undoubtedly, at least some of the hostility towards the Mongols can be attributed to this. One might (unintentionally or not) overlook or tone down the actions of one's own rulers, precisely because they are one's own, but not that of rulers as foreign as the Mongols. As Mongolians themselves point out, Napoleon and Alexander the Great were also responsible for much death and destruction, yet no one in the West seems to hold it much against them.[3]

Key to understanding this different picture I am painting here is to remember that the Mongolian "migration" was not a migration as such. Although pockets of descendants of the Mongols can be found scattered throughout Asia and Europe (there is, for example, a group in Afghanistan said to be descendants of the Mongol conquerors), the Mongolian "migrations" were in fact largely political and military exercises. The actual number of Mongols involved was relatively small.

For example, as David Morgan reminds us, one of the names of the Golden Horde (the Mongol rule in Russia) was the "Khanate of the Qipchaq," indicating that the Qipchaqs (a Turkic people) were still present after the Mongol invasions, and were apparently numerically greater than the Mongols (Morgan 1986, 141–2).[4] He goes on also to point out that less than 50 years after the conquests, Mongolian as a language—at least on coins—was being supplanted by Turkish (142).

Both scholarly and popular accounts of the Mongols have tended to focus on certain events, such as the destruction of Central Asian cities, or the "Tatar Yoke" endured by Russia. They did indeed occur. It is not my intention to argue otherwise. What I argue, however, is that these events often had no greater (or lesser) impact than many other events in the history of Eurasia. Rather, it was the western demonization of the Mongols that largely constituted the historical assessment with which we are familiar. I have tried, in the course of this chapter, to separate out these trends. In fact, as we shall see in the course of this chapter, the same scholars who argue for massive destruction at the hands of the Mongols often note the Mongols' tendency to bypass cities, and to foster economic growth once their conquests were complete. In adopting such an approach, I might be accused of siding too much with the Mongols. To a degree that is exactly my intention. Rather than simply demonize the Mongols and their deeds, we should seek to understand them.

The shape and foci of this chapter reflects this approach. I have not always dealt in great detail with certain topics, as might have been expected. Rather, I have attempted to provide an alternate reading of the record. To do justice to all of the topics I examine here would take at least a volume onto itself. Rather than attempting to condense such a work into a single chapter, I have chosen to highlight certain trends and issues that I feel needed to be reevaluated or emphasized.

It should also be noted here that I have applied the term "Mongol" rather narrowly. I have largely restricted this chapter to the period of the Mongol Empire, and where necessary, shortly after. I do not, therefore, deal with Timür the Lame (Tamerlane), for example. Although a Mongol by descent, he was not viewed as a legitimate claimant to any throne by them, marrying into the Genghisid line in an attempt to bolster his legitimacy. Further, by the time of Timür, Central Asia was largely Turkish in culture and language. He may himself have been a Mongol, but he could just as easily have been from any other background.[5]

Similarly, I have given a rather narrow meaning to the term Eurasia. Although not restricting myself totally, I have focused on the juncture of Europe and Asia—mostly in the areas of Russia and the former Soviet Union. Where necessary, I have expanded the discussion to include China, eastern Europe, and the Middle East (i.e., Persia).

One classic view of the impact of the Mongols can be summed up as follows: "[T]hese steppe nomads who conquered most of Asia created new concepts of absolutism and centralization. Every society they conquered, save the steppe societies, thereafter moved in the paths of absolutism, centralized control, and autocracy" (Schurmann 1956, 389). Other scholars argue that in the long run, the greater population of the conquered territories over-whelmed the Mongols, who in the end became assimilated (except for the case of the Golden Horde in Russia), and their impact, in the end, was min-imal. I have chosen to steer a course between these two interpretations. If areas the Mongols conquered became more absolutist, it was because they were already tending in that direction, or developed so later for different rea-sons. The Mongols preferred to rule indirectly, and usually maintained a cer-tain distance between themselves and their subjects, often ruling by intermediaries. It is worth noting in this regard that Kublai Khan, who did not follow this trend, and moved his capital to sedentary China, was re-garded by a good portion of the Mongolian population as something of a traitor. Certain modern Mongolian compilations and writings suggest such sentiment has not totally disappeared (see for example, the presentation in Sühbaatar 1992).

This legacy of indirect rule meant two things. First, it meant that the Mongols tended to remain in areas that were suitable to indirect rule. (Even China is not such an exception as it may first appear. Although all of China was not conquered until Kublai's reign, earlier rulers did control northern China from the steppe, rather than establishing a permanent base there.) This would suggest a correlation between existing political systems and the areas where Mongols retained control.[6] Second, it also meant that the Mon-gols maintained to a large degree a sort of cultural barrier between them-selves and their subjects. Even in China, where it is often assumed the Mongols were eventually Sinicized, they maintained a cultural distance from the bulk of their subjects, much like the later Manchu rulers of the Qing dy-nasty (see Crossely 1997).

The early European travelers to the Mongol courts, for example, needed Mongol or Turkic interpreters, not Chinese. In other areas, the cultural dis-tance was greater, as in Russia, where the Golden Horde eventually con-verted to Islam, while the Russians themselves remained Christian. Even in Persia, the Il-khans, who ultimately also converted to Islam, maintained a certain distance, and it is not clear that their allegiance to Islam necessarily ran very deep (Morgan 1986, 162–3). It is also worth noting that the Il-khans, who do provide the best case for an assimilationist argument, were the first Mongol dynasty to fall.

Another factor overlooked in the demonization of the Mongols is that their own rule was not as autocratic as it is portrayed. Although Genghis Khan, for example, wielded great power, he was in fact confirmed in his of-fice (and even first raised to it) by a *huraltai*, a council of nobles. For most of the empire's history as well, successions were by no means undisputed, and factional fighting was strong. Ostrowski argues, in effect, that this form was to be found in Muscovy as well. He writes that "a council of state" seems to have existed in both Muscovy and the Golden Horde. It "could act to limit the authority of the ruler; it was not merely an extension of the ruler's authority" (Ostrowski 1990, 533). If this is indeed the case, any autocratic tendencies must have come from elsewhere.

In the course of this chapter, I will argue the greatest impact of the Mongols in Eurasia took place in two interrelated spheres: the transmission of knowledge, and the economic impact. Even in this latter case, it is important that this not be misunderstood—although cities were indeed destroyed, many were rebuilt, and much evidence attests to the increase of trans-Eurasian trade under the Mongols. Indeed, as Jack Goody recently noted, when the Mongol dynasty in China collapsed, overland trade came to a halt, with a concomitant doubling of the price of Chinese silk and certain spices (Goody 1996, 57). One certainly would not have expected this to occur if the Mongols had brought nothing but death and destruction to Eurasia. The importance of trade is aptly summed up in David Morgan's assessment of the underlying principles of Mongol rule: "profit and military supremacy" (1982, 133). Ostrowski, in *Muscovy and the Mongols,* goes further, suggesting that the "primary strategic objectives" during the Mongols' campaigns were nothing other than the trade routes themselves (1998, 116).

Writing of the impact of the Golden Horde, Halperin observes: "The complexity of the Mongols' effects on the Russian economy . . . precludes any meaningful list of credits and debits. To calculate whether the benefits of being part of the Mongol hegemony outweighed the costs requires a balance sheet we can never fill out" (1985, 85). His point is well taken, and should be kept in mind throughout this chapter. If I at times seem to minimize the damage wrought by the Mongols, this is for two interrelated reasons. One, just stated, is that the impact appears to be exaggerated at times. The second is that even where the negative impact is not overstated, it is usually given more prominence than the other effects. It is with these other effects that I am most interested here.

As Thomas Allsen has noted, "even individual events are ofttimes difficult to evaluate in absolute terms: to one scholar the act of looting a local art treasure might well be categorized as simple theft motivated by greed, while to another it might be viewed, quite legitimately, as a mechanism of cultural diffusion" (1997, 5). This must be kept in mind even more than usual when dealing with the Mongols and their impact on Eurasia. Once one looks past the stereotypes, we find the Mongols encouraging trade and the exchange of knowledge.

It should be clear by now, but to reiterate, the bulk of this chapter will focus on the Mongol conquests of the thirteenth century and their aftermath. I do, however, also briefly consider the influence of the Mongols during other periods of history, including the migration of the group of Western Mongols who were to become known as the Kalmyk Mongols.

In order to contextualize the issues under discussion, it is necessary to start with the Mongol campaigns. It was, after all, their campaigns throughout Eurasia that made the Mongols infamous.

The Mongol Conquests

I do not recount here the full history of the campaigns of the Mongols. Any number of works on the Mongols can offer an overview of the campaigns (e.g., Morgan 1986, Ratchnevsky 1992, Saunders 1971). It is sufficient to note that the Mongols in fact made multiple forays into Russian territory and eastern Europe. The first, in the early 1220s, was from the Mongolian point of view, little more than a reconnaissance mission.

They did not linger on in these territories at first. They returned in 1236, victoriously campaigning in the region and expanding into Hungary and Poland before turning homeward in 1241 with the death of Ögödei Khan, ruler of all the Mongols (and son of Genghis Khan).[7] Further south, Baghdad fell to the Mongols under Hülegü's leadership in 1258, and Central Asia proper bore the brunt of the Mongolian campaigns. The Mongols never returned to Hungary, but they did return to Russia (from which they had also withdrawn in 1241) and ruled it for several hundred years. In Persia, the Mongols were not to remain in power long. The Il-khanate dissolved in the 1330s, but not before the khan Gazan had instituted reforms of Persian law. (Though with what, if any, lasting effect is not clear.)

Although both Hungary and Baghdad were devastated by the wars, both largely recovered. Other than terrifying and humiliating the European rulers, the European campaigns of the Mongols had no lasting impact on the internal politics of western Europe. The Europeans were able to neither unite against the perceived threat, nor join forces with the Mongols (at times equated with the legendary Christian king Prester John) against the Muslims during the Crusades. If the Mongol lords of later centuries were too busy fighting each other to offer a credible threat to neighboring regions, the same can be said of the European lords during the thirteenth and fourteenth centuries.

Sweeney (1994) has recently reminded us that the Mongol invasions also precipitated "invasions" of another kind: those of refugees. In terms of numbers alone, these were probably larger than the Mongol invasions themselves. "There can be little doubt that the historical evidence documents many shattered lives, but were the effects temporary or long-lasting in personal, social or material terms?" (37). Much work remains to be done on this topic, which is beyond the scope of this chapter. There is no doubt, however, that such refugee populations, whether they resettled permanently or not, would have had a substantial impact on the regions they inhabited, and they are worthy of more detailed study in the future.

In Persia and Central Asia, the impact, both immediate and longer term, was greater than in eastern Europe. Many cities were indeed leveled, and entire populations were exterminated by the Mongols' campaigns of terror. Many of these cities did not recover from their destruction. While we must not underestimate the damage the Mongols did, we should also not think the Mongols left nothing but a blackened swath of land in their wake. While many cities did not recover, many others did, and merchants grew rich upon the resurgent trade between Asia and Europe. Trade was to be one of the key components of the Mongol period. Where there was trade, cultures thrived. Those not on the trade routes, however, languished. But this is not a uniquely Mongolian trait.

In short, we can sum up the immediate impact of the Mongol conquests with the words of the Mongolist David Morgan. "The Mongol invasions were a truly awful, frequently a final, experience for those who had the misfortune to be in the way of the armies' advance; but that the impact was patchy, with some areas escaping fairly lightly, or even completely" (1986, 82). Additionally, it should be remembered that the total destruction of cities was not a foregone conclusion. Those that surrendered to the Mongols were largely left unharmed. (Many cities were even completely bypassed during the Russian campaigns.) It was only those who resisted that faced their full wrath. This was in large part due to the Mongolian use of terror as a military tactic designed to induce populations to surrender, rather than fight. Often outnumbered by their foes, the Mongolian armies relied on fear to do much of their work for them. This not only saved them the costs (in many senses) of a protracted military campaign, but it also had the benefit of handing the Mongolians a relatively unscathed region, ripe for economic exploitation. In leveling one town, the Mongols often succeeded in convincing other towns to surrender. Destruction, by and large, was undertaken with the aim of preventing even greater destruction and suffering.

It is interesting to note in this regard that in addition to the usual accounts of slaughter and destruction, the Armenian chronicle *History of the nation of the archers* makes what appear to be oblique references to this policy. Thus, we read, "but they did not kill the population, being without any order from the great Khan" (Blake and Frye, 1954, 323) and "if we remain in the manner without (y)asax [i.e., laws], and without a commander, this country will be wasted and the command of [Genghis Khan] will not endure. For he ordered us to subdue and hold the country through affection, and to build rather than destroy" (337).

The evidence from the Franciscan, John of Plano Carpini, who passed through the region shortly after the campaigns, is ambiguous. Carpini writes, "Kiev had been a very large and thickly populated town, but now it has been reduced to almost nothing, for there are at the present time scarce two hundred houses there and the inhabitants are kept in complete slavery" (Dawson 1980, 29–30). Yet later in his account, one gets a slightly different impression of Kiev. He writes of "a great feast" given on his return from the Mongols by a noble (70), and offers an extensive listing of merchants in Kiev who can vouch for his story, 11 by name and "many others, but I do not know their names" (71). While these and other incidents do not directly reflect on population numbers, it is hard to fathom that a village with "scarce two hundred houses" would be a worthwhile stopping point for at least a score of merchants. It seems safe to assume either exaggeration of the initial destruction, a quick recovery for Kiev (aided perhaps by the traders), or a combination of the two.

Carpini also notes, as did other travelers, "when we were journeying through that land we came across countless skulls and bones of dead men lying about on the ground" (29). But such a description is not unique to the Mongol campaigns. Years after the Persian conquest of Egypt, Herodotus still tells of the bones of the fallen soldiers lying on the ground (Herodotus 1972, 207).

As Fennell, in *The Crisis of Medieval Russia,* writes, "we are left with the picture of a Russia struck by yet another steppe invader, more formidable, more efficient in both war and peace and more enduring than the Pechenegs or the Polovtsy [Kipchaks]. But it was a Russia by no means as shattered, overwhelmed and dispirited as many modern historians would have us believe" (1983, 89). Citing this same passage (and pointing out the role of chauvinism in views of history), Morgan rebuts that "the problem for the Russians was perhaps more that, for centuries, the Mongols did not go away" (1986, 138). This is true, but only in a qualified way. The Mongols, indeed, did not go away, but neither did they settle in and among the Russians themselves.

For the purposes of this chapter, it is also important to remember, in the words of Denis Sinor, "from the very beginning of the Mongol expansion, military operations in the west had a low priority" (1975, 514–515). Although they couched their expansion in the rhetoric of global domination, it is a debatable point whether the Mongols would have continued their conquests to encompass all of Europe even without the death of Ögödei. Indeed, until the Khorezm Shah made his fateful mistake at Otrar, Genghis Khan claimed to be willing to split "world domination" between the two of them. Even attributing their withdrawal from Hungary in 1241 to Ögödei's death, it is still telling that the Mongols never bothered (or took the opportunity) to return to Europe to rule areas they had defeated militarily, although they did return to Russia and other areas.[8]

The Mongols, World Trade, and Taxes

As was already noted, one result of the conquests was an increase in trade between Europe and Asia. Conquered areas, such as Russia and Transcaucasia, benefited from Mongol-fostered trade (Halperin 1983, 243). More generally, Europe, and in particular, Italy, benefited. At least one merchant's handbook, that of Pegolotti, included discussions of East Asia. "[T]he number of Far Eastern business ventures steadily grew as long as and until the collapse of the Mongolian state did not make all trails impracticable" (Lopez 1952, 76). The existence of a single empire, at least for a while, along the length of the trade routes facilitated the flow of goods as well as people. It has been argued that one of the key reasons for this was that Mongolian military might was instrumental in lowering the "protection costs" of doing business overland (Seaman 1991, 13). In addition, "Genghis Khan's policies [of encouraging trade] were continued by his immediate successors, who, if anything, were even more encouraging to merchant interests providing, as they did, subsidized transport and above market prices for most goods" (Allsen 1997, 30). Not only was trade apparently safer under the Mongol Empire than before, but cheaper and more profitable as well. It was not only material goods that moved along these routes. As we shall see later in this chapter, Mongolian hegemony also allowed for the flow of information between two areas that hitherto had little knowledge of each other.

In order to understand why trade was important, it is necessary to digress and consider the political organization of the steppe nomads. Unlike many other scholars, I am not inclined to deny Inner Asia steppe nomads the ability for indigenous state formation. The received wisdom is that it is only in response to external pressures that nomads are able to form a state system (i.e., Krader 1980). The "tribal" (and hence, "egalitarian") nature of nomadic social structure is supposed to render the formation of autochthonous centralized political systems all but impossible. Wealth and power in a nomadic system cannot be easily stratified, it is argued, and even if it could, the populations one attempts to control are highly mobile. The nomads, this school holds, "developed the state in relation to, and in opposition to the state formation of the agricultural peoples" (138).

I am less convinced the evidence supports such a conclusion. Inner Asian nomads were able to, and did, form state systems without resorting to sedentary populations as a final cause. The nature of these state systems is important here. At least initially, these states appear to have followed Barfield's model (1989) of an "imperial confederacy." Such a system, he argues, was run like an empire when dealing with other political groups, but administered like a confederacy internally. In this vein, it should be noted according to the *Secret History*, the thirteenth-century Mongolian historical epic, Genghis Khan was appointed to his original position of power in 1189 (section 123; see Onon 1990, 46). He did not assume it without agreement from others. In a like manner, although this may have been a formality, the *Secret History* also notes that Temüjin was *given* the title Genghis Khan in 1206. Once again, he did not claim it for himself (sec. 202; see Onon 1990, 110).

Where I differ from Barfield is in his claim that it was outside circumstances that resulted in the formation of the imperial confederacies. He is correct in suggesting that the "state on the steppe was structured by its external relations" (Barfield 1989, 8). Structure, however, is not causality. The state may have been structured to exploit sedentary populations, but this does not necessarily deny the nomads the ability to form their own state. I do, however, think his general outline of the structure of the imperial confederacy has much to recommend it, and thus have elected to retain his terminology.

Barfield argues that it was only through the continued influx of trade or tribute that political leaders of the steppe groups were able to maintain control. (In the established Mongol khanates, this was to take the form of taxation as well as tribute.) As Barfield describes it, the confederacy was "autocratic and statelike in foreign and military affairs, but consultative and federally structured for dealing with internal problems" (36).

Drawing upon their privileged position with regards to foreign affairs, the leaders of the confederacy were able to buy the allegiance of their followers through their monopolization of luxury goods and wealth gained outside of the steppe. Failure to procure wealth in the form of tribute or the spoils of war would endanger standing of the leaders. The importance of trade is further underlined when we realize that trade was quickly established following military conquests. News of a military victory seems to have led to the formation of trade caravans almost immediately (Ratchnevsky 1992, 120–1).

One would not be remiss in seeing a strong element of Weber's charismatic leader at work in such a system, although the final picture is more complex. It is clear that there were certain "noble" lineages, such as Genghis Khan's, but this alone did not guarantee a position of power. Rather, it placed one in a position to contest for power. It should also be noted that no single, strong tradition of inheritance of power existed during the period of the Mongol Empire (cf. Fletcher 1986).

In the period following the death of Genghis Khan (in 1227), the same pattern could be seen in the Mongol Empire, writ large. At least initially, the rulers of the various khanates were subservient to the main khan in Harhorin (Karakorum). Thomas Allsen's description of the political structure of this period is reminiscent of Barfield's model: "The grand qan [i.e., khan] continued to enjoy an exclusive right to conduct relations with foreign states on behalf of the empire. . . . As regards internal affairs, the qaghan's [khan's] prerogatives were somewhat less extensive" (Allsen 1987, 43).

This model was to change in due time, although it is not evident that, again in Weberian terms, the entire Mongol Empire made the shift to a rationalized form of government. Although Ögödei (Genghis Khan's son and immediate successor) appears to have made such efforts, it was only after the splintering of the empire (under Kublai, Genghis's grandson) that such a change took place. In terms of Schurmann's analysis of tribute and taxation, we can see this, in China at least, as ultimately a return to what he terms the "political and social principles of the conquered sedentary societies" (1956, 305) rather than the creation of a uniquely Mongolian system of government. This return, however, did not occur in the case of the Golden Horde. (It should be pointed out that this return does not necessarily imply a "swamping" of Mongolian culture by that of the sedentary population. Rather, the use of such principles appears to be an example of the pragmatism of the nomadic rulers, who were aware that they themselves lacked the experience to administer sedentary populations.)

What this implies in the case of Mongolian rule in Eurasia (where Schurmann denies that rationalization ever took place, describing instead the situation as one of "confused multiplicities" [309]) is that we must rethink the standard descriptions of the monetary demands levied by the Mongols. It becomes apparent in this light that the obligations imposed by the Mongols on their subject populations were not necessarily an attempt to bleed sedentary populations dry. In fact, after the destruction of the military campaigns, "the Golden Horde, for reasons of self-interest, played a major role in providing the means for Russia's recovery" (Halperin 1985, 80). He goes on to note a few pages later that the length of time within which economic recovery was effected was about the same length as after the Time of Troubles (83). In other words, we see evidence to suggest that the impact of the Mongols was not unique in Russian history. Ostrowski again goes further, and cites a message from a leader of the Golden Horde in 1270 to a Grand Prince, noting in part, "whoever comes to me with arms, them I will deal with myself; but the merchant has unhindered passed through my domain" (Ostrowski 1998, 118). Trade, although it may have been disrupted temporarily by the campaigns, was clearly important to the Mongols.

The fiscal obligations imposed upon conquered groups, from the Mongols' point of view, were necessary as much to maintain power as anything else. It actually would have been in the interests of the Inner Asian nomads to merely exploit, rather than forthrightly conquer and rule, China or other sedentary populations. And indeed, in Russia, the Mongols remained on the steppe. Incursions into the settled parts of their domains were only undertaken when necessary to maintain power.

The Mongols were, for the most part, not interested in becoming part of sedentary populations themselves, but rather in maintaining a nomadic lifestyle augmented by the income conquered lands could provide. In the language of world systems theory, the sedentary populations served as periphery regions to the nomadic core. They existed, too, as both sources of materials and markets for nomadic goods. (An interesting reversal from how the settled people themselves like to think of things!) In this respect, it has been argued, the Mongols were no different than other world empires: "they shared many political and strategic objectives with maritime states like the Portuguese, the English and the Dutch" (Seaman 1991, 4).

It should be pointed out that the Mongols simply were carrying on a long steppe nomadic tradition. In their interactions with China, the various steppe nomads (such as the Hsiung-nu, the Hsien-pi, and others) usually evidenced little interest in actually ruling China. By and large they were more interested in letting someone else do the day-to-day running of the country, as long as they benefited economically. (Similarly, after the establishment of the Ming dynasty in China, the Mongols were once more interested in economic benefits to be extracted from the sedentary Chinese, rather than ruling per se.)

For the period at least immediately after the Mongol conquest in the region of the Golden Horde, "all that mattered to the Mongols was to exploit the Russian princes financially" (Spuler 1994, 48). In fact, Spuler goes on to suggest that it was precisely because the Muscovite nobility was so adept at collecting taxes and tribute that they were able to consolidate their power without drawing undue attention to themselves (52). If Spuler is correct, and I see no reason to argue his point here, then this only emphasizes the fact that the Mongols had assigned their outlying domains mainly economic roles. Politics qua politics within a given region played a minor role; minor enough, in fact, that power shifts could take place unchecked, as long as the financial situation did not deteriorate.

Even when dealing with taxes and tributes, one must approach the topic with a certain amount of caution. In his study of the impact of the Golden Horde on Russia, Halperin writes that "in the steppe, Mongol taxes, like those of most pastoral nomadic peoples, if not progressive, were at least proportional to wealth. *It was the Russian elite* who made the tribute regressive, forcing the poor to pay the most" (Halperin 1985, 78; emphasis added). In other words, the impact often attributed to the Mongols—

burdensome taxation—was as much, if not more, the work of the Russians themselves. The Mongols are merely convenient scapegoats.

As was mentioned above, the Mongols also had a vested interest in fostering the trade routes that ran through their empire. Cities fortunate enough to be on the trade routes that the Mongols encouraged did well for themselves. "There is every reason to believe that the international commerce the Mongols fostered was a major cause of Russia's new urbanization and economic recovery" (83). It also now appears that the international trade that was occurring at this time even trickled down to some degree to the peasants (81).

"The Mongolian conquest opened up new horizons" (Lopez 1952, 73). This seems a fair assessment. Trade was to be encouraged, for it could be, and was, taxed. Throughout the lands ruled by the Mongols—not just in Russia—trade was encouraged. This trade was not only long distance. Trade in and among the parts of the empire, especially between sedentary and nomadic populations, also occurred. This latter continued even after the collapse of the longer-distance routes (Rossabi 1989, 81).

Political Organization and Cultural Impacts

The Mongols were by no means the first group of Inner Asian nomads to make their way to the heartland of Eurasia, or even Europe. Others, such as the Huns and the Kipchaks, had made the trip before them (although the Mongols were the last to do so in any significant numbers). The fact that the Mongols were not the first group to reach Europe is not insignificant. While there were certain effects of the meeting of Inner Asian and sedentary European polities—including the fostering of long-distance trade—these were in place long before the Mongols first appeared (Kaplonski 1996). Also utilizing a version of the imperial confederacy, previous nomadic groups had fostered trade through the requirements of their leaders for goods with which to buy the loyalty of their followers. The result was an extensive network of Eurasian trade that included the nomads as a significant element, since trade is usually simpler and safer than conquest. The Mongols expanded upon and facilitated this trade, and provided the first direct links to Asia (as will be described further), but they were not the first Inner Asians to head West.

Once the Mongols had arrived in an area, where they did decide to settle in, their preferred pattern of rule was often indirect, relying on administrators and "overseers" rather than a complete replacement of the native system. In this regard, the Mongolian system had similarities to later colonial empires. While not totally negating the impact of Mongolian rule, this did have the result of mitigating much potential cultural change, although other policies precipitated unintended cultural and political changes. Ostrowski notes: "The ensuing assimilation, modification, and adaptation of these [Mongol] institutions resulted not from the Mongols' imposition of their system, but from the Muscovite princes' deliberate use of the khanate's administrative and military structures as a model for the creation of their own administrative and military structures" (Ostrowski 1990, 525).

More generally, the rulers of the Golden Horde were eventually to convert to Islam, but did not attempt to convert the Christian Russians, whom they were content to rule at a distance. It has even been suggested of the Golden Horde that "their Islamization, without enabling them really to share in the ancient civilization of Iran and Egypt, severed them finally from the western world and made of them . . . foreigners encamped on European soil, never to be assimilated" (Grousset 1970, 396). Without accepting in full Grousset's argument, I believe he makes an important point—namely that the Mongols of the Golden Horde, while not invisible in their presence, were never fully a part of the European cultural and political arena. In the blunt assesment of Dmitrii Obolenskii, "on the whole, it does not seem that [the Mongol] influence was very considerable" (1970: 7).

One of the reasons for adopting Mongolian practices, according to some, lay in the Mongolian choice of political system to administer their Russian holdings. Halperin notes that the Mongolians imported that Muslim *diwan* administrative system to Russia, rather than adopting the existing Russian system (Halperin 1983, 251). He suggests that the Russians did not copy this system in toto precisely because it was a Muslim, and hence infidel, system. (Although they did apparently adopt certain aspects of it.)

In general, the Mongols adopted a system that employed *baskak* (administrators, also spelled as *basqaq*), who were responsible for such administrative obligations as tribute, troop conscription and general maintenance of order (Buell 1979, 133). There was also another type of administrator, the *darugachi*. It is not entirely clear what the relation between the two was. Some scholars (i.e., Halperin 1985, 39) see the two as being distinct forms of administration, while others collapse them together (Buell 1979). This issue is further complicated by the fact that the exact duties and responsibilities of the two varied over time and geographical location (see Ratchnevsky 1992, 178–180). "In the later Mongol period a darugha / basqaq might be, in effect, a provincial governor, or he might be a kind of tax-collecting resident in conquered or partly autonomous territory. Revolts in such regions were generally and properly announced by the murder of the basqaq" (Morgan 1982, 129). Whatever the actual form this system took, it was a reflection of Mongolian administrative pragmatism, being adapted from the earlier Kara-Khitai.

The use of a foreign administrative system does not mean, obviously, that the Mongols had no impact whatsoever on the Russian political systems that followed. Indeed, they did. The Russians, for example, did adopt much of the Mongol system, including "taxes and the treasury, the organization and armament of the army, bureaucratic language, diplomatic forms, the postal service, and some aspects of criminal punishment and liability" (Halperin 1985, 90). Halperin also claims, however, that "paradoxically, the institutions Muscovy borrowed were characteristic less of the Golden Horde proper than of the world Mongol Empire of the thirteenth century" (94). The list of borrowings is extensive, but it is not clear that any of these were necessarily totally new introductions to Russian political culture. As Halperin himself writes shortly before, noting these various borrowings (a term that itself implies an active part on behalf of the Russians), "Russia's essential political structure predated the conquest, and the centripetal forces that eventually brought the feuding Russian principalities together into a single state derived from the internal processes of Russian history" (90). In other words, much may be attributed to the Mongol influence, but the changes were of degree rather than kind.

One rather intriguing aspect of this is the point that many Mongolian political practices were influenced by, if not derived from, the Chinese. As Herbert Franke phrased it, "We could even go one step further and ask how much of the government and taxation practices of the Golden Horde rulers in Southern Russia is of Chinese origin" (1966, 68). Ostrowski (1998, ch. 2) also argues that what influence the Mongols had on Russian administration was ultimately Chinese in origin.

While it has been traditionally argued that it was the period of Mongol rule that was responsible for the shift in Russian politics from Kiev to Moscow, this is a much- debated point. That it was Kiev that was the center of Russia before Mongol rule, and Moscow after, seems unquestionable. Yet just what role the Mongols played in this is far from clear. Other traditions beside that of Mongol rule have helped shape Russia. As de Hartog has noted, "the autocracy and despotism that are characteristic of the grand-principality of Moscow after the fifteenth century are only in part [if at all—CK] an inheritance from the Mongols. In this area, the influence of Byzantium is at least as great as that of the Golden Horde" (1996, 164). (Obolenskii [1970] argues that the influence of Byzantium was in fact much greater than that of the Mongols.) This becomes a relevant and understandable point once one is willing to look past the demonized image of the Mongols common in the West, and actually examine their political system on its own merits. Autocracy and despotism are linked to "barbarians" and only "barbarians" only if one does not make a real effort to understand those so labeled. As we have already seen, the Mongolian system was, in theory at least, as confederate as it was autocratic, although admittedly, this feature seems to have declined in prominence once the empire fractured into the separate khanates.

Given the intra-Russian political rivalry and maneuvering that character-ized Russia at this time, it is also far from clear that the Mongols were deci-sive in contributing to the decreased importance of Kiev. (Although some, such as Spuler, argue for a fairly direct influence [1994, 48].) Rather, it ap-pears as if Kiev, although nominally the "mother of all Russian cities," was already in decline before the appearance of the Mongols. Previous encoun-ters with nomadic groups (such as the Kipchaks) and disputed successions had as much to do with the decline of Kiev as the Mongols did. It was prior military defeats and squabbling among the nobility that helped contribute to the ease with which the Mongols carried out their conquests. The first Mongol invasion, in 1223, was remarkable for its minimal impact. Although the Russians were defeated militarily during Jebe and Subedei's reconnais-sance mission, the overall result was probably indistinguishable from previ-ous nomadic incursions into the sedentary regions, and Russia proper had fallen outside the path of the army.

Riasanovsky has noted, "the so-called 'Tatar Yoke' did not deeply influ-ence the course of [Russian] history or produce great social overturns in the life of the Russian nation. It accelerated some processes and held up others. But the processes themselves began without the influence of the Mongol-Tartar conquerors and continued independently of such influence" (1937, 261). Put in these terms, his claim perhaps is a little extreme—we have al-ready seen arguments suggesting *some* influence. Nonetheless, he is correct to suggest that much of the purported Mongolian impact was not in fact a result solely of the Mongolian invasions.

It seems fairly clear that although the Mongols had some impact on Rus-sian political life, much of it remained unaffected by the Mongols. One notes, for example, that much of the rivalry between the various Russian lords appears to have continued unabated during the period of the Golden Horde (see for example, Fennell 1988, ch. 5). The Mongols do indeed ap-pear to have a role to play here, but more as yet another factor to be taken into account in Russian politics, rather than *the* factor in Russian politics.

The eminent Mongolist Bertold Spuler perhaps offers the most succinct, cogent form of this argument: "Once the Russian states had submitted to Mongol authority, they had been left on the whole to their own devices, so long as they paid their tributes. . . . The Russians thus enjoyed the necessary respite in which to make a considerable recovery from the Mongol terror and recast their national life within the frame of the new order. Their efforts achieved success, for several reasons. . . . [T]he Mongols continued to leave the native principalities alone and intact, though individual princes were often deposed for lagging in their tribute payments, fighting among themselves or other offences" (Spuler 1994, 47).

Whatever one decides about the impact of the Mongols on Russian politics, the basic point seems to remain: ultimately, in Eurasia at least, the presence of the Mongols did not fundamentally affect the direction of political culture. Modifications were made, and ideas borrowed from the Mongols, but yet there was no fundamental shift from, say, democracy to autocracy. The Mongols had a political system that allowed for much autonomy of local rulers, as long as certain obligations were met. It was, in this manner, reminiscent of a feudal system. Those conquered by the Mongols may not have been familiar with their conquerors, but their system of rule can not have been that alien.

There is one area in particular, however, that is worth mentioning in terms of Mongolian influence, and that is the rise of the Russian church. Even if an unintended consequence, the period of Mongolian rule has been credited with facilitating the rise of the church. The reason for this is fairly straightforward. One of the hallmarks of Mongolian rule was the exemption of religious groups from taxation. It did not particularly matter if the Mongolians themselves were adherents to a particular religion or not. (Indeed, it will be recalled, the rulers of the Golden Horde converted to Islam.) The "tax breaks" afforded the Orthodox Church allowed it not only to rebuild after the destruction of the conquests, but even to expand its influence (Halperin 1985:113–4).

The case in Central Asia is much less clear than it is in the region of the Golden Horde. "In the fourteenth century the Chagatai khanate in Central Asia still had a long, though singularly obscure, life ahead of it" (Morgan 1986, 199). This was due in large part to the twofold nature of the area encompassed by the Chagatai khanate. While to the east, the region was still largely pastureland, to the west it was towns with a sedentary population. It was along these lines that the Chagatai khanate was to eventually split in 1346–47.

The Chagatai khanate was heir to some of the great oasis cities of Central Asia, such as Samarkand and Kashgar. It also included what was to become, in the nineteenth century, the Xinjiang region of China. A portion of it covered the area that had been the empire of the Khorezm shah. (The rest of his empire fell under the eventual jurisdiction of the Il-khans in Persia.)

This area probably suffered the most under the Mongol conquests, although it also received much attention and effort at rehabilitation. The Khorezm shah had the misfortune to kill an envoy of the Mongols, who had gone to protest the killing of a trade delegation by one of the shah's governors.

Genghis Khan, who considered ambassadors to be sacrosanct, responded by unleashing death and destruction on the Khorezm shah and his domains. It was "probably the greatest calamity ever to befall the people of the eastern Islamic world" (Morgan 1986, 68). The destruction was continued by Tolui (one of Genghis's sons, and father of Hülegü, the first of the Il-khans). This, it has been hypothesized, is an exception that proved the rule that the Mongolians were more interested in extracting resources than in wreaking havoc. It appears that Genghis did not originally plan to make the former empire of the Khorezm shah a part of his (69). If this is indeed the case, then there would have been little reason *not* to pursue a scorched-earth policy. (But as always, it must be remembered that even then, the destruction was concentrated, rather than total.) Aided in its recovery after the conquests (Spuler 1994, 43), Central Asia again suffered during the civil war between the brothers Arigböh and Kublai Khan.

Although Central Asia suffered due to its central location within the Mongol Empire, it was much more than a battleground to the Mongols. They were conscious of the riches of the region, and as one recent study notes of Mönh Khan's grandson, "although it is impossible to reconstruct an overall picture of Qaidu's internal policy, there seems to be sufficient proof that a great part of the responsibility for the prosperity of Central Asia belonged to him . . ." (Biran 1997, 105). The Mongols would also have had a vested interest in the rehabilitation of Central Asia for the simple reason that it served as a crossroads for much of the long-distance trade. Indeed, it has been suggested that a sort of "global peace" treaty signed by the different groups of Mongols in 1307 in part was the result of the desire to facilitate trade (72).

It is also worth noting here that several of the groups that inhabit Central Asia can trace their origins, directly or otherwise, to the Mongol conquests.

The Kazaks apparently came into being after the splintering of the White Horde in the fifteenth century (Olcott 1987, 1).[9] The Uzbeks ultimately derive their name from Özbeg, one of the khans of the Golden Horde. Further east, the groups known as Tatars can be traced to either the period of the Mongol conquests or the later migration of Western Mongols, also known as the Kalmyks.

Trans-Eurasian Information Flow

Perhaps the single greatest impact of the Mongols on Eurasian history was the result (intentional or otherwise) of the flow of information from Asia to Europe (and vice versa). One thinks of paper money and gunpowder, among others. The flow of information—and other, more tangible objects, such as disease—was considerable. The Europeans who reached China were well aware that in many ways, Chinese culture and political organization surpassed their own (Phillips 1988, 194).

The overall impact of the increased knowledge of Europe upon China seems to have been slight (Morgan 1986, 193). In fact, when viewed in terms of the other domains of the Mongols in the thirteenth and fourteenth centuries, Europe is perhaps best viewed as something of a cultural backwater, apparently contributing mainly furs, as well as some artisans, to the Mongol economy.[10] While suggesting that there was little if any lasting influence of Europeans during the Yüan dynasty in China, Franke remarks that "China [functioned] as a cultural center from which all kinds of influences spread west and reached Central Asia as well as Near Eastern countries" (1966, 67).

It is a debated point whether or not gunpowder and other Asian inventions traveled to the West via the Mongols, but it is clear that the Chinese and Mongols were using gunpowder during their campaigns, at least in the East. Even if we cannot be certain the recipe for gunpowder traveled from China to Europe, it is quite telling that one of the first persons to describe it in the West, Roger Bacon, had personally met with William of Rubruck shortly after his return from the East. The recipe appeared shortly after Rubruck's return. (For an account critical of the Chinese origin of many of the items traditionally ascribed as imported from there to Europe, see Woods [1996].[11])

Such information traveled along the trade routes both the southern Silk Road, and the more northerly routes that passed through the lands of the Golden Horde. It was these more northern passages, in fact, that served greater duty as linkages between Asia and Europe under the Mongols. The two great western observers of the Mongols, Carpini and Rubruck, for example, both traveled the northern routes (although Marco Polo took a more southerly approach, but one also under Mongol control.) John of Plano Carpini, travelling in the late 1240s, journeyed via eastern Europe into Russia. William of Rubruck took a slightly more southern route, passing through the Crimea, but still did not venture along the yet more southerly Silk Road.

These two travelers in particular bring up another important aspect of the Mongolian-facilitated information flow. It was the Mongol conquests that, intentionally or not, did much to spur on European interest in, and ultimately knowledge of, Asia.

It was not only information or trade goods that now flowed between Asia and Europe, courtesy of the Mongols. The Black Death that periodically ravaged Europe was certainly from Central Asia, and its transport was most likely facilitated by the Mongol Empire. Others, such as Adshead (1993, 95–102), have argued for a larger role of the Mongol Empire and Central

Asia in what he terms the "microbian common market," although the main "contribution" of the Mongol Empire in this regard seems to have been the plague. The spread of other diseases, such as cholera and smallpox, was facilitated by the Central Asian connection, but this was substantially after the Mongol period.

Asia had of course been known before the Mongols. Chinese silk, for example, was known in the Roman Empire, and the Romans complained of the economic drain of the Asian trade. Yet until the Mongols, little direct knowledge existed in Europe of eastern Asia. "It would . . . be a mistake to think that the exchange of commercial goods also implied an exchange of culture and ideas" (Olschki 1960, 43) prior to the Mongol period. It was travelers such as the Franciscans John of Plano Carpini and William of Rubruck, as well as later voyagers like Marco Polo (assuming we give him the benefit of the doubt; see Woods 1996), that first ventured into the unknowns of Asia. This led to what has been called "the basic information circuit" (Adshead 1993, 70).

Information, and not just trade goods, began to flow between Asia and Europe. This in turn led to "a unified conception of the world" (70), one in which its parts began to be seen in relation to one another. Other travelers soon followed the early Franciscans, at first largely to assess the potential Mongol threat, and to seek their aid against what was perceived as the common Muslim enemy. The effect was wider than this, however.

Prior to the expansion eastwards, Asia served for Europe not only as the source of silk, but as the Great Unknown. In it dwelled mythical beasts—groups of people with no heads, or the heads of dogs, and so on. It was also home to the mythical Prester John, a Christian king who would aid in the final overthrow of the enemies of Christianity. Christians did in fact exist in Inner Asia, but as Nestorians. Prester John never materialized.

The fact that he, or the mythical monsters, were never encountered in the various travels did not mean that they were immediately discarded. The short-term result was rather that their location was shifted even further eastward, and often onto islands (Phillips 1988, 208). It is not so much that the travels to the Mongol Empire led immediately to a complete revision in geography, but rather they helped lay the groundwork. It turned out that there were marvels enough without the need to invent them.

If one wishes, the argument can also be expanded in other geographical directions. It appears, for example, that the Mongols, by giving reason for Europeans to voyage to Asia, played a role in the death of the old belief that the heat at the equator was too great to live in, or travel through (195). (Doubtless, however, this belief would have fallen in time even without the presence of the Mongols.)

One should realize that while such travelers and their successors (in particular, missionaries—missions were established in China by the fourteenth century) helped expand knowledge, they were not immune to the beliefs of their own time. Marco Polo, for instance, gave a recognizable description of a rhinoceros, but fitted into a category he was already familiar with, that of the unicorn. "They are very ugly brutes," he observed. "They are not at all such as we describe them when we relate that they let themselves be captured by virgins, but clean contrary to our notions" (Polo 1958, 253).

This information flow did not deal only with east Asia and Europe. Although important for the later development of Europe, Europe itself was very much a backwater from an Asian point of view. Knowledge flow also increased between the advanced civilizations of the day—the Chinese and the Muslims. Translations from Chinese and Persian appeared in Persia and China, respectively. The Chinese translated works of Persian medicine and astronomy, while the Persians also translated Chinese medical texts (Ratchnevsky 1992, 210–11). It was between these two cultures that the most fertile exchange of knowledge took place.

The Kalmyk Mongols

We started this chapter by noting that one could not speak of a migration of Mongols during the Genghisid period, and that such terminology was misleading. There was one period, however, when one could indeed talk of the migration of Mongols in Eurasia. It is to this period that we now briefly turn.

The Kalmyk Mongols were originally a group of Western Mongols. In the sixteenth and seventeenth centuries, the Western Mongols were a major force on the steppe, making both the Russian and Qing (Chinese) empires uncomfortable. Groups of the Western Mongols eventually migrated ever further west over a period of roughly 150 years, largely as a result of pressures by the expanding Qing. The Torgut, one of the groups of Western Mongols, were the first to migrate, beginning their trek with about 200,000 people around 1616 (Rubel 1967, 13). By about 1632 they had settled in the region of the lower Volga, maintaining their nomadic lifestyle, at least initially. Various other groups of Western Mongols were to migrate and join the migrants over time.

Links were maintained with both the Zunghars in the homeland, and the Russian government. They also served as a source of cavalry for the Russian Empire, fighting at various times against both the Ottoman Empire and the Swedes (Hasland 1992, 208).

Throughout the eighteenth century, however, the Russian government attempted to exert increasing control over the Kalmyks, who both raided Russian villages from time to time and also provided a buffer from other steppe groups.

This attempt at increasing control was to precipitate yet another migration that was to end disastrously. A large group of Kalmyks undertook a return trek to their homeland in 1771. The vast majority, however, died en route. Of 400,000 who left the Russian steppe, less than 120,000 made it to the ancestral homeland (214).[12] Those (on the left bank of the Volga) who had remained behind and numbered about 70,000 were subjected to still more Russian control and attempts at sedentarization. By the end of the nineteenth century, they were largely sedentarized, and their lands were increasingly settled by Russian peasants.

Although not numerous when viewed in terms of the larger Russian population, the Kalmyks had provided a constant source of military strength, at least as long as cavalry remained a viable option. At the end of the nineteenth century, a Danish explorer acknowledged these contributions noting, "if the Kalmucks had not in past times helped the Russians the latter would hardly be what they are now in the Caucasus" (Kaarsberg, quoted in Haslund 1992, 215).

After the Russian Revolution, the Kalmyks briefly were granted their own Autonomous Region (in 1936). The area was occupied in part by the Nazis, who forcibly removed some of the Kalmyks during their retreat. In the winter of 1943–44, with the retreat of the Nazis, the Kalmyk Autonomous Soviet Socialist Republic (ASSR) was abolished, and the Kalmyk population exiled to Siberia. They were eventually allowed to return in 1958 (Tserel 1997:163–165). Eventually, those Kalmyks who had accompanied the Nazis were resettled after the war, winding up in a variety of countries around the world, including in New Jersey, in the United States. In the 1990s, the Mongolians of the independent country of Mongolia still saw a link existing between themselves and the Kalmyks in the United States.

To briefly recapitulate the argument: through this wide-ranging discussion, I have attempted to make a case that the impact of the Mongols upon Eurasia (and the world more generally) should be reassessed. The Mongols did indeed have an impact. They created the largest contiguous land empire ever, and opened new routes of trade and information between Asia and Europe.

These two items should be seen as interrelated. With a political system reminiscent of an "imperial confederacy," military expansion was one means with which to provide for a constant flow of goods and wealth to help the ruler maintain his position, through both booty and tribute. Trade was the flip side of this coin, for it allowed wealth, in the form of taxes and duties, to also bolster the nomadic hierarchy.

Starting from this view of the political system also allows us to understand why the Mongolians adopted a hands-off approach, at least in the steppe regions. The lands they controlled were not so much lands to be settled in as a reservoir of wealth. Thus Russia existed in the eyes of its Mongolian rulers not as a country, but as a source of revenue.

The Mongolian legacy did also include death and destruction, but we have argued that this was not unique to the Mongolians. Death and warfare was common during the thirteenth and fourteenth centuries. It was rather the fact that their enemies were unknown, and highly efficient, that led the Europeans to cast them as the "Devil's Horsemen," a label whose influence can be seen in accounts of the Mongols even today.

Notes

1. I wish to thank David Sneath for his input and comments on earlier versions of this chapter.
2. Ostrowski makes a similar point (1990, and especially 1998). His work, however, came to my attention after this chapter had been completed. I have attempted to incorporate his work, but have not been able to do so as fully as might be wished.
3. Andrei Bell pointed out in response to an earlier draft of this chapter that some people have indeed held it against Napoleon and Alexander. The Mongolian point, however, is still a valid one. The amount of relative outcry is staggeringly different.
4. The term Golden Horde is actually a relative late innovation, but since it is more common, I have elected to maintain its usage here.
5. Beatrice Manz does argue that the Mongol heritage played a role in Timür's administration, but it does not appear to have been the single overriding factor (Manz 1998).
6. There may well have been other factors as well, such as climate or available grazing pasture (see Sinor 1972). Yet the political correlation should not be overlooked.
7. A study such as the present one encounters difficulties when dealing with names and terms. Myriad spellings for different terms and names exist depending on which sources are consulted, and in which languages. In an attempt to impose some consistency on these spellings, where possible we have given the standard contemporary Halh spelling of names and terms.
8. One could also point out that, at least compared to Persia and China, where the greatest amount of cultural interplay seems to have occurred, Russia and eastern Europe were in many ways a backwater from the Mongolian point of view.
9. The White Horde was a Mongol khanate that was located east of the Golden Horde. Morgan notes, "Very little indeed is known about its history" (Morgan

1986: 113). Indeed, it is given slight, if any mention in many Mongolian sources (i.e., Maidar 1990; Sühbaatar 1992).

10. In Bira's recent (1993/4) article on East-West relations during the Mongol Empire, Russia and Europe more generally are notably absent from discussions on intercultural influences. China and Persia were the key sources and beneficiaries of this expanded contact.

11. For a critical review of Woods's position, see Morgan 1996.

12. Other sources say 70,000, out of an initial population of about 170,000, survived the trip (Halkovic 1985: 13).

CHAPTER 15

Migration, Its Role and Significance

When we look back at migration in temperate Eurasia in the last three thousand years, it becomes apparent that it shows two clearly defined patterns. The first one, from about the eighth century B.C. till around A.D. 1500, was characterized by a close interaction between areas of high civilization, the forest tribes, and the nomads. The second period, the time of European expansion and implosion, neatly falls between 1492 and 1992.

If the year 1492 signals an entirely new beginning in the West, in the East the time of the transition cannot be determined with similar precision. In the Eurasian context, the division of Inner Asia between Russia and China and the elimination of the nomads and the forest tribes as major players represented the triumph of high civilization and the conclusion of the first period. But at another, worldwide level, the Russian conquest of Siberia and the Far East was part of the European expansion, and the implosion that we witnessed in 1991—which is still far from over—was part of the general European implosion.

The advance of the Turkic nomads into the heart of Europe via Asia Minor and the Balkans—it reached its high point in 1529–1683—further complicates the picture. And it is not made simpler by the fact that, as they advanced into Europe, they were gradually sedentarized, so that by the time they reached Vienna, the Turks were no longer nomads but a somewhat unconventional (in the European context) sedentary empire.

Strictly speaking, Barfield's model of the triangular relationship among sedentary empires, nomads, and the forest tribes works better in the Far East. It was there that sedentary empires conjured up nomadic confederations, and the forest tribes interfered in the affairs of their more advanced neighbors almost on cue. In the West, although the interactions among the three were also a constant factor, they lacked the almost mechanical synchronicity evident in the Far East. The major determinant that would account for this divergence was the differences in the power configurations among the three contestants. In the West, the main protagonists were the high civilization and the forest tribe; in the East, the high civilization and the nomad.

The configurations were largely determined by geography. Geographical determinism has long gone out of fashion, and it is not my intention to resurrect it. But I cannot escape the conclusion that if the core European areas bordered on a wide expanse of the steppe or if China faced a densely forested zone in the north, their histories might have been very different, perhaps even reversed. It was Europe's good luck that its largest plain, the Alfold, is of modest size and lies on its eastern periphery. It was also fortunate that Alföld is a terminus of the steppe corridor, rather than its core area like Mongolia. That is why, for most of European history, the nomad was a nuisance rather than an overwhelming threat, like it was in China and Russia.

If the migration confirms the central role played by geography, it also deflates the role of climate as a decisive factor. While climate may have provided an extra push in completing the transition of certain tribes to nomadism, overall, it played a secondary role. Even then it was not so much the climate as the preadaptation of a given society, determined by social, cultural, and political factors, that decided the success or failure of a given society in competition with another (e.g., Vikings versus the Inuit in Greenland).

One also reaches the conclusion that at least in 460–1368 and, possibly, much earlier, China was the engine that "ran" Eurasian history. It worked like this: the unification of China brought forth nomadic empires; its disintegration led to their fall. The collapse of nomadic empires created chaos in the steppe, forcing losers in the struggle for power to flee. Most fled west because that is where the steppe corridor led (again, geographical determinism: if the plains had extended north and east, Europe might have had a much less turbulent history).

Of course, chain migrations in the Eurasian corridor have been known in earlier periods (e.g., the Andronovites), but these developed as a series of shorter movements that did not encompass the entire steppe. Unless someone can conclusively prove that the Huns were descendants of the Hsiung-nu, we can assume the steppe began to function as a cohesive unit only after 460, when a major Chinese victory over the nomads set off a wave of chain migrations with grave repercussions for the entire steppe and Europe. Some 60 years ago, Frederick Teggart noticed correlations in the histories of China and Europe: the pressure of the Chinese and nomadic tectonic plates against each other sent nomadic tsunami toward Europe.

If China was a major force in Eurasian history, its northern frontier was, historically speaking, static. It could conjure up the nomadic genie and put him back in the bottle, but it could not, until the middle of the eighteenth century, decisively defeat him. Until the development of technology reached a certain point, even a powerful and populous empire like China was at the receiving end in most confrontations with the nomads. Despite numerous attempts at colonization, the frontier zone between the Middle Kingdom and the nomad remained virtually unchanged.

In contrast, the frontier of high civilization in the West was periodically advanced, even before technology made Europeans invincible. Explanations can be sought partly in the advantages conferred by a more favorable geographical position (which influenced the configuration of its power relationship with nomads and forest tribes), but mostly in the structure of the European state system, its multipolarity. Unlike China, Europe failed to reestablish a unified empire. Byzantine attempts to reconquer the Western Empire came to naught, not least because, in addition to the nomads and the western foes it also had to contend with Persia and the Arabs (and later the Turks), while South China was relatively safe. Instead, a new, Frankish, empire arose in the West, astride and outside the old border. This empire was also divided in 843, leading to the formation of Germany and a new German empire almost completely outside the area of the old civilization. This grandchild of Rome (the true Third Rome, although without a "Rome" since it failed to establish a permanent capital) was strong enough to deflect most of the forest tribes and nomads from the core areas of high civilization and expand these areas at the European periphery, but not strong enough to reabsorb the old core areas (the failure of the Italian campaigns). But it had a major advantage that northern China lacked: it was buttressed by a string of middle-sized powers further east, stretching from Scandinavia to the Balkans, and two strong bulwarks, Russia in the east and Byzantium in the southeast.

This three-layered defense system proved adequate for protecting Europe. In the process, the outer bulwarks—Russia and Byzantium—were destroyed, but their resistance weakened the enemy. Its advance was further slowed down by the resistance of the eastern European powers. By the time the enemy arrived in Germany/Austria, it was a spent force. Where this three-layered system of defense was lacking—as in the south, against Muslims, or in the east, in Antiquity—the enemy had a free hand.

Only once did this system (almost) fail—with the Mongols. (But then the Mongols were exceptional in China as well.) Here, once again, the geographical factor had decisively kicked in: although the Mongols were recalled from Europe because of the succession struggle back home, the lack of adequate pastures and the impossibility of keeping adequate supplies of fresh mounts probably decided the issue. The Mongols could conquer, but they could not hold on to Europe in the long run.

This was indeed the predicament of nomads in Europe. That is why the high civilization in the West, repeatedly defeated and rolled back, continued to advance. Historically, it had the pattern of stop-and-go, with periods of expansion alternating with periods of defense or even retreat. What is striking is the continuity of expansion, despite tremendous differences in motivation, levels of development, power configuration, and position vis-à-vis other contestants.

The underlying force that made it possible, the spring that fed the river, was migration.

The earliest phase of the expansion, dominated by Phoenicians, Greeks, and, to a limited extent, Etruscans, was trade-driven, although other factors—political infighting in Greek city-states, population pressures (Miletus), and invasions (e.g., the Persian takeover of Phocas)—were also far from insignificant. At this stage, migration developed through the establishment of colonies by various city-states.

The incorporation of the entire Mediterranean region in the Roman Empire radically changed the contours and direction of migration. Metals and other raw materials lacking in the tiny city-states of the earlier period were now widely available (except for Baltic amber, and that was a luxury). Also available was the land for expanding population. The main task facing the empire was the consolidation of power and the successful incorporation of diverse populations whose allegiance was often in doubt. Hence, the implantation of Roman and then Roman-and-Latin colonies throughout the imperial domain. In addition, these colonies provided land for discharged veterans, indirectly contributing to the creation of a class of hereditary warriors, and also allowed the authorities to get rid of the excess numbers of a parasitic proletariat (the plebs) in the capital. Occasionally, however, the machine broke down and worked against the interests of the state it was designed to protect. This happened when veterans demanded—and got—land in Italy, which had long been secured, creating dangerous resentments among the expropriated landowners, the backbone of Roman power.

In general, the pace of the territorial expansion far outstripped its population resources. Compared to the vast territorial acquisitions of the empire, Rome's human resources (I am referring to Rome the city-state, not the empire) were simply inadequate. That was one of the main reasons that the number of "true" colonies was so small, at least in the imperial context (Caesar founded 32, and Augustus 74). With the consolidation of the empire and the increase in the number of citizens, the need for colonies decreased. And the grant of citizenship to all free inhabitants of the empire in 212 satisfied some of the fundamental reasons for colonization—promoting loyalty among subject populations and ensuring their gradual Romanization. By then, colonization had long ceased to be an instrument of external expansion or even internal consolidation. Historically, the cessation of migratory expansionism coincided with the high noon of Roman power and presaged the loss of the empire's vitality. We should also note that at this stage the pattern of Roman colonization resembled Chinese in the sense that it was mostly internal, confined to the imperial territory, unlike the earlier (Greek) or later (German) migrations. In both cases, internal migrations coincided with the high point in the historical trajectory of both empires and signaled their approaching demise.

The next episode of imperial expansion, the medieval German migration, started in the "Roman" fashion, with conquest and colonization in the east, but was then given further impetus by the new states of eastern Europe, which needed settlers and German expertise. This immigration, actively encouraged and promoted by the eastern European rulers (often against the wishes of their subjects), proved an effective instrument in integrating the eastern European periphery into the pan-European system. This peculiarity of German expansion—encouragement from within and from without—continued throughout German history. It is evident in the settlement-by-invitation in Russia in the eighteenth century, an unusual, perhaps unique example of one empire doing the colonizing in another. At the same time, colonization conducted by Austria in Bohemia in the seventeenth century and in Hungary in the eighteenth (and, briefly, by Hitler in western Poland in 1939–42) shows a more traditional pattern of imperial colonization that aims at consolidating imperial power in an unruly or a newly conquered province. Like its Roman predecessor, the German migration developed through an entire millennium, from 950 to 1950, and displays many patterns and variations.

The same can be said about the Russian colonization, which was "compressed" into "merely" five hundred years. Even within this limited time frame, it passed through several "time zones." It started when Russia was still a feudal polity and was carried on through rapid industrialization, a radical transformation into a totalitarian power, and almost to the very collapse of the Soviet Union, for as long as the Slavic majority retained its demographic force.

Clearly, such remarkable expansion under extremely diverse conditions was predicated upon some basic underlying factors. The same applies to the forest tribes and nomads, who also show an unmistakable tendency to expand under almost any circumstances. Population expansion in all three formations, despite famines, invasions, and high mortality, seems to have been a constant. It disproves the assumption that at each stage populations tend to reach an optimum size harmonized with the carrying capacity of their habitat. The history of the migrations—Greek, Germanic, even Seljuk—suggests otherwise. It would seem that, aside from the political factors, relentless population increase created an internal stimulus for expansion even where population densities were very low (as in Scandinavia). The fact that high civilization and, to a lesser degree, forest tribes expanded in all directions, even where natural conditions were less than favorable, confirms this. Another proof is provided by such customs as *ver sacrum* that, from the earliest times, sent excess young males away.

If we compare the three formations, high civilization was the most versatile and highly adaptable. It could build towns and create trade networks virtually anywhere. Its ability was greatly enhanced by the organizing and supporting power of the state.

The sedentary forest tribes were intrinsically no less versatile, but they lacked the organizing power of the state, which put them at a serious disadvantage vis-à-vis advanced civilizations, while their lack of mobility, in comparison to the nomads, made them vulnerable to nomads' attacks.

Among the three, the nomads were probably the most disadvantaged in the long run, limited as they were to a relatively narrow environmental niche and dependent on their sedentary neighbors for supplies of grain and even arms. But their vulnerability was concealed by their aggressive predation. Or rather, they were predatory because they were vulnerable—and because they had a major advantage: mobility.

At first glance, high civilization was the most vulnerable because it was the most attractive: it created large surpluses of wealth. What's more, these surpluses were concentrated in urban centers and monasteries, making them easy to skim. Indeed, early sedentary civilizations were extremely vulnerable vis-à-vis the nomad. But they had another tremendous advantage that ultimately allowed them to win the contest: a much greater (compared to their adversaries') ability to create and enhance technology. This book does not touch upon technology, but its role in the European expansion can hardly be overestimated. Although occasionally forest tribes and nomads achieved technological breakthroughs (e.g., masts and sails that allowed the Vikings to cross the open seas), in the long run high civilization was more successful in creating and implementing superior technology, which eventually helped it emerge as the winner. But "high civilization" in itself is too broad a category, since different civilizations produced and adopted technology at different rates at different times. Here, the contrast between Europe and China is very interesting. China was supposedly the first to invent the compass and gunpowder, but it was Europe that put them to widespread use. (And in Europe, as well, the Mediterranean led in the technological innovation until well into the Middle Ages, when it was overtaken by northern Europe.)

The attraction exerted by the high civilization did not necessarily lead to invasion. When sedentary empires were strong and could defend their borders, "barbarian" populations gravitated to the frontiers turned into zones of contact and interaction. Imperial wares and "gifts" to forest and nomad rulers played an important role in acquainting the barbarians with the luxuries of advanced civilization.

From luxury to necessity is but one step. Imports were highly prized and helped promote "civilized" influence among "barbarians." Ultimately, they helped high civilization to impose its terms of reference. Lindner showed that even the Huns at the height of their power had implicitly accepted these terms.

It was relatively easy for high civilization to absorb the forest tribes because the two were sedentary agricultural societies at different stages of development. It was only a matter of time before a forest tribe would erect towns, create writing, and build states—that is, join high civilization. Nomads were harder to incorporate because they belonged to a different formation. But they were not impervious to the attractions of high civilization either. They were prone to sedentarization, of which we have many examples (Scythians, Bulghars, Khazars, Magyars, and many others). With time, and in the absence of a threat from other nomads, they eventually sedentarized.

The second paradigm, the European expansion and implosion of 1492–1992, was radically different from the earlier one because it was carried out by high civilization alone and led to the imposition of this formation throughout the world.

However, both periods defy easy delimitation. In the west, Iberian exploration and expansion overseas was the continuation of eight hundred years of the *reconquista*. Their first targets were Muslim towns in Morocco. Symbolically, as well, the voyage of Christopher Columbus coincided with the conquest of Granada, the last Muslim entity in Iberia, and the expulsion of the Jews, whose confiscated wealth was used to finance the expedition.

In the east, Russian expansion across Siberia, undoubtedly a part of the European expansion, was also a continuation of the age-old interaction between high civilization and the nomad, although here the continuation was actually a reversal. The final point can be determined with great precision: 1771, the year of the Kalmyks' trek, and 1774–83, which saw the incorporation of the Crimean khanate, the last remnant of the (nomadic) Golden Horde into the Russian Empire. Thus, paradoxically, even though the European expansion was a radically new beginning, it also continued and fulfilled age-old patterns. (It is interesting that the *reconquista* motif is discernible in the Russian expansion as well, since the tsar was heir to the Great Khan and was even accepted as such by some Mongols. This "legalism" was later skillfully exploited in many episodes under various circumstances, for example in Russian attempts to penetrate Tibet in the late nineteenth and early twentieth century.)

The Seljuk and Ottoman advance into Europe adds another confusing variable into the complicated process of interaction between high civilization and the nomads. Starting in Central Asia, perhaps as early as the eighth century A.D., possibly as part of the Khazar kaghanate, the Turks conquered and absorbed Anatolia, destroyed what was left of Byzantium, and advanced through the Balkans to reach the gates of Vienna by 1529. This last and belated thrust of the nomadic world into the heart of high civilization occurred when European expansion was well on its way. However, by this time, the Turkic nomads were no longer nomadic: they had been sedentarized already in Anatolia as early as the twelfth and thirteenth centuries. By the time they reached Vienna their nomadism was a distant memory and a *mythomoteur.*

Is there a link between these seemingly disparate paradigms? I think there is: the creation of wealth and trade.

Even the earliest, the most primitive states were more adept at generating wealth than sedentary "barbarians" (the "forest tribes") or nomads who could not even produce enough grain to feed themselves. Already Mycenean palaces stored enough wealth to attract the greedy attention of the poorer outsiders.

With time, the differential between the sedentary state and other socioeconomic formations increased. It was enhanced by urbanization that concentrated wealth in well-defined locations, making it easier to "skim."

Trade was the motor of this process. It was trade and the search for metals that scattered Greeks and Phoenicians across the Mediterranean and beyond; trade and the search for wealth that sent the Vikings in all directions; trade and the search for gold and spices that later sent Europeans across the oceans.

Trade had another important function: it acquainted "barbaric" populations with the wealth of settled civilizations. Trade with Greeks "awakened" the Celts and the Scythians. Roman exports reached Germanic tribes on the Vistula and in Scandinavia. The first thing that both nomads and the forest tribes wanted to do when they encountered high civilization was to trade. Where the border was established and the empire was strong—along the Rhine with Rome and between China and the nomads—the frontier developed into a zone of exchange with a peculiar lingo, customs, and habits. Where the sedentary civilization was weak, the nomads and/or the forest tribes inundated the more developed areas, looting, pillaging, and imposing tribute, that is, extracting wealth. It was the search for wealth that sent Greeks across the Mediterranean and Europeans in the nineteenth century across the Atlantic; and it was the great disparity in wealth that produced many migratory flows of Germanic tribes into the Western Roman Empire, Slavs into the Balkans, and guest workers into industrial countries of Europe.

At first glance, the nomadic migrations in the Eurasian steppe do not conform to this pattern, especially the "domino" migrations west. These migrations were usually caused by the collapse of imperial confederations facing China and the internal upheavals that followed. However, we should bear in mind that the relationship between nomads and China was based on Chinese "gifts." The disintegration of China stopped the flow of gifts and trade and was an important factor in the collapse of the nomadic confederations. Thus, the extraction of wealth was an important factor in the East as well. That there were other factors involved—the structure of nomadic confederations and society; the geography of the steppe corridor, which contributed to making nomadic groupings in the East more numerous; the concrete political situation in Europe and in various segments of the corridor—merely proves that we should refrain from monistic explanations of complex phenomena. But the fundamental role of wealth disparity, search for wealth, and trade is beyond doubt.

The European expansion started long before industrialization. Indeed, the globalization of trade preceded both industrialization and the demographic transition.

While the process of expansion started virtually simultaneously in the West and East, its epicenter gradually shifted west. The reason was relatively simple: the opening up of the American colonies had shifted the global trade to the Atlantic seaboard. It was here that the most rapidly modernizing areas in Europe were located, in England, Holland, northern France, west Germany. They experienced rapid urbanization, attracting excess rural population. As industrialization spread east, so did the peripheral zone, which supplied much of the labor force. The westerly direction was further enhanced by the growing attraction of America and other overseas "new Europe" territories. In the Middle Ages, Germany supplied migrants to colonize the East. Starting in the eighteenth century, an increasing number of Germans went west. In short, the migratory flow "turned around."

This turnaround did not affect the old "core" areas of European civilization: the English, the French, the Italians, and the Iberians had never settled in the east in large numbers (with few exceptions, such as the *outre mer* after the first crusades). But Germans certainly had. By the end of the nineteenth century migrants from the European periphery were also going to western and central Europe and overseas. The turnaround was complete when Russian settlers in Kazakstan, Central Asia, and Siberia started moving back to Russia. Here, in the East, the turnaround "merged" with the general European implosion.

Historically, migration was the vehicle that expanded and defended the civilization (as in Greek, German, Russian) and the formation (sedentary high, sedentary low [forest tribes], or nomadic) of its bearers. Even the most spectacular conquests that were not sealed by sufficient migration proved ephemeral (e.g., Mongol, but also Alexander the Great). Conversely, migrations that were not supported by conquests (e.g., early Greek) could not be sustained in the long run either; their descendants eventually succumbed to assimilation.

This role of migration in promoting and reinforcing a particular formation and civilization is very clear in the trajectory of the European expansion. Migration was the glue that held European conquests together, the foundation on which the global European civilization was built. Without migration, there would have been no expansion.

Perhaps, the most important part played by migration was its "creative/destructive" role. Many migrations led to the destruction of the old and/or the creation of new states. In either case they changed the balance of power and the course of history. Here, migration is often inseparable from conquest and is often its vehicle.

The long-term success of migration and, ultimately, the maintenance of any civilization/formation depends on its demographic strength. The most prosperous state, unsupported by teaming millions, is doomed in a struggle with its competitors. (If this sounds Hobbsian, it is.) In a sense, migration is a sign of demographic vitality. In this context, the demographic transition acquires a particular importance.

Almost everywhere, modernization was accompanied by the demographic transition from high birth/high death rates to low birth/low death rates. High population growth rates typical of the last one hundred years were the result of plunging death rates brought about by better nutrition, better medical care, and better disease control. Birth rates also decreased, but at a much slower rate than death rates. The temporary difference between still high birth rates and already low death rates is what drives population growth in developing countries.

Virtually all European countries, with some exceptions (e.g., Albania), have completed their demographic transition sometime in the twentieth century, when other populations were only starting theirs. The European preeminence in world affairs was destroyed by the two world wars, the subsequent division of the European continent between the superpowers, and decolonization. And it was presaged and accompanied by the loss of demographic vitality.

With very few exceptions (e.g., Holland), European countries no longer have human resources to export. And while it will be simplistic to see European implosion only in terms of demography and migration, the role of both in the processes of expansion and collapse cannot be overestimated. The example of the Soviet Union is a further proof, if any is needed.

Eventually, the rest of the world will also complete the demographic transition. It will then turn into a static world without migration, without expansion, and, probably, without vitality. It does not mean that individuals would not change their place of residence or even emigrate. It only means that the mass, often transcontinental, migration of the last two centuries will come to an end. If that sounds implausible, look at Italy and Spain, even Portugal and Greece, where people no longer leave the less-developed regions.

It will probably be a safer world. But also a static world. Will it be the end of history?

APPENDIX A

Climate and Migration

William B. Meyer

In a book dealing with the history of migration on the Eurasian steppe, the role of climate and climatic change merit attention at some point. One reason has to do with the history of ideas on the topic. Climatic change was a factor invoked in some of the most ambitious early attempts to account for the long-term pattern and chronology of migrations in Eurasia. The excesses and deficiencies of the climatic determinism out of which these approaches arose tended in later years to discredit any investigation of the possible role of climate and left it largely unexplored. A more nuanced understanding of climate-migration and, more generally, climate-society relations offers a better likelihood than either of these extreme positions for shedding light on the migrations dealt with in this volume. The present chapter will assess the possibilities and problems involved in linking climate with migration and propose approaches for doing so.

There are few major movements of peoples or collapses of civilizations that some analyst has not tried to account for as the consequence of a shift in temperature or rainfall patterns. Far fewer, though, are the cases in which that interpretation even ranks among the leading ones given credence by most experts. Attributions of events in human history to climate and climatic change have always had to struggle against a number of handicaps. They include a general preference among social scientists for explaining social phenomena, as famously urged by Durkheim, strictly in terms of other social phenomena; the disrepute for its supposed reactionary political implications into which anything that suggests environmental or climatic determinism has fallen; and the reluctance of many scholars to accept anything that smacks of a simplistic single-factor interpretation of complex social processes. At the same time, such explanations enjoy certain advantages equally unrelated to their intrinsic merit in any given case. They include the inability of most social scientists to evaluate critically the climatic evidence and, indeed, much of the social evidence involved; a simplicity that can seem appealingly elegant as well as crudely reductive; and, in recent times, associations with a widespread public concern over global climate change and its possible impact. These associations can give an enticing aura of relevance to the claim that past societies collapsed or were otherwise transformed because of climate change, and that in any case may ease the acceptance of climate-change theses by accustoming the researcher to think in such terms.

The disadvantages have predominated for most of this century where climate and migration, and indeed climate and society generally, have been concerned. Prominent in most of the fledgling social sciences in their early years, environmental and climatic determinism were largely expelled from them in the decades that followed. So, in practice, were environment and climate themselves, whether or not addressed in deterministic terms. Even in geography, the field most hospitable to research linking the natural and social sciences, the reaction against the earlier prominence of climatic determinism, associated most notoriously with the work of Ellsworth Huntington, largely suppressed climate-society research until recently. Most studies of modern migration patterns fail to consider climatic variables in any detail (Kritz 1990). This studied neglect of the environmental dimension has left the social sciences embarrassingly ill-equipped to assess the human dimensions of global climate change. Any improvement of the base of knowledge regarding the relations of climate and society can help illuminate those issues, whether by their direct relevance or as offering more or less useful historical analogues for current and future situations (Meyer et al., forthcoming).

If, as a rule, the twentieth-century human sciences can be said to have ignored climate as a factor, there would seem to exist one prominent exception. The French historians collectively referred to as the Annales school are often described as giving precedence to climate and other environmental factors over the traditional ones of politics and ideas in human history. The reality is somewhat different. Among the originating themes of the Annales school, indeed, was not the introduction of the environmental dimension but its downgrading: the replacement of "determinism" by "possibilism" as its guiding perspective on human-environment relations, an emphasis on freedom of human occupants to use a given environment in many different ways rather than on the constraints that an environment places on its occupants.

The Annales historian from whose works—or perhaps merely from the titles of whose works—the image of a strong emphasis on the impacts of climate seems mainly derived is Emmanuel Le Roy Ladurie. He has indeed written extensively on the history of climate, but he has generally and quite explicitly eschewed any consideration of the role of climate and climatic change in social affairs. In his history of the European climate since the year 1000 (Ladurie 1971), and in his assorted essays on the relations of climate and history (collected in Ladurie 1973), Ladurie's avowed and actual aim has always been the modest and restrained one of aiding the meteorologist and climatologist in reconstructing past climates by examining certain data sources with whose uses and pitfalls historians are more conversant than natural scientists are. The title of the English translation of his main opus—*Times of Feast, Times of Famine*—notwithstanding, feast and famine and any other human consequences of climatic change were not Ladurie's concern. He quite explicitly eschewed any intention of trying to assess the significance for human society of the climatic changes he documented, and he was particularly dismissive of the possibility, at least in the near future, that scholars could relate migration convincingly and usefully to climate change:

> As regards migrations, the influence of climate is a completely ambiguous question. The Teutons of the first millennium before Christ are supposed to have left their countries of origin because of the cold. The Scandinavians of the period before A.D. 1000 are supposed to have done the same thing for exactly the opposite reason—the mildness of the climate, stimulating agriculture and thus also population growth, is said to have led to the departure of surplus male warriors. But what is one to conclude from such contradictory and unprovable speculations? (Ladurie 1971, 293).

One could conclude, certainly, that the seeming contradiction of which Ladurie is so scornful is not necessarily a contradiction at all. It is one only if particular climatic changes must be supposed to have precisely the same effects everywhere and at all times that they occur. It is evident from Ladurie's examples and many others that could be added that if there is something useful to be said about the relation of climate and migration, it will not come in that form, nor in the kindred form that simply invokes the coincidence of a climatic change with a societal discontinuity, such as migration or settlement abandonment as proof that the former caused the latter. That, unfortunately, is all too often the form in which it does come: the form paraphrased generically by McGovern (1991, 78) as "it got cold / hot / wet / dry and they died / flourished / migrated / intensified."

That was largely the form taken by the thesis, arising in the late nineteenth century, of a progressive desiccation of settled areas in Central Asia and consequent retreat of settlement. A variant, the "pulse of Asia" thesis put forward by Ellsworth Huntington (1907) in the early twentieth century, associated periods of agricultural retreat and of nomad invasions on the steppe over many centuries not with a unidirectional desiccation but with times of climatic deterioration, notably diminished rainfall. Arnold Toynbee (1934) adopted a version of the Huntington thesis, crediting climatic change for much of the long-term pattern of nomad movements on the Eurasian steppe. More recently, Gumilëv (1968) has renewed the argument in a considerably more nuanced form.

The question of whether an actual close correlation in time existed between climatic changes and nomad migrations has remained an important and ongoing debate. For the purposes of the present chapter, it is not a debate into which it is necessary to enter. For as pointed out by, for example, de Vries (1980) and McGovern (1991), even identifying such a regular correlation is not adequate to explain the social event. Why migration followed is a further question. For climate change does not automatically and mechanically, even among populations whose livelihoods are highly climate sensitive, compel relocation as the determinist thesis supposes. The occurrence of a climatic change can never be a sufficient explanation for a migration that ensued. Societies always possess a range of other ways of coping with any challenges that the shift presented, such as changing their activities or sharing losses, that may so buffer them from the effects of the change that the extreme step of moving elsewhere is not necessary.

Such was the gist of some of the criticisms raised against Huntington and his predecessors. The distinguished explorer of Central Asia Sir Mark Aurel Stein repeatedly pointed out that any climatic change would have driven the population from the area only if the adaptations available to the population were ineffective in coping with it. The effectiveness of those adaptations, such as irrigation, had varied over time, depending, for example, on state capacity and conditions of peace or war. Where some ascribed an outflow of an agricultural population to a climatic change's lessening the rainfall below what the system required, Stein pointed out that the evidence left it an open question whether the causal agent had been "a change in the physical conditions attending the supply of water" or social processes such as "neglect of irrigation works, caused probably by political troubles" (Stein 1904, 304).

Lattimore (1938, 3), with specific reference to the history of migration in Inner Asia, aptly recommended a careful study of the society exposed to a climatic change as "a step away from the excessively mechanical understanding of the geographical factor in history, and a step towards the more reasoned study of society as it functions in a geographical environment." Assessment of the effect of a change in climate requires detailed inquiry into the characteristics of society through which its effects were translated. Thus the classical determinist thesis that large-scale migration in marginal areas was the result of climatic shifts is not in itself adequate even if the shifts and the migrations coincided. At the same time, the discovery of any correlation between the two does open up possibilities that should not be ignored.

Arguments of a causal link between the two must do several things. First, of course, they must document the occurrence of a climatic change and its temporal association with a migration, or other social discontinuity. They must also show that the change was such as to cause significant stress to the livelihood system experiencing it. They must further show that the adaptive resources and repertoire of that system did not contain elements capable of dealing with that stress. They must take into account the conditions making a migration elsewhere feasible as necessary conditions instead of taking them for granted. Finally, other possible, non-climatic causes of the migration or societal discontinuity must be considered that may have represented elements or even as complete and adequate rationales in themselves for the observed change.

If one link between climate and migration is migration as a possible response to climatic change, a second is the change of climate that migrants can experience in moving from one place to another. A second deterministic thesis that was widely held at one time (e.g., Riis [1890] 1932, 29; Ward 1918, 276; Van Cleef 1940, 25) claimed that migration normally occurs only between areas of similar climate. "Similarity of climate . . . encourages penetration into regions similar to those left behind, in order that life may continue in accustomed ways" (Vidal de la Blache 1926, 179). Migrants will choose to move only to lands where they could carry on their livelihoods much as they had done before and to which their dress, dwellings, and constitutions were already adapted. Thus movement typically occurs within, rather than across, latitudinal or isothermal zones.

This thesis survives as the concept of "latitude pull" in certain corners of historical and geographical scholarship, but it plainly does not hold true in its strict form.

Exceptions abound, perhaps more so than confirming cases do. Lattimore (1937) assessed it as it was often cited in his time to explain the interwar patterns of outmigration from China and Japan. He found it of little use on closer examination. It ignored some significant movements, and the patterns that it did fit were readily accounted for on the basis of political and economic factors alone. "Explanations of this kind," he concluded, "are based on a limited range of evidence, and the range of evidence which they ignore is much greater" (Lattimore 1937, 120).

But this thesis, too, points to a set of relations potentially of great importance in connection with migration. The change of climate that migration may entail may indeed be a source of serious stress for the livelihoods and the health of the migrants in their new surroundings, and the change of climate may indeed be a major factor in their success or failure and prosperity or poverty, especially in the early years. The supposed rule may indeed hold true because the migrants themselves believed it to be a rule and took similarity of climate into account in choosing where to move. Even the fact that migrants moved to a different climate does not prove that they did not intend to stay in a similar one. They may have meant to but have chosen badly on the basis of an inadequate understanding of climatic patterns, as happened among the early English colonists of North America (Kupperman 1982).

Ladurie's dismissive reaction to the attempted linking of climate and migration is understandable, considering the character of much of the literature drawing a link. Still, his dismissal of the topic is not to be taken as the final word. Though the two deterministic theses examined so far do not work well, both have a basis in reality. It is certainly true both that climatic change can cause stress, to which a possible response is migration, and that migration can produce a change in climate that causes stress.

A more sophisticated concept that is likely to prove useful in organizing and clarifying both of these matters is that of "preadaptation," introduced by Newton (1974). (For a history and review, see Jordan 1989.) The concept originated and has been used mostly within the field of cultural geography, and has been applied mainly to the experiences of groups migrating from one environment to another. It calls attention to the fact that among the cultural traits that migrants carry with them, some will be well suited to the new environment. The migrants possessing those traits are described as preadapted to their new surroundings. They are likely to fare better there, other things being equal, than will other newcomers with traits poorly adapted to the new conditions.

The concept of preadaptation can be applied just as well, though to date it has not been explicitly, to a population that experiences a shift in climate in place. Just as certain preexisting traits among a society may be fortuitously well suited to dealing with a new climate encountered through migration, so too they may be well suited to dealing with a new climate encountered through climatic change. Certain others, of course, may hamper adaptation to the change, just as certain traits among migrants will work badly in the new climate. Societies preadapted to a change and well able to cope with and even profit from it will feel less pressure to migrate in response, whereas migration is a much more likely consequence of climatic change among societies poorly preadapted to the change.

Technical skills have been the focus of most studies in preadaptation. They are not, though, the only relevant factors. The concept can be broadened to include aspects of social organization that may be no less significant in aiding or hindering the successful use of a new environment. Social institutions themselves may facilitate or discourage the adoption of suitable technical changes, for example, or the buffering of the impacts of climatic change through the way losses are distributed.

Two examples will illustrate how an analysis can be conducted in these terms. The first is the decline and disappearance of the Norse settlements in west Greenland, coincident with the onset of the "Little Ice Age" during the fifteenth century. It represents one of the classical examples of a social discontinuity often attributed to climatic change. The work of McGovern (1980; 1981; 1991) and colleagues, from which the following discussion is drawn, both bears out the claim that climate played an important role in the collapse and demonstrates just how inadequate a simple attribution of it to climatic change would be.

The Norse settlements in west Greenland, founded in the late tenth century, were supported by a variety of activities: the grazing of sheep, cattle, and goats on pasture along the coast; the summer hunting of caribou and harp seal; and the winter hunting of walrus and polar bears for sale overseas. The climatic changes occurring at the start of the Little Ice Age did indeed impose a number of stresses on the system. They decreased the size and productivity of the pastures. They reduced the availability of caribou and harp seal by altering their migration patterns. They increased storminess along the coast and made navigation, both for hunting and for overseas trade, more hazardous.

In these senses, the system was highly vulnerable to the kind of climatic change that occurred, but that change was not in itself necessarily harmful for human occupancy of the region. The Inugsuk Inuit, who also inhabited west Greenland at the time, not only survived but "spread and prospered" (McGovern 1980, 270) during the same period that saw the Norse settlements die out. The Inuit possessed a number of traits that the Norse settlements did not that buffered them against the climatic changes and even helped exploit them. They had a more diversified livelihood system less vulnerable to fluctuations in the availability of one major component. Unlike the Norse, for example, they hunted ringed seal in the winter as well as harp seal in the summer. In addition, their clothing and dwellings were better suited to protection from the cold and their boats to rough weather.

The failure of the Norse, over a period of several centuries, to adopt any of these useful traits from the Inuit points to institutional as well as technical ways in which they were poorly preadapted to the climatic change they experienced. Theirs was from the start a markedly hierarchical social system. If anything, it became more so over time. Innovation was strongly discouraged and so was contact with the Inuit, from which useful techniques might have been learned. The Norse system, particularly its elaborate ecclesiastical establishment, was also highly demanding of wealth and labor, both in short supply in the colonies even before the onset of climatic change.

The disappearance of the Greenland settlements thus illustrates the inadequacy of simple correlation between climatic and social change—in this case, extinction, but, by a ready analogy, migration as well—to establish the former as sufficient cause of the latter. It represents, indeed, a case in which migration was evidently not attempted as a response to stress of a kind and degree that elsewhere have been supposed to have forced migration. Preadaptation offers a useful framework by which to organize the story. The climatic change had the effects it had because neither technically nor institutionally were the Norse settlements well preadapted to the climatic change that befell them.

A second case illustrates different degrees of preadaptation to a climatic change experienced as a result of migration rather than one experienced in place. Among the settlers of the United States Great Plains in the latter part of the nineteenth century were colonies of Russian Germans who emigrated there from the Volga steppe (Kloberdanz 1980). Their ancestors had migrated to the steppe in the 1760s, enticed there by guarantees of land and of linguistic and political rights offered by Catherine the Great. When those rights were revoked under Alexander II, many of the colonists chose to move elsewhere, many of them to the North American Great Plains.

Among the settlers of the plains, the Russian Germans were the only ones who came from a similarly subhumid climate (Baltensperger 1983). American settlers originated largely in the more humid Midwestern states east of the Mississippi. The Russian German agricultural system proved distinctly better suited than the American Midwestern one to the plains climate. Most American migrants to the region imported an agriculture emphasizing corn and livestock, a system well suited to their climates of origin but vulnerable to the lower average rainfall and more frequent drought on the plains. Russian German agriculture lessened the risks of drought with a greater diversity of crops, including rye, flax, oats, and barley. It also placed a much greater emphasis on crops, such as hard winter wheat, that were better suited than corn to the plains climate. During the severe droughts of the 1880s and 1890s it fared better than the Midwestern system (Baltensperger 1983). Russian German settlers also fared markedly better than two other immigrant groups on the plains, neither enjoying a farming system preadapted to the climate, with whom they have been compared: Swedes and French Canadians (McQuillan 1978).

The preadaptation of the Russian Germans may have been as much cultural as technical. Where Baltensperger (1983) emphasizes the latter, McQuillan (1978) stresses the former, arguing that it was the tight community cohesion and work ethic of the mostly Mennonite immigrants from the Volga steppe that principally accounted for their success. Both in this case were evidently important. A study of Mennonite and other colonization efforts in Paraguay, in an environment to which their agricultural techniques were much less preadapted than they were on the Great Plains, found that their form of community organization still made them the most successful of immigrant groups there (Hecht and Fretz 1983, 170). Elements of their farming system, notably the emphasis on hard winter wheat over corn, were so well suited to the climate of the plains that they set the pattern for much of the farming system that subsequently developed in the region (Malin 1944).

At the same time, especially in the early years, Russian German agriculture, though well suited to the plains climate, was not so well suited to the plains economy. Because there was little market for many of their favored crops, the settlers were obliged to change their practices somewhat, notably by growing drought-sensitive corn (Baltensperger 1983). This example points to a still wider sense of preadaptation. To be useful, a trait must be applied not just narrowly to the climate or the physical environment but to the entire environment in which a society operates. To adapt to the American market Mennonite agriculture had to lessen the role of some of the elements best adapted to the plains climate.

The example illustrates one of the risks in using the concept of preadaptation, the same risk that social scientists run when they employ the concept of adaptation itself. A means to an end may be wrongly judged ill-adapted because of a confusion as to what the end really is. Those who seem to be doing an exceptionally inefficient job at maximizing something given priority by the investigator may in fact be trying quite successfully to maximize something else. Growing some corn was ill-advised on agronomic grounds for the Russian Germans, but essential on economic ones. The *zemlianki,* or earth-covered dugout houses brought to the plains by the Russian Germans, made for a more even indoor temperature in the region's harsh winters and summers than did the American framehouse (Kloberdanz 1980). American settlers too built sod houses or dugouts but exchanged them as rapidly as possible for frame dwellings, preferring the "sawed house" to the "sod house" (Malin [1967] 1984, 95). Can one say that the Russian Germans were preadapted and that the Americans were not? Only if one takes a certain indoor temperature—and Russians of the period in any case liked a winter indoor temperature warmer than felt comfortable to most Americans—to be the entire goal of housing. That misses much of what the American settlers, no less than the Russian Germans, sought: to reproduce for outward show and personal satisfaction the house form to which they and their neighbors were accustomed. One could say, of course, that Russian Germans were better preadapted in the combination of their ends and their means than were the Americans, but that comes close to judging the ends themselves rather than means of attaining them.

This discussion has examined some of the dangers and some of the opportunities in relating climate and migration. Evidently, the importance of climate and climatic change will vary from society to society, region to region, and period to period. Evidently, they will not furnish the master key to the history of migration on the Eurasian steppe. At the same time, they raise important questions regarding any migration. Was it associated with a climatic change, and, if so, what connection can be established between the two? Did it entail a change of climate from origin to destination, and, if so, with what effects? In either case, how well and by what means—techniques, institutions, government assistance—were the societies involved preadapted for the change, and what were its consequences?

APPENDIX B

Some Controversies

I

J. H. Hexter divided historians into lumpers and splitters. Lumpers look for megatrends. They construct metanarratives and write metahistories. Splitters concentrate on the particular. They cut history into snippets and carefully chew each one. Their approach, to borrow a term from postwar Eastern European politics, can be called "salami tactics."

Historically, splitters have been on the ascendant, reflecting a general trend in all fields of knowledge toward narrow specialization and professionalism. Despite the great esteem for the Annales school, historiography has been increasingly hostile to all-encompassing theories. This hostility stemmed from several factors. Perhaps the most basic is that grand theories, of which Marxism is a good example, tend to favor monistic explanatory models and are inherently simplistic. On the other hand, our increasing awareness of the complexities of the world led to a growing acceptance of theories of chance and chaos. (For a discussion of chaos and history, see Prigogine and Stengers 1984, Eisler and Loye 1987, Dyke 1990, Hayles 1991, McCloskey 1991, and Reisch 1991.)

Then, there is the problem of uniqueness. "People, events, situations [are] so different," writes Hobsbawm, "that no generalizations about society [are] possible. There [can] therefore be no 'historical laws'" (Hobsbawm 1997, 60). This is the old argument of whether the term "caste" is applicable in any societies outside the Hindu civilization.

Finally, there has been "a rapprochement between history and the social sciences" (63) that has infused the study of history with analysis and statistics diverting it away from narrative (which has, nevertheless, made a timid comeback).

Thus, skepticism toward grand theory has deep roots. Fear of monism, fear of generalization, and an increasing use of statistical data and mathematical models (Tedlock once said that anthropologists secretly want to be lab technicians; in other words, even practitioners of soft sciences invest hard sciences with higher value) all conspire against the *longue* (and *grande*) *durée*.

The result is a growing specialization, often equated with professionalism. But there is a price to pay. Specialization creates barriers of incomprehension between different branches of history (Zeldin 1973, 5). We also need works of synthesis that compare societies, trace diachronic developments within one or several cultures, or examine comparable phenomena across civilizations (e.g., ethnicity). These types of study are complementary, rather than mutually exclusive. The smaller, more focused studies serve as building blocks for the larger ones, while the latter ones set the terms and direction of the subsequent smaller ones. (In particular, I am thinking of the works by Lucien Musset on invasions.) "I am . . . profoundly convinced that there are insights attainable by taking large views of the past which cannot be had from close inspection of the separated segments of history," wrote McNeill (McNeill 1986, 127). "Historians, however, through their idolization of written sources, have commonly allowed themselves to wallow in detail, while refusing to think about the larger patterns of the past which cannot be discovered by consulting documentary sources" (36).

There is one more aspect of the rejection of grand theory that has to be addressed: the divorce between history and philosophy. It is reflected in the rejection of speculative philosophies of history, exemplified by those of Spengler and Toynbee.

History, as a discipline, can be divided into two kinds: critical and speculative. This division is based on a similar division in philosophy (Broad 1923, ch. 1, in Nash 1969, xiv). While critical philosophy analyzes the universe, speculative philosophy attempts to provide a conceptual framework of the world. It strives to give us the "total picture." Hence the grandiose metaphysical constructs of Spinoza, Leibnitz, and Hegel.

Likewise, speculative history, from St. Augustine to Vico and Hegel, tried to uncover pattern and meaning in history. It sought to answer three questions (H. Dray 1964, 63ff): (1) What is the pattern of history? (2) What is the mechanism of history? and (3) What is the purpose or value of history? The answers, as might be expected, were diverse in the extreme: St. Augustine and Kant favored linear models, the Stoics and Nietzsche cyclical; while Vico and Spengler combined linear and cyclical into a spiral. The motor of change was similarly elusive: Hegel's World Spirit, Vico's Divine Providence, Marx's Economic Determinism, Toynbee's Challenge and Response, Spengler's biologism (Nash 1969, xiv-xvi).

Whatever its model, whether linear or cyclical, speculative philosophy stressed *development*. It sought to find a *pattern*. This is the Hegelian aspect of historiography, now decidedly unfashionable. But a search for pattern, that is, for meaning, is virtually inevitable. "There is nothing very mysterious to historians in looking for patterns in the past and finding them. We do it all the time" (McNeill 1986, 87). Without it, history turns into a mere jumble of incoherent facts, names of rulers, dates of battles, and an enumeration of articles of the constitution. As Spengler eloquently put it, "Is there a logic of history? Is there, beyond all the casual and incalculable elements of the separate events, something that we may call a metaphysical structure of historic humanity, something that is essentially independent of the outward forms—social, spiritual, and political—which we see so clearly? . . . Does world-history present to the seeing eye certain grand traits, again and again, with sufficient constancy to justify certain conclusions?" (Spengler 1980/1918, 3).

Ultimately, the topic should determine the scope of the study. This one could have been pursued on at least three levels. I could have written a monograph on a particular migration, for example, Goths or Bulghars; or I could have "done" a cluster of several interrelated ones, like the early Germanic or Slav migrations. Or, I could have looked for patterns of migration in a certain area through several historical periods.

I chose none of these approaches. The study started modestly enough, with an attempt to apply Barfield's model to Europe. But then, by the very nature of the study, I could not avoid looking for patterns of migration. In this, I followed not so much Spengler or Toynbee but Ortega y Gasset, who tried " . . . to elevate a particular, concrete historical 'phenomenon' [revolution] into something 'supra-historical'—a 'historical form' that has a 'general character' at least for the ancient Greeks and modern Western Europe, but not for the entire world and for all epochs. He was undertaking what he had called one of those 'metahistorical investigations' of historical epochs and rhythms in *Modern Times* (3:149), something he later called the 'method of epochs' as part of 'historiology'. In other words, he was developing out of history a transhistorical model, or schema, meant for a fairly general historical application" (Graham 1997, 41). He was looking for "the great historical rhythms" (Ortega 1923, 3:149, in Graham 1997, 173).

And so was I, in migration.

This does not mean that this book aspires to be a universal history. Nor am I trying to answer the great imponderables like what is the destiny of mankind? What universal laws govern history? What is God's role, if any, in history? Rather, I looked at migration through time and found, I believe, the "great historical rhythms." Although I did not expect to find a set of rules that governed, preordained, and predicted even one migration, I did not want to close my mind to the possibility that there was indeed a pattern to this confused Brown's movement. And if the scope extended over three thousand years—well, *tant pis*.

So, in this instance, I clearly belong to the lumper proletariat. I believe that "lumping," in historiography, can be profitable and intellectually stimulating. And I am not alone (I am glad to say). I have the support of William H. McNeill.

One day, he went for a stroll in Morningside Heights. "Below me ran the Henry Hudson Parkway, crowded with cars. When I glanced down at it, to my amazement I observed that the stop-and-go traffic on the Parkway constituted a longitudinal wave, with nodes and anti-nodes spaced at regular intervals . . . the pattern was most certainly there—clear and unambiguous. To recognize it required an observer, located at an appropriate distance, who possessed . . . the notion of longitudinal wave with which to generalize the infinite detail that assailed my eyes as particular cars formed ever-changing geometrical relations to one another" (McNeill 1986, 86). In this book, I invite the reader to take such a stroll across vast space and time.

II

There is an acrimonious debate going on in ethnic studies concerning essentialism, that is, creating entities where none exist. This controversy is significant in the context of the debates on nationalism, and particularly debates on the modernity of nations. Most "moderns" argue that nations and nationalism do not predate the end of the eighteenth century and link both with modernization and economic development. The "ancients"—the label is really a misnomer since even the leading "ancients" like Anthony D. Smith and John Breuilly acknowledge that the ideology of nationalism is modern—point out that some nations have deep ethnic roots that predate the era of nationalism.

This controversy concerns us because some "moderns" feel that the use of ethnic labels in describing ancient societies is unjustified. "It is highly unlikely that all the ancient peoples now known as Celts referred to themselves by that name, or indeed had any concept of a 'pan-Celtic' identity," writes Simon James. "Beyond their related speech, the ancient Celts . . . were no more an ethnic unity than, say, modern Argentinians, French and Romanians . . ." (James 1993, 8–9).

It may be true, although prolonged dealings with Greeks and Etruscans and confrontations with Romans and Germans seem to have awakened a certain degree of ethnic awareness among the Celts. But let's suppose, for the sake of the argument, that he is right: Celts did not see themselves as Celts but only as representatives of specific tribes. Does that make them non-Celtic? If someone belongs to a tribe that speaks a Celtic dialect, if he or she lives according to Celtic customs and worships Celtic gods, is he or she *not* a Celt, whether they know it or not?

For the purposes of this book, this controversy is a non-issue. Many concepts are complex constructs; they change and none more so than ethnic labels. Colin Renfrew noted that the term "Celtic" lends itself to seven interpretations; the concept of Germandom is even more varied, including or excluding a whole range of categories, such as Volksdeutsche, Aussiedler, German-speaking Swiss, and the like. A Turkish-speaking Greek Orthodox Christian may be considered Greek in Turkey and Greece because there religion is the badge of collective identity, yet millions of Catholics and Protestants consider each other German because to them language is more important.

The same applies in geography. The concept of Europe has certainly changed through time: initially, it stopped at the Don. It was only in the eighteenth century that V. Tatishchev "moved" the frontier to the Ural Mountains because he wanted to reassign Moscow from Asia to Europe (Hobsbawm 1997, 63). "That Europe is a construct does not, of course, mean that it did not or does not exist. There has always been a Europe, since the ancient Greeks gave it a name. Only, it is a shifting, divisible and flexible concept, though perhaps not quite so elastic as 'Mitteleuropa'" (218–19).

I find Hobsbawm's approach very reasonable. I am not arguing that the term "Celt" (or "German" or "Hun"), applied to ancient ethnies, is not a construct. Nor am I equating it with modern ethnicity. I merely use it as a convenient shorthand in reference to tribes who spoke Celtic and whose material culture was Hallstatt and later La Tène. And when they moved en masse to a new location, I call it a "Celtic migration."

III

There are several controversies surrounding migration. One of these is the problem of cultural change.

Few things are as permanent in history as change. And few things are as permanent in historiography as disputes about its provenance and direction.

Basically, two explanations are possible: evolution of an existing culture (often called "differentiation" or "evolutionism") or diffusion by migration and/or invasion. It is often assumed that the process of differentiation is gradual; migration, on the contrary, results in a rapid and drastic change.

Both processes have been well documented, historically and archeologically. But, for about a hundred years, from 1860 till 1960, the diffusionist models prevailed (Chapman, 12, in Chapman and Hamerow 1997). Each assembly of artifacts was identified with a culture, and each culture was assumed to correspond to a tribe. Whenever change in material evidence was sudden and drastic, indicating a break in the process of evolution, migration was presumed.

Diffusionist models had a great advantage: they could be easily integrated with virtually any theory. That was the secret of their appeal and acceptance. They were made even more attractive by the introduction of methodologies that allowed archeologists to delimit assemblages of material remains (which, inadvertently, also contributed to essentializing tendencies). One such was the method of horizontal stratification, introduced by Oscar Montelius, which allowed better chronological dating (Montelius 1903, in Chapman and Hamerow, 1997, 12). Another was a better spatial delimiting of groups with similar material cultures (Kosinna 1911, in Chapman and Hamerow, 1997, 12).

As each assemblage was associated with a specific culture, the spread of styles and artifacts was explained in terms of migration. (Needless to say, diffusionism was never the only game in town. Some scholars—Reinach and Bastian—leaned toward evolutionary models, while others, such as Myres and Arthur Evans, emphasized assimilation of borrowed traits [Chapman, 12, in Chapman and Hamerow 1997]. Another alternative model was offered by functionalism. Nevertheless, diffusionism remained the prevalent model.)

From the late 1950s/early 1960s, diffusionism lost ground. It was pronounced simplistic, hard to verify, and insufficiently rigorous. Critics emphasized two major shortcomings: gaps in chronological sequences and a static conceptualization of culture. It was natural that anyone disappointed with diffusionism would turn to alternative explanations, such as evolution.

Among the sins of diffusionism, probably the worst, was the conceptualization of archeological cultures as homogeneous entities (Binford 1972, in Chapman and Dolukhanov 1993). It rendered cultures static and the process of cultural change mechanical.

The breaks in chronological sequences were less serious, at least in their theoretical implications, because they ultimately rested on archeological evidence that was often patchy. Indeed, some migrations well known from documentary and literary sources left little or no archeological evidence at all. For example, the settlement of Galatians in Asia Minor is archeologically attested to by only three La Tène brooches! (See chapter on Celts.) The Inner Asian people of Wu-sun offer another example. In the five centuries of known history, there probably lived several million Wu-sun. Yet, fewer than 200 skulls have been identified. In 71 B.C., the Wu-sun took 39,000 Hsiung-nu prisoners (Groot 1921, 197, in Maenchen-Helfen 1973, 360), but no archeological evidence survived. About 150 B.C., a Chinese princess married a Wu-sun ruler. She was accompanied by several hundred servants and eunuchs, yet only one Chinese skull has been found (Groot 1926, 185, in Maenchen-Helfen 1973, 360).

Eventually, unreliability of archeological material led to the appearance of the "New Archeology" (Joseph Caldwell 1959). The "new" archeologists emphasized evolution determined by the environment, population growth, and internal dynamics inherent in each culture. They regarded diffusion and differentiation as two simultaneously operating processes of change (Nandris 1972, 61, in Chapman and Hamerow 1997, 3). Their stress on process, in contrast to their "static" predecessors, earned them the name of "processualists."

Indeed, "process" was their great contribution. Another was the insistence on rigorous scientific procedure and a systemic approach (Watson et al. 1971). On the negative side, there was a tendency toward excessive generalization and an overreliance on the environment and population increase as mechanisms of change (as opposed to migration).

There is little doubt that diffusionism needed a correction. The question is, why was anti-migrationism so successful?

Various explanations have been advanced, from decolonization (Clark 1966) to British insularity (Kristiansen 1989); generational experience, in the sense that the generation of archeologists who came to professional maturity in the 1960s had not witnessed massive population displacements (Chapman 14, in Chapman and Hamerow 1997); and even personality of individual archeologists (Adams et al. 1978).

None of these seem convincing. Decolonization hit Britain, where migrationism was rejected, and France, where it was not. Conversely, decolonization did not affect Germany, where migrationism continued to be accepted. The spread of processualism in Holland and Scandinavia, where the English influence has always been strong, points to cultural roots of this intellectual fashion.

British insularity is largely a fiction. The metropole of two large multilingual, multicultural empires in the last two hundred years and now a member of the European Union, with a long tradition of immigration and absorption of aliens, Britain has never been truly insular.

The lack of familiarity with mass migration among younger scholars who, ostensibly, did not witness millions of refugees during and after World War II is also implausible. They must have been aware of the flight of a million pieds noirs in 1962. They could not have failed to witness the escape of thousands of Hungarian refugees in 1956 or Czechs and Slovaks in 1968. Refugee crises in Africa and Asia have been endemic in the postwar period. Even if they had never opened a newspaper, they could not have been unaware of the 2.5 million immigrants from the former colonies.

The most plausible reason left (although not the only one, to be sure) is that the "new" archeologists wanted to define themselves in opposition to traditionalists. That is why they selected a strongly contrasting range of explanatory strategies

(Chapman and Hamerow 1997, 4). The controversy was largely generational. In other words, for many young archeologists, the break with orthodoxy opened doors. It launched them professionally. As William McNeill put it, "careers have been made and schools of historians have flourished on the strength of their discovery of flaws in received notions. . . . Hence the enthusiasm for revisionism" (McNeill 1986, 33). That, and not decolonization or British insularity, accounted to a large extent for the "retreat from migrationism."

There is yet another proof that the disregard for migrationism was rooted largely in academic politics. In 1968, when "new" archeology was no longer new, David Clarke produced a classificatory system of 12 social processes that could be derived from archeological material. The system—a hierarchy—contained 5 processes that involved migration (actually, the main mechanism of change was invasion, but it was often linked with migration): (1) culture group repatterning (through imperial colonization); (2) cultural intrusion/substitution (through military conquest or mass migration); (3) cultural assimilation (through military conquest followed by acculturation); (4) subcultural intrusion/substitution (through the substitution of one subculture by another in deliberate action); and (5) stimulus diffusion (through warfare as interaction to produce deliberate derivative development) (Clarke 1968, 411–31, in Chapman and Hamerow 1997, 3). Clarke's goal was to provide rigorous explanation of patterns of cultural change based on artifact assemblages. That Clarke's system failed to reverse the anti-migrationist trend testifies to the entrenched character of processual archeology and the need on the part of the "new" archeologists to maintain their position, even in the face of new evidence.

By the mid-1980s, anti-migrationism was so deeply entrenched that Irving Rouse wrote a book that was "intended to demonstrate to [his] anthropological colleagues that the inference of population movements from archeological evidence is still a viable pursuit" (Rouse 1986, xii). (Earlier, Adams, Van Gerven, and Levy made the same point in their article "Retreat from Migrationism" [1978].)

The late 1980s brought another shift in direction. Again, attempts have been made to link the new change with the transformations in Eastern Europe and the upsurge in migration (which largely failed to materialize). But it is once again hard to establish a direct link. More likely, a new generation of archeologists was ready to shake off the now old dogmas.

The new new archeologists—"the post-processualists"—rejected their predecessors' tendency toward generalization, positivism, and systemic approach. They stress the availability of data, its correlation with cultural change, and (probably their greatest contribution) the specificity of each situation. They also incorporate social network theory into their models.

For their part, recalcitrant processualists attack post-processualists for failure to formulate rigorous explanations for cultural change (Binford 1982 and Bintliff 1991, in Chapman and Hamerow 1997, 4). (This was, of course, one of the accusations hurled by the processualists at their predecessors.)

The rejection of migration was mostly confined to archeology. It was not rejected in other disciplines, such as geography, economics, and economic history. That is why David Clarke's assertion that archeology reflects the spirit of the times (Clarke

1979, 85) is debatable: clearly, the times it reflects differ significantly from those of other disciplines.

The above sketch provided an overview of the general trends in archeology regarding migration. Now, I suggest that we take a closer look at two cases of well-known migrations—Anglo-Saxons to England and Dorians to Greece—to see how the acceptance or rejection worked in practice.

The traditional account of the Anglo-Saxon settlement in England is based on a small number of sources that postdate the invasion by several centuries, mostly *The Ruin of Britain* by monk Gildas (sixth century), *History of the English Church* by Venerable Bede (eighth-century Northumbria), and the *Anglo-Saxon Chronicle*. These sources indicate that, after the departure of the Roman legions from Britain in 407, the province was ravaged by the Saxons. A chronicler in Gaul noted that "Britanniae Saxonum incursione devastatae" (Musset 1965, I, 154).

The Saxon incursion was only an episode in a string of depredations by Picts, Scots, and various Germanic tribes. They accelerated the process of decomposition that afflicted post-Roman Britain. Towns declined, trade with the continent came to a halt by 410–20. When St. Germain of Auxerre arrived in Britain in 429, he found no central authorities, although the local ones still functioned, e.g., in Verulamium (155). But by the time of his next visit in 440–44, even local authority had largely disappeared, and the power had passed into the hands of tribal chiefs (156).

Embroiled in internecine conflict and subject to constant attacks from barbarians, some of the local rulers invited Saxon mercenaries. According to Bede, this happened in 449; in 455, the mercenaries revolted and seized parts of southeastern England, starting a drawn-out process of conquest (156).

That some Anglo-Saxons arrived in England is beyond dispute. It is the size of the migration and the survival of the indigenous population that are the real bones of contention.

The traditional view held that the migration was massive and that the newcomers had either killed or expelled the earlier inhabitants: "There is every reason to believe that the Celtic inhabitants of those parts of Britain which had become English at the end of the sixth century had been as nearly extirpated as a nation can be" (Freeman 1888, 74, quoted in Crawford, 45, in Chapman and Hamerow 1997).

Indeed, the number of Anglo-Saxon burial grounds increased sharply from the fifth to the sixth century, as did their geographical range. And the cemetery population during this period also increased (Crawford, 45, in Chapman and Hamerow 1997). The distribution of certain types of jewelry found in graves showed a Saxon disembarkation point in East Anglia followed by "their unquestionable southwesterly advance en masse by the Icknield Way into Oxfordshire and Berkshire" (Leeds 1954).

Within a couple of generations, there was a rapid and widespread adoption of Germanic dress and funerary urns. At Mucking, on the Thames estuary, Roman-Celtic and Anglo-Saxon cemeteries were separate, and the chronological gap between the latest burials in the first and the first burials in the last was minimal (Hamerow 1993, 94, in Chapman and Hamerow 1997, 36).

Conversely, archeological evidence from Schleswig-Holstein suggests that the area experienced a sharp drop in population (Muller-Wille et al. 1988, quoted in Hamerow, 33, in Chapman and Hamerow 1997, 33). This fact corroborates Bede, who wrote that migration had depopulated the land of the Angles (33). That is why many scholars still subscribe to the traditional view that the combined archeological, documentary, and linguistic evidence suggests that "considerable numbers of Anglo-Saxons settled in southern and eastern England" (Hines 1984, 279; Harke 1989; Welch 1985, 14; 1992), although some Britons may have remained and could have been buried in Anglo-Saxon cemeteries.

Others, however, are more hesitant (Randsborg 1991). Some studies showed that the earliest Germanic burials from the fifth century were few (Hawkes and Dunning 1961). There was also considerable local variation. In Northumbria, it seems, Germanic settlers constituted a fraction of the population (Faull 1977; Crawford in Chapman and Hamerow 1997, 63). Similarly, until the sixth century, there was little Germanic settlement in Deira. The name itself is Celtic. It can be argued that here, at least, many Britons survived the Saxon takeover (63).

This would indicate a slow start and, perhaps, a chain of small migratory movements, rather than "a simultaneous and permanent movement of a substantial number of people" (Adams et al. 1978, 486).

As for migrants, three kinds of hypotheses have been advanced. Either they were a warrior elite, few in numbers but dominant by force of arms (Hodges 1989; Harke 1992); or they were farmers mostly interested in finding good agricultural land (Myres 1986; Hawkes 1982); or they were refugees fleeing unsettled conditions in their homelands (Arnold 1984, 17). Or they might have been any combination of these.

Among those who subscribe to the notion of limited migration, many believe that it was initially carried out by the predominantly male military elite (Hope-Taylor 1977; Arnold 1984, 61; Hodges 1989; Higham 1992, in Hamerow, 34, in Chapman and Hamerow 1997), although some ascribe it to peasant farmers (Miket 1977, O'Brien and Miket 1991). Musset believed that the turning point came after 500, with a second wave of Germanic migrants (Musset 1965, I, 157).

Three factors could have contributed to the growing Anglo-Saxon presence in Britain: continuing migration, natural increase, and adoption by the Britons of Anglo-Saxon burial practices (Campbell 1982, 36, in Crawford, 45, in Chapman and Hamerow 1997). The last factor may help to explain the drastic change of the fifth and sixth centuries in terms of acculturation: Britons aspiring to higher status would adopt Anglo-Saxon customs. Perhaps, they even tried to hide their origin, making identification of the Celtic element extremely difficult (Higham 1992, 181ff, in Chapman and Hamerow 1997, 35).

Yet, no Celtic cemeteries from this period have been identified (Crawford, 45, in Chapman and Hamerow 1997). If the Celts remained in German-occupied areas, they had to leave behind burials, at least in the initial stage of the Saxon penetration. Is it plausible that all Celts remaining in German-occupied areas chose to blend in with the invaders?

One way of testing various hypotheses would be to compare Anglo-Saxon cemeteries with their continental counterparts. Those studied by Crawford were rich in weaponry and other artifacts, compared to contemporary continental ones. He concluded that here was a new group that sought to establish its credentials by conspicuous consumption, including rich burials. These people were no poor farmers or refugees. They were clearly thriving. If their economic structure, agricultural technology, and social organization were similar, their success can only be explained by their aggressiveness and numerical advantage. Both "bring us perilously close to Gildas and Bede" (Crawford, 69, in Chapman and Hamerow 1997).

While archeologists have been increasingly reluctant to utilize migrationist paradigm, biologists have increasingly turned to the migratory model to explain regional blood group distribution (Falsetti and Sokal 1993). They found that nearly half of adult males were buried with weapons and that a correlation between height, certain epigenetic traits, and the presence of weapons could be established. This would indicate that weapons were restricted to particular lineages and that some of the weaponless males could be indigenes (Harke 1989, 1990, 1992; in Hamerow 1997, 37), although it is also plausible that they were Anglo-Saxon peasants.

Finally, there is a surprising lack of Welsh loan words in Old English, another indication that there was no prolonged contact between the two populations. Margaret Gelling (1993) postulates that the invaders and indigenes were farmers at comparable levels of development. There was little that the Celts could teach the invaders (Crawford, 68, in Chapman and Hamerow 1997). But languages borrow terms for which they already have words, and English borrowing from French after the Norman conquest is the nearest example.

All of this leads to the conclusion that the traditional account is basically sound, although it may stand some corrections. After Rome was forced to abandon the province, Britain experienced a marked deterioration accompanied by gradual deurbanization and a slow collapse of authority. Attacked from all sides, some notables invited Saxon mercenaries, who were thus given a chance to familiarize themselves with the country. Once they came to realize that they were stronger, they rebelled and took over parts of southeastern England, from where they expelled the autochthonous Celtic population. It is also likely that many Celts fled from the invaders, unwilling to accept enslavement or second-class status.

The original Anglo-Saxons, largely a warrior elite, were soon reinforced by other settlers. These were whole families, warriors and wealthy peasants, who arrived in a constant stream of small, well-armed groups seeking good agricultural land for settlement. (We should keep in mind that they arrived from Jutland and Schleswig, which do not lack in fertile soils.)

By the end of the century, the invaders had established several large beachheads along the lower Thames and the Humber, and in Kent and East Anglia, from where, reinforced by a second, large-scale migration after 500, they launched an attack on Celtic Britain. The struggle continued for another 150 years and brought most of what we now call England under Anglo-Saxon rule. Some 500 years would pass before the Anglo-Saxons, now the English, would continue their conquests into Wales, Scotland, and Ireland.

Another example is the controversy surrounding the Dorian descent into Greece.

Traditionally, the destruction of Mycenian palace complexes in Peloponnese was ascribed to the Dorian invasion from northern Greece. It was dated circa 1200 B.C., two generations after the fall of Troy (Huxley 1966, 19). (There has been considerable variation in dating the fall of Troy. Huxley follows Herodotus, who placed it in 1250 B.C. [Craik 1980, 26]. Eratosthenes dated it as of 1183 B.C. (26). And Thucydides [I.12.3] wrote that the Dorians occupied Peloponnese 80 years after the fall of Troy [Huxley 1966, 161, n.32], i.e., about 1280 B.C.) However, the earliest evidence for Dorian settlement in Argolis comes from circa 1075 B.C. and in southwestern Peloponnese from approximately 1000 B.C. (Huxley 1966, 161, n.32). So, it is not clear whether the destruction was wrought by the Dorians or whether they took advantage of destruction by others. But there is a growing consensus that it was a gradual infiltration, rather than a one-time massive migration (Craik 1980, 29).

Among contemporary scholars, Zeev Rubinsohn and Oswyn Murray (cited by Musti 1986, xxv, n.3 and n.15 respectively) support the traditional version. (Earlier supporters included O. Broneer and C. W. Blegen.) According to Murray, "even if it is impossible to prove that the Dorians had destroyed the Mycenean culture, it seems probable that they took advantage of the vacuum that had been created. This phenomenon had been known in other epochs: a people devoid of culture[?] who leaves no sign of its passage other than the destruction" (back translation from an Italian translation of the English original, Murray 1983, 17, in Musti 1986, xxv).

Some scholars sought alternative explanations to Greek invasions: (1) natural causes; (2) invasions by non-Greeks; (3) and internal rebellions (Snodgrass 1971, in Musti 1986, 52, n.16).

Among the first, Carpenter suggested drought and famine, leading to massive population outflows (Carpenter 1966, in Craik 1980, 27), which does not explain destruction of mainland palace centers. Kilian thought it looked like an earthquake, at least in some locations like Pylos (Kilian, in Musti 1986, 74, n.31). But this does not explain the building of "cyclopean" defenses in Attica and Peloponnese. Also, tablets in Linear B indicate the presence of an external threat (Musti 1986, 52–53). And earthquakes do not explain the drastic change in the economy and the sociopolitical structure that followed: the disappearance of writing (Linear B), the economy on a much smaller scale, and the like. (Kilian, in Musti 1986, 80).

The invasionist theories look more promising but cannot be proved beyond reasonable doubt. Palace archives from the last period, perhaps even (the very last) days of their existence have survived (Sacconi, in Musti 1986, 117–18). They come from Argolis (Mycenae and Tyrinth), Beothia (Thebes), and Messenia (Pylos). Nothing from Mycenae and almost nothing from Tyrinth or Thebes suggests danger. (Could the invaders have appeared suddenly, like the Vikings?) But in Pylos there was an interruption in the supply of bronze, extra sacrifices, and even refugees from Asia Minor and the Aegean among women working in the palace—all contemporaneous with the arrival of the People of the Sea. There was a general military alarm, and the coast guard patrolled the coast (Sacconi, in Musti 1986, 131).

Unfortunately, nothing in the archives indicates who the enemy may have been. Nor can we exclude the possibility of an uprising by the lower classes, who suddenly had a chance to overthrow their masters. What is beyond doubt is that life in the village continued as before. Mycenean culture, in the period between 1200 and 1050, survived, with "only" one difference: the central authority had disappeared, as did writing. Nothing in Greece of this time indicates an invasion or the presence of a new ethnic element (Sacconi, in Musti 1986, 132–33).

Another item of major importance was the decrease in population. In Mycenae, judging by graves, the upper strata were not renewed (Kilian, in Musti 1986, 74, nn.13, 14). In Argolis, 86 percent of dwellings were abandoned (Kilian, in Musti 1986, 75). However, in Achaea, 29 centers of IIIB were followed by 32 in IIIC with similar distribution (Papadopoulos, cited by Kilian, in Musti 1986, 75, n.49). Kilian concluded that the population of the abandoned centers did not flee but concentrated in the strongholds.

In Tyrinth, during IIIC, three waves of destruction are discernible. Of these, the first two seem to have been brought about by natural causes. But the last one, contemporaneous with the one in Mycenae, led to the abandonment of the site. It was also accompanied by at least two reductions in population in the surrounding area (Taylor, in Kilian, in Musti 1986, 77, n.77).

When the fog of the Dark Age lifted in the eighth century B.C., we find Dorians in possession of a large area in southern Greece, an area where they had not been before. It is simply impossible to doubt that they had migrated from elsewhere, most likely another part of Greece. The affinity of Arcadian dialect with Cypriot shows that Achaean—the basis of both—spread from inner Peloponnese. Tradition indicates a major migration of Achaeans toward Cyprus at the end of the Bronze Age. It is supported by archeology. Thus, one cannot doubt the post-Achaean Dorian immigration to Peloponnese (Hiller, in Musti 1986, 135).

Based on Eratosthene's dating of the Troyan War (circa 1190 B.C.), this must have occurred around 1100 B.C. Dialectology points to the northern or northwestern origin of Dorian dialects. The migration had to precede the destruction of Mycenean palaces that kept their records in non-Dorian dialects. The reason that some scholars mistrust the tradition is that no Dorian remains are still in existence (Hiller, in Musti 1986, 136). But Slavs left virtually no traces in Greece (Hood, Winters, in Grossland, in Musti 1986, n.3), nor Lombards in Italy, nor Celts in Anatolia. The lack of archeological remains is not a conclusive argument.

Even if we ascribe the destruction of Mycenean palaces to natural catastrophes, the problem of Dorians remains.

We should keep in mind several facts. Judging by ceramics, the Dorian area, culturally speaking, was a Mycenean periphery (Hiller, in Musti 1986, 137); its artifacts assemblage would not be strikingly different. It is believed that their arrival is announced by stone cyst graves, geometric style, incineration, and the use of iron, though none correspond exactly to the area of Dorian settlement (Hiller, in Musti 1986, 144). Since it is impossible, archeologically, to place the Dorian culture of the late Bronze Age with any degree of precision, we cannot trace Dorian invasion/migration either (Hiller, in Musti 1986, 145). Ultimately, we are forced to fall back on literary sources.

Attempts have been made to find a way out of the impasse. One is to link Dorians with the People of the Sea. Hiller believes that they originated in adjacent areas of the Balkan peninsula and their migration routes were parallel. The migration took the form of infiltration, settlement in enclaves, and assimilation by related surrounding population (Hiller, in Musti 1986, 143). Another possibility was to shift the time of the invasion to 1150–1050 B.C. and point the finger at Achaeans and/or Ionians (Musti 1986, xxvi).

But such drastic revisionism may be uncalled for: the tradition may have been misinterpreted. It did not describe the Dorian invasion as a catastrophe. In reality, it was a gradual movement from central Greece to Peloponnese, where migrants settled in fertile river valleys of Argolis, Laconia, and Messenia (which were fully Dorian by the eighth century B.C.). The conquest took many forms, with numerous local variations (Musti, 46–47, in Musti 1986). It is confirmed by the fact that tablets from Mycenae cease in the middle of IIIB, and those from Tyrinth and Pylos stop at the end of IIIB, while those from Thebes are discontinued either in III A2 or IIIB. And in Sparta there was a hiatus between the Mycenean layers and the arrival of new people circa 950 B.C. (Cartledge, 66, n.9, in Musti 1986).

The above leads us to the conclusion that the invasion was not an invasion but rather an infiltration that took 100 to 150 years. (In fact, tradition corroborates that.) The first move was short because it succeeded at the very beginning. The second attempt was stopped at the isthmus. The third one reached Patras in the bay of Corinth (Musti, 52, in Musti 1986).

The above examples suggest that we must revise our preconceived notions of mass migration. Unless it was a flight from an overpowering and victorious enemy, like the flight of the Goths from the Huns, migration usually took the form of slow infiltration: raids, counterraids, the establishment of bridgeheads, small-scale settlements by warriors followed by lineages looking for land. Even the flight of the Goths or the Celtic descent down the Danube were messy, drawn-out affairs. There were Goths who stayed under the Huns, others who fled to the empire, still others who found refuge in the Carpathian mountains, and others yet who were transferred to Pannonia. It took those who found themselves in the empire 15 years to reach Italy and 50 years to settle in Gaul, only to be evicted by the Franks some 90 years later and make the final move to Iberia. Likewise, it took the Celts who reached Anatolia about 40 years to "settle down."

In his book, Irving Rouse suggested that archeologists and anthropologists should learn from linguists.

Linguists generate migration hypotheses by mapping the distribution of languages and tracing their genealogies. Rouse believes that archeologists should do the same. They should start with delimiting the basic building blocks: local culture units.

These units should then be organized hierarchically into series and subseries of cultures, corresponding to the families and subfamilies of languages. The classificatory hierarchies may then show them whether diffusion, development, or acculturation had occurred.

The next step would be to generate hypotheses by plotting the distribution of the series and subseries on chronological charts and studying the changes that have taken place within these taxonomic units. Once philogenies have been established, time-space units can be added to them . . . and once chronologies have been prepared, lines of development can be inserted in them (Rouse 1986, 160). The last step would be to test hypotheses independently against different kinds of data (14).

Rouse provides two examples of successful application of the "hierarchies" method.

One concerns Polynesians. Earlier, anthropologists believed that they had come from the west. But this assumption was destroyed by Thor Heyerdahl, who sailed from Ecuador to the Tuamotu Archipelago on a South American–style raft (23).

However, linguistic research showed that the peopling of Polynesia proceeded from west to east via Melanesia. This conclusion was confirmed by archeologists who showed that the dates of the first habitation became progressively more recent from west to east (25). The linguists, archeologists, and physical anthropologists were more successful than Heyerdahl because they (1) used results of one another's research as models from which they could derive their own working hypotheses. They could check each other's progress and avoid wasting time and effort in needless trial and error; (2) formulated alternative hypotheses, instead of limiting themselves to a Ruling Theory as Heyerdahl had done; (3) traced migrations in terms of complexes of linguistic, cultural, or genetic traits, each indicative of a local population, instead of working with single traits as Heyerdahl had done; and (4) examined patterns of divergence from complex to complex, instead of working only with similarities as Heyerdahl had done (39).

Another example comes from the study of the Inuit. W. Boyd Dawkins (1874) and W. J. Solas (1924) made the same mistake as Heyerdahl: they "inferred migration from similarities at each end of a presumed route without also considering the alternative ways in which these similarities might have come into existence and without being able to test their hypothesis by examining the patterns of change in race, language, and culture along the route" (Rouse 1986, 47).

Physical anthropologists are "lucky" because they have material remains that lend themselves to laboratory analysis. In the Polynesian case, for example, they measured the relative frequency of leukocyte antigens in populations throughout Oceania to construct their phylogeny by calculating the degree of similarity and difference among them. Scholars studying the Inuit did the same with skeletally defined races. In both cases, they "studied past occurrences instead of using present resemblances to reconstruct the past" (161).

Cultural and social anthropologists are less fortunate because they (1) obtain data by observation and can never be sure that oral traditions and written records are not mythological; (2) concentrate on immigration, rather than population movement (Population movement is the original peopling or repeopling of an area; immigration is the intrusion of individual settlers into an already populated area); (3) work in terms of ethnic classifications made by the persons they study instead of developing their own scientific classifications, as do linguists, archeologists, and physical anthropologists. Often ethnic groups cannot be followed back into prehistory because it is impossible to identify them archeologically; (4) trace movements of societies on maps, which lack time depth, because such movements take place almost instantaneously (160–63).

However, social anthropologists are not without advantages of their own because social organization that they study is an important factor in migration.

Some societies, especially those with kin segmentation, are particularly prone to migration. They spread through lineage segmentation, like the Maya (Fox 1987, 1989, in Anthony, 23, in Chapman and Hamerow 1997). "Where privilege and prestige are allotted unequally among kin according to structural position within the kin group, migration offers the prospect of an improved lot for the structurally disadvantaged.... Migration ... is a social strategy through which kin groups improved their positions in competition for prestige and power" (Anthony, 23, in Chapman and Hamerow 1997).

Kin segmentation may also attract migrants because it makes inclusion and acceptance easier. For example, on the Pathan-Baluch border, constant warfare produced losers who joined lower-status, nomadic Baluch even though the Pathans were richer, more numerous, better armed, and more respected. The reason? Baluch segmentary lineages were open to new segments while in Pathan society even in-coming Pathans were incorporated only as powerless tenants. Also, Baluch pastoral economy offered the possibility of rapid growth, unlike Pathan agriculture, with its highly regulated system of land ownership. And the Baluch client-patron political system offered the possibility of upward mobility, unlike that of the Pathan, whose status and power depended on land ownership and long-cultivated local alliances with extended kin. Hence Baluch grew much faster (Barth 1981).

These factors can operate on an individual level. In societies where primogeniture is practiced, younger sons have few opportunities. The strong and the more ambitious leave (Kopytoff 1987, 18–19, in Anthony, 23, Chapman and Hamerow 1997).

We should note that economic rationality is not always a decisive factor. People often migrate to destinations where they can find relatives and compatriots on whose support they can count. This tendency may be helpful to archeologists who fail to find the economic factors in prehistoric migrations (Anthony, in Chapman and Hamerow 1997, 25). Kin migration is often a chain migration. The European Neolithic Linear Pottery culture probably represents a colonizing series of chain migrations (Anthony, 27, in Chapman and Hamerow 1997). Recent scholarship also indicates that kin-structured migration during the Neolithic is still detectable in modern European gene distributions (Sokal and Wilson 1991; Cavalli-Sforza, Menozzi and Piazza 1994, in Anthony, 27, in Chapman and Hamerow 1997).

To conclude: historically—and that includes prehistory—migration has been one of the most frequent, most common phenomena. Its acceptance or rejection in the academe was partly the result of earnest attempts to find the right answers to the right question, but also " ... embedded in paradigm shifts in archaeological theory, with all the sociopolitical factors of academic competition that are entailed" (Chapman and Hamerow 1997, 2).

Archeologically, migration can be inferred from patterns of change in cultural complexes. Gradual change and organic development of the new traits points to acculturation. Conversely, an abrupt change and a replacement of the original complex suggest a corresponding change in population. In a sense, we are back to square one.

It is not possible to corroborate each migration with sufficient archeological evidence. But where it is, archeological cultures should be treated as regional migration networks (Chapman and Dolukhanov 1993).

We must keep in mind that most migrations were actually a series of mini migrations that "unfurled" over extended periods of time. Another thing to remember is that migration is a social strategy, not an automatic response to overcrowding. The level of economic development is a major factor in determining the carrying capacity of a given area. Industrial societies can sustain a much higher density than agricultural ones; and these, in turn, sustain higher densities than hunter/gatherer societies.

With this in mind, we must not forget that there is little point in trying to find a model that would fit every historic or cultural context (Chapman and Hamerow 1997, 2).

Select Bibliography

Space constraints made it necessary to reduce the bibliography by about 50 percent.

Primary Sources

Classical and Byzantine

Arrian. *Actes contra Alanos: Scripta Minora.* Eds. A. G. Ross and G. Wirth. Leipzig: Teubner, 1968.

Julius Caesar. *The Gallic War and Other Writings.* Tr. M. Hadas. New York: Modern Library, 1957.

Cassiodorus. *Variae.* Tr. S. J. B. Barnish. Liverpool: Liverpool University Press, 1992.

Dio Cassius. *Historiarum romanarum quae supersunt.* Ed. U. P. Boissevain. Berlin: Weidmann, 1895–1931.

Marcellinus Comes. *Chronica Minora.* Ed. Theodor Mommsen. Monumenta Germaniae Historica, Auctores antiquissimi 11. Berlin: 1894.

Anna Comnena. *The Alexiad.* Tr. E. R. A. Sewter. Baltimore: Penguin Books, 1969.

Paulus Diaconus. *Historia Langobardorum.* L. Bethmann and G. Waitz, eds., Monumenta Germaniae Historicae. SS. Rer. Langob., vol. I. Hannover: Hahn, 1878.

Herodotus. *The History.* Tr. David Grene. Chicago: University of Chicago Press, 1987.

Theophanes Homologetes (The Confessor). *Chronographia.* Ed. Carl de Boer. Hildesheim: G. Olms, 1963/1883–85.

Jordanes. *The Gothic History.* Ed. C. C. Mierow. 2^d ed. Cambridge: Speculum Historiale and New York: Barnes and Noble, 1960/1912.

Josephus. *Antiquitates Judaicae: Opera Omnia.* Ed. S. Naber. 6 vols. Leipzig: Teubner, 1888–1896.

Lucanus. *De Bello Civili.* Ed. C. Hosius. Leipzig: Teubner, 1913.

Joannes Malalas. *Chronographia.* Tr. E. Jeffreys et al. Melbourne: Australian Association of Byzantine Studies, Dept. of Modern Greek, University of Sydney, 1986.

Ammianus Marcellinus. *Rerum gestarum libri.* Tr. W. Hamilton. New York: Penguin Classics, 1986.

Pliny the Elder. *Natural History* 2. Tr. H. Rackham. Cambridge, MA: Harvard University Press, 1947.

Polybius. *The Histories.* Tr. W. R. Paton. Cambridge, MA and London: 1960.

Constantine VII Porphyrogenitus. *De Administrando Imperio.* Ed. (Greek text) Gy. Moravcsik. Tr. R. J. H. Jenkins. 2^d ed. Washington, D.C.: Dumbarton Oaks Center for Byzantine Studies, 1967.

Priscus of Panium. *Fragments.* Ed. C. Miller. *Fragmenta Historicorum Grecorum* IV. Paris: 1868.

Procopius. *Bellum Gothicum.* Ed. J. Haury. 3 vols. Leipzig: Teubner, 1963/1905–13.

Menander Protector. *Fragmenta.* In Ludwig Dindorf, ed., *Historici Graeci Minores.* Vol. ii. Leipzig: 1871.

Michael Psellus. *Chronographia.* Baltimore: Penguin Books, 1966/1935.

Ptolemy. *Geographica.* Ed. C. Nubbe. Leipzig: Teubner, 1898.

Scriptores Historiae Augustae. Tr. D. Magie. 3 vols. New York: Putnam, 1922–32.

Seneca. *Thyestes: L. Annaei Senecae Tragoediae.* Eds. R. Peiper and G. Richter. Leipzig: 1902.

Diodorus Siculus. *Bibliotheca.* Tr. C. H. Oldfather. Cambridge, MA: Harvard University Press, 1961/1935.

Theophylacius Simocatta. *Historiae.* Ed. Carl de Boer. Rev. ed. P. Wirth. Stuttgart: Teubner, 1972.

Strabo. *Geographika.* Ed. Wolfgang Aly. 4 vols. Bonn: R. Habelt, 1957.

Tacitus. *Germania.* Eds. M. Winterbottom and R. M. Ogilvie. Oxford: Clarendon Press, 1975.

Medieval

Bertram Colgrave and R. A. B. Mynors, eds. *Bede's Ecclesiastical History of the English People.* Oxford: Clarendon Press, 1969.

Gregory of Tours. *Histories.* Tr. L. Thorpe. London: Penguin Classics, 1974.

Isidore of Seville. *Historia Gothorum, Wandalorum, Sueborum.* Ed. T. Mommsen. Chronica minora saec. Vol. XI. Reprint. Berlin: 1961/1894.

Liutprand of Cremona. *Antapodosis.* Tr. F. A. Wright. New York: Dutton, 1930.

Marco Polo. *The Travels.* Tr. R. E. Latham. London: Penguin Books, 1958.

Walafrid Strabo. *Liber de exordiis et incrementis quarundam in observationibus ecclesiasticus rerum, VII, Patr. Lat., cxiv,* col. 927. Ed. A. Knoepfler. Munich: Lentner (E. Stahl), 1899.

"The Tale of the Life . . . of Antonius the Roman." In the *Pravoslavnyi Sobesednik* II. Kazan: Kazanskaia Dukhovnaia Akademiia, 1858, 165–66.

Medieval Chronicles (except Byzantine)

The Anglo-Saxon Chronicle. M. J. Swanton, ed. and tr. New York: Routledge, 1998.

Annales Bertiniani. F. Grat, J. Vieillard, and S. Clémencet, eds. Paris: C. Klincksieck, 1964.

(The Venerable) Bede. *Chronica.* Ed. T. Mommsen. Chronica minora saec. Vol. XIII. Berlin: 1898.

Einhard. *Annales Regni Francorum.* Eds. E. H. Pertz and F. Kurze. Hannover: Hahn, 1895.

Fredegar. *Chronicle.* Bk. 4. Ed. and tr. J. M. Wallace-Hadrill. London: 1960.

The Homilies of Photius. Tr. C. A. Mango. Cambridge, MA: Dumbarton Oaks Studies 3, 1958.

Regino of Prüm. *Chronicon.* Ed. F. Kurze. Scriptores Rerum Germanicarum in Usum Scholarum. Hannover: Hahn, 1890.

The Russian Primary Chronicle. Eds. S. H. Cross and O. P. Sherbowitz-Wetzor. Cambridge, MA: The Medieval Academy of America, Publication no. 60, 1953.

Sagas

C. Fell, ed. and tr. *Egils Saga.* London: Dent, 1975.

Magnus Magnusson and Hermann Palsson, eds. and tr. *The Vinland Sagas.* Baltimore: Penguin Books, 1965.

————, eds. and tr. *Njal's Saga.* Baltimore: Penguin Books, 1960.

Snorri Sturluson. *Heimskringla: History of the Kings of Norway.* Tr. Lee M. Hollander. Austin, TX: University of Texas Press, 1964.

Chinese

Fang Hsuan-ling et al. *Chin-shu* (The History of the Chin Dynasties). Beijing: Chung-Hua Shu-Chu, 1974.

Lung-li Yeh, chin shih 1247. Tr. V. S. Taskin. *E Lun-li. Istoriia gosudarstva kidanei (Cidan'go chzhi).* Moscow: Nauka, 1979.

Ma Ch'ang-shou. *Pei-Ti yu Hsiung-nu* (The Northern Ti and the Hsiung-nu). Shanghai: 1962.

Pan Ku. *The History of the Former Han Dynasty (*Ch'ien Han shu*).* Tr. Homer H. Dubs. Baltimore: Waverley Press, 1938.

Ssu-ma Ch'ien. *Records of the Grand Historian of China* 2. Tr. Burton Watson. New York: Columbia University Press, 1961.

Muslim

Al-Biruni. *Athar al-Baqiyah.* Ed. E. Sachau. Reprint. Leipzig: Brockhaus, 1923.

Al-Istakhri. *Kitab Masalik al-Mamalik* (Viae regnorum). Ed. M. J. de Goeje, Bibliotheca Geographorum Arabicorum (*BGA*) I. Leiden: Brill, 1870.

Mahmud Al-Kashgari. *Divanu Lugat-it-Turk.* Ed. Besim Atalay. Ankara: Turk Dil Kurumu, 1941.

Al-Marwazi. *Taba'i al-Hayawan* (The Nature of Animals): *Sharaf al-Zaman Tahir Marwazi on China, the Turks and India.* Ed. and tr. V. F. Minorsky. London: The Royal Asiatic Society, 1942.

Al-Ya'qubi. *Ta'rikh* (The History). Beirut: 1970/1390.

Gardizi. *Zain al-Akhbar* (Adornment of Information). Excerpts in V. V. Bartol'd. "Izvlechenie iz sochinenija Gardizi zain al-Akhbar." In Akademik V. V. Bartol'd *Sochineniia,* 9 vols. Moscow: Izd-vo vostochnoi literatury, 1963–77.

Hudud al-Alam. *'The Regions of the World.' A Persian Geography.* Tr. V. F. Minorsky. London: Gibb Memorial Series, New Series, XI, 2d rev. ed. 1970/1937.

Ed. and tr. Zeki Validi Togan. *Ibn Fadlans Reisebericht, Abhandlungen für die Kunde des Morgenlandes* XXIV, 3. Leipzig: Brockhaus, 1939.

Ibn Kurdadhbih. *Kitab al-Masalik wa'l-Mamalik: Liber viarum et regnorum.* Ed. M. J. de Goeje. *BGA* VI. Leiden: Brill, 1889.

Ibn Miskawayh. *Tajarib al-Umam* (The Experiences of the Nations: The Eclipse of the 'Abbasid Caliphate'), 5 vols. Ed. H. F. Amedroz. Tr. D. S. Margoliouth. Oxford: Blackwell, 1920–21.

Ibn Rustah. *Kitab al-A'laq al-Nafisa* (The Book of Precious Gems). Ed. M. J. de Goeje. *BGA* VII. Leiden: Brill, 1892.

Other (Armenian, Hebrew, Syriac)

Evreisko-Khazarskaia perepiska v X veke. Ed. and tr. P. K. Kokovtsev. Leningrad: Izd-vo Akademii nauk SSSR, 1932.

Bar Hebraeus. *The Chronography.* Tr. Ernest A. Wallis Budge. London: Oxford University Press, H. Milford, 1932.

Movses Daskhurants'i. *Patmut'iwn Aghuanits': Movses Kaghankatuats'woy Patmut'iwn Aghuanits' asharhi.* Ed. M. Emin. Reprint. Tiflis: Elektratparan N. Agheneani, 1912.

Khazarian Hebrew Documents of the Tenth Century. Eds. Norman Golb and Omeljan Pritsak. Ithaca: Cornell University Press, 1982.

Secondary Sources

William Y. Adams. "On Migration and Diffusion as Rival Paradigms." In P. G. Dake et al., eds., *Diffusion and Migration: Their Roles in Cultural Development.* Calgary: Archaeological Association of the University of Calgary, 1978.

Samuel A. M. Adshead. *Central Asia in World History.* New York: St. Martin's Press, 1993.

Andrew Alföldi. "The Invasion of Peoples from the Rhine to the Black Sea." In *Cambridge Ancient History,* vol. 12. pp. 138–64. Cambridge: Cambridge University Press, 1939.

Thomas T. Allsen. *Mongolian Imperialism. The Policies of the Grand Qan Mongke in China. Russia and the Islamic Lands, 1251–1259.* Berkeley: University of California Press, 1987.

Bertil Almgren, ed. *The Viking.* London: 1966.

Franz Altheim. *Geschichte der Hunnen.* 2d ed. 4 vols. Berlin: De Gruyter, 1959–62.

A. Ambrosioni and S. Lusuardi Siena. *I Goti in Italia alla luce delle fonti scritti e delle testimonianze archeologiche.* Milan: 1985.

K. Ambroz. *Bospor: Khronologiia rannesrednevekovykh drevnostei,* "Bosporskii sbornik," I. Moscow: 1992.

Christo Anastasoff. *The Bulgarians. From their Arrival in the Balkans to Modern Times: Thirteen Centuries of History.* Hicksville, NY: Exposition Press, 1977.

Barbara A. Anderson. *Internal Migration during Modernization in Late Nineteenth-Century Russia.* Princeton: Princeton University Press, 1980.

D. Angelov. *Obrazŭvanie na bŭlgarskata narodnost.* Sofia: Nauka i izkustvo, 1971.

Holger Arbman. *The Vikings.* Tr. A. Binns. New York: Praeger, 1961.

André Armengaud. "Population in Europe, 1700–1914." In Carlo M. Cipolla, ed., *The Fontana Economic History of Europe,* vol. 3, *The Industrial Revolution.* London: Collins, 1974.

J. Arnold. *Roman Britain to Saxon England: An Archaeological Study.* Bloomington: Indiana University Press, 1984.

Mikhail I. Artamonov. *Istoriia Khazar.* Leningrad: Izd-vo gos. Ermitazha, 1962.

Jeremy R. Azrael and Emil A. Payin, eds. *Cooperation and Conflict in the Former Soviet Union: Implications for Migration.* Santa Monica, CA: Rand Center for Russian and Eurasian Studies, Center for Ethnopolitical and Regional Research, 1996.

A. Bacal. *Ethnicity in the Social Sciences. A View and a Review of the Literature on Ethnicity.* Coventry: Centre for Research in Ethnic Relations, 1991.

Bernard S. Bachrach. *A History of the Alans in the West. From Their First Appearance in the Sources of Classical Antiquity through the Early Middle Ages.* Minneapolis: University of Minnesota Press, 1973.

Elizabeth E. Bacon. *Central Asians under Russian Rule: A Study of Cultural Change.* Ithaca: Cornell University Press, 1966.

V. D. Baran. *Cherniakhivs'ka kul'tura za materialamy verkhn'oho Dnistra i Zakhidnoho Buhu.* Kiev: Naukova Dumka, 1981.

Thomas J. Barfield. "Inner Asia and Cycles of Power in China's Imperial History." In Gary Seaman and Daniel Marks, eds., *Rulers from the Steppe: State Formation on the Eurasian Periphery.* Los Angeles: Ethnographics Press/USC, 1991.

———. *The Perilous Frontier.* Cambridge, MA: Blackwell, 1989.

Graeme Barker and Tom Rasmussen. *The Etruscans.* Malden, MA: Blackwell, 1998.

Geoffrey Barraclough. "Introduction." In František Graus et al., eds., *Eastern and Western Europe in the Middle Ages.* New York: Harcourt Brace Jovanovich, 1970.

Ferruccio Barreca et al., ed. *L'espansione fenicia nel Mediterraneo.* Rome: Consiglio nazionale delle ricerche, 1971.

Fredrik Barth. *Ethnic Groups and Boundaries. The Social Organisation of Cultural Difference.* London: Allen & Unwin, 1969.

Antal Bartha. *Hungarian Society in the 9th and 10th Centuries.* Tr. K. Balazs. Budapest: Akadémiai Kiadó, 1975.

Roger P. Bartlett. *Human Capital: The Settlement of Foreigners in Russia, 1762–1804.* New York: Cambridge University Press, 1979.

Vladimir N. Basilov, ed., *Nomads of Eurasia.* Tr. Mary Fleming Zirin. Seattle: Natural History Museum of Los Angeles County in association with University of Washington Press, 1989.

Friedrich Behn. *Römertum und Völkerwanderung: Mitteleuropa zwischen Augustus und Karl dem Grossen.* Stuttgart: J. G. Cotta, 1963.

E. B. Bekmachanova. *Prisoiedineniie Kazakhstana k Rossii.* Moscow: Akademiia nauk, 1957.

Eugène Belin de Ballu. *L'histoire des colonies grecques du littoral nord de la mer Noire.* Leiden: E. J. Brill, 1965.

J. Bérard. *L'expansion et la colonisation grecque.* Paris: Aubier, 1960.

Volker Bierbrauer et al. *I Goti.* Milan: Electa Lombardia, Elemond Editori Associati, 1994.

Daniel A. Binchy. "The Passing of the Old Order." In B. O'Cuiv, ed., *The Impact of the Scandinavian Invasions on the Celtic-Speaking Peoples, c.800–1000 A.D.* Dublin: 1962.

Lewis R. Binford. *An Archaeological Perspective.* London: Seminar Press, 1972.

Michal Biran. *Qaidu and the Rise of the Independent Mongol State in Central Asia.* Richmond, Surrey: Curzon Press, 1997.

Helmut Birkhan. *Germanen und Kelten bis zum Ausgang der Römerzeit. Der Aussagewert von Wörtern und Sachen für die frühesten Keltisch-Germanischen Kulturbezeichnungen.* Vienna-Cologne-Graz: Österreichische Akademie der Wissenschaften, 1970.

José Maria Blazques Martinez. *Tartessos y los origines de la colonización fenicia en Occidente.* Salamanca: Universidad de Salamanca, 1975.

Dirk P. Blok. *Die Franken in Nederland.* 3d ed. Bussum: Fibula-Van Dishoek, 1979.

Jerome Blum. *Lord and Peasant in Russia: From the Ninth to the Nineteenth Century.* Princeton, NJ: Princeton University Press, 1961.

John Boardman. *The Greeks Overseas: Their Early Colonies and Trade.* London: Thames and Hudson, 1980.

Imre Boba. *Nomads, Northmen, and Slavs: Eastern Europe in the Ninth Century* (Slavo-Orientalia II). The Hague: Mouton, 1967.

I. Bóna. *Das Hunnenreich.* Germ. tr. G. Prohle. Stuttgart: K. Theiss, 1991.

Georges I. Bratianu. *La mer Noire. Dès origines à la conquête ottomane.* Munich: Societaţea Academică Română, 1969.

Iulian V. Bromlei, ed. *Sovremennye etnicheskie protsessy v SSSR.* Moscow: Nauka, 1975.

Johannes Brondsted. *Danmarks Oldtid.* København: 1965.

Charles E. P. Brooks. *Climate through the Ages. A Study of the Climatic Factors and Their Variations.* London: Ernest Benn Ltd., 1949.

Rogers Brubaker. *Nationalism Reframed. Nationhood and the National Question in the New Europe.* Cambridge: Cambridge University Press, 1996.

Philip Burnham. "Spatial mobility and political centralization in pastoral societies." In L'équipe écologie et anthropologie des sociétés pastorales, ed., *Pastoral Production and Society.* (Proceedings of the International Meeting on Nomadic Pastoralism. Paris, Dec. 1976.) Cambridge: Cambridge University Press, 1979.

Thomas S. Burns. *A History of the Ostrogoths.* Bloomington: Indiana University Press, 1984.

L. Cavalli-Sforza, P. Menozzi, and A. Piazza. *The History and Geography of Human Genes.* Princeton: Princeton University Press, 1994.

J. Campbell, Gen. ed., E. John, and P. Wormald. *The Anglo-Saxons.* Ithaca: Cornell University Press, 1982.

Patrizia Cannata. *Profilo storico del 1 impero turco (metà VI-metà VII secolo).* Rome: Istituto di Studi dell'India e dell'Asia Orientale, Università di Roma, 1981.

Stephen Castles and Mark J. Miller. *The Age of Migration: International Population Movements in the Modern World.* Houndmills, Basingstoke, Hampshire: Macmillan, 1993.

S. M. Cecchini. *I ritrovamenti fenici e punici in Sardegna.* Rome: Consiglio nazionale delle ricerche, 1969.

Nora K. Chadwick. *The Celts*. Harmondsworth: Penguin Books, 1970.

Timothy Champion. "Mass Migration in Later Prehistoric Europe. " In P. Sörbom, ed., *Transport Technology and Social Change*. Stockholm: Tekniska mus., 1980.

John Chapman. "The Impact of Modern Invasions and Migrations on Archaeological Explanation." In John Chapman and Helena Hamerow, eds., *Migrations and Invasions in Archaeological Explanation*. Oxford: Archaeopress, 1997.

John Chapman and Pavel M. Dolukhanov. "Cultural Transformations and Interactions in Eastern Europe: Theory and Terminology," pp. 1–36. In John Chapman and Pavel M. Dolukhanov, eds., *Cultural Transformations and Interactions in Eastern Europe*. Aldershot: Avebury, 1993.

John Chapman and Helena Hamerow, eds. *Migrations and Invasions in Archaeological Explanation*. Oxford: Archaeopress, 1997.

M. Chapman. *The Celts: The Construction of a Myth*. New York: St. Martin's Press, 1992.

E. V. Chernenko. *The Scythians: 700–300 B.C.* London: Osprey, 1983.

Raymond Chevallier. *La romanisation de la Celtique du Po, essai d'histoire provinciale*. Rome: École française de Rome, 1983.

Evangelos K. Chrysos. *To Byzantion ke i Gothi*. Thessalonika: Hetaireia Makedonikon Spoudon, Hidryma Meleton Chersonesou tou Heimou, 1972.

Grahame Clark. *World Prehistory: A New Outline*. London: Cambridge University Press, 1969.

Dietrich Claude. *Geschichte der Westgoten*. Stuttgart: Kohlhammer, 1970.

S. Esmonde Cleary. *The Ending of Roman Britain*. London: Batsford, 1989.

William G. Collingwood. *Scandinavian Britain*. London: Society for Promoting Christian Knowledge, 1908.

Roger Collins. *Early Medieval Spain: Unity in Diversity, 400–1000*. New York: St. Martin's, 1983.

Sarah Collinson. *Europe and International Migration*. London: Pinter Publishers for Royal Institute of International Affairs, 1993.

John Collis. *The European Iron Age*. London/New York: Routledge, 1997/1984.

Walker Connor. *Ethnonationalism. The Quest for Understanding*. Princeton, NJ: Princeton University Press, 1994.

Miron Constantinescu et al., eds. *Relations Between the Authochthonous Population and the Migratory Populations on the Territory of Romania*. Bucharest: Editura Akademiei Republici Socialiste România, 1975.

John M. Cook. *The Greeks in Ionia and the East*. New York: Praeger, 1963.

Sherburne F. Cook. *Prehistoric Demography*. Reading, MA: Addison-Wesley Modular Publications, 1972.

John X. W. P. Corcoran. *The Origin of the Celts: The Archaeological Evidence*. London: Pelican, 1970.

Elizabeth M. Craik. *The Dorian Aegean*. London: Routledge & Kegan Paul, 1980.

Roger J. Cribb. *Nomads in Archaeology*. New York/Cambridge: Cambridge University Press, 1991.

M. Cristofani. *La Civiltà degli Etruschi*. Milan: Electa, 1985.

Alfred W. Crosby. *Ecological Imperialism. The Biological Expansion of Europe, 900–1900.* Cambridge: Cambridge University Press, 1986.

R. A. Crossland and Ann Birchall, eds. *Bronze Age Migrations in the Aegean. Archaeological and Linguistic Problems in Greek Prehistory.* Park Ridge, NJ: Noyes Press, 1974.

Pamela Kyle Crossley. *The Manchus.* Cambridge, MA: Blackwell, 1997.

Barry W. Cunliffe. *The Ancient Celts.* Oxford/New York: Oxford University Press, 1997.

———. *Greeks, Romans, and Barbarians: Spheres of Interaction.* New York: Methuen, 1988.

Jan Czarnecki. *The Goths in Ancient Poland: A Study on the Historical Geography of the Oder-Vistula Region during the First Two Centuries of Our Era.* Coral Gables, FL: Miami University Press, 1975.

Krzysztof Dąbrowski, Teresa Nagrodźka-Majchrzyk, and Edward Tryjarski. *Hunowie Europejscy, Protobułgarzy, Chazarowie, Pieczyngowie.* Wrocław: Zakład Narodowy im. Ossolińskich, 1975.

Paolo Daffinà. *Il nomadismo centrasiatico.* Rome: Istituto dell'India e dell'Asia Orientale, Università di Roma, 1982.

P.G. Dake et al., eds. *Diffusion and Migration: Their Roles in Cultural Development.* Calgary: Archaeological Association of the University of Calgary, 1978.

O. I. Davidan. "Contacts between Staraja Ladoga and Scandinavia." In K. R. Schmidt, ed., *Varangian Problems* (Scando-Slavica, Supplementum I). Copenhagen: Munksgaard, 1970.

Hilda Roderick Ellis Davidson. *The Viking Road to Byzantium.* London: George Allen & Unwin, 1976.

Jeannine Davis-Kimball, Vladimir A. Bashilov, and Leonid T. Yablonsky, eds. *Nomads of the Eurasian Steppe in the Early Iron Age.* Berkeley: Zinat Press, 1995.

R. de Crespigny. *Northern Frontier: The Policies and Strategy of the Later Han Empire.* Canberra: Faculty of Asian Studies, Australian National University, 1984.

George J. Demko. *The Russian Colonization of Kazakhstan, 1896–1916.* Bloomington: Indiana University Press, 1969.

Émilienne Demougeot. *La formation de l'Europe et les invasions barbares.* Paris: Éditions Montaigne, 1969–1974.

Thomas K. Derry. *A History of Scandinavia: Norway, Sweden, Denmark, Finland, and Iceland.* Minneapolis: University of Minnesota Press, 1979.

Vincent Robin d'Arba Desborough. *The Greek Dark Ages.* London: Benn, 1972.

Jean-Paul Descoeudres, ed. *Greek Colonists and Native Populations.* New York: Oxford University Press, 1990.

Jan deVries. *Kelten und Germanen.* Bern and Munich: Francke, 1960.

Albert D'Haenens. *Les invasions normandes en Belgique au ix siècle.* Louvain: 1967.

Petre Diaconu. *Les Pétchénègues au Bas-Danube.* Bucharest: Éditions de l'Académie de la République Socialiste Roumanie, 1970.

István Dienes. *The Hungarians Cross the Carpathians.* Budapest: Corvina Press, 1972.

Pavel M. Dolukhanov. *The Early Slavs: Eastern Europe from the Initial Settlement to the Kievan Rus'.* London and New York: Longman, 1996.

Trude Dothan and Moshe Dothan. *People of the Sea: The Search for the Philistines.* New York: Macmillan, 1992.

John Drinkwater and Hugh Elton, eds. *Fifth-Century Gaul: A Crisis of Identity?* New York: Cambridge University Press, 1992.

I. V. Dubov. "The Ethnic History of Northwestern Rus' in the Ninth to Thirteenth Centuries." In D. H. Kaiser and G. Marker, eds. *Reinterpreting Russian History: Readings, 860s–1860s.* New York and Oxford: Oxford University Press, 1994.

D. M. Dunlop. *The History of the Jewish Khazars.* New York: Schocken Books, 1967/1954.

Francis Dvornik. *The Slavs: Their Early History and Civilization.* Boston: American Academy of Arts and Sciences, 1956.

Stephen L. Dyson. *The Creation of the Roman Frontier.* Princeton: Princeton University Press, 1985.

Wolfram Eberhard. *China und seine westlichen Nachbarn: Beiträge zur mittelalterlichen und neueren Geschichte Zentralasiens.* Darmstadt: Wissenschaftliche Buchgesellschaft, 1978.

Gunnar Ekholm. *Handelsforbindelser mellem Skandinavien och Romerska riket.* Stockholm: Svenska bokforlaget, 1961.

Peter Berresford Ellis. *Celt and Roman: The Celts of Italy.* New York: St. Martin's Press, 1998.

———. *Celt and Greek: Celts in the Hellenic World.* London: Constable, 1997.

L. A. El'nitsky. *Skifiia evraziiskikh stepei.* Novosibirsk: Nauka, Sib. otd-nie, 1977.

Hélène Carrère d'Encausse. *The Great Challenge: Nationalities and the Bolshevik State, 1917–1930.* Tr. Nancy Festinger, New York: Holmes and Meier, 1992.

R. T. Farrell, ed. *Viking Civilization; Contributions . . . from the Cornell Viking Series 1980.* London: 1982.

H. Fassmann and R. Munz, eds. *European Migration in the Late Twentieth Century.* Aldershot, Hants, England: Edward Elgar Publishing and Laxenburg: International Institute for Applied Systems Analysis, 1994.

M. Faull. *The Myth of the Dark Ages.* New York: St. Martin's, 1990.

John L. I. Fennell. *The Crisis of Medieval Russia, 1200–1304.* New York: Longman, 1983.

Alberto Ferreiro. *The Visigoths in Gaul and Spain, A.D. 408–711: A Bibliography.* Leiden and New York: E. J. Brill, 1988.

István Fodor. *In Search of a New Homeland: The Prehistory of the Hungarian People and the Conquest.* Tr. Helen Tarnoy. Budapest: Corvina, 1982.

Peter G. Foote and David M. Wilson. *The Viking Achievement: A Survey of the Society and Culture of Early Medieval Scandinavia.* New York: Praeger, 1970.

C. Daryll Forde. *Habitat, Economy and Society: A Geographical Introduction to Ethnology.* New York: Dutton, 1963/1934.

James Forsyth. *A History of the Peoples of Siberia: Russia's North Asian Colony, 1581–1990.* Cambridge: Cambridge University Press, 1992.

Herbert Franks. "The Forest Peoples of Manchuria: Kitans and Jurchen." In Denis Sinor, ed., *The Cambridge History of Early Inner Asia.* Cambridge: Cambridge University Press, 1990.

Morton H. Fried. *The Notion of Tribe.* Menlo Park, CA: Cummings Publishing Co., 1975.

Alfred Friendly. *The Dreadful Day: The Battle of Manzikert, 1071.* London: Hutchinson, 1981.

Richard N. Frye. *The Heritage of Central Asia from Antiquity to the Turkish Expansion.* Princeton: Markus Wiener Publishers, 1996.

Luis A. Garcia Moreno. *Historia de España visigoda.* Madrid: Cátedra, 1989.

Peter Garnsey, Keith Hopkins, and C. R. Whittaker, eds. *Trade in the Ancient Economy.* Berkeley: University of California Press, 1983.

V. F. Gening and A. Kh. Khalikov. *Rannie bolgary na Volge: Bol'she-Tarkhanskii mogil'nik.* Moscow: Nauka, 1964.

Bruno Genito. "Asiatic Steppe Nomad Peoples in the Carpathian Basin." In Gary Seaman, ed., *Foundations of Empire.* Los Angeles: Ethnographics Press/USC, 1992.

M. M. Gerasimova, N. M. Rud', and Leonid T. Yablonsky. *Antropologiia antichnogo i srednevekovogo naseleniia Vostochnoi Evropy.* Moscow: Nauka, 1987.

L. Gerevich, I. Erdélyi, and A. Salamon, eds. *Les questions fondamentales du peuplement du bassin des Carpathes du VIIIe au Xe siècle.* Budapest: 1972.

Adam Giesinger. *From Catherine to Khrushchev: The Story of Russian Germans.* Lincoln, NE: American Historical Society of Germans from Russia, 1981.

Aleksander Gieysztor et al. *History of Poland.* Tr. Krystyna Cekalska. Warsaw: Polskie Wydawnictwo Naukowe, 1968.

Marija Gimbutas. *Die Etnogenese der europäischen Indogermanen.* Innsbruck: Institut für Sprachwissenschaft, University of Innsbruck, 1992.

———. *The Slavs.* New York, Washington: Praeger Publishers, 1971.

Antonio Giuliano and Giancarlo Buzzi. *Etruschi.* Milan: Arnoldo Mondadori Editore, 1994.

Kazimierz Godłowski. *The Chronology of the Late Roman and Early Migration Periods in Central Europe.* Tr. Maria Walęga. Cracow: Nakładem Uniwersitetu Jagiellońskiego, 1970.

Walter Goffart. *Barbarians and Romans, A.D. 418–584: The Techniques of Accommodation.* Princeton: Princeton University Press, 1980.

Martin Gojda. *The Ancient Slavs. Settlement and Society.* The Rhind Lectures, 1989–90. Edinburgh: Edinburgh University Press, 1991.

Peter B. Golden. *An Introduction to the History of the Turkic Peoples: Ethnogenesis and State-formation in Medieval and Early Modern Eurasia and the Middle East.* Wiesbaden: Otto Harrassowitz, 1992.

———. "The Peoples of the Russian Forest Belt" and "The Peoples of the South Russian Steppes." In Denis Sinor, ed., *The Early History of Early Inner Asia.* Cambridge: Cambridge University Press, 1990.

Jack Goody. *The East in the West.* Cambridge: Cambridge University Press, 1996.

Colin D. Gordon. *The Age of Attila: Fifth-Century Byzantium and the Barbarians.* Ann Arbor: University of Michigan Press, 1966.

Heinrich Graetz. *History of the Jews.* Philadelphia: Jewish Publication Society of America, 1967.

J. Graham. *Colony and Mother City in Ancient Greece.* Manchester: Manchester University Press, 1964.

John T. Graham. *Theory of History in Ortega y Gasset. 'The Dawn of Historical Reason'.* Columbia, MO/London: University of Missouri Press, 1997.

James Graham-Campbell. *The Viking World.* London: Weidenfeld and Nicolson, 1980.

Vladimir V. Graivoronsky. *Ot kochevogo obraza zhizni k osedlosti: na opyte MNR.* Moscow: Nauka, 1979.

Bernhard Grambach et al., ed. *Germanen-Slawen-Deutsche. Forschungen zur ihrer Ethnogenese.* Berlin: Akademie-Verlag, 1968.

Michael Grant. *The Etruscans.* London: Weidenfeld and Nicolson, 1980.

Maria T. Grassi. *I Celti in Italia.* Milan: Longanesi, 1991.

František Graus et al. *Eastern and Western Europe in the Middle Ages.* New York: Harcourt Brace Jovanovich, 1970.

Miranda Green. *The Celtic World.* London/New York: Routledge, 1995.

John R. Gribbin. *The Climatic Threat: What's Wrong with our Weather?* London: Fontana, 1978.

Réné Grousset. *The Empire of the Steppes: A History of Central Asia.* Tr. Naomi Walford. New Brunswick. NJ: Rutgers University Press, 1970.

Lev N. Gumilëv. *Hunny v Kitaie: Tri veka voiny Kitaia so stepnymi narodami III-VI vv.* Moscow: Nauka, 1974.

I. A. Gurvich. *Pereseleniie krest'ian v Sibir'.* Moscow: 1899.

Rolf Hachmann. *The Germanic Peoples.* Tr. J. Hogarth. London: Barrie and Jenkins, 1971.

Ulf E. Hagberg, ed. *Studia Gotica: Die Eisenzeitlichen Verbindungen zwischen Schweden und Südosteuropa.* Stockholm: Almqvist & Wiksell, 1972.

Stephen Halkovic. *The Mongols of the West.* Bloomington: Research Institute for Inner Asian Studies, Indiana University, 1985.

Jonathan M. Hall. *Ethnic Identity in Greek Antiquity.* Cambridge: Cambridge University Press, 1997.

Charles J. Halperin. *Russia and the Golden Horde: The Mongol Impact on Medieval Russian History.* Bloomington: Indiana University Press, 1985.

Helena Hamerow. "Migration Theory and the Anglo-Saxon 'Identity Crisis.'" In John Chapman and Helena Hamerow, eds., *Migrations and Invasions in Archaeological Explanation.* Oxford: Archaeopress, 1997.

Franz Hancar. *Das Pferd in prähistorischer und frühistorischer Zeit.* Vienna and Munich: Verlag Herold, 1956.

Marcus Lee Hansen. *The Atlantic Migration, 1607–1860: A History of the Continuing Settlement of the United States.* Cambridge, MA: Harvard University Press, 1940.

William V. Harris. *Rome in Etruria and Umbria.* Oxford: Clarendon Press, 1971.

Leo de Hartog. *Russia and the Mongol Yoke: The History of the Russian Principalities and the Golden Horde, 1221–1502.* London: British Academic Press, 1996.

Henning Haslund. *Men and Gods in Mongolia.* Stelle, IL: Adventures Unlimited Press, 1992/1935.

Jean J. Hatt. *Celts and Gallo-Romans.* Tr. J. Hogarth. Geneva: Nagel, 1970.

Charles and Sonia Hawkes, eds. *Greeks, Celts and Romans, Studies in Venture and Resistance,* Archeology into History I. Totowa, NJ: Rowman & Littlefield, 1973.

Peter J. Heather. *The Goths.* Oxford, England and Cambridge, MA: Blackwell, 1996.

———and J. F. Matthews. *The Goths in the Fourth Century.* Liverpool: Liverpool University Press, 1991.

Alan Hecht and J. W. Fretz. "Food production under conditions of increased uncertainty: The settlement of the Paraguayan Chaco by Mennonite farmers." In Kenneth Hewitt, ed., *Interpretations of Calamity from the Viewpoint of Human Ecology.* Winchester, MA: Allen and Unwin, 1983.

Lotte Hedeager. *Iron Age Societies: From Tribe to State in Northern Europe, 500 B.C. to A.D. 700.* Tr. J. Hines. Oxford/Cambridge, MA: Blackwell, 1992.

———. "Empire, Frontier and the Barbarian Hinterland. Rome and Northern Europe from A.D. 1–400." In K. Kristiansen et al., eds., *Center and Periphery in the Ancient World.* Cambridge: Cambridge University Press, 1987.

Joachim Herrmann. *Wikinger und Slawen: Zur Frühgeschichte der Ostseevölker.* Berlin: Akademie-Verlag, 1982.

M. Hessenberger. *Aussiedler: Migration of People of German Origin from the Former Soviet Union to the Federal Republic of Germany and the Resulting Demographic and Social Problems.* Leeds: University of Leeds, School of Geography, 1994.

Nicholas Higham. *Rome, Britain and the Anglo-Saxons.* London: Seaby, 1992.

John Hines. *The Scandinavian Character of Anglian England in the Pre-Viking Period.* Oxford: Archaeopress, 1984.

Richard Hodges. *The Anglo-Saxon Achievement: Archaeology and the Beginnings of English Society.* London: Duckworth, 1989.

Thomas Hodgkin. *Italy and Her Invaders.* New York: Russell & Russell, 1982/1967.

Hans-Joachim Hoffman-Nowotny. *Migration: Ein Beitrag zu einer soziologischen Erklärung.* Stuttgart: Ferd. Enke Verlag, 1970.

Della Hooke, ed. *Anglo-Saxon Settlements.* Oxford: Blackwell, 1988.

J. Horedt. "The Gepidae, the Avars and the Romanic Population in Transylvania." In M. Constantinescu et al., ed., *Relations between the Autochthonous Population and the Migratory Populations on the Territory of Romania.* Bucharest: Editura Akademiei Republici Socialiste România, 1975.

Jean Hubert, Jean Porcher, and Wolfgang F. Volbach. *L'Europe des invasions.* Paris: Gallimard, 1967.

Charles O. Hucker. *China's Imperial Past: An Introduction to Chinese History and Culture.* Stanford, CA: Stanford University Press, 1975.

Ellsworth Huntington. *The Pulse of Asia: A Journey in Central Asia Illustrating the Geographic Basis of History.* Boston/New York: Houghton Mifflin, 1907.

George L. Huxley. *The Early Ionians.* New York: Humanities Press, 1966.

Helge Ingstad. *Westward to Vinland: The Discovery of pre-Colombian Norse House-sites in North America.* Tr. Eric J. Friis. New York: St. Martin's Press, 1969.

I. Ioniţa. "Probleme der Sîntana-de-Mureş-Cherniakhov-Kultur auf dem Gebiet Rumäniens." In Ulf E. Hagberg, ed., *Studia Gotica: Die Eisenzeitlichen*

Verbindungen zwischen Schweden und Südosteuropa. Stockholm: Almqvist & Wiksell, 1972.

William Irons. "Political Stratification among Pastoral Nomads." In L'équipe écologie et anthropologie des sociétés pastorales, ed. *Pastoral Production and Society.* Cambridge: Cambridge University Press, 1979.

Edward James, ed. *Visigothic Spain: New Approaches.* New York: Oxford University Press, 1980.

Simon James. *The World of the Celts.* London: Thames and Hudson, 1993.

Herbert Jankuhn. *Einführung in die Siedlungsgeschichte.* New York: De Gruyter, 1977.

J. Jaskanis and J. Okulicz. *Kultury oksywska i wielbarska.* In J. Wielowiejski, ed. *Prahistoria ziem polskih.* V. Warsaw: 1981.

Gwyn Jones. *A History of the Vikings.* London: Oxford University Press, 1968.

Huw R. Jones. *A Population Geography.* New York: Harper & Row, 1981.

Vladimir M. Kabuzan. *Izmeneniia v razmeshchenii naseleniia Rossii v XVIII-pervoi polovine XIX v. (po materialam revizii).* Moscow: Nauka, 1971.

Daniel H. Kaiser and Gary Marker, eds. *Reinterpreting Russian History. Readings 860s–1860s.* New York - Oxford: Oxford University Press, 1994.

B. Kandler-Palsson, ed. *Ethnogenese europäischer Völker.* Stuttgart/New York: Gustav Fischer, 1986.

Andreas Kappeler. *Russlands Erste Nationalitäten. Das Zarenreich und die Völker der Mittleren Wolga vom 16. bis 19. Jahrhundert.* Cologne and Vienna: Bohlau Verlag, 1982.

H. Jacob Katzenstein. *The History of Tyre, from the Beginning of the Second Millennium B.C.E. until the Fall of the Neo-Babylonian Empire in 538 B.C.E.* Jerusalem: The Schocken Institute for Jewish Research of the Jewish Theological Seminary of America, 1973.

Mikhail Kazanski. *Les Goths: Ier-VIIème siècles après J.-C.* Paris: Errance, 1991.

Anatoly M. Khazanov. *Nomads and the Outside World.* Tr. J. Crookenden. Madison, WI: University of Wisconsin Press, 1994/1984.

————. "Characteristic Features of Nomadic Communities in the Eurasian Steppes." In Wolfgang Weissleder, ed., *The Nomadic Alternative: Modes and Models of Interaction in the African-Asian Deserts and Steppes.* The Hague: Mouton Publishers, 1978.

Michael Khodarkovsky. *Where Two Worlds Met: The Russian State and the Kalmyk Nomads, 1600–1771.* Ithaca: Cornell University Press, 1992.

Russell King, ed. *Mass Migration in Europe: The Legacy and the Future.* London: Belhaven Press, 1993.

Peter Kivisto. *The Ethnic Enigma: The Salience of Ethnicity for European Origin Groups.* Philadelphia: Balch Institute Press, 1989.

T. J. Kloberdanz. "Plainsmen of three continents: Volga German adaptation to steppe, prairie, and pampas." In F. C. Luebke, ed., *Ethnicity on the Great Plains.* Lincoln, NE: University of Nebraska Press, 1980.

Frank A. Kmietowicz. *Ancient Slavs.* Stevens Point, WI: Worzalla Publishing, 1976.

Paul Kolstoe. *Russians in the Former Soviet Republics.* Bloomington: Indiana University Press. 1995.

Tamara S. Konduktorova. *Antropologiia naseleniia Ukrainy mezolita, neolita i epokhi bronzy.* Moscow: Nauka, 1973.

Józef Kostrzewski. *Prasłowiańszczyzna: zarys dziejów i kultury prasłowian.* Poznań: Księgarnia Akademicka, 1946.

Jovan Kovačević. Arheologija i istorija v*arvarske kolonizacije južnoslovenskih oblasti od iv do početka vii veka.* Novi Sad: Voïvodanski muzej, 1960.

Lawrence Krader. "The Origins of the State among the Nomads of Asia." In *Soviet and Western Anthropology.* Ed. Ernest Gellner. London: Duckworth, 1980.

Symposium, Bochum, July 1967. *Nomadismus als Entwicklungsproblem.* Bielefeld. Bertelsmann Universitätsverlag, 1969.

Kristian Kristiansen and Carsten Paludan-Muller, eds. *New Directions in Scandinavian Archaeology.* Copenhagen: The National Museum of Denmark, 1979.

Knud J. Krogh. *Viking Greenland.* Tr. H. Fogh and G. Jones. Copenhagen: The National Museum of Denmark, 1967.

Bruno Krüger, ed. *Die Germanen: Geschichte und Kultur der germanischen Stämme in Mitteleuropa.* Berlin: Akademie-Verlag, 1983.

Venčeslas Krůta. *I Celti in Italia.* Milan: Mondadori, 1999/1988.

———, O. Frey, B. Raftery, and Miklos Szábó, eds. *Les Celtes.* New York: Rizzoli, 1991.

Eugene M. Kulischer. *Europe on the Move: War and Population Changes, 1917–47.* New York: Columbia University Press, 1948.

Luc Kwanten. *Imperial Nomads: A History of Central Asia, 500–1500.* Philadelphia: University of Pennsylvania, 1979/1965.

Emmanuel L. Ladurie. *Times of Feast, Times of Famine: A History of Climate from the Year 1000.* Tr. B. Bray. Garden City, NY: Doubleday & Company, 1971.

H. H. Lamb. *Climate: Present, Past, and Future.* Vol. 2. London: Methuen, 1977.

John D. Langlois, ed. *China under Mongol Rule.* Princeton: Princeton University Press, 1981.

Owen Lattimore. *Inner Asian Frontiers of China.* Boston: Beacon Press, 1967/1940.

———. "The Mainsprings of Asiatic Migration." In Isaiah Bowman, ed. *Limits of Land Settlement: A Report on Present-day Possibilities.* New York: Council on Foreign Relations, 1937.

Gyula László. *Steppenvolker und Germanen.* Germ. Tr. H. von Thierry. Vienna/Munich, Schroll, 1970.

Gleb S. Lebedev. *Epokha vikingov v Severnoi Evrope: istoriko-arkhivnye ocherki.* Leningrad: Leningrad University Press, 1985.

James Lee. "Migration and Expansion in Chinese History." In William H. McNeill and Ruth S. Adams, eds., *Human Migration. Patterns and Policies.* Bloomington: Indiana University Press, 1978.

Christian Leiber. *Schätze der Ostgoten.* Stuttgart: Theiss, 1995.

G. J. Lewis. *Human Migration: A Geographical Perspective.* New York: St. Martin's Press, 1982.

Robert A. Lewis and Richard H. Rowlands. *Population Redistribution in the USSR: Its Impact on Society, 1897–1977.* New York: Praeger, 1979.

Robert A. Lewis, Richard H. Rowlands, and Ralph S. Clem. *Nationality and Population Change in Russia and the USSR: An Evaluation of Census Data, 1897–1970.* New York: Praeger, 1976.

Ivan I. Liapushkin. *Slaviane Vostochnoi Evropy nakanune obrazovaniia drevnerusskogo gosudarstva (VIII-pervaia polovina IX v.). Istoriko-arkheologicheskiie ocherki.* Leningrad: Nauka, Len-oe otd-nie, 1968.

John H. W. G. Liebeschuetz. "Alaric's Goths: Nation or Army?" In John Drinkwater and Hugh Elton, eds., *Fifth-Century Gaul: A Crisis of Identity?* New York: Cambridge University Press, 1992.

Pal Lipták. *Avars and Ancient Hungarians.* Tr. B. Belkay. Budapest: Akademiai Kiado, 1983.

Boris A. Litvinsky. "The Ecology of Ancient Nomads of Soviet Central Asia and Kazakhstan." In Gary Seaman, ed., *Ecology and Empire: Nomads in the Cultural Evolution of the Old World.* Los Angeles: Ethnographics Press/USC, 1989.

Frank Lorimer. *The Population of the Soviet Union: History and Prospects.* Geneva: League of Nations, 1946.

Ferdinand Lot. *Les invasions germaniques: la pénétration mutuelle du monde barbare et du monde romain.* Paris: Payot, 1945.

Henry R. Loyn. *The Vikings in Britain.* New York: St. Martin's Press, 1977.

Evgenii I. Lubo-Lesnichenko. "The Huns. Third Century B.C. to Sixth Century A.D." In Vladimir N. Basilov, ed., Mary Fleming Zirin, tr., *Nomads of Eurasia.* Seattle: Natural History Museum of Los Angeles County in association with University of Washington Press, 1989.

Herbert Ludat, ed. *Siedlung und Verfassung der Slawen zwischen Elbe. Saale und Oder.* Giessen: W. Schmitz, 1966/1960.

S. Lusuardi Siena. *I Goti in Italia. Le testimonianze archeologiche.* In A. Ambrosioni and S. Lusuardi Siena. *I Goti in Italia alla luce delle fonti scritti e delle testimonianze archeologiche.* Milan: 1985.

Carlile A. Macartney. *The Magyars in the Ninth Century.* Cambridge: Cambridge University Press, 1968/1930.

F. L. MacKellar, W. Lutz, Anthony J. McMichael, and Astri Suhrke. "Population and Climate Change." In S. Rayner and E. L. Malone, eds., *Human Choice and Climate Change,* vol. 1. *The Societal Framework.* Columbus, OH: Battelle Institute Press, 1998.

Paul L. MacKendrick. "Roman Colonization and the Frontier Hypothesis." In Walker D. Wyman and Clifton B. Kroeber, eds., *The Frontier in Perspective.* Madison: University of Wisconsin Press, 1957.

Colin Mackerras. *The Uigur Empire (744–840) According to the T'ang Dynastic Histories.* Canberra: Centre of Oriental Studies, Australian National University, 1968.

Otto Maenchen-Helfen. *The World of the Huns. Studies in Their History and Culture.* Ed. Max Knight. Berkeley: University of California Press, 1973.

D. Maidar. *Chinggis Khaan and the Great Mongolian State.* Ulaanbaatar: Ulsyn Khlevleliin Gazar, 1990.

James C. Malin. *History and Ecology: Studies of the Grassland.* Ed. R. P. Swierenga. Lincoln: University of Nebraska Press, 1984/1967.

Guido Achille Mansuelli. *La fine del mondo antico.* Turin: UTET, 1988.

Robert Marshall. *Storm from the East: from Genghis Khan to Khubilai Khan.* Berkeley: University of California Press, 1993.

T. H. McGovern. "The economics of extinction in Norse Greenland." In T. M. L. Wigley, M. J. Ingram, and G. Farmer, eds., *Climate and history: Studies in past climates and their impact on man.* Cambridge: Cambridge University Press, 1981.

William M. McGovern. *The Early Empires of Central Asia: A Study of the Scythians and the Huns and the Part They Played in World History.* Chapel Hill: University of North Carolina Press, 1939.

William H. McNeill. *Mythistory and Other Essays.* Chicago: University of Chicago Press, 1986.

————and Ruth S. Adams, eds. *Human Migration. Patterns and Policies.* Bloomington: Indiana University Press, 1978.

I. Melyukova. "The Scythians and Sarmatians." In Denis Sinor, ed., *The Cambridge History of Early Inner Asia.* Cambridge: Cambridge University Press, 1990.

Ramon Menendez Pidal, ed. *Historia de España,* vol. III. *España visigoda.* Madrid: Espasa-Calpe, 1992.

Nikolai Ia. Merpert. *Drevneishaia istoriia naseleniia stepnoi polosy Vostochnoi Evropy.* Moscow: Nauka, 1968.

William B. Meyer. *Americans and Their Weather.* New York: Oxford University Press (forthcoming).

William B. Meyer, Karl W. Butzer, Theodore E. Downing, Billie L. Turner II, G. W. Wenzel, and James L. Wescoat, Jr. "Reasoning by Analogy." In S. Rayner and E. L. Malone, eds., *Human choice and climate change,* vol. 3: *Tools for Policy Analysis.* Columbus, OH: Battelle Press, 1998.

Z. Mikić. "Die Ethnogenese der Südslawen unter Berücksichtigung von West- und Ostslawen aus der Sicht der Anthropologie." In B. Kandler-Palsson, ed., *Ethnogenese europäischer Völker.* Stuttgart/New York: Gustav Fischer, 1986.

G. Mildenberger. "Vor- und Frühgeschichte der bömischen Länder." In K. Bosl, ed., *Handbuch der Geschichte der böhmischen Länder.* Stuttgart: A. Hiersemann, 1966.

Sarunas Milisauskas. *European Prehistory.* New York: Academic Press, 1978.

Fergus Millar et al. *The Roman Empire and its Neighbors.* London: Weidenfeld & Nicolson, 1967/1968.

Martin Millet. *The Romanization of Britain: An Essay in Archeological Interpretation.* Cambridge: Cambridge University Press, 1990.

Pavel A. Minakir. "Chinese Immigration in the Russian Far East: Regional, National, and International Dimensions." In Jeremy R. Azrael and Emil A. Payin, eds., *Cooperation and Conflict in the Former Soviet Union: Implications for Migration.* Santa Monica, CA: Rand Center for Russian and Eurasian Studies, Center for Ethnopolitical and Regional Research, 1996.

Ellis H. Minns. *Scythians and Greeks. A Survey of Ancient History and Archaeology on the North Coast of the Euxine from the Danube to the Caucasus.* New York: Biblo and Tannen, 1965/1913.

Leslie P. Moch. *Moving Europeans: Migration in Western Europe since 1650.* Bloomington: Indiana University Press, 1992.

Roger Mols. "Population in Europe, 1500–1700." In Carlo M. Cipolla, ed., *The Fontana Economic History of Europe,* vol. 2, *The Sixteenth and Seventeenth Centuries.* London: Fontana/Collins, 1974.

Arnaldo Momigliano. *Storia e storiografia antica.* Bologna: Il Mulino, 1987.

David Morgan. *The Mongols.* Oxford: Blackwell, 1986.

Sabatino Moscati, Gen. ed. *The Celts.* Eng. tr. London: Thames & Hudson, 1991.

Viacheslav Yu. Murzin. *Proiskhozhdenie skifov: osnovnye etapy formirovaniia skifskogo etnosa.* Kiev: Naukova dumka, 1990.

Lucien Musset. *Les invasions: les vagues germaniques.* Paris: Presses universitaires de France, 1965.

———. *Les invasions: le second assaut contre l'Europe chretienne (VII-XI siècles).* Paris: Presses universitaires de France, 1965.

Domenico Musti, ed. *Le origini dei Greci: Dori e mondo egeo.* Rome: Editori Laterza, 1986.

John N. L. Myres. *Angles, Saxons, and Jutes.* Ed. Vera Evison. Oxford: Clarendon Press, 1981.

Ronald H. Nash, ed. *Ideas of History.* New York: Dutton, 1969.

Vitaly V. Naumkin, ed. *Central Asia and Transcaucasia: Ethnicity and Conflict.* Westport, CT: Greenwood Press, 1994.

V. A. Nazarenko. "Normanny i poiavleniie kurganov v Priladozh'ie." In A. D. Stoliar, ed., *Severnaiia Rus' i eë sosedi v epokhu rannego srednevekov'ia.* Leningrad: Leningrad University Press, 1982.

Birger Nerman. *Grobin-Seeburg. Ausgrabungen und Funde.* Stockholm: Almqvist & Wiksell, 1958.

Frank Nowak. *Medieval Slavdom and the Rise of Russia.* Westport, CT: Greenwood Press, 1970/1930.

Dmitri Obolensky. "Russia's Byzantine Heritage." In Michael Cherniavsky, ed., *The Structure of Russian History: Interpretive Essays.* New York: Random House, 1970.

Robert M. Ogilvie. *Early Rome and the Etruscans.* Atlantic Highlands, NJ: Humanities Press, 1976.

Volodymyr V. Onykiienko. *Kompleksnoe issledovanie migratsionnykh protsessov. Analiz migratsii naseleniia UkrSSR.* Moscow: Statistika, 1973.

Urgunge Onon. *The History and Life of Chinggis Khaan: The Secret History of the Mongols.* Leiden: E. J. Brill, 1990.

José Orlandis. *Historia del reino visigodo español.* Madrid: Ediciones Rialp, 1988.

Donald Ostrowski. *Muscovy and the Mongols.* Cambridge: Cambridge University Press, 1998.

Eric C. Oxenstierna. *The Norsemen.* Tr. C. Hutter. London: Studio Vista, 1966.

Massimo Pallottino. *The Etruscans.* Tr. J. Cremona. Bloomington: Indiana University Press, 1975.

Pedro de Palol and G. Ripoll Lopez. *Los godos en el occidente europeo: ostrogodos y visigodos en los siglos V-VIII.* Madrid: Ediciones Encuentro, 1988.

Ervin Pamlényi, ed. *A History of Hungary.* Tr. L. Boros et al. London: Collet's, 1975.

Larisa R. Pavlinskaya. "The Scythians and Sakians. Eighth to Third Centuries B.C." In Vladimir N. Basilov, ed., *Nomads of Eurasia.* Tr. Mary Fleming Zirin. Seattle:

Natural History Museum of Los Angeles County in association with University of Washington Press, 1989.

Emil A. Payin and Andrei I. Susarov. "The Political Context of Migration in the Former Soviet Union." In Jeremy R. Azrael and Emil A. Payin, eds., *Cooperation and Conflict in the Former Soviet Union: Implications for Migration.* Santa Monica, CA: Rand Center for Russian and Eurasian Studies, Center for Ethnopolitical and Regional Research, 1996.

T. Peisker. "The Asiatic Background. " *Cambridge Medieval History* I (1911): 323–59.

Patrick Perrin, ed. *Gallo-Romains, Wisigoths et Francs en Aquitaine, Septimanie et Espagne,* Actes des VIIe journées internationales d'archéologie mérovingienne. Rouen: Association française d'Archéologie mérovingienne. Musée des Antiquités de la Seine Maritime, 1991.

Franz Petri, ed. *Siedlung, Sprache und Bevölkerungsstruktur im Frankenreich.* Darmstadt: Wissenschaftliche Buchgesellschaft, 1973.

J. R. S. Phillips. *The Medieval Expansion of Europe.* New York: Oxford University Press, 1988.

Eustace D. Phillips. *The Royal Hordes: Nomad Peoples of the Steppes.* London: Thames and Hudson, 1965.

Richard A. Pierce. *Russian Central Asia, 1867–1917: A Study in Colonial Rule.* Berkeley: University of California Press, 1960.

S. A. Pletniova, ed. *Stepi Evrazii v epokhu srednevekov'ia.* Moscow: Nauka, 1981.

Walter Pohl. *Die Awaren: Ein Steppenvolk in Mitteleuropa. 567 bis 822 n.Chr.* Munich: Beck, 1988.

Karl Polanyi, Conrad M. Arsenberg, and Harry W. Pearson, eds. *Trade and Market in the Early Empires: Economics in History and Theory.* New York: The Free Press, 1965/1957.

Roger Portal. *The Slavs. A Cultural and Historical Survey of the Slavonic Peoples.* Tr. P. Evans. New York: Harper & Row, 1969.

Thomas G. E. Powell. *The Celts.* New ed. London and New York: Thames and Hudson, 1980.

Omelian Pritzak. "The Khazar Kingdom: Conversion to Judaism." *Harvard Ukrainian Studies* 2. Cambridge: Harvard Ukrainian Research Institute, 1978.

Teresa Rakowska-Harmstone. "Soviet Moslem Nationalism in Comparative Perspective." In S. Veinshtein, Ch. Lemercier-Quelquejay, and S. E. Wimbush, eds., *Turco-Tatar Past. Soviet Present.* Louvain: Éditions Peeters, 1986.

Klaus Randsborg. *The First Millennium A.D. in Europe and the Mediterranean.* Cambridge: Cambridge University Press, 1991.

H. D. Rankin. *Celts and the Classical World.* London: Croom Helm, 1987.

Colin Renfrew, ed. *The Explanation of Culture Change: Models in Prehistory.* London: Duckworth, 1973.

Colin Renfrew and Paul Bahn. *Archaeology: Theories, Methods, and Practice.* New York: Thames and Hudson, 1991.

Nicholas V. Riasanovsky. *A History of Russia.* New York: Oxford University Press, 1963.

Valentin A. Riasanovsky. *Fundamental Principles of Mongol Law.* Tientsin: 1937.

Tamara Talbot Rice. *The Scythians*. New York: Praeger, 1957.

Julian D. Richards. *Book of Viking Age England*. London: Batsford, 1991.

David Ridgway. "Phoenicians and Greeks in The West: A View from Pithekoussai." In G. R. Tsetskhladze and F. de Angelis, eds., *The Archeology of Greek Colonization. Essays dedicated to Sir John Boardman*. Oxford: Oxford University Committee for Archaeology, 1994.

Else Roesdahl. *Viking Age Denmark*. Tr. S. Margeson and K. William. London: British Museum Publications, 1982.

Renate Rolle. *The World of the Scythians*. Tr. F. G. Walls. Berkeley: University of California Press, 1989.

Eugeen E. Roosens. *Creating Ethnicity: The Process of Ethnogenesis*. Newburg Park, CA: Sage Publications, 1989.

Anne Ross. *Pagan Celtic Britain*. Rev. ed. London: Constable, 1992.

Mikhail I. Rostovtseff (Rostovtzeff). *Iranians and Greeks in South Russia*. New York: Russell & Russell, 1969/1922.

Irving Rouse. *Migrations in Prehistory: Inferring Population Movement from Cultural Remains*. New Haven: Yale University Press, 1986.

Michael Rowlands, Mogens Larsen, and Kristian Kristiansen, eds. *Centre and Periphery in the Ancient World*. Cambridge: Cambridge University Press, 1987.

Paula G. Rubel. *The Kalmyk Mongols: a Study in Continuity and Change*. Bloomington: Indiana University Press, 1967.

Dean S. Rugg. *Eastern Europe*. London and New York: Longman, 1985.

Steven Runciman. *A History of the First Bulgarian Empire*. London: G. Bell & Sons Ltd., 1930.

M. Rusu. "Avars, Slavs, Romanic Population in the 6th–8th Centuries." In M. Constantinescu et al., ed., *Relations between the Autochthonous Population and the Migratory Populations on the Territory of Romania*. Bucharest: Editura Akademiei Republici Socialiste România, 1975.

Leonid L. Rybakovsky. *Regional'nyi analiz migratsii*. Moscow: Statistika, 1973.

Michael Rywkin. *Moscow's Muslim Challenge: Soviet Central Asia*. Rev. ed. Armonk, NY: M. E. Sharp, 1990.

Michael B. Sakellariou. "Linguistic and Ethnic Groups in Prehistoric Greece." In George Christopoulos, Gen. ed., Ph. Sherrard, tr., *History of the Hellenic World*. Athens: Ekdotike Athenon, 1974.

———. *La migration grecque en Ionie*. Athens: Kentro Mikraiatikon Spoudon, 1958.

Edward T. Salmon. *Roman Colonization under the Republic*. London: Thames and Hudson, 1969.

Peter Salway. *Roman Britain*. New York: Oxford University Press, 1981.

Narciso Santos Yanguas. *Los pueblos germanicos en la segunda mitad del siglo IV*. Oviedo: Universidad de Oviedo, 1976.

P. H. Sawyer. *Kings and Vikings. Scandinavia and Europe, A.D. 700–1100*. London/New York: Methuen, 1982.

Piergiuseppe Scardigli. *Lingua e storia dei Goti*. Florence: Sansoni, 1964.

Chris Scarre and Frances Healy, eds. *Trade and Exchange in Prehistoric Europe*. Oxford: Oxbow Books, 1993.

Joseph B. Schechtman. *European Population Transfers, 1939–1945*. New York: Oxford University Press, 1946.

Herbert Schutz. *The Prehistory of Germanic Europe*. New Haven: Yale University Press, 1983.

Constantin C. Scorpan. *Limes Scythiae: Topographical and Stratigraphical Research on the Late Roman Fortifications on the Lower Danube*. Oxford: Archaeopress, 1980.

Franklin D. Scott. *World Migration in Modern Times*. Englewood, NJ: Prentice-Hall, 1968.

Gary Seaman. "Introduction: World Systems and State Formation on the Inner Eurasian Periphery." In Gary Seaman and Daniel Marks, eds., *Rulers from the Steppe: State Formation on the Eurasian Periphery*. Los Angeles: Ethnographics Press/USC, 1991.

Valentin V. Sedov. *Vostochnyie slaviane v VI-XIII vv*. Ed. B. A. Rybakov. Moscow: Nauka, 1982.

Hugh Seton-Watson. *The Russian Empire, 1801–1917*. Oxford: Clarendon, 1967.

Harlow Shapley, ed. *Climatic Change. Evidence, Causes and Effects*. Cambridge, MA: Harvard University Press, 1953.

Mark B. Shchukin (Ščukin). *Na rubezhe er. Opyt istoriko-arkheologicheskoi rekonstruktsii politicheskikh sobytii IIIv. do n.e.—IVv. n.e. v vostochnoi i tsentral'noi Evrope*. St. Petersburg: Farn, 1994.

Stephen J. Shennan, ed. *Archaeological Approaches to Cultural Identity*. London: Routledge, 1994.

Vasilii M. Sinitsyn. *Vvedenie v paleoklimatologiiu*. Leningrad: Nedra, 1967.

Denis Sinor, ed. *The Cambridge History of Early Inner Asia*. Cambridge: Cambridge University Press, 1990.

Aleksei P. Smirnov. "Ob etnicheskom sostave Volzhskoi Bolgarii." In L. Janin, *Novoie v arkheologii*. Moscow: Izd-vo Mosk-go u-ta, 1972.

———, ed., *Problemy arkheologii i drevnei istorii ugrov*. Moscow: Nauka, 1972.

Konstantin F. Smirnov. *Sarmaty i utverzhdeniie ikh politicheskogo gospodstva v Skifii*. Eds. V. Kropotkin and M. Moshkova. Moscow: Nauka, 1984.

Anthony D. Smith. *The Ethnic Origins of Nations*. Oxford: Blackwell, 1986.

Clifford T. Smith. *An Historical Geography of Western Europe before 1800*. New York: Praeger, 1978.

Thomas Sowell. *Conquests and Cultures: An International History*. New York: Basic Books, 1998.

Nigel J. Spivey and Simon Stoddart. *Etruscan Italy: An Archeological History*. London: Batsford, 1990.

Bertold Spuler. *The Mongol Period*. Tr. F. R. C. Bagley. Princeton: Markus Weiner Publishers, 1994/1969.

Ian M. Stead. *The Arras Culture*. York: Yorkshire Philosophical Society, 1979.

Ernst Stein. *Geschichte des spätrömischen Reiches*. Vienna: L. W. Seidel, 1928.

Stanislav M. Stetskevich, ed. *Ocherki istorii iuzhnykh i zapadnykh slavian*. Leningrad: Gosudarstvennoie uchebno-pedagogicheskoie izdatel'stvo ministerstva prosveshcheniia RSFSR, 1957.

Traian Stoianovich. *French Historical Method. The Annales Paradigm.* Ithaca: Cornell University Press, 1976.

A. D. Stoliar, ed. *Severnaiia Rus' i eë sosedi v epokhu rannego srednevekov'ia.* Leningrad: Leningrad University Press, 1982.

Karl Stumpp. *The German-Russians.* Tr. J. Height. Lincoln, NE: American Historical Society of Germans from Russia, 1978.

Orest Subtelny. *Ukraine: A History.* 2d ed. Toronto: University of Toronto Press/Canadian Institute of Ukrainian Studies, 1994.

Peter F. Sugar. gen. ed. *A History of Hungary.* Bloomington: Indiana University Press, 1990.

G. Suhbaatar. *The Cream of Mongolian Historical Writing.* Vol. 2. Ulaanbaatar: Textbook and Children's Books Publishing House, 1992.

Tadeusz Sulimirski. *Prehistoric Russia. An outline.* New York: Humanities Press, 1970.

James Ross Sweeney. "'Spurred on by the Fear of Death': Refugees and Displaced Populations during the Mongol Invasion of Hungary." In Michael Gervers and Wayne Schlepp, eds., *Nomadic Diplomacy, Destruction and Religion from the Pacific to the Adriatic.* Toronto: Joint Centre for Asia Pacific Studies, 1994.

Jing-shen Tao. *The Jurchen in Twelfth-Century China. A Study in Sinicization.* Seattle: University of Washington Press, 1976.

Frederick J. Teggart. *Rome and China: A Study of Correlations in Historical Events.* Westport. CT: Greenwood Press, 1983/1939.

Suzanne Teillet. *Dès Goths à la nation gothique: les origines de l'idée de nation en Occident du Ve au VIIe siècle.* Paris: Les Belles Lettres, 1984.

Alexei I. Terenozhkin. *Kimmeriitsy.* Kiev: Naukova Dumka, 1976/1971.

———and V. A. Il'inskaia. "Skifiia." In S. D. Kryzhit's'ky, ed., *Arkheologiia Ukrainskoi SSR.* Kiev: Naukova Dumka, 1986.

Charles Thomas. *Celtic Britain.* London: Thames and Hudson, 1986.

E. A. Thompson. *The Huns.* Cambridge, MA: Blackwell, 1996.

———. *Romans and Barbarians. The Decline of the Western Empire.* Madison: University of Wisconsin Press, 1982.

Malcolm Todd. *The Northern Barbarians, 100 B.C. - A.D. 300.* London: Hutchinson University Library, 1975.

Richard F. Tomasson. *Iceland, The First New Society.* Minneapolis: University of Minnesota Press, 1980.

Donald W. Treadgold. *The Great Siberian Migration: Government and Peasant in Resettlement from Emancipation to the First World War.* Princeton, NJ: Princeton University Press, 1957.

Piotr N. Tretiakov. *Finno-ugry, balty i slaviane na Dnepre i Volge.* Moscow: Nauka, 1966.

Tserel. *Some Questions on the Ethnic History of the Four Oirad and Related Ethnic Groups.* Ulaanbaatar/Uvs: Erdem Company, 1997.

Andrew B. Urbansky. *Byzantium and the Danube Frontier: The Study of the Relations Between Byzantium, Hungary, and the Balkans during the Period of the Comneni.* New York: Twayne Publishers, 1968.

László Varady. *Das letzte Jahrhundert Pannoniens (376–476).* Amsterdam: A. M. Hakkert and Budapest: Akadémiai Kiodó, 1969.

Vyacheslav Vashanov. "Economic Changes in the Post-USSR: Reasons for Mass Migrations." In Jeremy R. Azrael and Emil A. Payin, eds., *Cooperation and Conflict in the Former Soviet Union: Implications for Migration.* Santa Monica, CA: Rand Center for Russian and Eurasian Studies, Center for Ethnopolitical and Regional Research, 1996.

Alexander A. Vasiliev. *Justin the First: An Introduction to the Epoch of Justinian the Great.* Cambridge, MA: Harvard University Press, 1950.

Charles Verlinden. *Les origines de la frontière linguistique en Belgique et la colonisation franque.* Bruxelles: La renaissance du livre, 1955.

George Vernadsky. *The Origins of Russia.* Oxford: Clarendon Press, 1959.

Paul M. J. Vidal de la Blache. *Principles of Human Geography.* Tr. Millicent T. Bingham. New York: Henry Holt and Company, 1926.

Galina S. Vitkovskaya. "Relocation to Russia from the States of Central Asia: Understanding the Decision to Migrate." In Jeremy R. Azrael and Emil A. Payin, eds., *Cooperation and Conflict in the Former Soviet Union: Implications for Migration.* Rand Center for Russian and Eurasian Studies, Center for Ethnopolitical and Regional Research, 1996.

Friedrich Vittinghoff. *Römische Kolonisation und Bürgerrechtspolitik unter Caesar und Augustus.* Wiesbaden: Akademie der Wissenschaften und der Literatur in Mainz in Kommission bei Franz Steiner Verlag GMVH, 1951/52.

Mikhail V. Vorobiëv. *Chzhurchzheni i gosudarstvo Tsin' (Xv.–1234g.): istoricheskii ocherk.* Moscow: Nauka, 1975.

Spyros Vryonis Jr. "Religious Changes and Patterns in the Balkans, 14th–16th Centuries." In Henrik Birnbaum and Spyros Vryonis Jr., eds., *Aspects of the Balkans: Continuity and Change.* The Hague: Mouton, 1972.

Manfred Waas. *Germanen im römischen Dienst im 4. Jahrhundert nach Christus.* 2d ed. Bonn: Habelt, 1965.

Heinrich Wagner. *Studies in the Origins of the Celts and of Early Celtic Civilisation.* Belfast: Queen's University, 1971.

Lothar Waldmüller. *Die ersten Begegnungen der Slawen mit dem Christentum und den christlichen Völkern vom VI. bis VIII. Jahrhundert. Die Slawen zwischen Byzanz und Abendland.* Amsterdam: A. M. Hakkert, 1976.

Robert deC. Ward. *Climate, Considered Especially in Relation to Man.* 2d Rev. ed. New York: G. P. Putnam's Sons, 1918.

Patty J. Watson, Steven A. LeBlanc, Charles L. Redman. *Explanation in Archaeology: An Explicitly Scientific Approach.* New York: Columbia University Press, 1971.

Curt Weibull. *Die Auswanderung der Goten aus Schweden.* Goteborg: Erlanders boktr., 1958.

Wolfgang Weissleder, ed. *The Nomadic Alternative: Modes and Models of Interaction in the African-Asian Deserts and Steppes.* The Hague: Mouton Publishers, 1978.

Martin G. Welch. *Anglo-Saxon England.* London: Batsford, 1992.

Reinhart Wenskus. *Stammesbildung und Verfassung. Das Werden der frühmittelalterlichen Gentes.* Cologne and Graz: Bohlau, 1961.

J. N. Westwood. *Russia, 1917–1964.* London: Batsford, 1966.

Robert E. M. Wheeler. *Rome beyond the Imperial Frontiers.* London: Bell, 1954.

Hayden White. *Metahistory: The Historical Imagination in Nineteenth-Century Europe.* Baltimore: Johns Hopkins University Press, 1973.

Charles R. Whittaker. *Frontiers of the Roman Empire: A Sociological and Economic Study.* Baltimore: Johns Hopkins University Press, 1994.

Jerzy Wielowiejski. "Późny okres lateński i okres rzymski." In W. Hensel, ed. *Prahistoria ziem Polskich* V. Wroclaw: Zakład narodowy im. Ossolińskich, 1981.

Joseph Wiesner. "Die Kulturen der Frühen Reitervölker." In Eugen Thurnher. *Handbuch der Kulturgeschichte.* Frankfurt-am-Main: Akademische Verlagsgesellschaft Athenaion, 1968.

David M. Wilson. *The Vikings and Their Origins: Scandinavia in the First Millennium.* New York: McGraw-Hill Book Co., 1970.

Karl A. Wittfogel. *China und die osteurasische Kavallerie Revolution.* Wiesbaden: Otto Harrassowitz, 1978.

Ronald Wixman. "Applied Soviet Nationalities Policy: A Suggested Rationale." In Sevian I. Veinshtein, Chantal Lemercier-Quelquejay, and S. Enders Wimbush, eds., *Turco-Tatar Past, Soviet Present: Collectgion Turcica IV.* Louvain: Éditions Peeters, 1986.

Herwig Wolfram. *Das Reich und die Germanen: Zwischen Antike und Mittelalter.* Berlin: Siedler Verlag, 1990.

———. *Geschichte der Goten: Von der Anfangen bis zur Mitte des 6. Jahrhunderts.* Munich: Beck, 1990/1979.

Ian N. Wood. "The End of Roman Britain. Continental Evidence and Parallels. Gildas: New Approaches." In Michael Lapidge and David Dumville, eds., *Studies in Celtic History* 5. Woodbridge, Suffolk: Boydell Press, 1984.

Edward A. Wrigley. *Population and History.* New York: McGraw-Hill, 1969.

F. R. Wulsin. *China's Inner Asian Frontier.* Ed. M. E. Alonso. Cambridge, MA: Peabody Museum, 1979.

Shiba Yoshinobu. "Sung Foreign Trade: Its Scope and Organisation." In Morris Rossabi, ed., *China among Equals: the Middle Kingdom and its Neighbors, 10th–14th Centuries.* Berkeley: University of California Press, 1983.

C. Walter Young. "Chinese Immigration and Colonization in Manchuria. " *Pioneer Settlement.* New York: 1932.

Ying-shih Yu. *Trade and Expansion in Han China: A Study in the Structure of Sino-barbarian Economic Relations.* Berkeley: University of California Press, 1967.

A. Zásterová. "Les débuts de l'établissement définitif des Slaves en Europe méridionale." Vznik a počátký slovanů VII, Prague: Nakl. Československé akademie ved, 1966.

Zhanna A. Zaionchkovskaya. "Migration Patterns in the Former Soviet Union." In Jeremy R. Azrael and Emil A. Payin, eds., *Cooperation and Conflict in the Former Soviet Union: Implications for Migration.* Santa Monica: Rand Center for Russian and Eurasian Studies, Center for Ethnopolitical and Regional Research, 1996.

Z. Zinkjavicius and P. Gaucas. "Vostochnaia granica rasprostraneniia litovskogo iazyka v proshlom po dannym toponimiki." In Indulis E. Ronis, Gen. ed., *Problemy etnicheskoi istorii baltov.* Riga: Zinatne, 1985.

I. M. Zolotarëva, Gen. ed. *Etnogenez finno-ugorskikh narodov po dannym antropologii.* Moscow: Nauka, 1974.

Scholarly Articles

V. I. Abaev. "Diskussionnyie Problemy Otechestvennoi Skifologii." *Narody Azii i Afriki* 5 (1980):102–130.

William Y. Adams, D. P. Van Gerven, and R. S. Levy. "The Retreat from Migrationism." *Annual Review of Anthropology* 7 (1978):483–532.

David W. Anthony. "Migration in Archaeology: The Baby and the Bathwater." *American Anthropologist* 92 (1990):894–914.

David W. Anthony and Dorcas R. Brown. "The Origins of Horseback Riding." *Antiquity* 65 (1991):22–38.

Mikhail I. Artamonov. "Frozen Tombs of the Scythians." *Scientific American* 212 (1965):101–109.

I. I. Artiomenko (Artëmenko). "Archaeological Research in the Ukrainian SSR." *Soviet Anthropology and Archaeology* XVIII, 3 (1979–80):37–68.

Bernard S. Bachrach. "The Alans in Gaul." *Tradito* XXIII (1967):476–89.

Elizabeth E. Bacon. "Russian Military and Civilian Settlements, 1824–1917." *Central Asian Review* VI, No. 2 (XXXX):147.

E. Bakka. "Scandinavian Trade Relations with the Continent and the British Isles in Pre-Viking Times." *Early Medieval Studies* (Antikvarisk Arkiv 40). Stockholm, (1971):437–51.

Bradley H. Baltensperger. "Agricultural change among Great Plains Russian Germans." *Annals of the Association of American Geographers* 73 (1983):75–88.

Thomas J. Barfield. "The Hsiung-nu Imperial Confederacy: Organization and Foreign Policy." *Journal of Asian Studies* 41, No. 1 (1981):45–61.

Fredrik Barth. "The Land Use Pattern of Migratory Tribes of South Persia." *Norsk Geografisk Tidsskrift.* Bind XVII (1959–60):1–11 (The Bobbs-Merrill Reprint Series in the Social Sciences, A-11).

M. Bassin. "Geographical Determinism in Fin-de-siècle Marxism: Georgii Plekhanov and the Environmental Basis of Russian History." *Annals of the Association of American Geographers* 82 (1992):3–22.

Jerry H. Bentley. "Cross-Cultural Interaction and Periodization in World History." *American Historical Review* 101 (June 1996):749–770.

Daniel P. Biebuyck. "On the Concept of Tribe." *Civilizations* 16, No. 4 (1966):500–15.

Lewis R. Binford. "Archaeology as Anthropology." *American Antiquity* 28 (1962):217–25.

Sh. Bira. "The Mongol Empire (13th–14th centuries): The East and West Relations." *Bulletin of the International Association for Mongol Studies* (1993/94) 12(2)&13(1):11–31.

Marc Bloch. "Les invasions. " *Annales d'histoire sociale,* 1945 I:33–46 and II:13–28.

Dirk P. Blok. "Die Wikingen in Friesland." *Naamkunde* 10 (1978):25–47.

J. Bratzkus. "The Khazar Origin of Ancient Kiev." *Slavonic and East European Review* 22 (1944):108–24.

Maurice Broens. "Los Francos y el poblamiento de la península Ibérica durante los siglos VI y VII." *Ampurias* XVII-XVIII (1955–56):59–77.

———. "Le peuplement germanique de la Gaule entre la Méditerranée et l'Océan." *Annales du Midi* LXVIII (1956):17–38.

J. Brooks. "England in the Ninth Century: the Crucible of Defeat." *Transactions of the Royal Historical Society.* Fifth series, 29 (1979):1–20.

Terry A. Brown and Keri A. Brown. "Ancient DNA and the Archaeologist." *Antiquity* 66 (1991):10–23.

William R. Brubaker. "Citizenship Struggles in Soviet Successor States." *International Migration Review* 26 (1992):269–91.

Viktor V. Bunak. "Genogeograficheskiie zony Vostochnoi Evropy vydeliaiemyie po gruppam krovi ABO." *Voprosy antropologii* 32 (1969):6–28.

Thomas S. Burns. "Pursuing the Early Gothic Migrations." *Acta Archaeologica* 31 (1979):189–99.

W. Butzer and C. R. Twidale. "Deserts in the Past." *Arid Lands* (1966):127–44.

Joseph R. Caldwell. "The New American Archaeology." *Science* 129 (1959):303–307.

Luca L. Cavalli-Sforza. "Genes, People and Languages." *Scientific American* 265, No. 5 (1991):72–78.

Sonia Chadwick-Hawkes. "Soldiers and Settlers in Britain, 4th to 5th Century." *Medieval Archaeology* V (1961):1–70.

John Chapman and Pavel M. Dolukhanov. "The Baby and the Bathwater: Pulling the Plug on Migrations." *American Anthropologist* 94, No. 1 (1992):169–74.

Peter Charanis. "Ethnic Changes in Seventh-Century Byzantium." *Dumbarton Oaks Papers* (Washington) 13 (1959).

———. "On the Slavic Settlement in the Peloponnesus." *Byzantinische Zeitschrift* XLVI (1953):91–103.

Jan Chochorowski and Sergei Skoryi. "Prince of the Great Kurgan." *Archaeology* (September/October 1997):32–41.

J. Grahame D. Clark. "The Invasion Hypothesis in British Archaeology." *Antiquity* 40 (1966):172–89.

John N. Coldstream. "Mixed Marriages on the Frontiers of the Greek World." *Oxford Journal of Archeology* 12 (1993):89–107.

W. S. Cooter. "Roman Frontier Regions in Temperate Europe." *Comparative Frontier Studies* 3 (Summer):1–3.

Nicolà di Cosmo. "Ancient Inner Asian Nomads: Their Economic Basis and its Significance in Chinese History." *Journal of Asian Studies* 53, No. 4 (1994):1092–1126.

Károly Czegledy. "From East to West: the Age of Nomadic Migrations in Eurasia." *Archivum Eurasiae Medii Aevi* III, P. B. Golden, tr. (1983):25–125.

J. Czekanowski. "The Ancient Home of the Slavs." *Slavonic and East European Review* 24 (1946–47):356–72.

Eugène Darko. "Le rôle des peuples nomades cavaliers dans la transformation de l'Empire romain." *Byzantion* XVIII (1946):85–97.

Kingsley Davis. "The Migrations of Human Populations." *Scientific American* 231, No. 3 (September 1974).

Sue Davis and Steven O. Sabol. "The Importance of Being Ethnic: Minorities in Post-Soviet States—The Case of Russians in Kazakstan." *Nationalities Papers* 26, No. 3 (Sept. 1998):473–92.

Jan deVries. "Measuring the impact of climate on history: The search for appropriate methodologies." *Journal of Interdisciplinary History* 10, No. 4 (1980):599–630.

Hilda Ecsedy. "Tribe and Empire. Tribe and Society in the Turk Age." *Acta Orientalia Academiae Scientiarum Hungaricae* 31 (1977):3–15.

A. Falsetti and Robert Sokal. "Genetic Structure of Human Populations in the British Isles." *Annals of Human Biology* 20, No. 3 (1993):215–29.

Jensen G. Fellows. "The Vikings in England: A Review." *Anglo-Saxon England* 4 (1975):181–206.

Andrew Fleming. "The Genesis of Pastoralism in European Prehistory." *World Archeology* 4, No. 2 (1972):179–91.

Joseph Fletcher. "The Mongols: Ecological and Social Perspectives." *Harvard Journal of Asiatic Studies* 46, No. 1 (1986):11–50.

André G. Frank. "Bronze Age World System Cycles." *Current Anthropology* 34, No. 4 (1993):383–429.

Herbert Franke. "Sino-Western Contact under the Mongol Empire." *Journal of the Hong-Kong Branch of the Royal Asiatic Society* 6 (1966):49–72.

Frenkel. "Geography, Empire, and Environmental Determinism." *Geographical Review* 82 (1992):143–53.

Wolfgang H. Fritze. "Zur Bedeutung der Awaren für die slawisch Ausdehnungsbewegung im frühen Mittelalter." *Zeitschrift fur Ostforschung* 28 (1979):498–545.

Gachechiladze and M. J. Bradshaw. "Changes in the Ethnic Structure of Tbilisi's Population." *Post-Soviet Geography* 35, No. 1 (January 1994):56–59.

Dietrich Gerhard. "The Frontier in Comparative View." *Comparative Studies in Society and History* I (1959):205–29.

Henri Grégoire. "L'origine et le nom des Croates et des Serbes." *Byzantion* XVII (1944–45):88–118.

Henri Grégoire and P. Orgels. "Les invasions russes dans le Synaxaire de Constantinople." *Byzantion* XXIV (1954):141–45.

György Györffy. "Sur la question de l'établissement des Pétchénègues en Europe." *Acta Orientalia Academiae Scientiarum Hungaricae* 25 (1972).

Charles J. Halperin. "The Concept of the Russkaia Zemlia and Medieval National Consciousness from the Tenth to the Fifteenth Centuries." *Nationalities Papers* 8 (1980):75–94.

János J. Harmatta. "Goten und Hunnen in Pannonien." *Acta Antiqua* 19 (1971):293–97.

Hans W. Haussig. "Die Quellen über die zentralasiatische Herkunft der europäischen Awaren." *Central Asiatic Journal* II (1956):2–43.

Sonia Hawkes and G. Dunning. "Soldiers and Settlers in Britain. Fourth to Fifth Century." *Medieval Archaeology* 5 (1961):1–70.

Baymirza Hayit. "The Huns and the End of the Roman Empire in Western Europe." *English Historical Review* 110, N. 435 (1995):4–41.

Walter B. Henning. "The Date of the Sogdian Ancient Letters." *Bulletin of the School of Oriental and African Studies* 12 (1948):601–15.

Arie N. J. den Hollander. "The Great Hungarian Plain. A European Frontier Area." *Comparative Studies in Society and History* 3 (1960):74–88, 135–69.

Terry G. Jordan. "Preadaptation and European colonization in rural North America." *Annals of the Association of American Geographers* 79, No. 4 (1989):489–500.

Christopher Kaplonski. "The Nomads of Inner Asia and Their Impact on the Eurasian Steppe." Paper given at the American Association for the Advancement of Slavic Studies meeting. November 1996, Boston.

Mikhail Kazanski and R. Legoux. "Contribution à l'étude des témoignages archéologiques des Goths en Europe orientale à l'époque des Grandes Migrations: la chronologie de la culture de Cernjahov récente." *Archéologie Médiévale* 18 (1988):8–53.

Kiss. "Ein Versuch, die Funde und das Siedlungsgebiet der Ostgoten in Pannonien zwischen 456–471 zu bestimmen." *Acta Archaeologica Hungarica.* XXXI (1979): 229–239.

J. Kmieciński. "Kulturverbindungen Skandinaviens und südlicher Ostseeküste in der Latene und Römischen Kaiserzeit." *Peregrinatio Gothica* I (1986):39–60.

Z. Kobyliński, ed. *Ethnicity in Archaeology* (special theme). *Archaeologia Polona* 29 (1991).

Jerzy Kolendo. "Les influences de Rome sur les peuples de l'Europe centrale habitant loin des frontières de l'Empire." *Klio* 63 (1981):453–72.

Kristian Kristiansen. "Prehistoric migrations—the case of the Single Grave and Corded Ware cultures." *Journal of Danish Archaeology* 8 (1989):211–225.

Venčeslas Kruta. "Les Boïens de Cispadane, essai de paléoethnographie celtique." *Etudes celtiques* XVII (1980).

Yu. V. Kucharenko. "Le problème de la civilization 'gotho-gépide' en Polesie et en Volhynie." *Acta Baltico-Slavica* V (1967):19–40.

T. O. Kupperman. "The puzzle of the New England climate in the early colonial period." *American Historical Review* 82 (1982):1262–89.

V. A. Kuznetsov and V. K. Pudovin. "Alany v Zapadnoi Evrope v epokhu 'Velikogo pereseleniia narodov.'" *Sovetskaia Arkheologiia* II (1961):79–85.

Robert Latouche. "Aspect démographique de la crise des grandes invasions." *Population* II (1947):681–90.

Owen Lattimore. "The Geographical Factor in Mongol History." *Geographical Journal* XCI (1938):1–20.

W. Leasure and Robert A. Lewis. "Internal Migration in Russia in the Late Nineteenth Century." *Slavic Review* 27, No. 3 (1968):375–94.

Everett S. Lee. "A Theory of Migration." *Demography* 3, No. 1 (1966):47–58.

Paul Lemerle. "Invasions et migrations dans les Balkans depuis la fin de l'époque romaine jusqu'au VIII siècle." *Revue historique* CCXI (1954):265–308.

Rudi Paul Lindner. "Nomadism, Huns, and Horses." *Past and Present* 92 (1981):3–19.

Carlile A. Macartney. "The End of the Huns." *Byzantinisch-Neugriechische Jahrbücher* 10 (1934):106–14.

H. Machajewski. "The Wielbark Culture in Relation to the Przeworsk Culture in Wielkopolska." *Fontes Archaeologici Posnanienses* 29 (1978):49–64.

Otto Maenchen-Helfen. "Huns and Hsiung-Nu." *Byzantion* XVII (1944–45): 222–43.

Patrick Manning. "AHR Forum. The Problem of Interactions in World History. " *American Historical Review* 101 (June 1996):771–82.

Thomas H. McGovern. "Climate, correlation, and causation in Norse Greenland." *Arctic Anthropology* 28, No. 2 (1991):77–100.

D. A. McQuillan. "Farm size and work ethic: Measuring the success of immigrant farmers on the American grasslands, 1875–1925." *Journal of Historical Geography* 4, No. 1 (1978):57–76.

David Morgan. "Who Ran the Mongol Empire?" *Journal of the Royal Asiatic Society* 2 (1982):124–36.

K. Moszyński. "Przyczynek do tzw. etnogenezy słowian." *Slavia Antiqua* VIII (1961).

M. Muller-Wille, W. Dorfler, D. Meier, and H. Kroll. "The Transformation of Rural Society, Economy, and Landscape during the First Millennium A.D.: Archaeological and Palaeobotanical Contributions from Northern Germany and Southern Scandinavia." *Geografiska Annaler* 70B, No. 1 (1988):53–68.

M. Newton. "Cultural preadaptation and the upland South." *Geoscience and Man* 5 (1974):143–54.

Thomas S. Noonan. "Russia, the Near East, and the Steppe in the Early Medieval Period." *Archivum Eurasiae Medii Aevi* 2 (1982):269–302.

E. N. Nosov. "Poseleniie i mogil'nik kul'tury dlinnykh kurganov na ozere S'ezzhee." *Kratkiie soobshcheniia Instituta arkheologii AN SSSR* 166 (1981):64–8.

L. Oftedal. "On the Frequency of Norse Loanwords in Scottish Gaelic." *Scottish Gaelic Studies* 9 (1962):116–27.

Martha Brill Olcott. "The Settlement of the Kazakh Nomads." *Nomadic Papers* 8 (1981):13.

George Ostrogorsky. "Byzantium and the South Slavs." *The Slavonic and East European Review* XLII (1963):1–14.

Donald Ostrowski. "The Mongol Origins of Muscovite Political Institutions." *Slavic Review* 49, No. 4 (1990):525–42.

Tuomo Pekkanen. "On the Oldest Relationship between Hungarians and Sarmatians: From Spali to Asphali." *Ural-Altaische Jahrbücher* 45 (1973).

William Petersen. "A General Typology of Migration." *American Sociological Review* 23, No. 3 (1958):256–66.

Ludwik Piotrowicz. "Goci i Gepidowie nad dolną Wisłą i ich wędrówka ku morzu Czarnemu i Dacji." *Przegląd Zachodni. Miesęcznik* 5/6 (1951):60–76.

Xavier de Planhol. "Geography, Politics and Nomadism in Anatolia." *International Social Science Journal* XI, No. 4 (1959):525–31.

I. Pleinerová. "Germanische und slawische Komponenten in der altslawischen Siedlung Březno bei Louny." *Germania* 43, No. 1 (1965):121–38.

J. Rosen-Przeworska. "Ethnology and Archaeology in Foreign Areas." *Sovetskaia Arkheologiia* 3 (1963):17–27.

Michel Rouche. "Les Wisigoths en Aquitaine. Peuple ou armée?" *Peregrinatio Gothica* I (1986):283–94.

A. Rousseau. "Visigothic Migration and Settlement 376–418: Some Excluded Hypotheses." *Historia* 41 (1992):345–61.

J. H. Rowe. "Diffusionism and Archaeology." *American Antiquity* 32 (1966): 334–37.

R. S. Rykov. "Suslovskii kurgannyi mogil'nik." *Uchionye zapiski saratovskogo gosuniversiteta* 4 (1925):25–81 [in Maenchen-Helfen 1973].

Marshall D. Sahlins. "The Segmentary Lineage: an Organization of Predatory Expansion." *Anthropological Quarterly* 63, No. 2 (1961):322–46.

D. Schönberger. "The Roman Frontier in Germany: an Archaeological Survey." *Journal of Roman Studies* 59 (1969):144–97.

W. Schrickel. "Die Nordgrenze der Kelten im rechtsrheinischen Gebiet der Spätlatenzeit." *Jahrbuch des Römisch-Germanischen Zentralmuseums Mainz* XI (1964):138.

Ernst Schwartz. "Die Urheimat der Goten und ihre Wanderung ins Weichselland und nach Südrussland." *Saeculum* IV (1953):13–26.

Kenneth M. Setton. "The Bulgars in the Balkans and the Occupation of Corinth in the Seventh Century." *Speculum* XXV (1950):502–43.

Myra L. Shackley and Barry E. Wynne. "Viewpoint: Climate Reductionism." *Weather* 49 (1994):110–111.

Mark B. Shchukin. "K predistorii cherniakhovskoi kul'tury." *Arkheologicheskii sbornik Ermitazha* XX (1979):66–89.

Jonathan Shepard. "The Russian steppe-frontier and the Black Sea." *Archeion Pontou* 35 (1979):218–37.

Dezső Simonyi. "Die Kontinuitätsfrage und das Erscheinen der Slawen in Pannonien." *Studia Slavica Academiae Scienciarum Hungaricae* I, No. 4 (1955): 333–61.

István Sinkovics. "Der Angriff der Osmanen im Donautal im 16. Jahrhundert." *Études Historiques Hongroises* I (1975):347–81.

Denis Sinor. "Horse and Pasture in Inner Asian History." *Oriens Extremus* 19 (1972):171–84.

———. "Autour d'une migration de peuples au V siècle." *Journal Asiatique* 235 (1946–47):1–77.

Anthony D. Smith. "War and Ethnicity: The Role of Warfare in the Formation, Self-images and Cohesion of Ethnic Communities." *Ethnic and Racial Studies* 4 (1981):375–95.

Frank M. Stenton. "The Scandinavian Colonies in England and Normandy." *Trans. of the Royal Hist. Soc.,* XXVII (1945):1–12.

O. N. Trubachiov. "Iz opyta issledovaniia gidronimov Ukrainy." *Baltistica* IV, No. 1 (1968):31–53.

Richard P. Vaggione. "Over All Asia? The Extent of the Scythian Domination in Herodotus." *Journal of Biblical Literature* 92 (1973):523–530.

Eugene Van Cleef. "The Finns of the Pacific Coast of the United States, and consideration of the problems of scientific land settlement." *Annals of the Association of American Geographers* 30 (1940):25–38.

W. A. Van Es et al. "Dorestad." *Spiegel Historiael* 13, No. 4 (April 1978).

Charles Verlinden. "Frankish Colonization: A New Approach." *Transactions of the Royal Historical Society.* Fifth series, IV (1954):1–17.

George Vernadsky. "The Eurasian Nomads and Their Impact on Medieval Europe." *Studi Medievali.* Third series, IV, 2 (1963):401–34.

———. "The Date of the Conversion of the Khazars to Judaism." *Byzantion* XV (1941):76–86.

William Watson. "The Chinese Contribution to Eastern Nomad Culture in the pre-Han and Early Han Periods." *World Archeology.* 4, No. 2 (1972):139–49.

Martin G. Welch. "Rural Settlement Patterns in the Early and Middle Anglo-Saxon Periods." *Landscape History* 7 (1985):13–24.

Joachim Werner. "Die archäologischen Zeugnisse der Goten in Südrussland, Ungarn, Italien und Spanien." *Settimane di Studio* 3 (1956):127–30.

Other Scholarly Publications

Volker Bierbrauer. *Frühgeschichtliche Akkulturationsprozesse in den Germanischen Staaten am Mittelmeer (Westgoten, Ostgoten, Langobarden) aus der Sicht des Archäologen.* In "Atti del VI Congresso Internazionale di Studi sull'Alto medioevo." Spoleto: 1980.

Eric Birley, Brian Dobson, and Michael Jarrett, eds. *Roman Frontier Studies. Eighth International Congress of Limesforschung* (1969). Cardiff: University of Wales Press, 1974.

Solomon I. Bruk. "Etnodemograficheskie protsessy v SSSR (po materialam poslevoiennykh perepisei)," *Istoriia SSSR* 5 (1980).

Al. Bürmov. "Kům vůprosa za proizhod na prabůlgarite." *Izvestija na istoričeskoj družestvo v Sofija 22–4 (1948).*

I. A. Crawford. "War or Peace. Viking Colonization in the Northern and Western Isles of Scotland." *Viking Congress VIII* (1981):259–69.

Ivan Duichev. "Les Slaves et Byzance." *Études historiques à l'occasion du XI Congrès international des sciences historiques.* Sofia: 1960.

First Book of Demographics for the Republics of the Former Soviet Union, 1951–1990. Shady Side, MA: New World Demographics, L.C., 1992.

Heinrich G. H. Härke. "'Germans Heading for the Beaches': An Old Perspective on Protohistoric Migrations." Paper presented to the Theoretical Archaeology Group, Newcastle, 1989.

L. T. Hobhouse, G. C. Wheeler, and M. Ginsberg. *The Material Cultural and Social Institutions of the Simpler Peoples.* London: London School of Economics and Political Science, Monograph on Sociology No. 3, 1930.

I Normanni e la loro espansione in Europa nell'alto medioevo. Settimane di studio del centro italiano di studi sull'alto medioevo XVI (Spoleto 1969).

Herbert Jankuhn. "Der frankisch-friesische Handel zur Ostsee im frühen Mittelalter." *Vierteljahrschrift für Sozial- und Wirtschaftsgeschichte* XL (1953): 193–243.

M. Kritz. "Climate change and migration adaptations." Working Report 2.16. Ithaca: Population and Development Program, Department of Rural Sociology, Cornell University, 1990.

Josef Macurek, Gen. ed. *Magna Moravia. Sborník k 1100. Výročí příchodu byzantskémise na Moravu.—Commentationes ad memoriam missionis byzantinae ante XI saecula in Moraviam adventis editae.* Prague: Státní pedagogické nakl., 1965.

Fernand Mosse. Bibliographia Gotica. A Bibliography of Writings on the Gothic language to the End of 1949, in *Medieval Studies* 12 (1950): 237–324.

Peregrinatio Gothica II. Archaeologia Baltica VII. Łódź: 1989.

Walter Pohl. "Die Gepiden und die Gentes an der mittleren Donau nach dem Zerfall des Attilas Reiches." In Herwig Wolfram and Falko Daim, eds., *Die Völker an der mittleren und unteren Donau im fünften und sechsten jahrhundert,* Denkschriften der Österreichische Akademie der Wissenschaften. Vienna: Österreichische Akademie der Wissenschaften, 1980.

P. H. Sawyer. "Conquest and Colonization: Scandinavians in the Danelaw and in Normandy." *Viking Congress* VIII (1981):123–31.

E. Schönbäck. "Progress Report on Archaeological Fieldwork at L'Anse-aux-Meadows, June to October 1975." *Parks Canada Research Bulletin* 30, Ottawa, 1976.

D. Straume and E. Skar, eds. *Peregrinatio Gothica* III. Oslo: Universitets Oldsaksamlings, 1992.

Frederick J. Turner. *The Significance of the American Frontier in American History.* Washington. D.C.: Annual Report of the American Historical Association for 1893, 1894, pp. 199–227.

Max Vasmer. "Die ältesten Bevölkerungsverhältnisse Russlands im Lichte der Sprachvorschung." *Preuss. Akad. Der Wiss., Vorträge und Schriften,* Heft 5, 1947.

Daniele Vitali, ed. "Celti ed Etruschi nell'Italia centro settentrionale dal V secolo a.C. alla Romanizzazione." *Proceedings of the International Colloquium at Bologna.* Imola: University Press, 1985.

F. T. Wainwright. "Danes and Norwegians in England." *IV Congrès international des Sciences Onomastiques.* Uppsala (1952):530–40.

Joachim Werner. *Die archäologischen Zeugnisse der Goten in Südrussland, Ungarn, Italien und Spanien.* In *I Goti in Occidente,* "Settimane di studio del centro italiano di studi sull'alto medioevo," III (Spoleto 1956):127–130.

Herwig Wolfram and Falko Daim, eds. *Die Völker an der mittleren und unteren Donau im fünften und sechsten jahrhundert.* Denkschriften der Österreichische Akademie der Wissenschaften, 1980.

Herwig Wolfram and Walter Pohl, eds. *Typen der Ethnogenese unter besonderer Berücksichtigung der Bayern.* Denkschriften der Österreichische Akademie der Wissenschaften, 1990.

World Climate from 8000 to 0 B.C. Proceedings of the International Symposium Held at Imperial College, London, 18–19 April 1966. London: Royal Meteorological Society, 1966.

Dissertations

Peter R. Meffert. "The Population and Rural Economy of the Kazakh Soviet Socialist Republic." Ph.D. diss., Stanford University, 1988.

István Mócsy. "Radicalization and Counterrevolution: Magyar Refugees from the Successor States and Their Role in Hungary. 1918–1921." Ph.D. diss., University of California, Los Angeles, 1973.

V. V. Sedov. *Slaviane verkhnego podneprov'ia i podvin'ia do XIV v.* Diss., Moscow University, 1966.

Encyclopaedias

Bol'shaia Sovetskaia Entsiklopediia. 1st ed. Moscow: Izd-vo Sovetskaia entsiklopedia, 1926/1947.

Aleksandr A. Kaufman. "Pereseleniie. " *Entsiklopedicheskii Slovar'.* St. Petersburg: Brokgauz and Efron, 1898.

La Grande Encyclopedie. *Paris: Larousse, 1902/1886.*

Atlases

Paul Robert Magocsi. *Historical Atlas of East Central Europe.* Seattle and London: University of Washington Press, 1993.

Magazines and Other Publications

Aziatskaia Rossiia. St. Petersburg: Izdanie Pereselencheskago Upravleniia Glavnago Upravleniia Zemleustroistva i Zemledeliia. 3 vols. and atlas, 1914.

Die Geteilte Heimat. *Bonn: Aktion Gemeinsinn e.v., 1994.*

Germany. British Geographical Handbook, Naval Intelligence Division. Vol. II, 1944, p. 90.

Helsinki Watch Report. *"Punished Peoples" of the Soviet Union: The Continuing Legacy of Stalin's Deportations.* New York: Human Rights Watch, 1991.

Info-Dienst Deutsche Aussiedler. *Bonn: Bundesregierung für Aussiedlerfragen, Oct. 1996.*

Pereselencheskoie Delo. Otchiot po revizii Turkestanskogo kraiia proizvedionnoi po Vysochaishemu poveleniiu senatorom gofmeisterom grafom K. K. Pahlenom. St. Petersburg: 1910.

Volk auf dem Weg: Deutsche in Russland und in der GUS, 1763–1993. Stuttgart: Landsmannschaft/Kulturrat der Deutschen aus Russland e.v., 1993.

Vosstaniie 1916 goda v Kazakhstane: dokumenty i materialy. Alma Ata: ANKazSSR, 1947.

Index